BLUTOPIA

BLUT

Duke University Press   Durham & London   1999

GRAHAM LOCK

OPIA

Visions of the

Future and

Revisions of the

Past in the

Work of Sun Ra,

Duke Ellington, and

Anthony Braxton

© 1999 Duke University Press
All rights reserved Printed in
the United States of America on
acid-free paper ⊗ Typeset in Joanna
by Tseng Information Systems, Inc.
Designed by Amy Ruth Buchanan
Library of Congress Cataloging-in-
Publication Data appear on the last
printed page of this book.

for Val Wilmer and

Victor Schonfield,

guiding lights,

generous spirits

Contents

Acknowledgments

My original and most crucial debt of gratitude is to the members of the School of American and Canadian Studies at Nottingham University who gave me the opportunity and the funds to carry out the research that led to this book. I would like, first and foremost, to thank my supervisor, David Murray, both for his astute and helpful criticisms of the manuscript and for support and generosity well beyond the call of duty. Had he not "taken a chance on chance" and agreed to supervise my research—on a topic (black music history) that is still not regarded in the UK as a necessary component of American Studies programs— then this book never would have been written. I am also indebted to members of the School's regular work-in-progress seminars and, in particular, to Richard King and Peter Ling for their comments on earlier drafts of this material.

I am, of course, immensely grateful to the many musicians who have taken the time to share their knowledge with me over the years. Chief among those who have had a direct influence on this book are Sun Ra, whom I was lucky enough to interview twice at length, and several members of his Arkestra (particularly Marshall Allen, John Gilmore, and Tyrone Hill) plus Marilyn Crispell, Mark Dresser, and Gerry Hemingway from the Anthony Braxton Quartet. I would like to say a special thank you to Anthony Braxton, who graciously consented to several new interviews to supplement those I had conducted with him in the 1980s and who also made available a wealth of unpublished material, including librettos, scores, and private concert recordings. He and his family invited me to visit them, too, a favor I repaid by promptly falling ill and groaning on their couch for several days. My meetings with Messrs Braxton and Ra have proved defining points in my life, and their music continues to provide many of its most joyful hours.

Because so much of the writing and research on creative music has taken place outside the academic domain, I have been extremely reliant on help from an international network of writers and aficionados. The following people have made particularly valuable contributions to this book. Victor Schonfield's detailed and insightful comments helped enormously to sharpen the manuscript, and he generously allowed me free access to his library, record collection, and inestimable expertise. Jack Collier took time from a busy schedule to read and comment on the manuscript; his constant support and encouragement have long been a source of inspiration. The same is true of Chris Trent, who also supplied me with many rare audio- and videotapes, read sections of the manuscript, and made available his own extensive archives. I am especially grateful to John F. Szwed for the time, wisdom, and support he has bestowed on this project. When we discovered, back in 1993, that we were both working on Sun Ra, he was happy to swap references and information, and we also exchanged initial drafts of our respective first chapters. His *Space Is the Place* is an exemplary model of jazz biography. My thanks, too, to Mike Heffley for the chance to see an early draft of his *The Music of Anthony Braxton*, definitely the most comprehensive overview of a most commodious subject! Another vital transatlantic contact was Allan Chase, who not only loaned me his master's dissertation on Sun Ra but also sent me many hard-to-find articles that had defeated the best efforts of the Inter Library Loan system. Alan Cohen and Brian Priestley kindly read sections of the manuscript and provided references; Francis Davis and Mark Sinker generously allowed me to see the unpublished portions of their interviews with Sun Ra.

Many other people have helped in ways too numerous to detail here. My thanks to Ben Andrews, Charles Blass, Nickie Braxton, Marilyn Charlton, Donald Clarke, Aaron Cohen, John Corbett, Andrew Crompton, Nicole Dalle, Hugo de Craen, Derek Drescher at BBC Radio 3, Leo Feigin at Leo Records, Joe Fonda, Alun Ford, Paul Gilroy, Jerry Gordon at Evidence Records, Andy Hamilton, Colin Harrison, Peter and John Hinds of Omni Press, Andy Isham, Jan and Janet Kopinski, Art Lange, Roz Laurie, Janet Law, Rupert Loydell, Nathaniel Mackey, Kerstan Mackness and Steve Sanderson at New Note, Trevor Manwaring at Harmonia Mundi, Fred Maroth at Music & Arts, Francesco Martinelli, Chrissie Murray, Chris Parker, Velibor Pedevski at Braxton House Records, Caroll Pinkham, Karen Pitchford, Peter Pullman, Ted Reichman, Alan Rice, Tony Russell, Bill Smith at *Coda*, Paul Smith at Blast First Records, Douglas Tallack, Werner X. Uehlinger at Hat Hut Records,

Nick White, Val Wilmer, and Anthony Wood. Thanks also to the various organizers of the BAAS Postgraduate Conference at Nene College, Northampton, in December 1995 and the *Jazz Contexts* colloquium at Nottingham University in June 1998, at which I was able to present papers relating to the material in this book.

A number of people in both academic and nonacademic institutions have also been extremely helpful. I am particularly grateful to the following: Julie Crawley at the Audio Visual Collection in Exeter University Library; Reuben Jackson at the Duke Ellington Collection, Archives Center, National Museum of American History, Smithsonian Institution, Washington, D.C.; Ken Jones at the National Jazz Foundation Archives in Loughton Library, Essex; Graham Langley at the British Institute of Jazz Studies, Crawthorne, Berkshire; Andrew Simons at the British Library National Sound Archive, London; Alison Stevens in the Inter Library Loan Department of Nottingham University Library; and the staff at the Institute of Jazz Studies at Rutgers University, Newark, N.J.

My editorial contacts at Duke University Press, Katie Courtland, Bob Mirandon, Pam Morrison, and Ken Wissoker, deserve many thanks, too. I very much appreciate their facilitating the smooth transformation of this work from manuscript to book form.

In conclusion, I would like to express the deepest gratitude to my parents, George and Una Taylor, for their continuing love and support.

"Where there is no vision

the People Perish."

—James Hampton

Introduction: Blutopia

It's the remembering song. There's so much to remember. There's so much wanting, and there's so much sorrow, and there's so much waiting for the sorrow to end. My people, all they want is a place where they can be people, a place where they can stand up and be part of that place, just being natural to the place without worrying someone may be coming along to take that place away from them.

There's pride in it, too. The man singing it, the man playing it, he makes a place. For as long as the song is played, *that's* the place he's been looking for.

—*Sidney Bechet* [1]

[Black American] music is produced by, and bears witness to, one of the most obscene adventures in the history of mankind. It is a music which creates, as what we call History cannot sum up the courage to do, the response to that absolutely universal question: *Who am I? What am I doing here?* . . .

So much for that European vanity: which imagines that with the single word, *history*, it controls the *past*, defines the *present*: and, therefore, cannot but suppose that the *future* will prove to be as willing to be brought into captivity as the slaves they imagine themselves to have discovered, as the *nigger* they had no choice but to invent.

—*James Baldwin* [2]

You really have to struggle, to fight. For example, they want you to accept that Africa has been a dark continent, that there was no civilization. This makes your body die. But then you start to read and you discover how people put history wrong. For me this meant a very important process of learning. Your art becomes your evolution. It tells you that there is something else, another reality: the immaterial. This opens up certain things, and might lead to the fact that the breath of your poetic visions becomes more beautiful.

The exploration of history is a spiritual process, in order to be able to judge one's self.

—Cecil Taylor [3]

The three quotations above point to the main themes I will be exploring in this book: music as an alternative form of history, music as the gateway to "another reality," and the self-representation of African American musicians in relation to the "invented nigger" of racial stereotyping. Sidney Bechet's eloquent testimony to the power of African American music identifies the presence of two major impulses: a utopian impulse, evident in the creation of imagined places (Promised Lands), and the impulse to remember, to bear witness, which James Baldwin relates to the particular history of slavery and its aftermath in the United States. These impulses might be, and sometimes have been, regarded as antipathetic: the utopian associated with space, the future, the sacred, and the spirituals, the remembering with time, the past, the secular, and the blues. What I hope to show in studying the work of Sun Ra, Duke Ellington, and Anthony Braxton is that these impulses can fuse, forming a crossroads in the creative consciousness where visions of the future and revisions of the past become part of the same process, a "politics of transfiguration," [4] in which accepted notions of language, history, the real, and the possible are thrown open to question and found wanting.

The word I use to situate these visions and revisions is Blutopia. "Blutopia" is the title of a brief instrumental composition by Duke Ellington, which he performed at his orchestra's Carnegie Hall concert in December 1944. [5] Musically unexceptional, it does not seem to have featured in his subsequent repertoire and warrants only a passing mention in his autobiography. When I first saw the Carnegie Hall recording, I read "Blutopia" as signaling a utopia tinged with the blues, an African American visionary future stained with memories.[6] In this reading of the word, it is the refusal to forget its history that distinguishes Blutopia from other utopian futures. And if that history, largely shaped by the "obscene adventure" of slavery, has made the vision of a better future that much more necessary as an aid to survival, its particular horrors also must have made such a vision harder to sustain, requiring an optimism-against-the-odds (and a means of expressing it) that might be regarded as impossible or even insane.

Cue Sun Ra, no stranger to accusations of insanity, who cheerfully embraced the impossible—declaring in the 1960s that it attracted him because "everything possible has been done and the world didn't change"[7]—and spent the rest of his life traveling the spaceways, "from planet to planet," not only promoting but enacting a vision of future utopia. Cue Anthony Braxton, with his plans for a music played by a hundred orchestras linked by satellite, for a music played by orchestras on different planets, in different galaxies—projects that, as Mark Sinker has shrewdly noted, "make political and philosophical demands just by the instrumentation."[8] And cue Duke Ellington, who hailed the New World A-Comin', which he envisioned as "a place in the distant future where there would be no war, no greed, no categorisation, no nonbelievers, where love was unconditional, and no pronoun was good enough for God."[9] If Ellington, unlike Ra and Braxton, has not been deemed mad, it is probably because his utopianism was largely channeled through conventional religious forms, most extensively in the three Sacred Concerts of his final years, examples of an African American Christian tradition of affirmative music that can be traced back to the slaves' spirituals. These spirituals represent one of the guiding forces in black culture, not least because their detailed evocations of heaven are among the earliest documented examples of African Americans creating, in music and song, Bechet's "place where they can be people . . . where they can stand up and be part of that place"; a line such as "I'm gonna walk all over God's heaven" (from the spiritual "All God's Chillun Got Wings") denotes a sense of belonging no less than a sense of freedom. But whereas Ellington compositions like "Heaven" and "Almighty God," from the Second Sacred Concert,[10] adhere to and reiterate the basic tenets of a Christian mythology voiced in the spirituals, the musics of the non-Christian Braxton and the anti-Christian Ra transform the celestial landscapes that the slaves imagined into new utopias that realize other, more personal belief systems. This may explain why the utopian impulse is addressed more urgently in Ra's and Braxton's musics than in Ellington's. They have to create anew what he has only to reaffirm. Their envisioned futures are provisional; his is guaranteed by God.

Certainly, it is the impulse to bear witness that seems the stronger force in Ellington's music. The subtitle to *Black, Brown and Beige*, his most ambitious work, was "A tone parallel to the history of the American Negro," a phrase that could stand as an epigraph to his entire oeuvre. John Edward Hasse reports that Ellington's personal library contained 800 books on black history, a clear indication of his interest in the subject.[11] Ellington broached the idea of composing a history of black America as early as 1930, and it remained a central theme in his work, a thread that ran through extended projects such as *Jump for Joy*, *Black, Brown and Beige*, *The Deep South Suite*, and *My People*, as well as through many of the shorter pieces for which he is better-known—"Black and Tan Fantasy," "Harlem Air Shaft," Ko-Ko."[12] His pride in black history brought him into conflict both with prevailing white versions of that history—for him Nat Turner and Denmark Vesey were heroes[13]—and, more particularly, with the kinds of racial stereotyping that attended media images of black life and often framed black performance. His well-known dislike of artistic categorization can probably be read, at least in part, as an attempt to evade the racial stereotyping that was frequently implicit in such categorization and that generally had the effect (and presumably the intention) of restricting the fields of activity in which African American artists were "permitted" to function.[14]

In his angry rejection of such critical presuppositions, Ellington can be compared to Anthony Braxton, whose trenchant attacks on jazz journalism also form part of a wider critique of the racial stereotyping and misdocumentation that he considers endemic to Western society and that he attributes to white attempts to portray slavery, "the raping of Africa," as "not a negative act towards a civilized people."[15] Like Ellington, Braxton sees accepted definitions of jazz as constrictive and implicitly racist; like Ellington, he refuses to confine his work to these "sanctioned zones" and instead aims for the stars—as in his ideas for "a music to heal deserts . . . a music that can help to prevent earthquakes . . . music as a practical tool to help create planets,"[16] a "breath of poetic visions" that makes the critics' obsession with questions such as "But is it jazz?" and "Does it swing?" seem grotesquely small-minded.

Sun Ra, who not only aimed for but claimed to come from the stars, was less concerned with history per se than with expounding an alternative *mythic past* to that proposed in the Christian spirituals. Yet his assertions of alien-ness can perhaps be read as a deliberate riposte to the history of white American refusal to treat black Americans as human beings; and his reinvention of himself, as Herman Blount became Le Sony'r Ra, has much in common with the transformative process that many African Americans underwent in moving from slavery to freedom, an experience that entailed not only a change in status but virtually a whole new way of being. In throwing off what he called a "manufactured past," Sun Ra was able to embrace the future of the "alter-destiny," thus demonstrating on a personal level the mental emancipation that he felt was necessary for all African Americans.

In the musics of all three artists there is a sense that the utopian impulse cannot be fully realized until the truths of the "remembering song" are acknowledged by black and white alike. The distortions found in white versions of black history need to be revised. Braxton in particular explicitly states that Western value systems, too, will need to change, that more attention must be given to that other reality which Cecil Taylor calls "the immaterial," if a better future is to be had. The occasional apocalyptic scenarios that Braxton and Sun Ra evoke in their work warn that failure to effect this change will result not in utopia but in likely global catastrophe. What is at stake in this music, for these twentieth-century musicians no less than for the slaves, are issues of life, death, and the fate of the human race. "My Lord, what a mornin' / When the stars begin to fall." [17]

— • • • ———

I should explain that this book has been shaped by the context in which it was written. That is, the text is closely based on the doctoral thesis that I wrote as a student in the School of American and Canadian Studies at Nottingham University from 1993 to 1997. Since jazz is still relatively uncharted territory academically, at least in the context of American Studies, there were few models for the approach I adopted, which was to draw at times on biography, cultural theory, musicology, and social history while trying to focus primarily on what the musicians themselves have said about the music.[18]

This last aim was not as straightforward as it might sound. While Ra, Ellington, and Braxton are unusual in that they have each produced a substantial body of written and/or spoken commentary on their work, much of this material is problematic for one reason or another. What, for example, are we to make of Sun Ra's repeated claims that he was "not of this planet"? Or Anthony Braxton's insistence on titling his compositions with diagrams and pictures rather than words? I began with the assumption that these were expressions of personal systems of metaphysics that should be treated with respect, however strange they initially seem. One of the main goals I set myself in this book was to outline these systems and to trace their possible sources. Nevertheless, my subjects proved slippery metaphysicians, as questioning of language as they were of history, often decrying it as a powerful weapon that was employed to the detriment of black people and black creativity.[19] As a result, they each tend to use language in specific, self-conscious modes: Ra given to wittily subversive wordplay, Ellington to extreme circumspection, Braxton to generating neologisms and compound phraseology in a bid to rise above what he has termed the "mono-dimensional" language of jazz criticism. One consequence is that their words—written and spoken—can take on an elusive, equivocal quality; it becomes difficult to gauge how "serious" they are being, whether they "mean" what they say or if it is a put-on. Such use of ambivalence is a traditional feature of African American culture, where strategies of signifying, tricksterism, mimicry, parody, masking, encoding, and other forms of indirection have long been popular.[20] And necessary, too. As Paul Gilroy notes:

> Created under the very nose of the overseers, the utopian desires which fuel the complementary politics of transfiguration must be invoked by other, more deliberately opaque, means. This politics exists on a lower frequency where it is played, danced, and acted, as well as sung and sung about, because words, even words stretched by melisma and supplemented or mutated by the screams which still index the conspicuous power of the slave sublime, will never be enough to communicate its unsayable claims to truth.[21]

Certainly, Ra, Ellington, and Braxton are cagey self-presenters, and I daresay it would be possible to construct a thesis that simply traced the various forms of indirection at play in their words and music (and an element of playfulness is often present). However, while I have pointed on occasion to specific instances of signifying or trickster tactics, this was not the kind of book I wanted to write, one that I feared might end up imposing a reductive formalism on the music.[22] (Signifyin(g), in particular, to use the word in its Gatesian guise, seems to have become the postmodern equivalent of "natural rhythm," in that all African American musicians are now presumed to have it in their music—and those who do not are deemed in some way "inauthentic.")[23]

The genesis of the book I have written can possibly be traced to my initial meeting with Sun Ra in 1983, when for much of our interview I simply had no idea what he was talking about. At the time I attributed this incomprehension more to his "weirdness" than to my ignorance, a common response I imagine when you don't know that you don't know. Two factors changed my mind. One was a series of interviews I conducted with Anthony Braxton in 1985, when I began to realize just how much I didn't know about African American music. The second was simply listening to, and thinking about, Sun Ra's music, to which I found myself increasingly drawn. The more I learned about Ra, the more implausible seemed the insinuations of his detractors that he was a clown, a con man, or a maniac. Such dismissive epithets had no explanation for the beauty of his music, for his ability to maintain and motivate a band for thirty years, for his unswerving commitment to a singular vision that brought neither financial reward nor critical acclaim. When he died in 1993 and the obituarists trotted out the same dismissive epithets, trying to understand that singular vision assumed a new urgency, even became a personal responsibility, given my dual involvement as a jazz writer and a fan of Ra's music.

My feelings about the work of Braxton and Ellington have followed a similar course: attraction to the music, dismay at its representation in the media, determination to better understand what it meant to its creators. What, for them, was their music *about*? This became the central question that I wished to address.

I should emphasize that *explication* has been my primary goal here. I was not interested in trying to fit my subjects into a theoretical paradigm nor in offering a critical analysis of what they had to say. I realize some readers may find this noninterventionist policy exasperating at times, and there are certainly occasions when I could have taken a more critical stance toward this or that statement or piece of music. That I have chosen not to follow such a course reflects both my priorities—I wanted to *make sense of,* not *argue with*—and the customary limits of available time and space. In particular, Anthony Braxton's *Tri-axium Writings*,[24] a unique endeavor in African American music philosophy, deserves a more detailed and extensive engagement than I have been able to provide here, where my chief focus has been on the relatively small section of his work that is concerned with a critical discussion of jazz journalism. I had better make clear that in sketching in the philosophical background to this critique, I have compressed many of Braxton's arguments to the point of oversimplification, often omitting the qualifications and provisos of his original text. As a result, several of his statements about Western society and civilization appear to be rather more sweeping than is actually the case. However, even when Braxton's initial assertions might be construed as controversial or provocative, I have generally let them pass unchallenged for the reasons that I just mentioned; I have neither the space nor the inclination to be disputatious. While I do not necessarily endorse everything that Braxton says, and would probably rephrase many of his arguments were I putting them myself, I can think of no substantive point he makes with which I strongly disagree. Therefore, I see no point in picking an argument for the sake of it or simply to assert a spurious "objectivity." There is already a long and ignoble tradition of white commentators being only too ready to sit in judgment on the works and viewpoints of black musicians. This book will, I hope, be seen as a contribution to the dismantling of that tradition and the implicit racial arrogance that it so often has embodied.

Let me be clear on this point. In tracing examples of racial stereotyping in a variety of reviews and articles (which I do throughout the book, and especially in chapter 5), I am not suggesting that individual writers were being deliberately racist or knowingly Eurocentric. As Braxton argues in Tri-axium Writings, racial stereotypes and Eurocentric attitudes permeate the fabric of Western culture; they are symptoms of a malaise that affects us all and shapes our thinking, often despite our best intentions. Nor am I suggesting that critics are obliged to like a piece of music simply because it challenges stereotypical definitions of jazz. What I am saying is that the terms of this critical discourse need to change; the preconceptions, the expectations, the projected desires that have framed and distorted white perceptions of black music should be interrogated and all extraneous baggage dumped. This is as true for academic writers as it is for journalists. Attempts in the 1980s and 1990s to refigure contemporary jazz in terms of postmodernist practice seem to me no less of an imposition than attempts in the 1920s and 1930s to inscribe the jazz of that era as a form of primitivism. As Ingrid Monson has pointed out, theoretical constructs derived from Western philosophy may not be the most useful tools for gaining insight into the workings of African American music.[25]

Which tools are the most useful remains a moot point. As someone who currently has a foot in both academia and journalism, I have tried in Blutopia to draw on the particular strengths of each discipline. Of course, there is always a danger that those attempting to bridge such gaps will find themselves stuck between a rock and a hard place. Indeed, if Krin Gabbard is right in his alarmingly bleak forecast of a future in which scholars and journalists become warring camps, set on producing two mutually exclusive forms of jazz discourse, then the kind of book I have tried to write here will soon be a virtual impossibility.[26] Still, I take heart from Sun Ra's line on the impossible, and from the Braxton/Ellington line on resisting categorization. And if their music does create a place where, to echo Bechet, people can be people, then that is the place where I hope Blutopia will find its home.

Part I Sun Ra: *A Starward Eye*

"Who heard great 'Jordan roll'?

Whose starward eye

Saw chariot 'swing low'?"

—*James Weldon Johnson,*

"O Black and Unknown Bards"

1 Astro Black: Mythic Future, Mythic Past

But if you would tell me who I am, at least take the trouble
to discover what I have been.

—Ralph Ellison [1]

In April 1993 the American magazine *Jazz Times* appeared on the news-
stands with a front cover headline that read: "Sun Ra: Visionary or Con
Artist?" If the question was, as John Corbett later claimed, "insult-
ing and ignorant," it was not entirely unprovoked. As Corbett himself
wryly noted: "Of course, anyone claiming to be from the planet Saturn
will be the subject of continuing ridicule no matter how irrefutably
out of this world and truly prophetic their music is." [2]

Indeed, the insensitivity of the *Jazz Times* headline was soon eclipsed
by that shown in some of the obituaries that followed Sun Ra's death on
30 May 1993. In the *Daily Mail*, Benny Green referred to Sun Ra's "galactic gobbledegook," portrayed him as "wearing a short interplanetary
Noddy bonnet," and complained: "The trouble has always been to
know where to draw a firm line between the tomfoolery of an enter-
taining charlatan and the sincere missionary beliefs of a considerable
musical pioneer." [3] In the *Independent*, Steve Voce, while also acknowledging Sun Ra's "serious contribution to the music," nevertheless poked
fun at his clothes and his philosophy, describing him as a "nutter"
who "had only one joke." [4] These remarks may have been exceptionally facile, yet their disbelieving tone was certainly not unprecedented
in commentary on Sun Ra. Allan Chase has pointed out that "naivete,
cynicism, facetiousness, inconsistency, and insanity" have all been put
forward to explain what he calls Sun Ra's "differentness." [5] Even writers

sympathetic to Ra have tended to dwell on his singularity, perhaps not surprisingly given his claim that "I am not of this planet. I am another order of being. I can tell you things you won't believe."[6]

It is clear from the above quotations that the controversy about Sun Ra has not been primarily musicological. Though critics have differed in their degrees of appreciation, few have had any problem relating his music to the African American creative tradition. Robert Campbell, for example, reported that in the 1980s a typical Sun Ra concert "contained Fletcher Henderson and Duke Ellington charts, freakouts, standards, blues for piano and organ, slices of R&B, you name it," and back in the 1970s Val Wilmer similarly noted that Ra's music "can range from swing to neo-bop to free collective improvisation, all in a single night."[7] What provoked the accusations of chicanery and/or madness was the "galactic gobbledegook," or what I will call the "Astro Black Mythology," that filtered through the music, alluded to in song titles and lyrics, poems and interviews, and a pervasive influence as well on the design of his record jackets and many aspects of his onstage performances, not least the colorful attire worn by Sun Ra and his band, the Arkestra, which Wilmer has described as deriving from "midway between Africa and the realms of science fiction."[8]

("Astro Black Mythology" is a phrase from Ra's poem/song lyric "Astro Black."[9] In this chapter I use it to refer to what I see as possibly the axis of the Ra cosmology, that is, the creation of an alternative mythic future and mythic past for African Americans. In this context, "Astro Black Mythology" is an appropriate shorthand term for two reasons: it emphasizes Sun Ra's conscious creation of a mythology, and it conveniently encapsulates the two dominant facets of that mythology, the Astro of the outer space future, and the Black of the ancient Egyptian past.)

In an earlier discussion of this Ra mythology, I suggested that it should be looked at as "part of a black historical continuum that reaches back through the blues and slavery to an Egyptian civilization that began 5,000 years ago."[10] My aim in this chapter is to further explore that contention by looking in particular at the two principal components of Ra's Astro Black Mythology: ancient Egypt and outer space. I should stress that I am by no means attempting to explicate Sun Ra's entire philosophy, which would require at least a book to itself.[11] Nevertheless, as I hope will become clear, ancient Egypt and outer space were significant, perhaps core, factors in Sun Ra's mythology, and the fact that he linked them provides us with a key to better understanding what that mythology was about. At the least, I believe I can show that some of the apparently more eccentric and "insane" elements of Sun Ra's works were grounded in a particular cultural context and that a useful way of beginning to make sense of his work is to look more closely at its relationship to certain aspects of African American history.

— • • • ——

Sun Ra's concern with ancient Egypt can be approached by means of both its immediate musical context and the broader African American intellectual context. Norman Weinstein has shown that an interest in Africa, including Egypt, has been a feature of African American music since the early years of the twentieth century, and Frank Kofsky has documented a specific upsurge of African references in the American jazz of the 1950s, a phenomenon he attributes to "the growth of nationalist feelings among black musicians," and one undoubtedly fueled by the number of African nations that achieved independence from European colonial powers during this period.[12] Insofar as Sun Ra was involved in nationalist activities in Chicago in the 1950s,[13] when he also formed the Arkestra, and his composition titles at the time included "Africa," "Nubia," and "Aiethopia" [sic], he can be seen as a participant in the growth of these feelings among African American musicians. And insofar as this interest in Africa affected the actual sound of the music, Sun Ra can be counted among the leading participants. The Arkestra began to use two or three drummers, and Ra encouraged all the band members to play miscellaneous percussion instruments. According to Wilmer: "This emphasis on percussion, combined with chants set up by the musicians, was the first sign of *conscious* Africanisms to appear in the music since Dizzie [sic] Gillespie's Afro-Cuban period."[14] And Chase, writing with reference to Ra's increasing use of "exotic" Latin dance rhythms in the late 1950s, points to both the direct African element in the composition titles and the more circuitous African influences in the rhythms. "Sun Ra's titles enhanced the association of these rhythms with the exotic, and with Egypt and Africa in particular: 'Tiny Pyramids,' 'Nubia,' 'Africa,' 'Watusa,' 'Ancient Aeithopia' [sic], 'Kingdom of Thunder,' 'Paradise.' The rhythms used were more Caribbean than strictly African, but those Caribbean rhythms derived largely from African (and Iberian) sources."[15]

If an LP like 1959's *The Nubians of Plutonia* (originally titled *The Lady with* the *Golden Stockings*) or the 1958 track "Aiethopia" perhaps demonstrated some of the more imaginative uses of such "Africanisms" at the time,[16] what really set Sun Ra apart from his other Africa-inspired contemporaries was a deep fascination with Egypt, particularly ancient Egypt, that continued to play a major part in his work for the next three decades. This fascination was evident not only in his choice of name (Ra being the ancient Egyptian sun god), but also in many composition and record titles ("Ahnknaton" [sic], "Pyramids," "Sunset on the Nile," *I, Pharaoh*), in the occasional renaming of his Saturn record label as Thoth (after the ibis-headed Egyptian moon god), and in the use of Egyptian hieroglyphics and motifs both on record jackets and on stage sets and costumes.[17]

That Sun Ra's references to ancient Egypt were intended, at least in part, to rekindle awareness of black achievement and black history is suggested by a lyric such as "When the black man ruled this land / Pharaoh was sitting on his throne / I hope you understand." [18] This impression was confirmed by my interviews with Arkestra members Marshall Allen and Tyrone Hill in 1990:

> The importance of ancient Egypt's *blackness* is attested to by current Arkestra members. Altoist Marshall Allen answers my queries with "Well, there are a lot of ancient Egyptians in America." You mean black people? "That's right. People from all over Africa are there. You gotta have some kind of identity." And trombonist Tyrone Hill (ex-MFSB) states it even more plainly: "Knowing about ancient Egypt makes me feel better as a person, 'cause those were black people. Our race don't know very much about ourselves. In America, education and the mass media tell you black people got nothing to offer, but we've done many beautiful things. Sun Ra made me aware of this." [19]

Hill's remarks point to Sun Ra's use of ancient Egypt as part of an attempt to revise the history of black people as represented by the white cultural and academic establishments. If the political critique implicit in this attempt differentiated Ra from the more general cultural nationalism espoused by his fellow musicians in the 1950s,[20] it also placed him within an existing African American intellectual tradition.

A small number of African American writers, including W. E. B. DuBois, had previously broached the topic of ancient Egyptian civilization,[21] but it was only in 1954, with the publication of George G. M. James's *Stolen Legacy*, that prevailing white academic ideas about ancient civilization were comprehensively challenged. James's book, whose full original title was *Stolen Legacy: The Greeks Were Not the Authors of Greek Philosophy but the People of North Africa, Commonly Called the Egyptians*, claimed not only that Greece, supposedly the cradle of Western civilization, had "stolen" much of its religious, philosophical, and scientific thinking from Egypt, but also it took for granted that the ancient Egyptians had been black Africans, a fact long denied by many white historians.[22] James's book had a considerable impact in African American circles, but it was largely ignored by mainstream academics until its theses were developed some thirty years later by Martin Bernal in his *Black Athena*.[23] Ironically, Bernal points out that James's ideas had been common currency before the eighteenth century, but that "*after the rise of black slavery and racism, European thinkers were concerned to keep black Africans as far as possible from European civilization.*"[24] DuBois too had made this point, noting that "it is one of the astonishing results of the written history of Africa that almost unanimously in the nineteenth century Egypt was not regarded as a part of Africa." He concluded: "There can be but one adequate explanation of this vagary of nineteenth-century science: it was due to the slave trade and Negro slavery. It was due to the fact that the rise and support of capitalism called for rationalization based upon degrading and discrediting of the Negroid peoples."[25] (As Tyrone Hill's comments above make clear, such "discrediting" has remained a major part of American mainstream culture, and Sun Ra's invocations of ancient Egypt were intended to counter this negative view of black history.)

It seems that Sun Ra had embarked on his study of ancient Egypt before *Stolen Legacy* was published, and it is certain that he was using the name Ra by 1952.[26] He confirmed to both Chase and me (in 1990) that he had read *Stolen Legacy*, but unfortunately he did not say when.[27] It is curious that on one of his earliest releases, the 1957 LP *Jazz by Sun Ra* (later reissued as *Sun Song*), he actually dedicates a track not to the Egyptians but to the ancient Greeks! "CALL FOR ALL DEMONS . . . In *ancient Greece the word* DEMON *meant living spirit. The Grecians were not an ignorant people, they had both culture and wisdom. This song is my tribute to them.*"[28] It seems unlikely that Sun Ra would have written this, at least without mentioning that the Greeks' "culture and wisdom" were probably derived from the Egyptians, had he already read *Stolen Legacy*.

Later recordings and pronouncements by Ra, however, reveal some interesting parallels with James's account of ancient Egypt. For example, James noted the significance of the notion of discipline in what he called the "Egyptian Mystery System";[29] Sun Ra wrote a series of numbered compositions under that general rubric ("Discipline 15," "Discipline 27-11," "Discipline 99," etc.), and he often stressed the importance of discipline in both music and life.[30] James also explored the Egyptians' belief in a heliocentric universe and the central importance of the sun god in their cosmology, topics frequently alluded to by Sun Ra in titles such as "The Sun Myth," "Sun Song," *The Heliocentric Worlds of Sun Ra, Secrets of the Sun, When Sun Comes Out*, as well as in his use onstage of sun-shaped instruments and symbols.[31] In our 1990 interview, Sun Ra complained bitterly about the destruction of sun iconography in Egypt and South America by Christians who, he said, "were trying to put this planet in darkness." He decried it as "a planned strategy to get rid of what they called sun-worship; but it wasn't sun-worship, it was the truth."[32]

This hostility toward Christianity, coupled with a concern for the social situation of African Americans in the 1950s, is possibly the most significant of the similarities between Sun Ra's work and that of James. James, like Ra, was hoping to effect a revision of black history that would not only see the world accord African Americans new respect but would also "mean a most important change in the mentality of Black people: a change from an inferiority complex, to the realization and consciousness of their equality with all the other great peoples of the world who have built great civilizations."[33] James argued that some of the later Roman emperors had championed Christianity as a means to suppress the Egyptian Mystery teachings: "In keeping with the plan of Emperors Theodosius and Justinian to exterminate and forever suppress the Culture System of the African continents the Christian church established its missionary enterprise to fight against what it has called paganism. Consequently missionaries and educators have gone to the mission field with a superiority complex, born of miseducation and disrespect. . . ."[34] As a corrective, James proposed his "New Philosophy of African Redemption," a reeducation program that would enlighten the world "as to the real truth about the place of the African continent in the history of civilization,"[35] one that would produce a change of belief and behavior in the black population: "*It really signifies a mental emancipation, in which the Black people will be liberated from the chain of traditional falsehood,* which for centuries has incarcerated them in the prison of inferiority complex and world humiliation and insult."[36]

One immediate form of action that James advocated was "a perpetual protest" against the Christian church's misrepresentations of black culture and black history.[37] He seems to have had in mind what he calls "missionary policy" regarding contemporary depictions of African society, but for Sun Ra it was the Christian church's role in African American society that caused more concern. Wilmer has summarized Ra's early rejection of the Christian church: "At home, in the South . . . he evoked parental wrath when he turned his back on the church, but he detested the palliative effects of religion and the way it led to the resigned acceptance of the status quo by the people around him. Later, in Chicago, he attempted to show the Black urban proletariat ways of improving their situation. 'I felt that the Black people of America needed an awakening,' he said."[38]

Certainly in the 1950s Ra issued pamphlets in Chicago that offered reinterpretations of parts of the Bible, which he insisted was not the Good Book but the Code Book, its real truths suppressed by orthodox Christianity but still available to those who had the key to unlocking its secrets.[39] A vital component of this decoding operation was the process that Sun Ra called "doing the equations," a form of play on the structure and meaning of words that could also involve numerology.[40] It was a process that he demonstrated when he taught briefly at the University of California at Berkeley in 1971: "A typical class (according to Paul Sanoian, one of his students) found Sun Ra writing Biblical quotes on the board and then 'permutating' them—re-writing and transforming their letters and syntax—into new equations of meaning. His lecture subjects included . . . a radical reinterpretation of the Bible in light of Egyptology."[41] While this process might be adduced by some as evidence of Sun Ra's "insanity," it might also have its roots in African American folk beliefs, in the use of what a character in Zora Neale Hurston's anthropological study *Mules and Men* calls "by-words": " 'They all got a hidden meaning' just' like de Bible. Everybody can't understand what they mean. Most people is thin-brained. They's born wid they feet under the moon. Some folks is born wid they feet on de sun and they kin seek out de inside meanin' of words.' "[42] Sun Ra could certainly be said to have had his feet on the sun! Note, too, the apparently commonplace belief that the Bible is full of "hidden meanin.' " The importance to Ra of finding "de inside meanin' of words" is underlined by his brief poem, "To the Peoples of Earth," which reads:

> Proper evaluation of words and letters
> In their phonetic and associated sense

Can bring the peoples of earth
Into the clear light of pure Cosmic Wisdom.[43]

My own interviews with Sun Ra in 1983 and 1990 confirmed his antipathy to Christianity. At our first meeting he spoke critically of what he termed "righteousness," saying that righteous people had often tried to ban music—"and music is the spiritual language, so that would make them truly unspiritual"—and adding that "this has happened in the black race too, the righteous people got in control there and they put up churches and things and then they didn't need music so they didn't support art and beauty . . . you might as well say goodbye to America, it can't survive without art."[44] In 1990 he was even more forthcoming, and I would like to quote three extracts in particular that I believe will help us understand Astro Black Mythology as a specific response to aspects of Judeo-Christian mythology.

> GL: Why are you so interested in ancient Egypt?
>
> SR: I deal with the foundation of things. Everything started in Egypt. I mean, civilization. So naturally I got interested in the basic things. Egypt is basic. More than other nations. Other nations might have had their religions and all that, but Egypt had the culture. It had the truth too. Another kind of truth, which the world will have to recognize—although it went another way after Moses did his job. But it's proven that the world's in the condition it is today because of Moses, not because of Pharaoh.
>
> . . .
>
> GL: I've read that from an early age you rejected Christianity and were opposed to gospel music, the spirituals?
>
> SR: I wasn't really opposed to it. I looked at the condition of black people in America and I judged the tree by the fruit. I knew that [inaudible word or words] good for them couldn't possibly be good for me because they don't deal with progress. They back there in the past, a past that somebody manufactured for 'em. It's not their past, it's not their history. They don't know nothin' about their history . . . and all that enslavement and all that ignorance and whatever they got, they was forced to have it and it became a habit. They got a habit of being ignorant.
>
> . . .
>
> SR: Moses said, fear the Creator. Why should a person fear the Creator, be afraid to express themselves? They talk about Hitler,

the worst dictator was Moses . . . They call him a wise man—
what's wrong with them? That man was a murderer, a liar,
and a deceiver. Moses wasn't good for this planet, I don't care
who sent him. The Egyptian government, they contributed so
much to humanity—he ain't left no art, no beauty, no alpha-
bets. Nothin'. All he did was go out there and kill people. . . .
He was a magician. He learned magic along with the Ra priests
and then he took it and used it against them. Bit the hand that
fed him. Turned against Pharaoh. He was a thief too, he took a
book out of the Bible, the Book of Jason. I researched it, 'cause
I'm a scientist.[45]

This extraordinary attack on Moses takes us to what I see as the crux
of Sun Ra's disagreement with the church and its Judeo-Christian mythology: that by causing African Americans to identify with the Old
Testament stories of the Israelites, it has trapped them in a false history and, in doing so, cut them off from their true historical legacy,
the black civilization of Egypt, which first gave beauty and culture to
the world.

To reclaim the "truth" about Egypt, however, required not only a
revision of history but, as Sun Ra was keenly aware, a revision of mythology, too. The vehemence of his remarks is best understood in the
context of the uniquely significant role that Moses and the Exodus
story have played in African American culture. Many commentators
on the institution of slavery have remarked on the importance of this
liberation narrative in what Albert Raboteau has called the slaves' creation of a mythic past:

Slaves prayed for the future day of deliverance to come, and they
kept their hopes alive by incorporating as part of their mythic past
the Old Testament exodus of Israel out of slavery. The appropriation of the Exodus story was for the slaves a way of articulating
their sense of historical identity as a people. That identity was
also based, of course, upon their common heritage of enslavement. The Christian slaves applied the Exodus story, whose end
they knew, to their own experience of slavery, which had not
ended. In identifying with the Exodus story, they created meaning and purpose out of the chaos and senseless experience of
slavery. Exodus functioned as an archetypal event for the slaves.
The sacred history of God's liberation of his people would be or
was being repeated in the American South.[46]

Raboteau goes on to quote a Union Army chaplain, working with freedmen in Alabama, who in 1864 wrote disapprovingly of the ex-slaves' religion: "There is no part of the Bible with which they are so familiar as the story of the deliverance of the Children of Israel. Moses is their *ideal* of all that is high, and noble, and perfect in man. I think they have been accustomed to regard Christ not so much in the light of a Spiritual Deliverer, as that of a second Moses who would eventually lead *them* out of their prison house of bondage."[47] Evidence of such sentiments can be found in numerous spirituals from the antebellum and immediate postbellum periods: "Go Down, Moses" ("Tell ole Pharaoh to let my people go"), "Didn't Ole Pharaoh Get Los'," "Ride On, Moses," "My Army Cross Over" ("O Pharaoh's army drownded!"), "O, the Dying Lamb" ("I wants to go where Moses trod"), and these lines from a freedmen's hymn: "Shout the glad tidings o'er Egypt's dark sea / Jehovah has triumphed, his people are free!"[48]

Though the glad tidings quickly turned to disillusionment with what Raboteau has called "the chaos, disappointment, and disaster of Reconstruction,"[49] the identification with a Chosen People destined for a Promised Land has remained a potent force in African American culture. Two particular examples are of relevance here. Jon Michael Spencer has shown that the great black migration of the interwar years was often described in terms of an exodus, and he takes issue with the conclusion of Arna Bontemps and Jack Conroy (in their book *They Seek a City*) "that the great black migration had no Moses."[50] Spencer argues that the *Chicago Defender* newspaper, which constantly encouraged blacks to leave the South, "was the movement's Moses, personified in its editor, Robert S. Abbott," and he notes that the *Defender's* twenty-fifth anniversary issue in 1930 carried a portrait of Abbott captioned, "Twentieth Century Moses." Spencer concludes: "From the beginning, the great migration was given a religious interpretation by the movement's Moses, who saw it as an 'exodus' from pharaoh's land of oppression."[51] This exodus is worth noting, since it is one in which Sun Ra himself was a participant, albeit a late one. In 1946, at the age of thirty-two, he left his native city of Birmingham, Alabama, and, after working briefly in Nashville, settled in Chicago, where he would spend the next fifteen years.[52] But rather than a Promised Land, he found himself scrabbling for a living in a sleazy underworld of gangsters, burlesque shows, and strip joints. (Corbett reports him playing piano "behind a curtain at whites-only strip joints in Calumet City" in 1951,[53] and John Szwed has suggested that the opening scenes to the film *Space Is the Place* were based on a real incident at Chicago's Club DeLisa, where Ra worked in the mid-1940s, "when a mobster threatened him.")[54]

The second major example of the Exodus myth in action that I would like to consider is its co-option by the civil rights movement in the late 1950s and 1960s. One can imagine Sun Ra's frustration at the resurgence of this Judeo-Christian version of black history. Just at the point when his own research and James's scholarship were poised to reaffirm the rightful history of black achievement in ancient Egypt, this truth was swept aside by renewed recourse to the Moses/Exodus story, which swiftly became a primary metaphor for the civil rights struggle. The resonances of this "past that somebody manufactured for 'em" continued to sound through the 1960s, up to and including the final speech of Dr. Martin Luther King Jr. Appealing for black unity, King specifically identified ancient Egypt with white racist America: "We've got to stay together and maintain unity. You know, whenever Pharaoh wanted to prolong the period of slavery in Egypt, he had a favorite, a favorite formula for doing it. What was that? He kept the slaves fighting among themselves."[55] Later, in the famous climax to the speech, made the night before he was assassinated, King's own identification with Moses reached its tragic apotheosis:

> Well, I don't know what will happen now. We've got some difficult days ahead. But it doesn't matter with me now. Because I've been to the mountaintop. And I don't mind. Like anybody, I would like to live a long time. Longevity has its place. But I'm not concerned about that now. I just want to do God's will. And he's allowed me to go to the mountaintop. And I've looked over. And I've seen the promised land. I may not get there with you. But I want you to know tonight, that we, as a people, will get to the promised land.[56]

Though Sun Ra did not record them until 1974, lines from the enigmatic "There Is Change in the Air" perhaps reveal his feelings about such promises and promised lands: "The people and the leaders walk hand in hand / They're on the right road / They're going the wrong direction."[57]

Despite his disagreements with the civil rights movement's use of the Moses myth—and the espousal of "freedom songs" (when *discipline* was the attribute required)—I think that for Sun Ra "the wrong direction" did not indicate a criticism of any particular political strategy so much as a skepticism about conventional political activity per se. When in 1983 I asked him what he thought about Dr. King, he replied:

> Well, I don't really think too much of anyone who doesn't speak for music. But one time I did read an article in the U.S. where he said that no nation will move forward without the artists moving forward first. That's pretty close. But I don't think the people in America buy that. . . .
>
> What they [the leaders of the civil rights movement] were talking about may have been correct, but the advances — the so-called advances — that the darker people have made in America, that was cut off by Reagan. So, really, what good was his death? However, if people would base what they done on culture and beauty, they would immediately become part of the nation of the world that knows beauty is necessary for survival.[58]

Sun Ra never stopped promoting ancient Egypt as a source of beauty, though in later years references to Egypt seemed to play a less prominent part in his music. The two major exceptions to this rule, the compositions "I, Pharaoh" and "Sunset on the Nile," were, significantly, valedictory in tone. ("I, Pharaoh," first recorded in the mid-1970s, is a twenty-minute monologue by Ra in the role of Pharaoh, looking back at a time when "My kingdom was splendid, without compare," lamenting that "the nations of the world destroyed my kingdom, enslaved my people, now I, Pharaoh, am all alone" and complaining that while "they got a Christmas Day, they got an Easter Day" yet "they never give me no glory, they never tell my story." There is a slight sting in the tail in that the "one thing" Pharaoh has still got left is "the secret of immortality," but overall the mood is one of rueful poignancy.)[59] Ra's tone was notably less valedictory in 1979, however, when at a talk he gave in New York City, he declared that no matter how "dark-skinned" you were, you were only entitled to call yourself "black" if you were "from ancient Egypt" and "belonged to Pharaoh."[60] By 1990 his mood had changed again and, perhaps despairing of ever persuading African Americans to adopt Pharaoh as their mythic hero in place of Moses, he told Francis Davis (apropos of his greater popularity elsewhere in the world): "The main problem in America is black folk worshippin' the wrong thing. You can't get 'em to change because they think what they doin' is quite appropriate."[61]

If Egypt became a less dominant presence in his music, Ra found an alternative symbol of black achievement and beauty to promote. From the mid-1970s he began to feature in his Arkestra concerts the repertoire of early big band leaders such as Duke Ellington and Jimmie Lunceford; in particular, he drew on the repertoire of his idol, Fletcher Henderson (with whom he had worked briefly in Chicago in 1946–47), performing compositions like "Big John's Special," "Blue Lou," "Can You Take It?," "Christopher Columbus," "King Porter Stomp," "Limehouse Blues," "Queer Notions," "Slumming on Park Avenue," and "Yeah Man." [62] Ra told Tam Fiofori in 1970 that the early big bands he'd heard as a teenager represented "truly natural Black beauty," [63] and in 1987 he explained to Phil Schaap: "in the Deep South, the black people were very oppressed and were made to feel like they weren't anything, so the only thing they had was big bands. Unity showed that black men could join together and dress nicely, do something nice, and that was all they had. So big bands are very important in the South. . . ." [64] He even went so far as to suggest that Fletcher Henderson and Coleman Hawkins were not men but angels (which he also said of himself), [65] and that the decline of the big bands was "a planned strategy by people to bypass particular Black musicians that were the masters." [66] So what we have now is "an empire of false musicians," comprising imitators, egotists and "the money-minded," who play "false jazz" and try to keep the true creators "out of the way." [67] In Sun Ra's view, the history of jazz too, it seems, had become "a past that somebody manufactured" and he attempted to revise this false history by presenting real "Black beauty" in his concerts; typically, he also devised a chant to underline what he was doing: "They tried to fool you / Now I got to school you / About jazz, about jazz." [68]

Later Ra extended the Arkestra's repertoire to feature the work of white composers too who, he told Mark Sinker, he felt had not been accorded "proper status—or proper honour" in the United States (a process that culminated in 1989 with several concerts devoted to compositions from Walt Disney films): "I'd been doing Duke Ellington, Fletcher Henderson, Basie—first I did that. The black folks still asleep, they didn't help me with that. So then I decided to take the white race and honour their brothers, because they hadn't done it either. So then I did George Gershwin, Irving Berlin, Cole Porter—and then finally I did the Disney thing. . . ." [69] Playing the music of such composers, Ra explained, would create "a shield of beauty" to protect the world from "the cosmic forces" that might otherwise "come and destroy people." [70] The scope of this ambition, to save the planet, echoed through many interviews and in lyrics such as "I can't give you civil rights / I can give you universal rights,"[71] and perhaps explains Sun Ra's lack of interest in conventional politics. Indeed, if politics is the art of the possible, this is exactly the kind of activity that Sun Ra considered the most pointless. "The impossible attracts me," he declared in the 1960s, "because everything possible has been done and the world didn't change."[72] And: "The impossible is the watchword of the greater space age. The space age *cannot* be avoided and the *space music* is the key to understanding the meaning of the *impossible* and every other enigma."[73]

Whether it can help us to understand the second key element of Sun Ra's Astro Black Mythology, his fascination with outer space, is the issue to which we must now turn. Before we do so, however, it is perhaps worth pointing out that by most standards he did achieve the impossible. That a black pianist from a poor family in Alabama was able to travel the globe in space clothes proclaiming himself "another order of being" is unlikely enough; that he also kept a band together for nearly forty years and released well over a hundred LP recordings, the great majority of them on his own record label, is more incredible still. Ra's own life and work became prime examples of the black creativity he so tirelessly promoted. Certainly, Arkestra trombonist Tyrone Hill was in no doubt that in revising history Sun Ra was also making history and restoring black people to their rightful place as participants in history: "It's like I'm part of . . . this is history, you know. I feel history was made last night when we played and as I'm sitting here talking to you. So I feel I'm part of something they'll talk about in the future. Sun Ra is an integral part of world history."[74]

— • • • ⸺

I hope I have established that Sun Ra's evocations of ancient Egypt were not the ravings of a "nutter" but can be seen as part of an ongoing debate about the origins of civilization and the uses of different mythic pasts as metaphors for African American history. Nevertheless, the future was the main focus of Ra's music, and it was his vision of the future that attracted the most ridicule and misunderstanding. What I hope to show is that Ra's "galactic gobbledegook" becomes more explicable when viewed in the context of certain African American cultural traditions. Call it the "celestial road," as Ra did in 1979, or call it the "heavenly way," as DuBois did in 1903, but African Americans have been traveling along it for well over two hundred years.[75]

Sun Ra's interest in the future, indeed his enthusiastic anticipation of it, is evident from one of his earliest releases, the 1957 LP *Jazz by Sun Ra* (later reissued as *Sun Song*). His notes to the music begin with a poem, "New Horizons," that evokes "a new world of sounds. . . . A new world for every self / Seeking a better self and a better world" and closes with the promise of:

> Music rushing forth like a fiery law
> Loosening the chains that bind,
> Ennobling the mind
> With all the many greater dimensions
> Of a living tomorrow.[76]

Already music is configured here as something akin to a cosmic force ("fiery law") that can free us from the limitations of the past and prepare our minds for the wonders to come. Composition titles on the recording—"Future," "Transition," "New Horizons"—confirm Ra's declaration that "most of my compositions speak of the future," while he describes the track "Sun Song" as "the reach for new sounds, a spacite picture of the Atonal tomorrow."[77]

That Ra's music continued to "speak of the future" in general terms is indicated by LP titles such as 1961's *The Futuristic Sounds of Sun Ra*, *Art Forms of Dimensions Tomorrow* (released in 1965), and *A Tonal View of Times Tomorrow, Vols. 1 and 2* (alternative titles for *Space Probe* and *The Invisible Shield*, both released in 1974). The music itself was appropriately innovative and often sounded otherworldly, thanks in large part to Ra's highly individualistic arrangements, the Arkestra's groundbreaking development of large-ensemble collective improvisation, and Ra's imaginative use of electronic keyboards, in which field he was certainly a pioneer.[78] This embrace of new technology had been signaled on *Sun Song* by the track "Brainville," not so much by the music as by Sun Ra's notes on the composition, which he declared was "dedicated to scientists, space pilots, those of the medical profession and all others who are of daring mind."[79] What's more, "Brainville" itself is a utopian vision of "a city whose citizens are all intelligent in mind and action," where "Musicians are called SOUND SCIENTISTS and TONE ARTISTS. Every being is healthy and there is no extinction of being. Yes, Brainville is a wonderful city, and we like the thought of it."[80]

By the beginning of the 1960s, this confluence of music, science, and utopia was being expressed by Sun Ra almost exclusively in terms of space travel. While a scattering of his song titles in the 1950s had alluded to space themes ("Saturn," "Planet Earth," "Star Time"), two discs recorded between 1959 and 1961 put outer space at the center of the Arkestra's repertoire.[81] *Rocket Number Nine Take Off for the Planet Venus* (aka *Interstellar Low Ways*) comprised the titles "Somewhere in Space," "Interplanetary Music," "Space Loneliness," "Space Aura," and the two title tracks; *We Travel the Spaceways* included the title track "Tapestry from an Asteroid" and different versions of "Interplanetary Music" and "Space Loneliness."

From this point on, outer space became the dominant reference in Sun Ra's music. Other space titles recorded in the early 1960s were "Lights from a Satellite," "Space Mates," "Space Jazz Reverie," "Friendly Galaxy," "Love in Outer Space," "Next Stop Mars," "Voice of Space," and "Spiral Galaxy."[82] Although many of these pieces were purely instrumental, titles such as "Friendly Galaxy" and "Love in Outer Space" suggest that Ra viewed outer space as a benign location; later lyrics such as 1979's "On Jupiter, the skies are always blue" not only confirm this impression but show that space retained its utopian resonances for Sun Ra.[83] Perhaps his most explicit statement of this view was "Space Is the Place," first performed in the early 1970s and thereafter a regular feature in Arkestra concerts:

> Outer space is a pleasant place
> A place that's really free
> There's no limit to the things that you can do
> There's no limit to the things that you can be
> Your thought is free
> And your life is worthwhile.[84]

It is possible to see space playing a variety of roles in Sun Ra's music. Perhaps his most straightforward use of outer space is as an image of the imminent technological future. Val Wilmer has written that his activities in Chicago in the 1950s included "distributing pamphlets in which he pointed to the technological developments taking place in the world and the practicality of pursuing studies in the fields of electronics or engineering. His exhortations to 'stay in school' predated James Brown's by more than a decade."[85] Arkestra tenor saxophonist John Gilmore has recalled that Sun Ra, even in the early 1950s, "was always telling people to be ready for the Space Age, computers. He said there were gonna be electronic instruments that you could blow . . . that we were gonna walk on the moon and that, all of it happened."[86] Several early statements by Sun Ra himself make clear his concern with preparing people for the future. Sometimes this concern was directed specifically toward African Americans:

> Many different musicians all over the planet . . . are experimenting, particularly the white musicians who are trying to do something to change their race over another way, 'cause they knew something was going to happen to them if they don't change. . . . In the Black race, it hasn't been like that. Musicians weren't planning nothing for their people as far as change is concerned. I had dedicated a so-called lifetime to doin' exactly that 'cause I knew we was gonna need it.[87]

At other times his concern was all-inclusive. In his notes to *Sun Song* he set out what sounds like a credo for his entire oeuvre: "The real aim of this music is to co-ordinate the minds of peoples into an intelligent reach for a better world, and an intelligent approach to the living future. By peoples I mean all of the people of different nations who are living today."[88]

Other notes and poems on this 1957 recording indicate that Sun Ra was also using outer space as a metaphor for inner space, the realm of the imagination, as in this extract from the poem "Enticement":

> Imagination is a magic carpet
> Upon which we may soar
> To distant lands and climes;
> And even go beyond the moon to any planet in the sky.[89]

In the same notes he also offered his *Instructions to the Peoples of Earth*, which concludes: "You must learn to listen because by listening you will learn to see with your mind's eye. You see, *music paints pictures that only the mind's eye can see.* Open your ears so that you can see with the eye of the mind."[90] Other poems in the booklet refer to visiting outer space, yet intriguingly there is no mention of space ships. In "New Horizons," it is again "imagination . . . ! / With wings unhampered, / Unafraid . . . . / Soaring like a bird" that travels to "the heart of tomorrow,"[91] and this bird imagery also pervades "Sun Song," in which Ra claims rather bizarrely that "Yes, I have a nest; / Out in outer space on the tips of the world."[92]

This decidedly unscientific approach to space travel (to which I return in a moment) is puzzling, not least because science and science fiction were prominent themes in American culture at the time. This was the era of stories by Ray Bradbury and Arthur C. Clarke, of films like *It Came from Outer Space* and *Invasion of the Body Snatchers*, of sputniks and satellites—all plausible sources for prompting Sun Ra's interest in outer space, yet offering no clue as to why he was relatively *late* in adopting the science fiction imagery of his subsequent space chants.[93] Certainly, Ra was by no means the first jazz artist to make use of science fiction motifs. In 1955 Shorty Rogers released *Martians Go Home*, quickly followed by *Martians Come Back*. According to Ira Gitler, "'Martians Go Home,' with its cover photo of Shorty—his head enclosed in a space bubble—was one of the most visible, and audible, albums of the time."[94] In 1956 Duke Ellington recorded his *A Drum Is a Woman* project (a version of which was broadcast on national television in 1957), in which the heroine Madam Zajj visited the moon, accompanied by a "Ballet of the Flying Saucers." And in 1958 West Coast bassist Curtis Counce recorded his *Exploring the Future* LP, its cover shot depicting him in a space suit floating through the cosmos, and its list of tracks included the compositions "Into the Orbit," "The Countdown," and "Race for Space." "Race for Space" is a thought-provoking phrase. As its use by Counce implies, it was much in vogue in the United States in the late 1950s, as the Soviet Sputnik 1 beat the American Explorer satellite into space by three months. This same period saw a crisis in race relations, initiated by the Brown vs. Board of Education verdict in 1954 and climaxing in the standoff in Little Rock, Arkansas, in September 1957, just a month before the launch of Sputnik 1.[95] Duke Ellington, alert to the ambiguity of the phrase, wrote an essay titled "The Race for Space," in which he argued that the Russians were winning that race because "so many Americans persist in the notion of the master race" and so prevent the racial harmony necessary for progress.[96] Ellington's essay was apparently unpublished, but it seems likely that Sun Ra also, with his sensitivity to language, might have noted that ambiguity and contemplated the notion that, whoever won, the race for space seemed destined to be the white race. Perhaps this thought prompted him to prepare the black race, too, for a future in outer space. But whenever and for whatever reason he made that decision, he would have known that according to one cultural tradition, African Americans had been traveling the spaceways well before his own arrival on the planet in 1914. It is to that tradition that I would now like to turn.

In his 1912 novel *The Autobiography of an Ex-Colored Man* James Weldon Johnson describes a Southern camp meeting at which a particularly electrifying sermon is preached by a traveling preacher called John Brown, whose eloquence he likens to the creation of "tone pictures":

The most striking example of John Brown's magnetism and imagination was his "heavenly march." I shall never forget how it impressed me when I heard it. He opened his sermon in the usual way, then, proclaiming to his listeners that he was going to take them on the heavenly march, he seized the Bible under his arm and began to pace up and down the pulpit platform. The congregation immediately began with their feet a "tramp, tramp, tramp," in time with the preacher's march in the pulpit, all the while singing in an undertone a hymn about marching to Zion. Suddenly he cried: "Halt!" Every foot stopped with the precision of a company of well-drilled soldiers and the singing ceased. The morning star had been reached. Here the preacher described the beauties of that celestial body. Then the march, the "tramp, tramp, tramp," and the singing were again taken up. Another "Halt!" They had reached the evening star. And so on, past the sun and moon—the intensity of the religious emotion all the time increasing—along the milky way, on up to the gates of heaven.[97]

Such sermons could be heard in Southern Baptist churches in the late nineteenth and early twentieth centuries, though a decade or two later the march was replaced by the gospel train. In 1927 the popular black preacher the Rev. A. W. Nix recorded his striking sermon, "The White Flyer to Heaven," in which he exhorts his congregation to accompany him on a special gospel train that will transport them through the "First Heaven, the Heaven of Clouds" and into outer space:

> Higher and higher! Higher and higher!
> We'll pass on to the Second Heaven
> The starry decked Heaven, and view the flying stars and dashing meteors
> And then pass on by Mars and Mercury, and Jupiter and Venus
> And Saturn and Uranus, and Neptune with her four glittering moons.[98]

Sixty-three years later, on the last track of his *Live in London* 1990 CD, you can hear Sun Ra exhort his congregation of concertgoers to take a similar (if more astronomically accurate) trip and "travel the spaceways" with him to Venus, Jupiter, Neptune, and "Pluto too."[99] What makes this resemblance especially intriguing is that the Rev. Mr. Nix was, like Sun Ra, a native of Birmingham, and may have preached this very sermon at the Tabernacle Baptist Church that Sun Ra attended as a child in the company of his grandmother. Whether or not Sun Ra ever heard Nix, in person or on record, it seems indisputable that the space trip format he employed in the 1990 London concert—and similar space trips were often a feature of Arkestra performances—was deliberately based on the heavenly journey of the Baptist sermon tradition.[100]

This sermon tradition may also account for the bizarre bird imagery of "Sun Song," quoted above. Paul Oliver has noted that verse 11 in Deuteronomy 32, "As an eagle stirreth up her nest, fluttereth over her young, spreadeth abroad her wings, taketh them, beareth them on her wings," was an especially popular text for preachers, so much so that several different sermons on it were released on record. One from 1928 by the well-known Rev. J. M. Gates shares some notable similarities with "Sun Song," in particular its linking of the bird with the sun: "He can fly, and watch the sun / He's the only bird that can view the sun in the morning / And read the message written in the sun." [101] Insofar as the eagle was, according to Oliver, often seen as a symbol of Christ, Ra could perhaps be said to be proposing the sun god as an alternative savior, and his reference to a "fiery nest of many mansions" certainly echoes the phraseology of the spirituals,[102] as for example in "The love of God shines in his eyes / He tells of mansions in the skies" or "I want to live up yonder / In bright mansions above." [103] What I suggest is happening here is that Sun Ra is deliberately invoking the sermon traditions of the heavenly journey and the eagle-Christ in order to emphasize that he is offering an alternative vision, specifically, an alternative future to that proposed by the Christian church. My guess is that Ra quickly abandoned his references to the Eagle sermon because the allusions were too arcane, too much within the Baptist tradition, whereas the heavenly journey, presented anew in the contemporary language of science and science fiction, had a much wider resonance throughout the culture.[104]

I have pointed to Sun Ra's dislike of Christianity and in particular his objection to the mythic past that the church had, in his view, "manufactured" for African Americans. Ra was no less opposed to the mythic future that the Christian religion offered black people. That his own vision of the future, what he called "the alter-destiny," was shaped by his antagonism to Christianity is suggested by his comment: "if you are dissatisfied with yourself in the scheme of things and the altar has not changed conditions, perhaps you should consider the alter." [105] In particular, he criticized what he regarded as the church's refusal to embrace the science and technology that promised a better future. As he told Mark Sinker (with reference to the 1950s): "I was talking about computers, I was talking about spaceships, I was talking about flying into outer space. I was talking about satellites! A black minister told me, 'Hey, this ain't in the Bible.' I'd say, they're going to the moon, they going to go further. I don't care what it says in the Bible—that's what's going to happen." [106]

Sun Ra was not the first African American to feel this way. Spencer has reported that from the 1920s onward, the *Chicago Defender* ran innumerable articles that comprised "constant criticism of old-time religion" and "repeated petition for religion to keep up with the findings of science," sentiments that he sees as part of a wider process of secularization and urbanization that accompanied the Great Migration.[107] In particular, he notes that the spirituals became associated with the sorrows and submissiveness of slavery and the postbellum South. One 1932 letter to the *Defender* even predicts that the spirituals will soon be replaced by a new kind of song, informed by the language of science: "from the deep and boundless soul of the Negro will rise a new idea, filtering through a new vocabulary enriched by scientific discovery, recognizing the supremacy of a divine master and interpreting the beauty and grandeur of a glorious creation." [108] This is a fair summary of what Sun Ra's space chants later attempted to do. So we can say that in addition to using outer space as a metaphor for both the actual scientific future and the inner space of fantasy and imagination, Sun Ra also presented outer space as the site of a mythic future that he proposed as the alter(native) destiny to the Christian notion of heaven.

I will return in a moment to the question of how precisely he went about this. First, though, I would like to consider the point that the two poles of Ra's Astro Black Mythology—ancient Egypt and outer space—are linked by virtue of their being alternatives to, in turn, a Christian mythic past, the Exodus myth, and a Christian mythic future in God's heaven. Yet these two elements of Judeo-Christian mythology were themselves linked in a very special way in African American history in the "sacred world" that, according to Lawrence Levine, the black slaves created and described in their spirituals. Levine derives his concept of the "sacred world" from the work of the religious historian Mircea Eliade, in particular Eliade's hypothesis that "for people in traditional societies religion is a means of extending the world spatially upward so that communication with the other world becomes ritually possible and extending it temporally backwards so that the paradigmatic acts of the gods and mythical ancestors can be continually re-enacted and indefinitely recoverable." [109] This concept of the sacred, argues Levine:

> gets at the essence of the spirituals and through them at the essence of the slave's worldview. . . . They extended the boundaries of their restrictive universe backward until it fused with the world of the Old Testament, and upward until it became one with the world beyond. The spirituals are the record of a people who found the status, the harmony, the values, the order they needed to survive by internally creating an expanded universe, by literally willing themselves reborn. [110]

This seems to me an uncannily apt description not only of Sun Ra himself, who, as I hope to show in chapter 2, indeed willed himself reborn, but also of the processes implicit in his work—but with the crucial difference that Ra proposed his Astro Black Mythology in place of the Christian beliefs that shaped the slaves' worldview (and which, for him, had itself become a "restrictive universe"). So he extended his myth-world back to the glories of ancient Egypt rather than to the Old Testament patriarchs and upward to a heaven that he depicted not as the location of a promised afterlife but, in the light of astronomy and modern technology, as the site of a real, living future in outer space.

To amplify this point, I would like to look more closely at Sun Ra's space chants and their relationship to the spirituals. A distinct and significant subgenre within Ra's music, where they constitute the great bulk of his vocal material, the space chants are brief, repetitive, and antiphonal, comparable in form to the spirituals, whose themes and imagery they constantly echo. [111] These echoes range from direct quotation to specific allusions to more general similarities. As their name suggests, most space chants are about outer space but at least one, "Children of the Sun," seems more about challenging the Christian mythic past, its lines "The same sun is shining now / That was shining then" apparently countering the lines "An de God dat lived in Moses' time is jus' de same today" from the spiritual "He's Jus' de Same Today." [112] One other non-space chant that may be related to a spiritual is "I Am the Brother of the Wind," the lyrics to which—"I, the wind, come and go as I choose and none can stop me"—appear to be a direct refutation of "Hold the wind! Hold the wind! Hold the wind, don't let it blow." [113] Far more frequent, however, are space chants that quote or allude to spirituals in the context of outer space. Sometimes Sun Ra incorporated direct quotations into his chants: spirituals he quoted most frequently include "All God's Chillun Got Wings," "No Hiding Place," "Sometimes I Feel Like a Motherless Child," "Swing Low, Sweet Chariot," and "This World Is Not My Home."[114] Some of these spirituals are presumably quoted because they fit easily into Ra's own cosmology: "This World Is Not My Home" and "Sometimes I Feel Like a Motherless Child," for example, accord with his claim to be "not of this planet"; "Swing Low, Sweet Chariot" resembles his various chants about spaceships, such as "U- U- UFO / Take me where I want to go."[115] His use of "No Hiding Place" is more pointed, seemingly a jibe at the church's refusal to embrace the space age. He quotes this spiritual on the LP *Beyond the Purple Star Zone*, during a version of "Rocket Number Nine"; the song suddenly changes, and Ra introduces a new chant, in which he proclaims:

> The space age is here to stay
> Ain't no place that you can run away
>
> If you run to the rock to hide your face
> The rock'll cry out, no hiding place
>
> It's gonna be just like your ancestors said
> Even though they're cold and dead.[116]

The two middle lines come from "No Hiding Place" and originally referred to the inescapability of God's judgment.[117] Ra not only transforms the message into his own Astro Black Mythology, in which you cannot escape the alter-destiny of the space age, but by slyly recontextualizing the original sentiment he signifies on it.[118] This "space age" chant also can be heard on the 1976 LP *The Soul Vibrations of Man*, where it segues into a Ra version of the heavenly journey—"Mercury is the first heaven, Venus is the second heaven" (and so on through all nine planets)—that incorporates lines from the spiritual "All God's Chillun Got Wings" (aka "Heaven"), specifically "Everybody talkin' 'bout heaven ain't goin' there" and "When I get to Heaven, I'm goin' to put on my shoes, I'm goin' to walk all over God's Heaven."[119] (Again, the first line in particular could be seen as Ra signifying on the church by repeating, in a different context, a line that might originally have been used to signify on, for example, slave masters who professed to be Christians.)

At times Ra will allude to a spiritual without quoting it directly. A good example occurs in the medley of space chants that I mentioned earlier on the *Live in London 1990* CD. Toward the end of the medley, Ra tells the audience:

> You're on the Spaceship Earth
> And you're outward bound
> Out among the stars
> Destination unknown
> But you haven't met the captain of the spaceship yet, have you?
> You'd better pay your fare now
> Or you'll be left behind
> You'll be left hanging
> In the empty air
> And you won't be here and you won't be there.[120]

Compare his pointed references to "the captain" and paying your fare to these lines from the spiritual "The Old Ship of Zion":

> King Jesus is her captain, Hallejuh! [sic]
> O get your ticket ready, Hallelujah!
> She is coming in the harbor, Hallelujah!
> She will land you safe in heaven, Hallelujah![121]

Compare, too, Ra's warning about "hanging in the empty air" with this similar warning from the spiritual "The Downward Road Is Crowded": "You can't ride the empty air / And get to heaven that day"; while the spiritual "Hail! Hail!" includes the lines "When I get in the middle of the air / You know I can't stay here / Not a sinner will be there."[122]

Several other space chants seem to echo more fleetingly the language and/or the themes of certain spirituals, translating their religious messages into the context of Ra's own cosmological trinity of space, music, and the future. Compare, for example, Ra's "Have you heard the latest news from Neptune" with "Good news! O good news! De angels brought de tidings down / Just comin' from de trone";[123] "The 21st century is knocking at your door" with "Somebody's knocking at your door / Sounds like Jesus";[124] "You gotta face the music / You gotta listen to the cosmo-song" with "Got to go to judgment / Got to stand your trial."[125] One or two of Sun Ra's more enigmatic LP titles may also refer to spirituals. *The Night of the Purple Moon*, for example, could refer to the evocation of Judgment Day in "Didn't My Lord Deliver Daniel": "De moon run down in a purple stream / De sun forbear to shine;"[126] while *Monorails and Satellites* suggests that we compare and contrast the heavenly transport of the spirituals—"Ain't but one train on this track / It runs to heaven and runs right back"—with the more circumambulatory routes of contemporary satellites.[127] And its resemblance to a spiritual may explain why at a handful of 1990 concerts Sun Ra chose to sing "Down Here on the Ground," a 1968 pop ballad by Gale Garnett and Lalo Schifrin. The song portrays the singer "down here on the ground, wanting something better," enviously watching the birds "flyin' sort of free" and hoping that "one morning sure I will find / Wings on my mind / To take me high," an image very similar to one that recurs in many spirituals: "One of these morning bright and fair / Take my wings and cleave the air."[128]

As Chase notes of "Down Here on the Ground," the lyrics "become a surprisingly appropriate expression of Sun Ra's avowed alienation from the world around him, his desire for transformation or escape," and in this context they take on a "special pathos."[129] In this respect, however, "Down Here on the Ground" is relatively exceptional in Sun Ra's repertoire. Given DuBois's well-known description of the spirituals as "sorrow songs,"[130] it is worth noting that Ra's space chants often explicitly disavow sorrow: for example: "We sing this song for a new tomorrow / We sing this song to abolish sorrow" and "Enlightment [sic] is my tomorrow / It has no plane of sorrow."[131] Ra underlined this point in interviews with Cole Gagne and Phil Schaap, telling Schaap: "Well, Jazz is what the Creator likes . . . . The rest of the stuff that's sad and sanctimonious he doesn't like. But he likes my music."[132] It is as if Sun Ra was concerned to propose an alternative not only to the Judeo-Christian mythology of the spirituals but also to their association with a history of African American sorrow and submissiveness that had so bothered the *Chicago Defender*.[133] The focus on happiness was evident as well in other areas of Ra's music, signaled by titles such as "Days of Happiness," "Blithe Spirit Dance," *Sound of Joy*, and *Sun Sound Pleasure!!* as well as by his performances of standards like "Happy as the Day Is Long" and " 'S Wonderful."[134] In 1957 Ra declared that the aim of his compositions was to "depict happiness combined with beauty," and thirty years later he was still saying "I want to make people happy."[135] (This sentiment was becoming somewhat vitiated by the mid-1980s as Sun Ra performed a small group of songs like "Down Here on the Ground" and Jerome Kern and lyricist Otto Harbach's "Yesterdays" that, as Chase has argued, "seemed to express deeply personal feelings of separation, nostalgia and longing when Sun Ra sang them."[136] A feeling of isolation was definitely palpable in 1990 when Ra, then seventy-six years old, told me: "I left my family, I left my friends, I left for real. I left everything to be me, 'cause I knew I was not like them. Not like black or white, not like Americans. I'm not like nobody else. I'm alone on this planet.") [137]

I would like to make two further points that I think establish beyond question that Sun Ra's space chants were drawing from and referring to the mythic world of the spirituals. Levine has noted that one characteristic of the slaves' religious mythology was that "God and Christ and Satan were not symbols but personages with whom meetings or confrontations were quite possible." [138] A similar familiarity with supernatural beings is assumed in early Sun Ra LP titles such as *Angels and Demons at Play* and *When Angels Speak of Love* and reaffirmed on later titles such as *Music from the Private Library of God* and *A Fireside Chat with Lucifer*, [139] the latter of which recalls not only "The White Flyer to Heaven," in which the Rev. Mr. Nix promises that, once arrived in heaven, "I'm gonna sit down and chat with the Father / And chat with the Son," [140] but also the numerous earlier spirituals that had made similar claims: "Going to chatter with the angels . . . Going to walk and talk with Jesus." [141] Sun Ra's declared intimacy with Lucifer can perhaps be seen as strategic to his quarrel with Christianity, though he also claimed similarly close acquaintance with God, describing himself on one occasion as an "archangel . . . representing the living God," [142] and telling Schaap: "I'm very well in tune with the angel of death, and with God, and Lucifer and the Devil and whatever you got. They're all my friends. . . ." [143]

A final example of Sun Ra's familiarity with the Creator, or at least the Creator's language, is the story that Francis Davis recounted in 1991 and is worth repeating here because it also provides a good example of Ra's wit and deadpan humor—unmistakable in concert but perhaps not so immediately apparent on the printed page. The story concerns an incident in the 1960s when a Nigerian poet (unnamed, but possibly Tam Fiofori) who was part of Sun Ra's entourage at the time became involved in a fracas with some New York City policemen in the subway and fell to the ground. As "about a dozen cops" came racing along the platform, their nightsticks drawn, Davis relates:

> the prone poet did as Sun Ra had told him to do when in physical danger: he shouted out "Creator, help me!"
>
> According to Sun Ra, a deep, disembodied, peremptory voice then commanded: "LEAVE THE MOTHERFUCKER ALONE."
>
> "The police didn't know where it came from, but they left him

alone after that," Ra told us. "But if he had said, 'God, help me,' they would have beaten him up."

But here's the part I like.

"I didn't know the Creator used that kind of language," the Nigerian supposedly told Sun Ra afterward.

"He speaks to each man in his own tongue," Ra assured him.

"Why would he speak to you in a language that you wouldn't understand?" he asked us, as though nothing could be more absurd.[144]

The clinching piece of evidence that Ra intended his space chants as alternatives to the spirituals concerns the manner of their performance. Whenever there was room, most members of the Arkestra would leave their seats and come to the front of the stage where, clapping and chanting, they would dance in a counterclockwise circle, just as in the ring shout, the central ceremony of African American slave worship and originally one of the main arenas in which the spirituals, too, were stomped and shouted.[145] A defining characteristic of the ring shout, which was almost certainly a retention from West African religious ceremonies, was that the circle of dancers always moved in a counterclockwise direction. This counterclockwise dance occurred in every Arkestra concert I have seen, either in person or on film.[146] Levine records an account of a black camp meeting in 1818 at which the dancers, circling and chanting "We're traveling to Immanuel's land / Glory! Halle-lu-jah," enacted Joshua's victory at the Battle of Jericho. He notes: "The shout often became a medium through which the ecstatic dancers were transformed into actual participants in historic actions: Joshua's army marching around the walls of Jericho, the children of Israel following Moses out of Egypt."[147] Or, some 150 years later, Sun Ra leading his Arkestra on a heavenly trip around the solar system, proclaiming (in the *present* tense), "We travel the spaceways, from planet to planet." And, as happened at the old ring shouts, watchers are urged to join in—"We do invite you / Be of our spaceworld"— the price of the ticket (as it were) being no more than an act of faith in the power of our imaginations:

If you find Earth boring
The same old same thing
Come on and sign up
With Outer Spaceways Incorporated.[148]

So, just as the slaves' "sacred world" brought together past and future, time and space, in the eternal now of the ring shout, so Sun Ra united ancient Egypt and outer space in his myth-world and celebrated the union in his sacred arena, the concert, where costumes and instruments alike linked the worlds of Africa and science fiction, and the entire spectrum of black creative music was enacted in ceremonious and colorful spectacle. John Corbett is surely correct to say that Sun Ra's music was "about the formal construction of vehicles to travel in self-created space. Ra called for listeners to do the impossible, to make manifest a fantastic journey, a highly politicized, poetical trip into unknown worlds. His work was predicated in the concretization of metaphor and the materialization of space as a musical and mental— but altogether real—place." [149] Corbett goes on to compare this facet of Ra's work with Mikhail Bakhtin's concept of the "chronotype"—"the intrinsic connectedness of temporal and spatial relationships." [150] But examples of this "connectedness," of the "concretization of metaphor," can be found closer to home in the African American cultural tradition of transformation that took early form in the ring shout and later shape in sermons like John Brown's heavenly march or "The White Flyer to Heaven," in which the Rev. A.W. Nix, as Oliver says, "made the vision real by projecting himself into the scene and carrying the congregation with him on the heavenly train." [151] Making the vision real was obviously a central impulse in Sun Ra's work, and if the vision in question was essentially futuristic, the means he used to actualize it were steeped in tradition—the better, perhaps, to emphasize that his outer space utopia, his alter-destiny, was specifically offered as an alternative to the mythic spaces traditionally invoked by those traditional means.

In view of Ra's attacks on "the righteous," it is worth noting that well before the end of the nineteenth century, a growing number of black clergymen were attempting to abolish the ring shout on the grounds that it was primitive, heathenish, and, in the words of A.M.E. Bishop Daniel Alexander Payne, "disgraceful to themselves [i.e., the participants], the race and the Christian name." [152] Perhaps it was such attitudes that Ra had in mind when he declared that this planet "has never done anything for me but try to stop me, try to make my so-called life ugly like it did the rest of black people, and tried to make me worship a god that they made." [153] Certainly his appropriation of the ring shout for his concerts could be construed as another facet to his argument with the more orthodox and "righteous" elements of the African American church.[154] Yet I doubt that simple provocation was his primary intent. The Arkestra's dances relate to the ring shout as their space chants relate to the spirituals; that is, there may be degrees of humor and mimicry in play, but Sun Ra's main aim appears to have been a massive act of re-vision, whereby the Christian vision of a mythic future is transformed and translated into the language and imagery of futuristic science. In 1993, bell hooks argued: "the Church wasn't just a place for conventional religiosity but a place for a transcendent vision of life that allowed for the formation of utopian discourses. One of the things that we ought to be asking is this. If we do away with the power of the Church, as has happened in black experience in the US, then what takes its place as something legitimizing the imagination of a future outside the existing social reality?"[155]

Sun Ra's work demonstrates that music, actually the site of many of those "utopian discourses" within the church, can play the same role outside the church in the new and different context of scientific potential. Or, as Ra told his audience at New York's Soundscape in 1979, "You've outlived the Bible, which was your scenario." Rather, he declared, we're living "in a science fiction film now."[156] Astro Black Mythology was the personal "utopian discourse" he proposed to help people in general, and African Americans in particular, to negotiate that change, fulfilling what he said back in 1957 was the "real aim" of his music: "to co-ordinate the minds of peoples into an intelligent reach for a better world, and an intelligent approach to the living future."[157]

— • • • ———

Sun Ra's vision of that "living future" was, as I have shown, essentially utopian, but it had its negative potentialities too. Like the spirituals, Ra's space chants constantly evoked heaven yet made little mention of hell. They did, however, offer the occasional intimation of apocalypse, as did the spirituals in their depictions of Judgment Day.[158] Ra's most notable, and humorous, version of apocalypse was 1982's "Nuclear War":

> It's a motherfucker, don't you know
> If they push that button, your ass gotta go
> Gonna blast your ass so high in the sky
> You can kiss your ass goodbye, goodbye.[159]

This was followed a year later by the instrumental "Hiroshima," but apocalypse was a topic that Ra addressed more in his interviews than in his music, and then it was only in his later years that dire warnings about the fate of humanity and the planet began to feature as interview topics.[160] If, in the Ra cosmology, heaven was the real future in outer space, it seems that hell was the equally real and likely apocalypse on an Earth whose inhabitants refused to change their ways. Ra certainly warned of this, urged people to change, and stressed that "beauty is necessary for survival," [161] but for the most part he adhered to his early intention "to depict happiness combined with beauty" and left hellfire and damnation to the preachers of the church he so disdained.[162]

One final comparison with the spirituals may shed light on Sun Ra's references to Saturn as his home. This claim has, I think, been widely misunderstood. As Chase has noted, "contrary to many writers' comments, I have found no statement from Sun Ra saying that he was 'born' on Saturn." [163] Just as, perhaps, when a slave sang "My home is over Jordan," he or she was not claiming to have been born in Palestine. Depending on context and circumstances, mentions of "home" in the spirituals might refer to the heaven to come, to a return to Africa (though many slaves had not been born there), or they might be a coded allusion to freedom in Canada or the North.[164] Sun Ra's references to Saturn were often enigmatic and occasionally contradictory,[165] but they do seem to include or to play with these same meanings. As a regular stop on his travels of the spaceways, Saturn was a part of Ra's mythic future, and, like most of the other planets, it had its own space chant: "Saturn rings / Rings around Saturn." More particularly, it was also a site of (mythic?) origin; as he told me in 1990, "I had to deal with Saturn, 'cause I feel that a lot of black people came from planet Saturn." [166] In this context Saturn was "home" for Ra in the same sense that Africa was "home" for a slave who had been born in the United States. Finally, Saturn was associated with freedom to the extent that Ra once stated that "the foundation of all freedom is discipline," [167] and as Arkestra vocalist June Tyson sings on "Journey to Saturn," "Saturn is the planet of discipline / Saturn is a hard task-master." [168] In a more general sense we can perhaps say that Saturn occupies a place in the Ra cosmology similar to that of Zion in the slaves' mythic world, as a "home" that can symbolize both the mythic future *and* the mythic past.

John Corbett has written that the funeral program for Sun Ra read, "Graveside obsequies celebration of the Homegoing of Sun Ra," to which he commented: "Not a homecoming, but a homegoing—Birmingham was both Ra's landing-spot and his launching pad." [169] John Szwed, in his account of the "homegoing," noted that Sun Ra was "laid to rest in a white robe and cap trimmed in black" and that his headstone read "Herman Blount (aka Le Son'y Ra)." [170] Even this brief description evokes the world of the spirituals: "Goin' Home," "I'm goin' to put on my robe," "the angels done changed my name." [171] It is to issues of renaming, rebirth, and self-representation that I would like to turn in chapter 2, as we trace the transformation of Herman Poole Blount from Alabama into the "spirit being" Le Sony'r Ra aka Sun Ra.

> I looked at my hands and my hands were new
> I looked at my feet and my feet were too
> I know the angels done changed my name
> Done changed my name for the coming day. [172]

2 Of Aliens and Angels:
Mythic Identity

O nobody knows who I am

Till the judgment morning [1]

The horns set up an eerie wailing as singer June Tyson begins the chant: "*The Sun is coming, the Sun is on his way*"; and from the backstage depths a portly figure waddles ceremoniously into view flanked by writhing dancers. A rainbow of lights illuminates the stage and we can see that tonight he has discarded his space-age skullcap and the customary lurex cape festooned with images of suns, stars and the ringed Saturn, his home planet: instead he is clad in a large fur hat and full-length leopard-skin cloak. Tonight he is not a Space Magician, he is an African Doctor.

He flings up his arms and the band fall silent.

"I have many names," he intones softly into the microphone. "Some call me Mister Ra, some call me Mister Re. You can call me Mister Mystery."

The audience raise a ragged cheer at the familiar greeting. His arms drop and the band launch into a melee of frenzied sound. Sun Ra permits a sly grin to crease his ancient face, then his arms shoot skyward. Silence. Down: cacophony. Up: silence.

"I am not a part of Earth history," he tells his startled listeners. "I belong to the Kingdom of Mythology." [2]

In this chapter I want to address the mystery of Mister Ra, to look at issues of renaming, rebirth, and representation. My hope is to illuminate Sun Ra's "Kingdom of Mythology," or at least some primary aspects of it, by locating its probable sources within the contexts of African American history and culture. And given that his notions of a mythic future and a mythic past were posited as alternatives to the Judeo-Christian mythology of the spirituals, perhaps it is not unreasonable to suppose that Ra's creation of what I will term a "mythic identity" may also be related to elements of slave culture.

Before embarking on an investigation of this hypothesis, however, it might be as well to relate a few basic biographical facts about Sun Ra. It seems he was born on 22 May 1914 in Birmingham, Alabama, and was originally called Herman Poole Blount. Though he spent a year majoring in teacher training at the State Agricultural and Mechanical Institute for Negroes in Normal, Alabama,[3] Ra worked as a professional musician, playing around the South and Midwest in the mid- and late 1930s under the names Sonny Blount and Sonny Lee. During World War II he was a conscientious objector, and after spending a short time in jail, he was excused from public service work on medical grounds.[4] In 1946 he settled in Chicago, later moving to New York in 1961 and then to Philadelphia in 1968, where he lived until his death in 1993. It seems that soon after his arrival in Chicago he began calling himself Le Sony'r Ra, the name he legally adopted on 20 October 1952 and which thereafter appeared on his passport.[5] Nevertheless, nearly all of his recordings and poems have appeared under the name of Sun Ra, which, together with Sonny, is the name that his band members and close associates used in talking about him.[6]

— ... ——

Perhaps the first point to make is that renaming is an issue that figures prominently in African American history and culture. To quote Ralph Ellison: "our names . . . must become our masks and our shields and the containers of all those values and traditions which we learn and/or imagine as being the meaning of our familial past."[7] In jazz, the music closest to Sun Ra's heart, there was an early tradition in New Orleans of the black community renaming its most eminent musicians "King," the best-known example being King Oliver. Later, the white press appropriated this practice, dubbing white bandleader Paul Whiteman "King of Jazz" and white bandleader Benny Goodman "King of Swing," much to the disgust of many black musicians.[8] Still, titles like *Duke* Ellington and *Count* Basie were widely seen as badges of distinction,[9] as was Lester Young's sobriquet of *Prez* (short for President), and Sun Ra arrived in Chicago in 1946 in the company of *Sir* Oliver Bibb, who dressed his band as eighteenth-century aristocrats. If

Ra's act of renaming was influenced by this tradition, it seems likely to have been in reaction *against* the proclivity for titles derived from the European aristocracy; taking the name of an Egyptian god suggests a very different set of "values and traditions." Ra's renaming seems more in line with the blues practice that Julio Finn has described as taking "a black name," exemplified in his comments on bluesman John Lee "Sonny Boy" Williamson, who sang, "I hear my black name a-ringin' / All up and down the line":

> Like a herald, come to deliver a timely message, he announced to black folk that they ought to be proud of their colour, their people and their origin. He also touched on one of the rites of initiation in the blues. In blues lore, this 'black' eponym denotes the *nom de guerre* he assumed when he became a bluesman. Significantly, he doesn't say 'blue name'; in using the word 'black' he is bragging about the colour of his skin. This black name is the antithesis, the refutation of his 'white' one, that ignoble hang-over from slavery. The bluesman's black name is the one he chose when he realized that his mission was to be the interpreter and praiser of his people. In light of this, it would never do for him to appear in his new role under a misnomer bequeathed him by the white slaver. When John Lee Williamson renamed himself 'Sonny Boy' he set the seal of his awareness on his 'new' self, and proclaimed to the world that he had renewed the bond between himself and his roots.[10]

There can be little doubt that Herman Blount deliberately took a "black name" in calling himself Sun Ra, although it was a name that carried the additional implication that the "roots" he was claiming for himself lay specifically in the civilization of ancient Egypt.

Another group of African Americans who took new and grand-sounding names were messianic religious leaders such as Noble Drew Ali (Timothy Drew), Father Divine (George Baker), and Elijah Muhammad (Robert Poole), their new names signifying both a spiritual re-birth and—in the cases of Noble Drew Ali and Elijah Muhammad—the adoption of a new cultural identity (that entailed the creation of a new mythic past for African Americans).[11]

I will return to the question of renaming in a moment; there are, however, a few other points of similarity between Sun Ra and these religious leaders that are worth noting. Father Divine, for example, shared Sun Ra's refusal to discuss personal origins. When asked where he came from, Divine was wont to reply, "I was combusted one day in 1900 on the corner of Seventh Avenue and 134th Street in Harlem," and when questioned as to his age, he answered with the biblical quotation, "Before Abraham was, I am." [12] Curiously, Ra also claimed the same method of arrival on one occasion, telling writer Jeff Levenson in 1985 that he "arrived from a distant solar system and combusted in the Magic City—Birmingham, Alabama." [13] Usually he was far more circumspect, parrying Bret Primack's query "When were you born?" with "Actually I don't know. I don't remember. I have no record of that." [14] And he refused to discuss his birthdate with Robert Rusch on the grounds of its "controversial aspects. I arrived on this planet on a very important day, it's been pinpointed by wisemen, astrologers as a very important date . . . a very controversial arrival, so that's the only reason I don't talk about it." [15] And, like Father Divine, he also alluded to great age, informing Phil Schaap that he had come to Earth "around 1055 or so. I didn't just arrive on the planet you know. I have been around for quite some time." [16]

The black religious leader whose pronouncements most closely resemble those of Ra is Elijah Muhammad, first leader of the Nation of Islam, who like Ra was based in Chicago in the 1940s and 1950s. According to both Alton Abraham, a close associate of Ra's in Chicago, and Arkestra tenor saxophonist John Gilmore, there was definitely contact between Ra and members of the Nation of Islam in the 1950s, with Gilmore claiming that the Black Muslims stole several ideas from Ra: "They would sort of antagonise him, in order to get him to talk." [17] Arguments about who influenced whom are not my concern here; instead, let me simply indicate some of the similarities between Ra's philosophy and that of the Black Muslims. The Muslims, like Ra, were antipathetic to the Christian church, laid emphasis on the value of discipline, and believed that the Bible needed decoding. To quote Elijah Muhammad in "What the Muslims Believe": "(3) WE BELIEVE in the truth of the Bible, but we believe that it has been tampered with and must be reinterpreted so that mankind will not be snared by the falsehoods that have been added to it." [18] Black Muslim mythology also resembles Sun Ra's Astro Black Mythology in its revision of certain Old Testament stories to create new mythic pasts and mythic futures for African Americans. Essien-Udom, in his study of Black Nationalism, argues:

The eschatology of the Nation of Islam is full of Old Testament images which help to convey the sense of social estrangement of the urban lower-class Negro. According to Muhammad, all persons of African descent in North America, "the lost-found Nation of Islam in the wilderness of North America" or the so-called American Negroes, belong generally to the "Asian Black Nation" and specifically to the ancient tribe of Shabazz. The origin of the Nation is traced to Abraham of the Old Testament, who is the "patriarch" of the "Black Nation" or of the "Asian Black Nation."[19]

Another Old Testament prophet, Ezekiel, is involved in the Muslims' apocalyptic mythic future, which, like that of Ra, takes us into outer space. Essien-Udom first paraphrases, then quotes Elijah Muhammad directly:

> Muhammad claims that Allah has warned that He will destroy the world with bombs, poison gas, and fire which will consume and destroy everything of this present world so that none of white civilization will be left. A dreadful plane "made like a wheel" was pointed out to him in the sky by Allah. Its dimensions were half a mile by half a mile. It was a "human-built planet": "(I won't go into all of the details here, but it is up there and can be seen twice a week; it is no secret.) Ezekiel saw it a long time ago. It was built for the purpose of destroying the present world."[20]

Sun Ra's space chant, "The satellites are spinning / A better day is breaking / The galaxies are waiting / For planet Earth's awakening,"[21] perhaps puts a more positive "spin" on this vision of cosmic change. And his notion of a "shield of beauty" that protects the world from "cosmic forces" that might otherwise "come and destroy people" can perhaps be read as a sly rebuttal of this Muslim eschatology, especially as Ra's "shield" was made by music, which the Muslims disdained.[22]

Renaming was a vital part of the process of initiation into the Nation of Islam. Essien-Udom notes that the "names which individuals bore before becoming registered Muslims are said to be 'slave names,'" and he quotes the Muslim minister Jones: "We still have names like Anderson, Robinson, Culpepper, and these are white man's names. Negroes go into college named Culpepper and they come out still named Culpepper. They don't even know who they are."[23] Nevertheless, despite dropping their 'slave' names, Essien-Udom reports that few Muslims "have been able to obtain their 'real' names" and that "many followers . . . hope that some day Allah will bestow upon them their real names."[24] This notion of a new name being handed down from God is not only similar to one of Sun Ra's stories about getting his name (which I discuss below), but was again prefigured in slave culture in spirituals such as "The Angels Changed My Name" (quoted at the close of chapter 1). Until such time as divine guidance intervened, however, many Black Muslims marked the loss of their original African names by adopting a simple "X" in its stead.

It is not my intention to pursue a detailed comparison between the mythologies of Sun Ra and Elijah Muhammad. I think this brief glance at the beliefs of the Black Muslims is enough to show that Ra was not alone in formulating a new mythic past and mythic future for African Americans nor in his desire to construct a new mythic identity for black people. The importance of renaming to both Sun Ra and Elijah Muhammad points to its importance in the wider cultural context of African American history, and it is to this topic that I now turn.

Sterling Stuckey has identified the significance of naming in the West African societies from which the majority of the slaves originated—"Among the Negro peoples a man's name is often identified with his very soul, and often with the souls of his ancestors"—and the consequent traumatic impact on African slaves of having new names imposed on them by slaveholders in America.[25] He adds that even "for black people not born in Africa, resentment at not having a surname and at having a Christian name of another's choosing were causes for distress."[26] Consequently, renaming was one of the first actions undertaken by freed slaves, an important symbolic reclamation of personhood. James Olney, in his analysis of the autobiographical slave narratives that became the predominant genre of black writing in the nineteenth century, lists as one of their major characteristics: "taking of a new last name (frequently one suggested by a white abolitionist) to accord with new social identity as a free man, but retention of first name as a mark of continuity of individual identity."[27] The comment in parentheses indicates a bitter irony here; even the new name of the ex-slave was often suggested by a white person and nearly always was of European origin. Christianity played a major role in such renaming, providing not only "Christian" names but Christian surnames, too. Stuckey quotes Sojourner Truth's statement: "I went to the Lord an' asked him to give me a new name . . . the Lord gave me Truth, because I was to declare the truth to the people." He also reports that she had decided to discard her slave name because she "had not wanted to keep 'nothin' of Egypt on me.' "[28]

Sun Ra, to the contrary, used the renaming tradition to reaffirm his links with Egypt and made absolutely sure that neither of his new names could be construed as Christian—to the extent of naming himself after a rival deity. His choice of a new first name also signals that this change did not incorporate "a continuity of individual identity" so much as announce a total reinvention of the self.[29] It is true that there was a thread of continuity in that both before and after his change of name, Ra's close associates called him "Sonny" (or "Sunny"), but this was already a new name, a "black" name if Julio Finn is correct. In what may have been an attempt to deny any Christian connotations even in his original Christian name, Ra claimed that he had been named Herman after the famous African American magician Black Herman, who was active in the early decades of the century.[30] (Presumably this is the same Black Herman, the "noted occultist," who features in Ishmael Reed's novel *Mumbo Jumbo*,[31] where the "ribbon of red and black" he wears denotes his allegiance to Thoth's descendent Elegba and to African mystery systems.)[32] Ra also denied repeatedly that his original surname was Blount (though his biographer John F. Szwed has confirmed to me that this is the name that appears on Ra's birth certificate), telling one interviewer that his parents' name was Arman, which "comes from ancient Egypt,"[33] presumably an attempt to assert a mythic genealogy in place of that of the slave master.

Accounts differ of how Herman Blount first came by the name Le Sony'r Ra. The version below, related to me by John Gilmore, sounds suspiciously like Ra signifying on the kind of Christian renaming tale epitomized by the Sojourner Truth story.

> Well, he [Sun Ra] was working at the Club DeLisa, I believe, in the late 40s, before I met him. And a fellow called Sammy Dyer was the choreographer and show producer there: he took care of hiring all the girls and the band. Sun Ra used to rehearse the chorus girls before they'd play with the band, and he'd write out all the music too. So, one day, Sammy came in and he told Sunny —"Your name is Le Sony'r Ra." It just came out of his mouth: "That's your name—Le Sony'r Ra." So Sun Ra realised something was telling him that this was his spiritual name. And from that moment, he used Le Sony'r Ra.[34]

Though not confirming the details of this account, Sun Ra did tell Ira Steingroot that he became known as Sun Ra "when the Creator spoke to me one day and called me that,"[35] and he stated on several occasions that the Creator often spoke to him through other people.[36] How Le Sony'r Ra metamorphosed into Sun Ra remains a mystery. Ra himself said on one occasion: "I always called myself Sun Ra. I can't remember having any other name."[37] But later he told John Corbett: "Sun Ra is not a person, it's a business name . . . and my business is changin' the planet."[38]

Renaming, then, marked the assertion of a new identity for both Ra and the writers of the slave narratives. There is also a curious correlation, by way of contrast, between their respective attitudes to birth. Olney has noted the extraordinary number of slave narratives that begin with the words "I was born," which he argues are "intended to attest to the real existence of a narrator."[39] Ra, intent on establishing a mythic existence, was not only evasive about the details of his birth (as we saw above), but he frequently denied that he had been born at all, and even made the same claim on behalf of the Arkestra. As John Gilmore told me: "Sun Ra doesn't allow us to say that we were born. He says we arrived on the planet."[40] (Ra tended to explain this claim by pointing out that only those who had been born had to die, which is perhaps just another way of saying, as he often did, that myth lies outside history.)[41] Similarly, Ra's declaration of extraterrestrial origins—"I am not of this planet"—was followed by his assertion that "I can tell you things you won't believe."[42] Compare this to the slave narrative's characteristic concern to establish its authenticity as a "factual and truthful" account, which was often expressed, writes Olney, in such assurances as "nothing exaggerated, nothing drawn from the imagination."[43] It is as if Sun Ra was deliberately reversing the formal conventions by which the slave narratives claimed to be documented truth, perhaps to signal that he was breaking his historical links (as an African American) with the fact and condition of slavery. Indeed, the point at which many slave narratives end—with the act of renaming—is the point at which Sun Ra's new narrative of mythic identity begins: a shift from history to mystery, past to future, time to space. As he says in the film *Sun Ra: A Joyful Noise*: "history is only his story. You haven't heard my story yet."

— • • • ——

Before we look more closely at Sun Ra's representation of his mythic identity, one other area of slave culture will repay further exploration, a special subgenre of slave narrative that takes us immediately into the realms of myth and mystery. Baptist conversion testimonies were specifically concerned with the process of rebirth into a new identity. Zora Neale Hurston included a few examples in Nancy Cunard's 1934 compilation Negro,[44] but a more comprehensive selection of these testimonies, originally taken from ex-slaves by a Fisk University graduate student from 1927 till 1929, was later published in the book God Struck Me Dead, edited by Clifton H. Johnson.[45] These conversion experiences were a standard part of Baptist practice, in that unless you could testify to a spiritual "rebirth," you were not fully accepted into the church. Baptists, like the Black Muslims, regarded the unconverted as "dead."[46]

Of particular interest here are the various resemblances between these anonymous visionary accounts and Sun Ra's description of an alien abduction experience that he said took place in 1936. (Some striking similarities also can be seen between these conversion testimonies and the spirituals—not surprisingly, since both were steeped in the same biblical imagery and mythology.) To begin with a general example, several of the former slaves describe first hearing a divine voice (usually that of God or an angel) in early childhood;[47] Ra told Phil Schaap that the Creator had first spoken to him "at three years old."[48] His subsequent remark that he had spent much of his childhood "out to lunch with the Creator"[49] is both a punning colloquialism and, perhaps, an allusion to the image of sitting in heaven at the welcome table, which recurs in sermons, spirituals, and conversion testimonies. "The angels would come up to the table, take one mouthful of food, and go away shouting and rejoicing, saying 'Praise God!' "[50]

Many of the ex-slaves describe visions in which they visit heaven and hell, often by either flying through the air ("I was not asleep but had just closed my eyes when I saw, in a vision, a beautiful little white chariot floating through the air; and I was in it. There was no one with me nor was I guiding the chariot, but it just went along sailing through the air.")[51] or by traveling along a remarkably narrow path: "The path we were traveling was no bigger than my little finger, but my foot just fitted it"; "Suddenly I saw a path no larger than a pencil and I went down that."[52] (Similar images of flying and of a narrow route to heaven are common in the spirituals. "Swing Low, Sweet Chariot" exemplifies the former; these lines from "Ezek'el Saw the Wheel" illustrate the latter: "Watch out my sister how you walk on the cross / Yo' foot might slip and yo' soul get lost.")[53] Sun Ra's accounts of his initial visit to what he identified as "another planet" incorporate both the elements of flying and traveling along a narrow route.

> I did go out to space through what I thought was a giant spotlight shining on me. . . . I had to go up there like that [imitates a mummy], in order to prevent any part of my body from touching the outside, because I was going through time-zones, and if any part of my body touched the outside I wouldn't get it back. So this spotlight—it seemed like a spotlight, but now I call it the energy car—it shined down on me, and my body was changed into some beams of light . . . and I went up at terrific speed to another dimension, another planet.[54]

Some of the conversion testimonies refer to seemingly similar experiences. One reports: "A light seemed to come down from heaven, and it looked like it just split me open from my head to my feet."[55] (Again, this image is prefigured in a spiritual: "On a my knees when the light pass'd by . . . Tho't that my soul would rise and fly.")[56] Other converts report being "struck dead" or at least struck dumb by a great surge of energy that transports them into what could be called another dimension, where a voice speaks to them. Sometimes the convert is transported directly to heaven, but more often he or she is taken first to the gates of hell, from where they are snatched and saved in a second abrupt transportation. Compare these reports with the way that Sun Ra's account continues:

> So then they called my name, and I realised I was alone, a long way up from here, and I didn't know what they wanted of me— and I stayed up in the dark. And they called my name again, but I refused to answer. And all at once they teleported me down to where they were. One split second I was up there, next I was down here. So they got the power. Then they talked to me, they had antennas, and they had red eyes that glow like that.[57]

Compare:

> When he [the voice] said that . . . I felt his power. It was like lightning; it came so quick. I was killed dead. The next thing I remember was that I was standing on the brink of hell . . . I saw my old body lying at hell's dark door. Quicker than a flash I was caused to turn away by the power of God.[58]

Sun Ra's experience differs from the conversion testimonies in that his second transportation is not from hell to heaven but simply from the top of "a huge auditorium" to the middle, where he meets the rather devilish beings with their antennae (horns?) and glowing red eyes. One of the ex-slaves reports seeing "the devil, a terrible clubfooted man, with red eyes like fire,"[59] though another describes the "little man" who, recurringly in these visions, leads the sinner back to God, as having "eyes . . . like fire."[60] If the red eyes are ambiguous, Sun Ra's later remark that the space beings "had on robes, that's why I wear robes now,"[61] would seem to ally them with heaven rather than hell, since many of the converts speak of seeing angels—and themselves— dressed in robes (which is another echo of the spirituals, of course).

Ra's story also shares a similar conclusion to those of several of the ex-slave converts, with the celestial beings exhorting their visitors to take back a message of salvation to mankind. Despite, sometimes, an initial reluctance, the converts finally accept their role as divine messengers-cum-preachers. Here is Sun Ra's version:

> Anyway, they talked to me about this planet, and the way it was headed and what was going to happen to teenagers, and governments, and people. They said they wanted me to talk to them. And I said I wasn't interested. So then they said I was the only one that could do this job. . . . They showed me [how] to be a ruler of people. . . . They told me, "When it reaches the stage that everything's going to collapse—talk to them. We're going to teach you a kind of music that will talk in that type of language to them. They will listen."[62]

Now extracts from two conversion testimonies (the converts have both been taken to heaven):

> While I was viewing the city a voice came to me saying, "Go into yonder world and tell them what a dear saviour you have found." I didn't want to leave. I said, "Lord, they won't believe me if I go." He said, "I command you to go, and you shall go. Speak, and I will speak through you."[63]

And:

> Mary and Martha put a robe on me and dressed me up. I sat down to a table with a host of angels. They all went away, though, in a flash. A voice said, "You are born of God. My son delivered your

soul from hell, and you must go and help carry the world. You have been chosen out of the world and hell can't hold you." [64]

And whereas Ra was told he would be taught to play a heavenly music (space music?), several of the former slaves speak of hearing singing or heavenly music in their visions: "and while I laid there the prettiest music came to me. I told the Lord I wanted to see where the music came from, and I looked above me and saw many angels and heard the flapping of their wings." [65]

The points of similarity between Sun Ra's account of his abduction and the former slaves' conversion testimonies seem too numerous to attribute to coincidence. There is the spotlight from heaven, the flying, the narrow pathway, the sudden transportations, the sense of being struck dumb (or refusing to speak), the hearing of voices, the strange beings with red eyes and/or robes, the commands to return to this world and preach (with divine guidance as to language), the heavenly music. Did Ra have a "real" experience, similar to those of the converts, but which he described in the very different context of science fiction? Or was the story a part of his constructed mythic identity, a rebirth parable based on the kind of religious visions he would undoubtedly have heard about in his childhood? Rather than speculate on such imponderables, I think the point to make is that Ra's abduction story certainly evokes what for many African Americans was a very "real" and often life-changing experience, [66] but that it revises and updates that experience in the futuristic language of science fiction — just as the space chants revise and update the cosmology of the spirituals. Whether Ra's trip to "another planet" was physical or psychic, visionary or imaginary, its significance perhaps lies more in the way he represented it, not in biblical terms but as a science fiction scenario, as if to signal to African Americans that the only way to define a personal identity, to experience a spiritual rebirth, to be "saved," in fact, was not by following the old ways of the Christian church but by embracing the future and traveling to outer space.

A final point to make here is that Sun Ra's tale of a meeting with extraterrestrials, which could be taken as prima facie evidence that he was a "nutter," turns out on closer inspection to be culturally rooted, a contemporary variation on an experience that was not uncommon among a significant percentage of the black population during a certain period of their history. (There is also the fact that in the last fifteen years or so an increasing number of non-African Americans have attested to alien abduction experiences. Intriguingly, there are many similarities between these contemporary accounts and the ex-slaves' conversion testimonies, including the recurring appearance of the "little man" [or men] as the initial abductor. Even the theme of biological/genetic experimentation, which seems a dominant motif in recent abduction experiences, was prefigured in at least one African American religious vision, which occurred on 20 March 1867: "He [the Lord] laid me upon a table in my vision. I was naked and He split me open. And there was two men there—one on each side of de table. I could hear de knives clicking in me, inside. And after dey got through wid me, they smothed [sic] they hand over de wound and I wuz healed.")[67] Though I doubt that Steve Voce intended his use of the word "nutter" to be taken literally as a medical diagnosis, such glib ascription of insanity to African Americans has certainly occurred within serious medical discourse. Thomas Szasz, for example, has disinterred the work of one Samuel A. Cartwright, M.D., who proposed that African American slaves were "nutters" for trying to escape from slavery and its hardships. In 1851 Cartwright "claimed to identify two new diseases peculiar to Negroes: one, which he called 'drapetomania,' was manifested by the escape of the Negro slave from his white master; the other, which he called 'dysnesthesia Aethiopis,' was manifested by the Negro's neglecting his work or refusing to work altogether."[68] That the slave's desire to escape slavery could be construed as evidence of mental illness—and "cured" by whipping, which Cartwright also advocated as a "preventive measure against absconding or other bad conduct" (so you were whipped if you tried to escape and whipped if you didn't!)[69]—should perhaps act as a warning to commentators, including jazz critics, to think more carefully before handing out labels like "nutter" and "charlatan."[70]

(A comparable example in jazz commentary might be James Lincoln Collier's description of Charlie Parker as a "sociopath," a choice of terminology that drew a passionate response from James Baldwin: "I am attacking, of course, the basis of the language—or perhaps the *intention* of the language—in which history is written. . . . This is exactly how the music called *jazz* began, and out of the same necessity: not only to redeem a history unwritten and despised, but to checkmate the European notion of the world. For, until this hour, when we speak of history, we are speaking only of how Europe saw—and sees—the world."[71] It is one of my main contentions in this book that the work of Sun Ra, Duke Ellington, and Anthony Braxton indeed tries "not only to redeem a history unwritten and despised, but to checkmate the European notion of the world.")

And while it was not slavery, I think there can be little doubt of Sun Ra's desire to escape the kind of world in which he found himself. As he told me in 1990: "I ain't part of America. I ain't part of black people. They went another way. Black people are carefully supervised so they'll stay in a low position. But I'm not down there, yet I come from one of the most discriminating states in the whole world—Alabama."[72] Indeed, the second and third decades of the century—the period of Sun Ra's childhood—were not a good time to be black in the South. According to C. Vann Woodward: "The war-bred hopes of the Negro for first-class citizenship were quickly smashed in a reaction of violence that was probably unprecedented."[73] In this postwar frenzy of racism, "Mobs took over cities for days at a time, flogging, burning, shooting, and torturing at will . . . . During the first year following the war more than seventy Negroes were lynched, several of them veterans still in uniform."[74] In the mid-1920s the revived Ku Klux Klan reached its peak of membership, a reputed 5 million, and although the Klan was active nationally, Woodward notes that within the South its influence "toward the inflaming of prejudice, the encouragement of race violence and the strengthening of the segregation code was powerful."[75] In fact, in the 1920s and early 1930s "the Jim Crow laws were elaborated and further expanded,"[76] as segregation was extended to all walks of life, including the most trivial activities. The truth of Sun Ra's contention that Alabama was "one of the most discriminating states in the whole world" can be illustrated by a single example. In 1930, his home city of Birmingham passed an ordinance "making it 'unlawful for a Negro and a white person to play together or in company with each other' at dominoes or checkers."[77] Legislation of this kind bespeaks a mentality so petty and obsessive that we are entitled to ask who is the more "insane" here, the people who made such laws or someone who tried to escape and disavow the kind of world where such laws held sway, even if to the extent of declaring himself "another order of being"?

— • • • —

But precisely what "order of being" did Sun Ra claim to be? Questions of renaming and rebirth lead us to questions of representation, to the details of his mythic identity. John Corbett, in his essay "Brothers from Another Planet: The Space Madness of Lee 'Scratch' Perry, Sun Ra, and

George Clinton," takes a very different and much more positive approach to the notion of Ra's "madness" than Steve Voce.[78] I think this essay is worth a closer examination, even though in the end I will want to argue that Corbett misrepresents the way that Sun Ra represented himself. Corbett begins by observing that "in African-American slang there is a longstanding constellation of terms that revolves around the interrogation of sanity," and he points to a particular group of words that link "madness with excellence and innovation," a notion he says that is "most fully developed and deployed in relation to music, especially jazz and blues."[79] After listing a number of titles to illustrate the point (e.g., Thelonious Monk's "Nutty," Eric Dolphy's *Out to Lunch*), Corbett continues:

> Although the subtle shades of meaning that differentiate these various uses of craziness could fill a volume, what we are concerned with is the way that this discursive web sets the stage, in a fundamental sense, for the rhetorical and identificatory tactics of Ra, Clinton, and Perry, all of whom utilize the overarching idea of insanity liberally in their work. Each of them doubles the intensity of this metaphor with a superimposed metaphor of outer space. In the tropology of madness, one is "close to the edge" or "out of one's mind." The mind, and more specifically the *reasonable* mind, is configured as a terrestrial zone, as earth; sanity is the "ground," from which one departs in "flights" of fancy. Hence, the connection is established between "going way out" (a common phrase in jazz for a solo that transgresses a widely held musical code, such as the established harmonic framework), and leaving earth. Tradition = earth; innovation = outer space. In the language of black music, madness and extra-terrestriality go hand in hand.[80]

While I would agree with much in this essay, and much in this extract, there are three assumptions in particular here with which I take issue. I am not convinced that Sun Ra fits into this "discursive web" as easily as Corbett suggests, nor do I believe that he "utilize[s] the overarching idea of insanity liberally" in his work, nor am I persuaded that, "In the language of black music, madness and extraterrestriality go hand in hand." Not necessarily, as the spirituals surely demonstrate. Extraterrestriality there encodes a heavenly site of order and justice that represents a vision of *greater sanity* than the terrestrial world of slavery, apprehended by the slaves as cruel, arbitrary, and irrational. Indeed, the creation of that vision was possibly the very means by which the slaves preserved their sanity in the "howling wilderness" of this world. To quote Levine: "The spirituals are the record of a people who found the status, the harmony, the values, the order they needed to survive by internally creating an expanded universe, by literally willing themselves reborn."[81] Paul Radin in his foreword to *God Struck Me Dead* argues the same point: "What the slave desired was a status that he himself had ordained, not a fictitious one imposed from without. Such a status he could only secure in the realm of dreams, fantasies and visions."[82] (Or as Ra said, "history is only his story. . . . I'm more a part of the mystery, which is my story.")[83] Nor was there any room for doubt or disbelief; these dreams and visions had to be taken as the ultimate reality. "There was no other safety for people faced on all sides by doubt and the threat of personal disintegration, by the thwarting of instincts and the annihilation of values."[84] Ra's revision of these extraterrestrial visions required an equal commitment of faith. Like the slaves, he did not play with tropes of madness, and, unlike Lee Perry and George Clinton, he did not represent himself as being mad. The only evidence that Corbett cites of Ra's supposed troping of madness is the LP title *Cosmic Tones for Mental Therapy*, which I read as signifying exactly the opposite— Ra associating his music with mental health—and evoking the traditional African American belief in the beneficial power of music, as exemplified by Albert Ayler's proclamation that "Music is the healing force of the universe."[85] Nor have I found any evidence of Ra alluding to Corbett's "discursive web" of madness, though he does make frequent recourse to the language of myth, dream, and fantasy—the realm where, according to Radin, he could affirm a status or identity of his own rather than live the fictional role imposed on him by the "his story" of history.

What I am trying to suggest is that Ra was more interested in questioning accepted notions of reality (and proposing an alternative) than in questioning accepted notions of sanity (and pretending madness). Of course, ideas of reality and sanity are closely linked, but in this context I think it is important to differentiate between them. Unfortunately, Corbett, in an otherwise insightful argument about Ra's claims to extraterrestrial origins, conflates the two:

> while this E. T. metaphor—if it can be considered a metaphor— may indicate the *insanity* of its maker, it also cuts back in the other direction, suggesting the fundamental *unreality* of existence for people imported into New World servitude and then disenfran-

chised into poverty. Thus Ra, Clinton, and Perry may force us not just to question their sanity, but to question our own. *Is it sane to believe them? Is it sane not to believe them? Is it "reasonable" to believe that they are from space? Is life on this planet not an unreasonable, otherworldly existence in itself?*[86]

Well, yes, but let me say again that as far as I can see Ra did not pursue this discourse along the lines of a sanity/insanity debate—for example, he never proclaims insanity as Lee Perry does in "I Am a Madman"—rather he poses questions about *reality* (which includes history) and about humanity.[87]

There are numerous examples in his music and in his interviews of Ra's questioning of reality. In the song "Somebody Else's World" he states clearly that what we accept as real is only a partial and subjective version of what is and what could be:

> Somebody else's idea of somebody else's world
> Is not my idea of things as they are
> Somebody else's idea of things to come
> Need not be the only way to vision the future.[88]

(And a later line makes the claim that the past too can be re-"visioned": "What seems to be need not be what we had to be.") He expanded on this concept in a 1988 interview with Ira Steingroot (Sun Ra is speaking):

> It's a magic kingdom here. People think certain thoughts and they start coming to be. Sickness and death and all that. It's not proper. What they're talking about could become a reality. So if they believe they die and go to hell, undoubtedly they do. But it ain't real. It's all fixed up according to their imagination.
> [IS:] When did you feel that other dimensions of reality were impinging on your own?
> [SR:] From the time I was three years old. I remember things—images and scenes and feelings. I never felt like I was a part of this planet. I felt that all this was a dream, that it wasn't real. And suffering . . . I just couldn't connect.[89]

That mention of suffering hints at a political edge to Ra's mythology, and there is certainly a racial dimension in his response to the young black people in the 1974 film *Space Is the Place* when they ask him if he's "for real": "I'm not real, I'm just like you. You don't exist in this society.

If you did, your people wouldn't be seeking equal rights. You're not real. If you were, you'd have some status among the nations of the world. So we're both myths. I do not come to you as a reality, I come to you as a myth. Because that's what black people are, myths. I come to you from a dream that the black man dreamed long ago."[90] White denial of black existence was undoubtedly part of the reality that Ra was trying to oust,[91] as was white denial of black history (e.g., Egypt) and white denial of black access to the future (e.g., outer space). Race was, I think, a crucial factor in Ra's mythology, though his focus was also sufficiently broad to encompass the planet, the universe, and what he called the omniverse (since he claimed this universe was only one among many). "I was sent here to help the planet," he told me in 1990;[92] and to quote from the moving obituary by John F. Szwed, Ra's spirit was "too lavishly universalistic . . . to stop at the vulgar limits of race and history."[93] Ra's Astro Black Mythology seems to have been devised in part to outflank the "vulgar limits" of history (though the template here was white misrepresentation of black history). "Myth was here before history," he declared. "When they started history the truth couldn't move, 'cause they put a lot of lies in there too."[94] Myth may also be here after history. Ra explained in 1965: "Myth permits man to situate himself in these times and to connect himself with the past and the future. What I'm looking for are the myths of the future, the destiny of man . . . . I believe that if one wants to act on the destiny of the world, it's necessary to treat it like a myth."[95] The resulting "mythocracy" might perhaps be a lie, Ra would acknowledge, but a lie that was possibly of more use and that offered more potential to the planet than the lie on which reality was based. As he told his audience at Soundscape in 1979:

> Your only hope now is a lie. In fact, the Christian Church is based on a lie. They're dealing with Paul, and Paul said, "If you believe my lie . . ." He was smart enough to see that the truth couldn't help. So then the white race took the lie and the kingdoms they got are based on Paul's lie. But I don't call a lie a lie. I call it a myth. I'm telling people that they've tried everything and now they have to try mythocracy. They've got a democracy, a theocracy—but they should try a mythocracy. The mythocracy is what you never came to be that you should be.[96]

In this context, we can perhaps read Ra's claim to be from outer space as the most outrageous, impossible "lie" in his mythic identity.[97]

This claim, what Corbett calls the "E.T. metaphor," was not, I think, designed to raise questions about our or Sun Ra's sanity but to initiate a discourse on Otherness, which in the case of Ra's mythology took an extreme form: he declared himself not mad but *alien*, other than human.

In 1914, Thomas P. Bailey, an educator from the American South writing about the North's failure to oppose the rising tide of racism in both North and South, asked the question: "Is not the South being *encouraged* to treat the negroes as *aliens* by the growing discrimination against the negro in the North, a discrimination that is social as well as economic? Does not the South perceive that all the fire has gone out of the Northern philanthropic fight for the rights of man?"[98] The salient points to note here are that Negroes are identified with aliens and that aliens are contrasted with men—or "man" (in the sense of their not being fully human. I am not suggesting that anyone in 1914 was claiming African Americans came from outer space.) I will return in a moment to the links between black and alien.

First, I would like to look briefly at Sun Ra's disowning of the word "man." There is definitely a "discursive web" (to borrow Corbett's phrase) of African American cultural perspectives around issues of manhood. One is the very forceful assertion of manhood, specifically in response to the white racist practice of calling all black males under the age of fifty or so "boy." Muddy Water's signifying title "Mannish Boy" alludes to this practice, and the 1955 lyric literally spells out his reply: "I'm a man, spell it m-a-n."[99] Sun Ra took a different line. As Chase has argued: "He often demonstrates his contempt for human baseness by refusing to pronounce the word 'man,' instead spelling it 'm-a-n,' as if the very word was repellent to him."[100] Both responses could be described as in-your-face refutations of racism, but whereas Muddy Waters was asserting equality, Sun Ra was affirming difference. On London's Jazz FM radio in 1990, Ra declared: "I'm not a man, I'm an angel. . . . I will not take responsibility for what man has done. 'Cause the things they do, I don't do those things, I don't approve of them. . . ."[101] One of man's actions of which he disapproved was the Atlantic slave trade, specifically because of what he called "the great shame" of its "*dehumanisation* of black people in America" (my emphasis):

> How can anyone survive coming into a country as a thing, rather than as a man or a woman? The nations of the world got to face

that. They allowed it to happen. . . . They let America bring people in without passports. They broke international law . . . and they broke cosmic law to do that. I suppose dogs came in through the Commerce Department—and birds and bees—and things. Like the black people of America. They came in as things. . . . They are not even existing, as far as law is concerned in this country.[102]

Ra took a somewhat different approach to this same conceit in an earlier interview with Rich Theis. Here, perhaps, is an example of his mythologizing in action, as he offers an alter-destiny to the dehumanization of the slaves and turns a racial epithet like "alien" into a mark of mystery and potential:

You have to realize this planet is not only inhabited by humans, it's inhabited by aliens too. . . . So, in mixed up among the humans you have angels. The danger spot is the United States. You have more angels in this country than anywhere else. . . . Never in the history of the world has there been a case where you take a whole people and bring 'em into the country in the Commerce Department . . . . It happened here . . . . It was possible for aliens and angels and devils and demons to come into this country. They didn't need no passport. So then they'd come as displaced people.[103]

As Corbett has observed, here "Ra takes the disempowerment of slavery and turns it into an inventive situation in which the absolute identity of African-Americans—as people or as angels—is unknown to anyone but African-Americans themselves."[104] Or, as the slave spiritual had it, "O nobody knows who I am / Till the judgment morning."[105] Nor, Ra might have added, *what* I am. Denied status as a "man" both by the historical fact of slavery and by the Jim Crow laws that reached a peak of oppression in the first three decades of the twentieth century, Sun Ra declined to assert equal status with the oppressors and instead turned racist dehumanization on its head by claiming to be of a different race altogether: "I'm really of the Angel race. There ain't but two kinds of races here, you got the Angel race and the human race. The Angels are a race, most people don't know that. I belong to the Angel race."[106] Ra not only denies terrestrial racism here (all humans are one race), but he also literally rises above it—"Angels like their minds and spirits to take wing"—to a "celestial plane" where happiness brings immortality and "music is happiness."[107] Ra's mythology then celebrates alien-ness and offers a way for African Americans to turn the dehumanizing "alien" status imposed on them by slavery and racism into a new and positive mythic identity as "another order of being."

This context allows us to see Sun Ra's assertions of his alien-ness—his disparaging comments on "man," his various claims to be "an immortal spirit," "another order of being," "an angel," "an archangel" ("I've been promoted lately," he explained),[108] his space costumes, his space music, his extraterrestrial origins—as elements of what Houston A. Baker has called "deformation of mastery," an African American cultural strategy that involves the *display* of difference. Drawing on examples from zoology, Baker likens deformation to a "phaneric mask": "the phaneric mask is meant to advertise. It distinguishes rather than conceals. It secures territorial advantage and heightens a group's survival possibilities."[109] The particular example that Baker cites is of gorilla "display" when "Man—the master of 'civilization'—enters forests and triggers a response."[110] An important part of this display, which involves a kind of danced demonstration of power and ferocity, is the "hooting" sound that the gorilla makes. Baker comments:

> The gorilla's deformation is made possible by his superior knowledge of the landscape and the loud assertion of possession that he makes. It is, of course, the latter—the "hoots" of assurance that remain incomprehensible to intruders—that produce a notion (in the intruder's mind and vocabulary) of "deformity." An "alien" *sound* gives birth to notions of the indigenous—say, Africans, or African-Americans—as *deformed*.[111]

Baker discusses "deformation of mastery" as a characteristic African American literary strategy employed in particular by Paul Laurence Dunbar and W. E. B. DuBois, but I think the idea can usefully be applied to Sun Ra, too. His "alien sound" (his space music, his "galactic gobbledegook") has indeed provoked accusations of various kinds of "deformity" ("nutter," "con artist," "charlatan"), and, more particularly, his "advertising" of his alien-ness could be said both to heighten the "survival possibilities" of African Americans, by transforming racism's traumatic dehumanizations into the potential for a new mythic identity, and to "secure territorial advantage," in that his habitation of outer space claims it as the rightful place for African Americans, both in the sense of a "celestial plane" that puts them on a higher spiritual level than "men" and in the sense of a real scientific future in which they are fully entitled to participate.

Mention of DuBois should also remind us that Sun Ra was not the first African American intellectual to explore the notion that (to quote Greg Tate) "black existence and science fiction are one and the same." [112] In an unpublished story, "A Vacation Unique," written in 1899, DuBois likened black experience in America to living in "the Fourth Dimension," a place in which the inhabitants' "feelings no longer count, they are no part of history." [113] And if Sun Ra had required a more contemporary source for his claims of extraterrestrial origin, he could have found it in this scene from Richard Wright's novel *The Outsider*, published in 1953:

> A tall Negro lifted his voice with loud authority over the rolling laughter.
>
> "Where there's lots of rumors, there's bound to be some truth in 'em," he pronounced.
>
> "You mean to tell me you believe flying saucers are *real?*" a short, brown boy demanded with indignation. "You got better sense than *that!*"
>
> Cross had heard a hundred such arguments in bars and cafes and he was ready to relax and listen to yet another one, to see to what heights of fantasy it would soar.
>
> "I say these white folks is hiding something," the tall Negro maintained, "and what they're hiding *scares* 'em!"
>
> "And what're they hiding?" the waitress asked.
>
> "Things they don't want *you* to know," the tall Negro said cryptically . . . .
>
> "Know what they found in one of them flying saucers?" the tall man demanded. "One of 'em was full of little men, about two feet high, with skin like peach fuzz—"
>
> Laughter showered in the cafe.
>
> "But what the white folks so scared about?" someone asked. "Little men can't hurt nobody."
>
> Silence. All eyes were turned expectantly to the face of the tall man.
>
> "THEM LITTLE MEN THE WHITE FOLKS FOUND IN THEM SAUCERS WAS COLORED MEN AND THEY WAS FROM MARS!" The tall man spoke in deep solemn tones. "That's why they hushed up the story. They didn't want the world to know that the rest of the universe is colored! Most of the folks on this earth is colored, and if the white folks knew that the other worlds was full of colored folks

who wanted to come down here, what the hell chance would the white folk have?"

Screams of approval, leaping from their chairs, and clapping of hands. . . .

"But how come you reckon they so scared?" an elderly man asked.

" 'Cause they're guilty," the tall man explained. "And guilty folks are *scared* folks! For four hundred years these white folks done made everybody on earth feel like they ain't human, like they're *outsiders*. They done kicked 'em around and called 'em names. . . . Now our colored brothers are visiting us from Mars and Jupiter and the white folks is sweating in a panic — "

Negroes rolled in laughter, feeling that the powerful white world had been lowered to their own humble plane by the magic of comic words.[114]

This scene, set in Chicago in the mid-1940s, is interesting not only because Wright depicts the appeal of the "E.T. metaphor" and confirms Ra's appreciation of the "magic" power of words, but also because he suggests that such discussions were a common feature of black life at the time ("Cross had heard a hundred such arguments").[115] It is tempting to speculate that Wright might have heard Sun Ra and his associates engage in just such a discussion, but this seems extremely unlikely as Wright left Chicago to live in New York in 1937 and then moved to Paris in 1947 (though he did spend a few weeks in Chicago in September 1949 while filming *Native Son*). Nevertheless, it is clear that the identification of black people with aliens has long been a recurring motif in African American culture, one to which allusions continue to be made in, for example, the music of George Clinton,[116] the conversation of bebop tenor saxophonist Johnny Griffin ("I'm not really from this planet. I did something wrong on my planet and they sent me here to pay my dues. . . . I must be from someplace else in the universe because I'm a total misfit."),[117] and in the 1995 statements of novelist Ishmael Reed: "We're not believed. We're like aliens trying to tell our experiences to earthlings. . . . There's always been this feeling in this country that we're aliens, that we don't belong here."[118]

One black writer who definitely did hear Sun Ra talking about extraterrestrial origins was Henry Dumas, an associate of the Arkestra in the 1960s.[119] His poem "Outer Space Blues" is dedicated to "Sun Ra Myth." Here are the concluding two stanzas:

So when the spaceship land
    I aint runnin too fast
I say, I reckon I might not run too fast
I might run over into Mississippi
    and you know I can't pass

Hold it people, I see a flying saucer comin
    guess I wait and see
Yeah, a spaceship comin
    guess I wait and see
All I know they might look just like me.[120]

— • • • ——

In conclusion, I would like to look briefly at the film *Space Is the Place*, made in 1972, and the only fictional representation we have of Sun Ra's "mythic identity." John F. Szwed describes the film as "part documentary, part science fiction, part Blaxsploitation [*sic*], part revisionist Biblical epic."[121] The plot, he writes,

> is easy to summarize (if not so easy to understand): having been travelling in space for some years in a rocket ship propelled by music, Sun Ra locates a planet, which he deems suitable for a resuscitation of the Black race. He returns to earth and lands in Oakland, circa 1972 (where in real life the Arkestra was staying and where the Black Panthers were under attack by the police and the FBI). Throughout the film Ra battles with the Overseer, a supernatural pimp who profits from the degradation of Black people. Sun Ra offers those who would follow him into space an "alter-destiny," but the Overseer, the FBI and NASA ultimately force him to return to space prematurely.[122]

Szwed warns that it would be a mistake to take the film as a literal exposition of Sun Ra's own beliefs. While many of Ra's ideas were incorporated into the script, Szwed reports that producer Jim Newman "says that no one was sure of all the meanings of the film, as it was collectively written and considerably re-edited."[123] But even if we cannot be sure of the precise degree of Sun Ra's involvement, the indications are that his influence was preeminent. Szwed notes that Newman's initial intention had been to make a documentary, yet *Space Is the Place* turned into something else that accords closely with Ra's Astro Black

Mythology. (The first music heard in the film is June Tyson singing, "It's after the end of the world / Don't you know that yet?," as if to signal that we are stepping outside time and history and into the world of myth.) I would also say that there are few significant differences between the Sun Ra who appears in *Space Is the Place* and the Sun Ra we know from other contexts.

Like Astro Black Mythology, *Space Is the Place* alludes to characteristics of slave culture. Sun Ra's descent to Earth from outer space with the intention of leading the black race to freedom on another planet recalls the earlier trips of leaders such as Harriet Tubman, who would "descend" from Canada or the North to guide fleeing slaves out of captivity. Then there is Ra's ongoing duel with the Overseer. James Olney, in his essay on slave narratives, lists "description of a cruel master, mistress, or overseer" as a principal element common to most of them.[124] In *Narrative of the Life of Frederick Douglass, an American Slave*, one of the most famous and influential slave writings, Douglass's fight with the overseer Covey proved to be a turning point so crucial that it could be compared to a form of spiritual rebirth: "I felt as I never felt before. It was a glorious resurrection, from the tomb of slavery, to the heaven of freedom." [125]

If the black Overseer in *Space Is the Place* is not physically "cruel" in the way depicted in the slave narratives, he can be said to represent a similar (if more contemporary) sellout to white values, betraying any sense of racial solidarity in exchange for personal gain.[126] Thus, in the horse race that is a side bet in their cosmic duel, Sun Ra backs "Alter Destiny" while the Overseer backs "Earthly Delights" (which wins but is then disqualified after a drug test!). And, in another episode of the duel, in which they each draw a card from what appears to be a version of the Tarot pack, Ra picks one depicting his spaceship above the word "Judgment," while the Overseer chooses a card on which the large Cadillac he drives throughout the film is pictured above the words "The Chariot." Perhaps one gloss of this coded iconography is to see Ra's spaceship as representing the future, the "alter destiny," while the Overseer's Cadillac denotes a preference for the present-day materialistic comforts of "earthly delights." (But I wonder if more levels of meaning were intended as well. One of the more bizarre aspects of Ra's spaceship is that it looks like a pair of giant eyes; the association with "Judgment" is perhaps intended to evoke the eye of Horus, symbol of divine judgment in ancient Egyptian hieroglyphics. In contrast, to label the Overseer's Cadillac "The Chariot" seems to introduce a note of discrepancy, even of irony, as if to indict a failure of spiritual leadership. Was Sun Ra trying to link the accommodationist strategies of the black church to the self-serving practices of the Overseer, signifying that the spiritual promise of "the chariot"—symbol of deliverance for the slaves—had given way to the earthly comforts of the expensive car?) [127]

Space Is the Place also makes clear the link between Sun Ra's Astro Black Mythology and the emigration that has long been an important strand in African American political and cultural discourse. If space, for Ra, was the site of a mythic past, the "home" of extraterrestrial origin, it was also the site of a mythic future, the "home" of ultimate destination. *Space Is the Place* focuses more on the mythic future, a response perhaps to the heated debates on nationalism and separatism that engaged African Americans in the 1960s and that were given a wide public airing by the rise of the Black Muslim and Black Power movements.

These issues had been addressed by a long succession of African American political leaders and writers—Marcus Garvey, W. E. B. DuBois, Booker T. Washington, Alexander Crummell—that can be traced back to the first half of the nineteenth century; they were first given substantial voice in the writings of Martin Delany. In particular, Delany's *Official Report of the Niger Valley Exploring Party*, an account of his 1860 trip to Africa to inspect land for possible future settlement by African Americans, was republished in 1969 under the title *Search for a Place*. [128] Not only does *Space Is the Place* "answer" that title (and the chief question of a century of nationalist debate), but the film's opening scenes, in which Ra travels to a distant planet to test its suitability for future settlement by African Americans—"We could set up a colony for black people here," he muses—seem deliberately to echo the aims of the Delany expedition. [129] (They also echo the lines of an old spiritual:

> From this world o' trouble free,
> > Stars beyond!
> > Stars beyond!
> There's a star fo' you an' me,
> > Stars beyond!) [130]

Certainly, the issue of *place* is of central importance to *Space Is the Place*, and, unlike the space chants where Ra's invitation to "sign up with Outer Spaceways Incorporated" appears to be all-inclusive, it is specifically the place of and for black people that is the film's primary concern: "My Kingdom is the Kingdom of Darkness and Blackness," Ra intones in one scene, "and none can enter except those who are black in spirit." I will return to the question of *place* shortly. First, I would like to point out that if the notion of black emigration to Africa had a long history in African American culture, the notion of black emigration to another planet had also been aired before the appearance of *Space Is the Place*—not in black culture but in American science fiction.

In his 1951 novel *The Martian Chronicles* Ray Bradbury includes a chapter, "Way in the Middle of the Air," which describes the departure of the black population of the American South in rocket ships headed for Mars. Bradbury's depiction of black emigration seems based, at least in part, on Marcus Garvey's vision of black economic cooperation: "It was happening all along the way. Little white boys, barefoot, dashed up with the news. 'Them that has helps them that hasn't! And that way they *all* get free! Seen a rich man give a poor man two hundred bucks to pay off some'un! Seen some'un else give some'un else ten bucks, five bucks, sixteen, lots of that, all over, everybody.'"[131] Compare this with Essien-Udom's comments on Garvey: "He sought to organize Negroes in the United States into a vanguard for African redemption from colonialism and hoped eventually to lead them back to Africa. The major instrument for the achievement of these objectives was economic cooperation through racial solidarity."[132] But Bradbury's story is particularly fascinating because, through the voice of the white racist Samuel Teece, he makes a link between this science fiction scenario (set in the year 2003) and the promises of the spirituals:

> "I reckon you think you're goin', just like that song—what's the words? 'Way up in the middle of the air'; ain't *that* it?"
> "Yes, sir." The Negro waited.[133]

And later:

> "I suppose you got names for your rockets?"
> They looked at their one clock on the dashboard of the car.
> "Yes, sir."
> "Like Elijah and the Chariot, The Big Wheel and The Little Wheel, Faith, Hope, and Charity, eh?"
> "We got names for the ships, Mr. Teece."
> "God the Son and the Holy Ghost, I wouldn't wonder? Say, boy, you got one named the First Baptist Church?"
> "We got to leave now, Mr. Teece."
> Teece laughed. "You got one named Swing Low, and another named Sweet Chariot?"

The car started up. "Good-bye, Mr. Teece."

"You got one named Roll Dem Bones?"

"Good-bye, mister."

"And another one called Over Jordan! Ha! Well, tote that rocket, boy, lift that rocket, boy, go on, get blown up, see if I care!" [134]

Bradbury, as narrator, makes a similar link himself in a passage that recalls the spiritual "I'll Hear the Trumpet Sound": "In that dreadful Judgment Day / I'll take wings and fly away." [135] Describing the debris-strewn landscape en route to the launching site, Bradbury writes that the scene was "as if a whole city had walked here with hands full, at which time a great bronze trumpet had sounded, the articles had been relinquished to the quiet dust, and one and all, the inhabitants of the earth had fled straight up into the blue heavens." [136] Since Sun Ra was an ardent fan of science fiction,[137] and since "Way in the Middle of the Air" was one of the few science fiction stories of the period to address the topic of black life,[138] it seems reasonable to suppose that Ra would have read the story, though to what degree it influenced the creation of his mythology in general or the plot of Space Is the Place in particular can only remain a matter for speculation.[139]

What is certain is that debates about place have resounded through-out African American history. To quote C. Vann Woodward: "Slavery was only one of several ways by which the white man has sought to define the Negro's status, his 'place,' and assure his subordination." [140] Woodward uses or quotes the word "place" in a similar context on several occasions, each time emphasizing the idea of it as narrow and confining.[141] The title of Space Is the Place refutes any such limitations, and in several scenes the film itself takes up this debate. Black people are described as being at "the bottom of the totem pole," while Ra tells the black youths in the club that they neither exist in present-day society nor is there any apparent place for them in a future society: "They [white people] take frequent trips to the moon. I notice none of you have been invited." White attitudes to the "place" of black people are epitomized in the film by a hilarious example of musical signify-ing. In order to make Sun Ra tell them the secrets of space travel and "transmolecularisation," the FBI agents, having kidnapped him and tied him to a chair, fit him with headphones and force him to listen to a recording of "Dixie." To fully appreciate the significance of this action, we need to look briefly at that composition's history. The writing of "Dixie" has long been attributed to the well-known blackface (i.e., white) minstrel Dan Emmett, who first performed it in New York in April 1859.[142] Purporting to depict a Negro's longing to be back "in de land ob cotton," the song quickly won enormous popularity among whites, especially in the South and not least among slaveholders, who were not slow to recognize the implicit political message of a lyric that portrayed blacks as unhappy in the "free" North and longing to return to the "good old days" in the South: "My master mean to us. We used to watch for him to come in the big gate, then we run and hide. He used to come to the quarters and make us children sing. He make us sing 'Dixie.' Sometime he make us sing half a day. Seems like 'Dixie' his main song. I tell you I don't like it now. But have mercy. He make us sing it. Seems like all the white folks like 'Dixie.' I's glad when he went away to war." [143]

The song proved such a hit in the South that, on secession from the Union in 1861, it was adopted as the national anthem of the Confederacy (with modified lyrics) and played at the inauguration of Jefferson Davis: "so momentous was the event that historians thought to preserve the bandleader's cornet in the state archives museum." [144] "Dixie" preserved its status and its popularity in the postbellum South and was played, for example, at the Atlanta Exposition in 1895, just before the famous address given by Booker T. Washington (thus putting him in his place).[145] It continues to polarize opinion in the South, its performance at a range of occasions from state functions to football games still provoking protests from African Americans.[146] "Dixie" can thus be seen as a song that whites have traditionally used to remind blacks of their "place," that is, "away, away, away down South in Dixie," in the land of segregation and inferior status. The figure of the homesick Negro, wishing "to lib and die in Dixie," long persisted as a stereotype in American culture, another part of that "past that somebody manufactured for 'em" that Sun Ra was so keen for African Americans to throw off. In the musical symbology of Space Is the Place, "Dixie" stands for the false history (his story) to be found in white misrepresentation of black life and black status, while "Space Is the Place" exemplifies the utopian vision of Sun Ra's mythic future (my story) in outer space, a place where:

> There's no limit to the things that you can do
> There's no limit to the things that you can be
> Your thought is free
> And your life is worthwhile.[147]

The film ends with the Earth torn apart by apocalyptic convulsions as Ra and a small band of black survivors head for a new life out among the stars. If, as I have argued elsewhere in these chapters, apocalypse and separatism were not generally characteristic of Ra's work, perhaps their presence here serves to emphasize the starkness of the choice that he saw facing black people—between a "real" world in which they were trapped in a history of slavery and racist dehumanization, or a "myth" world in which black creativity was celebrated from the splendors of ancient Egypt to the spaceways of a future heaven.

— · · · ———

I have tried to outline how Herman Poole Blount, renamed, reborn, and reinvented, became Le Sony'r Ra, the impossible embodiment of his own Astro Black Mythology: "I am the alter-destiny, the presence of the living myth," as he declared in *Space Is the Place*. Though I have also tried to show how elements of this mythology can be traced to sources in African American history and culture, many other aspects of Ra's work, ranging from possible links to the philosophy of Madam Blavatsky to his wonderfully deadpan uses of humor,[148] await further elucidation. Ra could be teasingly evasive at the best of times, as Mark Sinker discovered in 1989 when Ra suddenly informed him:

> I'm not here, you see—this is not me talking, this is just my image and shadow. I wouldn't be caught dead on a planet like this. So my real self is somewhere else, and I'm talking with this self. The same way you sit and look at a TV set. I'm one of the miracles of the Creator—I can sit and talk to you from a nice safe place, out of all the danger on this horrible planet. And I can talk through my spirit. There have been times when men have seen my real self. If I feel ill or something, my other self will stand right there in the room watching over me . . . . My other self is darker than [sic], but absolutely the same. So I do have what the Egyptians call a double. I'm connected with ancient Egypt, I'm connected with the Pharaoh.[149]

Though Ra characteristically locates himself in the context of ancient Egypt, the kind of duplicity he claims here is reminiscent of the West African trickster gods Legba and Esu, who came to the New World in the slave ships and have continued to exert their influence on all facets of African American culture, from blues to literature to art.[150] Like Ra, the trickster gods are divine messengers and interpreters of cosmic codes who travel between the sacred and mundane realms of heaven and earth, unconfined by the boundaries of terrestrial "reality." [151] Traditionally, their haunt is the crossroads, where, like Ra, they traverse the intersections of time and space, making the impossible happen with a mischievous glint in the eye.[152] I do not want to lay undue emphasis on these parallels because, as far as I'm aware, this is one network of Black Atlantic mythologies to which Ra did not allude or refer: ancient Egypt remained his single lodestar where African mythology was concerned. Yet the similarities are at least worth noting, both because Legba and Esu will reappear in the chapters on Anthony Braxton and because they demonstrate again that so much of Ra's mythology can be related, directly or indirectly, to some aspect of African American culture. Ra may have been, in John Paroles's phrase, "a self-made myth," but the contours of the myth were shaped by a kind of symbiotic dialogue, an intertextual relationship, with the main narrative threads of African American history.

This myth was not the work of a madman or a con man, but one of the most brilliant and comprehensive acts of self-representation in black culture. Herman Blount, obscure pianist from Alabama, was reborn as Le Sony'r Ra, ancient African god from outer space, a living myth at "the crossroads whence dimensions meet." [153]

Part II   Duke Ellington: Tone Parallels

The only true history of America is recorded

in its music. The music says what's really

happening here.

—Jeanne Phillips

3 In the Jungles of America:
History Without Saying It

The American Negro must remake his past

in order to make his future.

—*Arthur A. Schomburg* [1]

Two of the earliest documented interviews with Duke Ellington appeared in December 1930. The first, in the *Christian Science Monitor*, ended with him stating, "I am just getting a chance to work out some of my own ideas of Negro music," and lamenting that "so few records have been kept of the Negro music of the past. It has to be pieced together so slowly. But it pleases me to have a chance to work at it." [2] The second interview, which appeared in the *New York Evening Graphic Magazine*, contained the first of his many disclaimers regarding the word "jazz"—"I am not playing jazz, I am trying to play the natural feelings of a people"—and also the first report of a project that, in various guises, would continue to occupy him for virtually the rest of his life: "At present he is at work on a tremendous task, the writing, in music, of 'The History of the Negro,' taking the Negro from Egypt, going with him to savage Africa, and from there to the sorrow and slavery of Dixie, and finally 'home to Harlem.'" [3] Three months later, Ellington was able to develop his views at greater length when his first published article appeared in the British magazine *Rhythm*:

> I have already said that it is my firm belief that what is still known as "jazz" is going to play a considerable part in the serious music of the future . . . that from the welter of negro dance musicians now before the public will come something lasting and noble I am convinced.

The music of my race is something more than the "American idiom." It is the result of our transplantation to American soil, and was our reaction in the plantation days to the tyranny we endured. What we could not say openly we expressed in music, and what we know as "jazz" is something more than just dance music. . . .

To-day we are an important and intrinsic part of the population of the great United States of America. In Harlem we have what is practically our own city; we have our own newspapers and social services, and although not segregated we have almost achieved our own civilisation. The history of my people is one of great achievement over fearful odds; it is a history of people hindered, handicapped and often sorely oppressed and what is being done by Countee Cullen and others in literature is overdue in music.

I am therefore now engaged on a rhapsody unhampered by any musical form in which I intend to portray the experience of the coloured races in America in the syncopated idiom. This composition will consist of four or five movements, and I am putting all I have learned into it in the hope that I shall have achieved something really worthwhile in the literature of music, and that an authentic record of my race *written by a member of it* shall be placed on record.[4]

Several points emerge from these articles: Ellington's racial pride, his view of jazz as "serious music," his belief that music can be used to say that which cannot be stated openly. In particular, it is clear that from a relatively early stage in his career he considered it a major aim of his music to represent black history and black experience in America. In this chapter I outline the development of these representations, looking both at Ellington's own music and writings and at the larger cultural contexts in which they took place, not least the various other representations of blackness that served to frame and mediate his own. Mark Tucker has traced Ellington's views on music and black history to the cultural and political milieu of Washington, D.C., where Ellington was born in 1899 and lived with his respectable, fairly well-to-do family until 1923.[5] I examine these early influences in more detail later, but I begin by looking at Ellington in the context where he first became famous, as a performer in Harlem's Cotton Club. Here, the young composer found himself playing music for depictions of black life, in jungles and on plantations, that crassly misrepresented the very history he was keen to document. How Ellington negotiated this paradox and how these experiences possibly influenced his later work are lines of inquiry that I intend to pursue.

— • • • ———

"The world's most glamorous atmosphere. Why, it's just like the Arabian nights."[6] Ellington's initial reaction to Harlem on his arrival there in 1923 was, if characteristically fanciful, still a fair indication of the allure that Harlem held for a great number of African Americans in the 1920s. Harlem was, according to James de Jongh, "virtually unprecedented in the African diaspora" as "a place for blacks to be themselves, as they saw fit."[7] Despite a wide range of social problems common to many African American communities, such as low wages, high rents, and high death rates:

> What figured in popular culture were the ways in which it was different, and better. Affirmation of the wonder of it seems to have been the characteristic attitude about black Harlem in the 1920s. Harlem was taken to be a harbinger of change in who blacks were and their position among the races of the world. Although they sensed tensions and even contradictions in their optimism, blacks seemed to regard Harlem as a liberated black community, freed from the worst oppressions of racism. In Harlem, at least, a black had a chance to succeed and fulfill his selfhood, and new kinds of Negroes, with new ways of thinking, could flourish.[8]

If Harlem was, as de Jongh maintains, a "liberated" community, it nevertheless contained pockets of "tensions and contradictions," and the Cotton Club, which by the end of the 1920s had become Harlem's most celebrated nightspot, was one such pocket. Owned and run by white gangsters, it operated with a whites-only admission policy while employing only black performers, and it catered to a show-business vogue that had whites flocking uptown to witness the "exoticism" of black entertainment. Ellington's music contributed to this vogue. His orchestra had moved into the Cotton Club in December 1927, and when CBS began nationwide broadcasts from the club in 1928, Ellington's reputation soared; he quickly became one of the club's major attractions. Given his respectable upbringing and his burgeoning ambition to represent black history in music, it is extremely ironic that Ellington's initial fame was associated with his being the leading exponent of what was called "jungle music." This style of jazz, characterized by wailing, growling brass, was used to accompany the Cotton Club's speciality of the time — "jungle skits," in which dancers in "primitive" costumes (i.e., feathers, beads, and little else) would perform erotic dances that supposedly depicted life in the African jungle. Jazz historian Marshall Stearns has described one such skit that he saw at the Cotton Club:

> I recall one where a light-skinned and magnificently-muscled Negro burst through a papier-mache jungle onto the dance floor, clad in an aviator's helmet, goggles and shorts. He had obviously been "forced down in darkest Africa," and in the center of the floor he came upon a "white goddess" clad in long golden tresses and being worshipped by a circle of cringing "blacks." Producing a bullwhip from heaven knows where, the aviator rescued the blonde and they did an erotic dance. In the background, Bubber Miley, Tricky Sam Nanton, and other members of the Ellington band growled, wheezed, and snorted obscenely.[9]

Such depictions of "Africa" were by no means new to American culture. Nineteenth-century minstrel shows had occasionally featured acts such as the "Nubian Jungle Dance";[10] later, from the early years of black musical theater, came shows like Bert Williams's and George Walker's In Dahomey (1902) and In Abyssinia (1906), while "jungle" songs were a standard part of black musical revues in the 1920s.[11] (Jungle films were also popular in the 1920s and 1930s. The 1930 Golden Dawn, for example, based on a musical play by Oscar Hammerstein II and Otto Harbach, resembled the skit that Stearns saw in its portrayal of a white princess courted by a whip-brandishing black overseer.)[12] Mark Tucker has argued that these jungle production numbers, despite the crude stereotyping involved, were popular with both black and white audiences,[13] yet blacks were deeply divided not only about the relative merits of jungle songs, but also about the status of all black vernacular musics. This cultural division reflected class differences, with the middle-class "dicty" blacks looking to Europe for their models of high art and generally disregarding jazz and blues as not worthy of attention. When Langston Hughes published his first book of poems, The Weary Blues, in 1926, in which he used jazz and blues motifs to signal black life in Harlem, the response from the middle-class black community was, reports de Jongh, overwhelmingly negative:

We may have to remind ourselves that Hughes's identification of Harlem with jazz and blues, which now seems so natural—perhaps even a bit trite—was severely criticized by black authority figures and rejected in its own time. The initial negative reaction to *The Weary Blues* objected as much to Hughes's using jazz and blues as literary material as to the flexible sexual morality of the cabarets. The spirituals had come to be accepted by the Negro elite as dignified and ennobling folk forms, but blues and jazz were embarrassing reminders of a status they were trying to escape.[14]

This viewpoint is borne out in part by the essays on music in *The New Negro*, the 1925 anthology of new black writers and artists compiled by Alain Locke, which became one of the central documents of the largely literary-based Harlem Renaissance. Locke himself contributed a long piece in which he extolled the virtues of spirituals and, following the example of W. E. B. DuBois, hailed them as "the most characteristic product of the race genius as yet in America."[15] In a briefer essay on jazz, J. A. Rogers, after defensively admitting to "the vulgarities and crudities of [jazz's] lowly origins" and "the only too prevalent cheap imitations," nevertheless insisted that "jazz has a great future," though he ruefully concluded that because of financial constraints on blacks it was "white orchestras of the type of the Paul Whiteman and Vincent Lopez organizations that are now demonstrating the finer possibilities of jazz music."[16]

Ellington, of course, was not mentioned in *The New Negro*; in 1925 he was still little-known. But even in 1928, given his association with "jungle music," it seems unlikely that de Jongh's "black authority figures" would have endorsed him as an example of the "New Negro."[17] We know that his middle-class family in Washington, D.C., was very taken aback when they first heard his music on the radio. According to his sister, Ruth: "It was quite a shock. Here we were, my mother and I, sitting in this very respectable, Victorian living room in Washington, my mother so puritanical she didn't even wear lipstick, and the announcer from New York tells us we are listening to 'Duke Ellington and his *Jungle* Music'! It sounded very strange and dissonant to us."[18] The reference to the "strange and dissonant" sounds perhaps offers a clue as to why Ellington's "jungle music" caused a stir. Jungle songs and sketches may not have been new in American popular culture, but the kinds of musical settings that Ellington was creating for them certainly were. Significantly, Ellington's own matter-of-fact account of "jungle music" in his 1973 autobiography, *Music Is My Mistress*, focuses on how those "strange" sounds were made and how they expanded the group's musical capabilities.

> During one period at the Cotton Club, much attention was paid to acts with an African setting, and to accompany these we developed what was termed "jungle style" jazz. (As a student of Negro history I had, in any case, a natural inclination in this direction.) Its most striking characteristic was the use of mutes—often the plumber's everyday rubber plunger—by Bubber Miley on trumpet and Joe "Tricky Sam" Nanton on trombone. They founded a tradition we have maintained ever since. This kind of theatrical experience, and the demands it made upon us, was both educative and enriching, and it brought about a further broadening of the music's scope.[19]

One critical debate has led to speculation about Ellington's own feelings toward the "jungle" tag. James Lincoln Collier, proposing that Ellington's above-quoted statements "may seem self-serving, a rather tony way of looking on performances that verged on the pornographic," has argued that Ellington and his commercially astute manager Irving Mills "seized on the idea of 'jungle music'" as a gimmick around which to promote and publicize the band.[20] A contrary view has been put forward by Norman Weinstein, who dismisses Collier's argument as a "comical conspiracy theory" and claims rather that Ellington had deliberately employed titles such as "Jungle Nights in Harlem" "to suggest that African folkways had not completely disappeared from America's cities." Collier's theory, asserts Weinstein:

> lacked even a shard of hard evidence and more; he lacked a rudimentary understanding of what the twenties and thirties meant for African Americans in Harlem. . . .
> Would any critic think mention of African jungles in jazz was a scam if he'd joined the crowd lining a Harlem street to watch the army of Marcus Garvey supporters pass? . . . Their handbills and pamphlets celebrated what African freedom meant to African Americans.[21]

It seems to me that neither of these views of Ellington—as cynical opportunist or ardent Africanist—stands up to examination. There is no evidence that Ellington either initiated or was particularly enthusiastic about the "jungle" label being attached to his music. Irving Mills's business acumen may be discernible in the fact that, after moving to the Cotton Club, the Ellington orchestra recorded a number of tracks under the name of the "Jungle Band" and also recorded a handful of compositions with the word "jungle" in the title. But this hardly constitutes a major exploitation of the "jungle" label. The "Jungle Band" was merely one of several names that the Ellington band recorded under—others included the "Whoopee Makers," the "Washingtonians," the "Harlem Feet Warmers," the "Memphis Men," the "Ten Black Berries," and the "Harlem Hot Chocolates"—while their recordings for their main outlet, the Victor label, were done under the name "Duke Ellington and His Cotton Club Orchestra." [22] Similarly, of the scores of compositions that Ellington recorded during his residency at the Cotton Club from 1927 to 1931 (the period when, if he had wanted to exploit the "jungle" tag, it would presumably have been most advantageous to do so), only *three* include the word "jungle" in the title: "Jungle Jamboree" (1929), "Jungle Blues," and "Jungle Nights in Harlem" (both 1930).[23] By the same token, this relative scarcity of "jungle"—or, indeed, any kind of African—references in Ellington's music also undermines Weinstein's "Africanist" thesis.[24] And other weaknesses can be found in his argument. The Garvey movement had peaked and was in decline by the time that Ellington began to record his "jungle music"; Ellington himself never showed the slightest interest in Garveyism and its "back to Africa" philosophy; instead,—as I hope to show below— he was concerned almost exclusively with the Negro *in America*, both in the past and in the future.[25] And while it is true that Garveyism may have prompted many African Americans to become more curious about Africa, it does not follow that they would have become more enthusiastic about *jungles*, or "jungle music." (Langston Hughes in *The Big Sea* describes a disastrous performance of O'Neill's *The Emperor Jones* that took place in Harlem in the mid-1920s, the audience at one point hooting with laughter and loudly advising the Emperor, "Why don't you come on out a' that jungle—back to Harlem where you belong?")[26] Perhaps it is worth reiterating that the Cotton Club's "jungle" skits were devised by whites for a white audience; it was white visitors to Harlem, not black locals, who were fascinated by "jungle" representations, a show business parallel perhaps to modernist art's fascination with the supposedly "primitive."

Ellington's own view of "jungle music" and the relationship to Africa of both the music and the Cotton Club's skits can, I think, be gauged more accurately from the following two quotations than from Collier's and Weinstein's differing speculations. (The first statement is admittedly anecdotal, the second somewhat more conclusive.) In his 1978 biography of Ellington, Derek Jewell writes: "Leopold Stokowski often came to hear the band at the Cotton Club. He was enthused at the time with ethnic music, wanting to incorporate Oriental and African styles within symphonic tone poems. 'You and I should go to Africa and hear that music,' he observed one evening to Ellington, who gave him a sardonic look and replied: 'The only thing I could get in Africa that I haven't got now is fever!' "[27] And in the first biography of Ellington, published in 1946, Barry Ulanov recounts in detail the opening moments of a musical comedy that Ellington had written, *Air-Conditioned Jungle*. It makes very clear what Ellington thought of white representations of Africans as jungle primitives:

> In a particularly chic living-room, decorated in the best of urbane good taste, but not given to flamboyant extravagances, sit the King and Queen of one of the ancient African tribes. She's dressed in a gown by Schiaparelli; he's in a sleekly fitted dinner jacket. They are drinking their after-dinner brandy and coffee in relaxed comfort: the house is air-conditioned. A muffled bell rings. The King picks up the telephone.
>
> "Yes," he says, "yes, yes. Mmm-hmm. Oh, bother. Well, if there's nothing we can do about it." He slams the receiver down on its cradle and turns unhappily to his consort.
>
> "What is it, darling?" she asks.
>
> "There's another of those expeditions coming over from America. Trying to discover the original source of their jazz, you know."
>
> "Oh, damn," the Queen curses.
>
> "Yes, my dear," the King says, "we shall have to get out our leopard skins again."[28]

Ellington's irony was rarely so upfront in his work, but even in the extract from *Music Is My Mistress* quoted earlier, he makes it clear that his "jungle style" jazz had nothing to do with Africa. It was, he wrote, something "we developed," whose "most striking characteristic" was "the use of mutes—often the plumber's everyday rubber plunger"; an everyday implement in Harlem, that is, but presumably not so in jungle life.[29]

If Ellington exploited the "jungle" label at all, it was not commercially but artistically. The chief irony here is that the Cotton Club's "jungle" skits—plus the various other "exotic location" sketches that were featured [30]—really did enable Ellington, as he claimed in *Music Is My Mistress*, to broaden the scope of his music, not least by developing and extending the use of techniques such as the growl and the plunger. Yet because of the context in which these techniques were presented, they were generally seen not as innovatory but as forms of primitivism in themselves.[31] Typical reviews of the time portrayed the music in terms such as "hot" and "dirty." *Variety's* Abel Green, for instance, called Ellington's orchestra "one of the hottest bands on the air. . . . One torrid trumpet brays and blares in low-down style."[32] In another piece, he referred to the group's propensity for "a real wicked ditty."[33] For Ellington himself, the Cotton Club seems to have been a workshop in which he could experiment with those "strange and dissonant" sounds, transmuting them into a music of singular beauty; it provided an opportunity, in the words of Mark Tucker, "to explore new sounds, textures, harmonies and emotional states—a catalyst for his musical imagination."[34]

One critic did see beyond the "primitivist" connotations of epithets like "hot" and "low-down" to provide a more astute account of what Ellington was achieving. R. D. Darrell wrote a regular "Dance Records" column for the *Phonograph Monthly Review* from 1927 until 1931. In his earlier columns, Darrell uses terms such as "stunts" and "effects" to describe Ellington's orchestrations, though he also notes that they are "exceptionally original and striking."[35] Before long, phrases like "symphonic ingenuity," "unique genius," and "inimitable masterpiece" begin to appear. In his January 1931 column Darrell remarks of "Dreamy Blues" (aka "Mood Indigo"): "It is a poignantly restrained and nostalgic piece with glorious melodic endowment and scoring that even Ravel and Strawinski might envy."[36] And later in the same column he writes of "Jungle Nights in Harlem" that it "contains some more amazing piano and orchestral effects (Rimsky-Korsakov would rub his ears on hearing some of the tone colors here!). Note the parabolic flights in particular. Fantastic music, astoundingly played."[37] In a longer piece on Ellington that he wrote in 1932, Darrell points tellingly to the tendency of "my neighbor" to see "only mud where I see gold, ludicrous eccentricity where I find an expressive expansion of the tonal palette, tawdry tunes instead of deep song, 'nigger music' instead of 'black beauty.'"[38] Yet if Darrell correctly identified a general failure to appreciate the significance of Ellington's music (and other jazz), his writing also revealed an allegiance to European cultural values that prevented him from recognizing the singular and idiomatic nature of what John Gennari has called jazz's "aesthetic agenda." That Darrell's 1932 article compared Ellington to, variously, Debussy, Delius, Mozart, Schubert, Stravinsky, Rimsky-Korsakov, and Wagner serves to underline Gennari's comment that Darrell's writings "testify to a deep-seated assumption that jazz could become art only by transcending its milieu, that jazz's creative breakthrough still required the legitimating, sanctifying influence of the elite European tradition before it could assume a place in the modernist canon alongside Stravinsky's *Rite of Spring*." [39]

This Eurocentric perspective would return to trouble Ellington in later years, but in the 1920s and 1930s, for the most part, those who enthused about his music tended to take the Abel Green line that it was good because it was "low-down." [40] If the "jungle" label functioned as a shield, enabling Ellington to attain levels of experimentation and subtlety that might not have been possible in other contexts, it also served to blind many people to those subtleties. Nearly thirty years after Darrell's columns had appeared, the English critic Vic Bellerby still thought it necessary to make the point.

> The free use of the term "jungle style" is often to be deplored in its indiscriminate reference to Ellington's work, the more so because it is found typifying a style which is essentially subtle and sophisticated. A classical critic would probably be horrified if *Le Sacre du printemps* were called "jungle music"; yet in its simulation of barbaric tribal rhythms, the Stravinsky masterpiece is far nearer to the pulse of African rhythm than *Echoes of the Jungle*, which is essentially the richly-coloured, detached impressionism of a sophisticated Negro city dweller. [41]

In the 1920s and 1930s many white Americans would have found it hard to comprehend the notion of a sophisticated Negro and a sophisticated Negro music. Even the leaders of the Harlem Renaissance may have had trouble with the idea of a sophisticated *jazz musician*, since their concept of culture tended to follow literary-based or "high art" European models. Ellington, meanwhile, working willy-nilly behind the "jungle" mask, was laying the foundations for one of the great bodies of work in twentieth-century music.

An intriguing coda to the "jungle" issue is provided by 1963's "Money Jungle," one of the relatively few late Ellington pieces to mention "jungle" in its title. As the name of both the composition and the recording on which it appeared, "Money Jungle" featured Ellington in a trio with black political radicals Charles Mingus and Max Roach. In his notes to the original LP, George Wein points out that "Money Jungle" "sounds like a title that might have been thought of by the protest conscious Mingus or Roach. But no . . . it is a product of the Ellington imagination."[42] The assumption here is that Ellington is using "jungle" in a perjorative sense, and it seems likely that Wein was right. Ellington's career was punctuated by financial crises; some of his most cherished projects were circumscribed by a lack of money, and meeting the costs of maintaining a full-time orchestra was a constant struggle. His views on this money jungle come across vividly in *Music Is My Mistress*, a book characterized not only by Ellington's refusal to say anything negative about anybody or anything but also by his repeated emphasis on optimism for the future. Then, near the end of the autobiography, a reference to money triggers this extraordinary outburst of apocalyptic bitterness:

> There is hardly any money interest in the realm of art, and music will be here when money is gone. After people have destroyed all people everywhere, I see heaping mounds of money strewn over the earth, floating on and sinking into the sea. The animals and fish, who have no use for money, are kicking it out of the way and splattering it with dung. Money and stink, the stink of dung, the stink of money, so foul that in order for the flowers to get a breath of fresh air, the winds will come together and whip the sea into a rage, and blow across the land. Then the green leaves of trees, and grass, will give up their chlorophyll, so that the sea, the wind, the beasts, and the birds will play and sing Nature's old, sweet melody and rhythm. But since you are people, you will not, unfortunately, be here to hear it.[43]

The irony of the air-conditioned jungle and the bitterness of the money jungle cast their shadows back on the "jungle music" of the 1920s and 1930s and lend credence to the statements of Professor Howard "Stretch" Johnson, who worked as a dancer in the Cotton Club in the early 1930s:

> We didn't know at the time that the splendid sound of the Ellington organization was not jungle music but a creative form of irony which masked the commercial pandering to an upper-class white audience thrilled at the opportunity to hear and witness what it thought was genuine black exotica. . . . At the club, the

sensitivity and lyricism of the Ellington band, even when "growl-ing," made it clear that the jungle did not have to be African.[44]

Indeed, Ellington's use of "jungle music" could perhaps be cited as one of his first major successes in navigating the jungles of America.

— • • • ———

The Cotton Club's framing of its African American entertainers as jungle savages was a voguish attraction, but a less-discussed kind of framing was provided by the club's permanent decor, as noted by Ellington's son, Mercer: "The stage was set up to represent the Land of Cotton with a plantation cabin, rows of cotton bushes, and trees that shot up when the show started . . . . The concept of the Cotton Club represented not the South of the aristocrats but the South of the Negro. The people who came there wanted what they thought was the red-hot feeling of the South as depicted by Negroes."[45] This description of the Cotton Club's interior was confirmed by Cab Calloway, who also made it clear that the decor's implications were not lost on the per-formers: "The bandstand was a replica of a southern mansion, with large white columns and a backdrop painted with weeping willows and slave quarters . . . the whole set was like the sleepy-time-down-South during slavery. Even the name, Cotton Club, was supposed to convey the southern feeling. I suppose the idea was to make whites who came to the club feel like they were being catered to and enter-tained by black slaves."[46]

Evocation of the Old South was widely reflected in the choice of names for clubs that featured black performers: the Cotton Club and Club Kentucky in New York, Club Alabam in Los Angeles, the Planta-tion Club in Chicago. Another Plantation Club, on New York's Broad-way, was indeed fitted out as "a southern plantation, complete with log cabins, Negro mammies, picket fences around the dance floor, a twinkling summer sky, and a watermelon moon. Aunt Jemima herself stood in one of the cabins, flipping flapjacks."[47]

These depictions of slave quarters and plantation life were a throw-back; such scenes figured both in white antebellum minstrelsy and later black versions, such as the "Black America" extravaganza of 1895 when a "plantation" was re-created in Ambrose Park, Brooklyn.[48] The contradictions begin to accrue in layers here. Not only in the midst of 1920s "New Negro" Harlem did the old minstrel stereotypes continue to operate, but also the early twentieth-century modernist appropriation of "blackness" as a sign of the elementally sensual became entangled with and underpinned by this older representation of the Slave South as the location of what was seen by whites as authentically black, not least the "red-hot feeling" that Mercer Ellington claimed they flocked to see and hear in Harlem's clubs and cabarets (where the minstrel trappings perhaps served to frame this potentially explosive "feeling" in a familiar and thus less-threatening setting). In fact, minstrelsy and minstrel stereotypes continued to play a prominent part in American popular culture well into the twentieth century. Minstrel shows and revues remained popular in rural areas of the South and West, where a minstrel offshoot, the "Uncle Tom Show," proved particularly ubiquitous. In the 1930s, minstrelsy was even government-sponsored. The Works Progress Administration and the Federal Theatre Project produced minstrel shows and puppet minstrel shows as well as distributing minstrel publications such as the 1938 *56 Minstrels*. Aimed at juvenile community groups like the Boy Scouts, this book included arrangements of "The Darktown Follies," "Watermelon Minstrel," and "Plantation Days with the Snowflake Family."[49] In the 1920s and 1930s, minstrelsy also began to permeate the newer forms of media. The first popularly celebrated talking picture, 1927's *The Jazz Singer*, featured Al Jolson in a blackface role, and the first nationally syndicated radio program in the United States was the *Amos 'n' Andy* show, another blackface entertainment so successful that it ran without interruption for fifteen years on radio (1928 to 1943).[50] What also survived, and even flourished, was the tangle of patronizing assumptions and delusions that surrounded the images of minstrelsy, not least the notion that these were "authentic" representations of black life.[51] In 1929, for example, *Hearts of Dixie*, one of the first films to look at black plantation life (and to give a major role to black actor Stepin Fetchit), was reviewed by a columnist in the *Los Angeles Examiner*: "There is nothing in *Hearts of Dixie*, however, at which either race can take offense. It is such a true and sympathetic picture of the colored folk. The pitiful superstitions of some of the uneducated Negroes, their simplicity, their love of a good time, and their psychology are all graphically presented . . . . The real Southern plantation melodies are so sincerely sung that one glimpses the real soul of the Negro."[52]

In 1930 the Ellington orchestra temporarily left the Cotton Club—where the latest "Blackberries of 1930" revue included items titled "Cotton Club Minstrels" and "Swanee River Rhapsody"[53]—and traveled to Hollywood, where they were to appear in their first major feature film, *Check and Double Check*.[54] The stars of the film were Amos 'n' Andy, but they were not the only performers in blackface. Two light-skinned members of the Ellington orchestra, the Puerto Rican Juan Tizol and the Creole Barney Bigard, were forced to put on black makeup to make it clear that the band was not integrated, the reason being that many whites, especially in the South, opposed any kind of racial mixing.[55] Indeed, film historian Thomas Cripps adds that RKO, thinking the film could be a hit, later "covered up Ellington in the billing 'due to the Southern angle.'"[56] A case, it seems, of being blacked up and then blacked out! Nevertheless, the film almost certainly helped Ellington build on the reputation he was gaining from his recordings and radio broadcasts. Irving Mills, who had negotiated the orchestra's appearance in *Check and Double Check*, may also have been responsible for the title of one of the compositions written for the film. "Ring Dem Bells," credited to Mills and Ellington as co-composers, is an extreme rarity among Ellington titles in its use of dialect.[57] Another Ellington piece played in the film may have contained a more subversive message; "Old Man Blues," as critic Dan Morgenstern has noted, "is, as the title tells us but few musicologists seem to have heard, Ellington's answer to Ol' Man River—a hip message indeed to insiders, since the film itself starred Amos 'n' Andy."[58] (Presumably Morgenstern takes the tune to be a critical comment on the stars' blackface roles, since *Showboat*, the source of "Ol' Man River," used black actors to play the black roles on film.[59])

This cryptic "hip message" aside, Ellington seems to have had little choice but to go along with such minstrel trappings in the 1920s and 1930s. "Following instructions," to use Irving Mills's phrase,[60] was simply necessary for survival in the show-business milieu of the period, and blackface and dialect were commonplace features of popular culture. The great vaudeville star Bert Williams, to whom Ellington wrote a musical tribute, was obliged to perform in dark makeup because he was a light-skinned black,[61] and in her autobiography Billie Holiday recounted with some venom an occasion in Detroit when she too was forced to black up. (Her comments also shed light on the kind of financial pressures under which Ellington would have had to work.)

> Next they told Basie I was too yellow to sing with all the black men in his band. Somebody might think I was white if the light didn't hit me just right. So they got special dark grease paint and told me to put it on.

It was my turn to flip. I said I wouldn't do it. But they had our names on the contracts and if I refused it might have played hell with our bookings, not just for me, but for the future of all the cats in the band.

So I had to be darkened down so the show could go on in dynamic-assed Detroit. It's like they say, there's no damn business like show business. You have to smile to keep from throwing up.[62]

Such "darkening down" could also be enforced metaphorically. In a 1935 article in the *Philadelphia Record* the journalist Gama Gilbert appears to make use of minstrel stereotyping to cast Ellington as a staple figure from minstrel shows, the simple, bemused Negro (a figure that Stepin Fetchit was concurrently portraying on film). With what reads like an air of amused condescension, Gilbert recounts a meeting with Ellington and the "dusky maestro"'s reaction to recent praise from English critics and composers.[63]

When Duke was making life gayer for the patrons of exclusive London night clubs last year, he had a strange experience. He was taken up by the musical intelligentsia of the British capitol. He was "discovered" by the highbrows, and great was the hue and cry thereof. It was the greatest British triumph since Dr. Livingstone's adventures in Darkest Africa.

Constant Lambert, English composer and critic, who is a very brilliant but very young man, wrote a book about modern music ("Music Ho!"). He had a lot of nice things to say about Duke's music, practically smothering the jazz boy's "Blues" in an admiring avalanche of fancy critical verbiage. . . .

Apparently all this adulation left honest Duke slightly bewildered. Your correspondent found the idol of Mayfair one night last week in a local temple far removed from Kensington Gardens, Hyde Park or the studios of London's Bohemia. In fact, your correspondent found the dusky maestro in a rather select but noisy night club in Manayink, doing his stuff in a smoke-laden, purple-lighted cabaret to the syncopated delight of a crowded dance floor.[64]

Cornering Ellington in his dressing room during an intermission, Gilbert reads out extracts from Lambert's book and notes Ellington's reactions:

"I know nothing in Ravel," read your reporter (from Lambert's pages), "so dextrous in treatment as the various solos in Ellington's ebullient 'Hot and Bothered' and nothing in Stravinsky more dynamic than the final section . . . it is a genuine melodic and rhythmic counterpoint."

A look of simple wonder appeared on Duke's countenance. "Is that so," he gasped. "Say, that fellow Lambert is quite a writer, isn't he?"

Your reporter read some more. "In Ellington's compositions jazz has produced the most distinguished popular music since Johann Strauss."

Duke's face lit up in a broad grin. "Hot damn!" he said. "I guess that makes me pretty good, doesn't it?"[65]

Then, after Ellington explains how the sound of a recording of "Mood Indigo" was caused in part by a faulty microphone, Gilbert interjects:

"Yes," we said, "that was what one English critic called 'Ellington's weird and dulcet harmonizations such as were never [heard] on land or sea, recalling the opalescent subtleties of Debussy.' "

"How come?" said Duke.

"That's what an English critic said about that record."

"Is zat so?" said Duke. "Opalescent subtleties. Don't those London fellows push a mean pen?" . . .

The intermission was over. The reporter left. But the Duke still lingered. Stretched out in his chair with a dreamy expression in his eyes, he was scratching his head, "The greatest popular dance music since Johann Strauss—hot damn!" he said.[66]

Certain stylistic features of this piece may be attributable to the journalese of the period, but clearly Gilbert is implying that the English "musical intelligentsia," and particularly Lambert, with his "avalanche of fancy critical verbiage," are ridiculous and affected, and consequently their high regard for Ellington's music ("his stuff") need not be taken seriously—that, in fact, it makes them figures of fun. Ellington himself is presented in an extremely patronizing manner, evident not only in the sarcastic undertow of such phrases as "the jazz boy," "honest Duke," "the idol of Mayfair," and "the dusky maestro," but also in the attempts to portray him as slightly simple-minded, with his bewilderment, his "look of simple wonder," his head-scratching and his repeated gasps of "Is zat so?" and "Hot damn!" In short, the article is framed by a minstrel stereotyping that ensures not only that Ellington himself is demeaned, but the acclaim accorded his music is also undermined, the implication being that his work's rightful place is not in the company of Ravel, Debussy, and Stravinsky but in a "smoke-laden, purple-lighted cabaret." Thus, Ellington is "darkened down," lest anyone mistake him for a white composer. Yet rereading the article today, with our awareness of Ellington's capacity for irony, it is possible to excavate other levels of meaning in the text. Perhaps Ellington's replies were a typically wry and discreet means of distancing himself from the extravagant praise of the English. Or perhaps his series of casual questions—"Say, that fellow Lambert is quite a writer, isn't he?" or "I guess that makes me pretty good, doesn't it?" or "Don't those London fellows push a mean pen?"—was a subtle way of goading the disdainful Gilbert, by emphasizing that, yes, this was high praise and it was for him.[67]

That Ellington was extremely sensitive to minstrelsy's representations of black life and black history became clear in 1941, when he worked as one of the main collaborators on the musical revue Jump for Joy. Others involved included composer Hal Borne, lyricist Paul Francis Webster, and sketch writers Sid Kuller and Hal Fimberg. Ellington and Borne wrote the music, and the Ellington orchestra performed throughout the show's eleven-week run in Los Angeles, from 10 July to 27 September. Interviewed during this run by journalist John Pittman, Ellington explained the rationale behind the show:

> "'Jump for Joy' provided quite a few problems. There was the first and greatest problem of trying to give an American audience entertainment without compromising the dignity of the Negro people. Needless to say, this is the problem every Negro artist faces. He runs afoul of offensive stereotypes instilled in the American mind by whole centuries of ridicule and derogation. The American audience has been taught to expect a Negro on the stage to clown and 'Uncle Tom,' that is, to enact the role of a servile, yet lovable, inferior."[68]

Some thirty years later, Ellington recalled Jump for Joy in his autobiography in very similar terms, describing it as an "attempt to correct the race situation in the U.S.A." The show's aims, he said, had been to "take Uncle Tom out of the theatre, eliminate the stereotyped image that had been exploited by Hollywood and Broadway, and say things that would make the audience think."[69] One of the original sketches for the show, he added, had featured Uncle Tom on his deathbed. While his children danced around him, singing, "Let him go, God bless him!," producers from Hollywood and Broadway desperately tried to keep him alive by injecting adrenalin into his arms![70]

Jump for Joy brought together an impressive array of black talent and white Hollywood liberal support. Langston Hughes and Mickey Rooney contributed items to the show; Countee Cullen and John Garfield attended many of the rehearsals. All of the performers were black. In addition to the Ellington orchestra with singers Ivie (initially Ivy) Anderson and Herb Jeffries, they included actresses Marie Bryant and Dorothy Dandridge, comedians Wonderful Smith and Pot, Pan and Skillet, and, later, blues singer Big Joe Turner. Whites were involved in the writing, producing, and financing of the show. Lana Turner and Groucho and Harpo Marx were among the sponsors, while celebrities who went to see it included Marlene Dietrich, Mae West, and Orson Welles, who was so impressed that the next day he contracted Ellington to codirect a film on the history of jazz.[71] Unfortunately, Jump for Joy's initial success was not maintained, in part because a dispute between ASCAP (American Society of Composers Authors and Publishers) and U.S. radio stations meant that no music from the show could be broadcast, and hopes to take Jump for Joy to Broadway were dashed. For Ellington, however, the show represented a major artistic and political statement, and in Music Is My Mistress he spends several pages discussing its merits. One point he stresses is the care that was taken to avoid any kind of racial stereotyping; fifteen of the writers who contributed to the show would meet backstage after each performance and reexamine the material. The turnover of sketches and songs was high, with items coming in or going out on a daily basis. "We were always on guard against the possibility of chauvinism creeping in," Ellington recalled, "of saying the same things about other races we did not want said about Negroes." Attending these meetings for twelve weeks was, he concluded, like "a full college education in social significance."[72] In her excellent essay that accompanies the Smithsonian Institution's LP issue of material from Jump for Joy, Patricia Willard reveals that these social concerns were shared by all of the performers; at one point the chorus girls staged a walkout because the choreographer asked them to talk in dialect.[73]

The issue of blacking up was also addressed. It was banned from Jump for Joy. In Music Is My Mistress, Ellington specifically states that he was the person who ruled it out.

I had stopped all the comedians from using cork on their faces when they worked with us. Some objected before the show opened, but removed it, and were shocked by their success. As the audience screamed and applauded, comedians came off stage smiling, and with tears running down their cheeks. They couldn't believe it. I think a statement of social protest in the theatre should be made without saying it, and this calls for the real craftsman.[74]

Singer Herb Jeffries, in an interview with Willard, confirmed Ellington's vehement dislike of blacking up. Actor John Garfield, one of the Hollywood eminences grises unofficially helping out with the show, had advised Jeffries backstage to darken his skin to match that of his co-performer Clarence "Frenchy" Landry:

He called in Frenchy and the make-up man and had him match me to Frenchy with the Max Factor Egyptian #39 or something. Now it's my cue for act 2. I'm out there singing, "If Life Were All Peaches and Cream." Duke looks up from the pit and he's horrified. I can't figure out what is upsetting him so much because I'm thinking about the song, not how I look, and besides, I don't know how I look. I thought maybe my fly was open. I was afraid Ellington was going to have apoplexy.

Right after the finale, Duke storms into my dressing room, furious: "What in the hell are you playing—Al Jolson? We don't do blackface in Jump for Joy!"[75]

Ellington's declaration that social protest was best made "without saying it" explicitly was one of his guiding aesthetic principles.[76] Yet Jump for Joy was possibly the most outspoken project he was involved in. A fast-paced succession of songs, skits, comic turns, and dances, the show ranged across many facets of black life and, in addition to giving us musical gems such as Ivie Anderson's exquisite rendition of "I Got It Bad and That Ain't Good," may have helped to promote the enormous popularity among young black men of the "zoot suit with the reet pleat."[77] Not every item aspired to "social significance," but in those that did the satire pulled no punches. What Jump for Joy made particularly clear was the contempt that blacks felt for various white representations of blackness, not least the figure of Uncle Tom and the notion that blacks belonged—and were happy—in the South.[78] Early in the show, Ellington spoke directly to the audience:

Now, every Broadway colored show
According to tradition,
Must be a carbon copy
Of the previous edition,
With the truth discreetly muted
And the accent on the brasses.
The punch that should be present
In a colored show, alas, is
Disinfected with magnolia
And dripping with molasses.
In other words,
We're shown to you
Through Stephen Foster's glasses.[79]

The show's theme song took up the same issues:

Fare thee well, land of cotton,
Cotton lisle is out of style, honey chile,
Jump for joy.

Don't you grieve, little Eve,
All the hounds, I do believe,
Have been killed, ain't you thrilled,
Jump for joy.[80]

Other songs included "Uncle Tom's Cabin Is a Drive-In Now" ("Je-mimah doesn't work no more for RKO / She's slingin' hash for Uncle Tom and coinin' dough")[81] and "I've Got a Passport from Georgia," which stated its message so unmistakably that it sparked a campaign of violence and intimidation from the Glendale, California, chapter of the Ku Klux Klan and was eventually dropped from the show after a series of death threats.[82] Sample verses were:

I've got a passport from Georgia
And I'm sailin' for the U.S.A.
Where it's hello to a fellow,
Be he black or white or yellow
In New York with Fiorello it's okay. . . .

I've got a passport from Georgia
And I'm goin' up where life's a cinch
Where the cravat's a correct tie

Where you wear no Dixie necktie
Where the signs read "Out to Lunch" not "Out to Lynch." [83]

Perhaps it was verses such as these that Ellington had in mind in the 1960s when, in reply to demonstrators who asked, "What is your position on civil rights? Why don't you ever make a statement?," he said, "I made my statement in 1941 in *Jump for Joy* and I stand by it." [84]

Ellington's claim that the show represented his statement about civil rights raises some questions about authorship to which I will return. First, though, I would like to conclude this brief survey of Ellington's work apropos of minstrelsy and the South by looking at one of his last major pieces to address the issue directly.

The Deep South Suite was premiered in November 1946 at Carnegie Hall. A purely instrumental work, it comprised four sections to which Ellington gave the titles "Magnolias Just Dripping with Molasses," "Hearsay," "There Was Nobody Looking," and "The Happy-Go-Lucky Local." In *Music Is My Mistress* he discusses these sections, beginning with "Magnolias" and "Hearsay":

> The Deep South is many things to many people but here we were content to reproduce what might be called the Dixie Chamber of Commerce dream picture, with beautiful blue skies, Creole girls with flashing eyes, fried chicken, watermelons, and all those good old nostalgic memories. . . . "Hearsay" was concerned with other things that were told about the South, things that were not in accordance with the Chamber of Commerce dream picture, things that were at times almost directly the opposite.[85]

Ellington's reluctance to make direct political statements, even in 1973, is evident here in his use of irony and euphemism. Yet he does drop hints to the alert reader that a more pointed subtext is present. The most obvious clue is the title "Magnolias Just Dripping with Molasses," which not only echoes his *Jump for Joy* monologue that criticized white representations of black life in the South ("The punch that should be present/In a colored show, alas, is/Disinfected with magnolia/And dripping with molasses") but compounds the effect by bringing magnolias and molasses together in a single, over-the-top image of sickliness. Other clues, like the references to such stereotyped signifiers of black life as fried chicken and watermelon, should dispel any doubts that Ellington's tongue was firmly in his cheek. Mercer Ellington, in his memoir *Duke Ellington in Person*, later made very clear the intention behind these pieces, calling them "satirical and bitter": "*Deep South Suite*, in its first movements, was sharply critical. 'Magnolias Just Dripping with Molasses' ridiculed the Dixie Chamber of Commerce dream picture. 'Hearsay' referred to events that the Chamber of Commerce would not wish extensively publicized and the South's evil record of lynchings." [86]

Yet if "Magnolias Just Dripping with Molasses" is an example of Ellington saying in music something he did not want or feel able to say more directly, the response of critic James Lincoln Collier highlights the possibility that such musical barbs are no less open to misinterpretation than Ellington's elusive prose. In his biography of Ellington, Collier suggests the piece is a straight portrait of "the happy face of the South," further argues that "this rather charming picture of the South confused critics, who assumed that Duke viewed the South with a good deal of disdain," and then concludes: "In fact, despite the violent racism that existed there, Ellington had a sneaking fondness for the area, and his tone pictures of it are usually appreciative." [87] If any critic is confused here, it is surely Collier, who seems blithely unaware of just how deep *The Deep South Suite* is. Significantly, Collier does not mention Mercer Ellington's contradictory interpretation of "Magnolias Just Dripping with Molasses," nor does he offer any evidence for his contentious claim that Ellington had a "sneaking fondness" for the South. It is also curious that while his description of the music refers to Lawrence Brown's trombone solo ("playing a very pretty melody"), he fails to note that this solo includes brief snatches of "Dixie" and "The Old Folks at Home," quotations that undermine Collier's perception of the piece.[88] "The Old Folks at Home" was by Stephen Foster, another of the targets of Ellington's *Jump for Joy* monologue, while the old minstrel song "Dixie," which had long been the anthem of the white South, was possibly the most hated song in Black America.[89] It is hard to see how the allusions to these songs could signify anything other than Ellington's "disdain," his belief that the "dream picture" they represented was a total lie. The clinching piece of evidence can be found in the South itself, which witnessed a particularly ugly outburst of racial violence just ten weeks before the suite's debut. According to Klaus Stratemann, "Ellington was to have played a series of one-nighters and concerts through Texas and other Southern states. Because of racial disturbances in the area at the time, which included the murder of four blacks at Athens, Ga., Ellington asked the William Morris agency to cancel those commitments and return all deposits for his appearances in the South." [90] With such horrors fresh in his mind, it is surely inconceivable that the race-proud Ellington would have set about composing a straight portrayal of "the happy face of the South."

Collier's comments on "Magnolias Just Dripping with Molasses" are perhaps exceptionally obtuse, but they do illustrate the dangers of Ellington's preference for indirection. With *The Deep South Suite's* third movement, "There Was Nobody Looking," his policy of not "saying it" becomes even more problematic. Here is the relevant "explanation" from *Music Is My Mistress*:

> "There Was Nobody Looking" illustrated the theory that, when nobody is looking, many people of different extractions are able to get along together. It had to do, I explained, with a pretty little flower in the middle of a field and a small dog who was fascinated by the flower. As the puppy reached over to caress the flower, a light breeze blew it out of his reach, and every time he tried to touch it the flower was carried off in a different direction by the breeze. There was, nevertheless, no animosity or friction between dog and breeze, for each respected the other's right to court the flower. Moreover, the puppy and the flower were both too young to be influenced away from their natural tendencies, and, most important, there was nobody looking! [91]

I doubt that anyone could make much sense of this "explanation," and the music, a jaunty piano solo with a hint of stride, offers no further clues. We have to turn to Mercer Ellington's later explication to discover precisely which facet of Southern life the piece was addressing:

> In *The Deep South Suite* he dealt with another subtlety, something that for years was both accepted practice and common knowledge below the Mason-Dixon line: the classic liaison of *white man* and *black woman*, reverse freedom as it were. The work "Nobody Was Lookin'" [sic] referred directly to this, to the master going over the fence, figuratively and literally. Because in the early days this was how it was done: over they went and up they came with the woman. In later years—and maybe we're talking about what goes on to this day, when things are not so hidden anymore—the accepted thing was for the white man to have a colored woman on the side. . . . On the other hand, if this situation was reversed it was always a horrible thing in everyone's mind.
>
> Ellington thoroughly disliked this sort of dishonest thinking, and there was every reason for him to be concerned about mis-

cegenation. Within our own family we have witnessed mixtures deriving from more than one such occurrence. Ellington knew people who had experienced blacks as persons and personalities and, vice versa, he knew blacks who had known whites. This inequality was a practice he was unable to swallow.[92]

Even Mercer's normally transparent prose seems to get nervously opaque in this extract. Perhaps he was reluctant to say that Ellington had "every reason to be concerned with miscegenation" because he had had affairs with white women. Yet he makes this clear elsewhere in his book, both when he alludes to the possible animosity caused by the fact that Ellington's companion on at least one of his State Department-sponsored tours abroad in the 1960s was a white woman,[93] and when he remarks that in the 1920s Ellington "had an encounter with high society and its prejudices. His attentions had been invited by a Park Avenue socialite, but they were resented by her relatives, who managed to involve the police in discouraging the affair."[94] If Ellington felt personally vulnerable on this issue, perhaps it is no surprise that his commentary on "There Was Nobody Looking" took such a circuitous and obfuscating form as the parable of the flower, the puppy, and the breeze. Mercer's reference to the police also serves as a reminder that miscegenation was not simply a sensitive issue; in many places it was officially taboo. "Until 1967, seventeen American states had laws against intermarriage . . . . Until recently in many American states it was illegal to *advocate* intermarriage."[95] To the extent that "There Was Nobody Looking" implicitly advocated miscegenation, perhaps it was necessary that its message stay hidden. Yet the problem remains: given that Ellington's music, title, and commentary make no tangible reference to miscegenation, on what grounds can Mercer justify his claim that the piece "referred directly to" and "dealt with" the issue? That may have been Ellington's intention, but perhaps this is one occasion on which his policy of indirection was pursued so rigorously that it proved self-defeating.

This opinion was apparently shared by William Morris Jr., head of the touring agency to which Ellington had signed after he left Irving Mills. Ellington writes in *Music Is My Mistress* that, at the party following the suite's performance at Carnegie Hall, Morris "really pitched a bitch. 'You should have said it plainer,' he kept insisting. 'You should have said it plainer!' He was for out-and-out protest, but as with *Jump for Joy* I felt it was good theatre to say it without saying it. That is the art."[96]

Ellington's equation of *The Deep South Suite* and *Jump for Joy* as works that "say it without saying it" is rather curious. While the former piece fits that description, the witty and incisive lyrics of a song like "I've Got a Passport from Georgia" could hardly "say it" more plainly. What is also curious is that while the coded approach of *The Deep South Suite* was far more characteristic of Ellington's approach to protest, it was *Jump for Joy* to which he seems to have been particularly attached, devoting several pages to it in his autobiography (where he also reprints the first-night program), listing it in a 1952 *Down Beat* article as one of his top ten career highlights,[97] and, as noted earlier, citing it in the 1960s as his definitive statement on civil rights. This attachment is especially intriguing given that *Jump for Joy* was a collective project. Ellington wrote much of the music but only one of the lyrics and none of the sketches (many of which were written by whites)—which raises the question of how the show could be described as *his statement* at all. But perhaps it was the very fact of this collectivism that Ellington was citing as his statement on civil rights (without actually "saying it," of course!): the fact that blacks and whites *could* work together without black representations of blackness and whiteness being undermined or constrained or replaced by white misrepresentations. Without, that is, recourse to stereotypes. According to *Jump for Joy* writer Sid Kuller, "traditionally, black humor had been performed by blacks for white audiences from a white point of view. Our material was from the point of view of black people looking at whites."[98]

That Ellington felt strongly not only about miscegenation but about racially mixed artistic cooperation was signaled by his involvement in the 1947 musical *Beggar's Holiday* (based on John Gay's *The Beggar's Opera*), in which both the cast and the production team were racially mixed. Ellington stresses this point in *Music Is My Mistress*, adding, "It was a long time before its time so far as social significance was concerned. Again it was a matter of saying things without saying them. . . . Alfred Drake (a white actor) played the part of Macheath the mobster, and the chief of police and his daughter were both black. Mack and the colored girl fell in love. Now that's a silly show in 1947! There were no such things then."[99]

Mercer, too, has testified to his father's belief in an integrated society. "With reference to the world in general, ours was obviously not a society that needed to be separated. Pop firmly believed it should be mixed, and he wrote a number of things directly related to this point of view."[100] One of the last of these things was a score for a 1969 film based on a particularly bizarre premise. *Change of Mind* was about the transplanting of a white man's brain into a black man's body. David Meeker in his *Jazz in the Movies* reports that "racial harmony is the message behind this story," while Ellington himself merely remarks that the subject was "provocative" and the film "not too popular."[101] What a wonderful irony that this intended image of integration—the white brain in the black body—can also be seen as an image of the Ultimate Minstrel, a white man in blackface so "authentic" it won't come off! It's not hard to imagine Ellington smiling wrily at the film's implications.[102] After all, the thesis, which I take to be implicit in *Change of Mind*, that racial harmony will not be possible until whites learn to come to terms with the reality of black experience and abandon their false representations of blackness, is one that Ellington's music had carried, directly and indirectly, for more than forty years.

—· · · ———

Though important, Ellington's undermining of primitivist and minstrelsy stereotypes was secondary to his main purpose—a more accurate, and positive, portrayal of black life in the United States. The interviews and the article quoted at the beginning of this chapter show that by the start of the 1930s Ellington was already thinking in terms of representing black history and images of blackness in his music. Mark Tucker in *Ellington: The Early Years* cites two events that took place in Washington, D.C., in the second decade of the century that might have given impetus and initial shape to these ideas. In 1911 the Howard Theater, Washington's first black theater, presented a musical show titled *The Evolution of the Negro in Picture, Song, and Story*, whose program—Overture, Night of Slavery-Sorrow Songs, Dawn of Freedom, Day of Opportunity—could, Tucker speculates, have been the template for later Ellington works such as *Symphony in Black* and *Black, Brown and Beige*.[103] And in 1915 W. E. B. DuBois's spectacular pageant *The Star of Ethiopia* was mounted in Washington's American League baseball park. Tucker notes that rehearsals for the pageant took place at Ellington's high school, and he quotes from the program: "The Story of the Pageant covers 10,000 years and more of the history of the Negro race and its work and suffering and triumphs in the world. This Pageant combines historic accuracy and symbolic truth."[104] The pageant was divided into five scenes or historical periods—"Gift of Iron," "Dream of Egypt," "Glory of Ethiopia," "Valley of Humiliation," and "Vision Everlasting"—and featured "music by colored composers, lights and symbolic dancing."[105] Whether or not Ellington attended the pageant, it seems safe to assume that he would have known about it, as he would many of the other musical and cultural activities that typified black middle-class society in Washington at the time.[106]

Another early influence to whom Tucker draws attention was Ellington's high school principal and English teacher, Miss Boston. Ellington himself had this to say of her, and of his schooling, in Music Is My Mistress: "She taught us that proper speech and good manners were our first obligations, because as representatives of the Negro race we were to command respect for our people. This being an all-colored school, Negro history was crammed into the curriculum, so we would know our people all the way back. They had pride there, the greatest race pride. . . ."[107] (Race pride was a prominent issue in Washington, D.C., in this period. The imposition of segregation on federal employees' dining and toilet facilities by the incoming Woodrow Wilson administration in 1913 outraged middle-class blacks, while attempts to desegregate the schools were resisted by "the proud Negroes of Washington," who felt the white children were "not good enough" to mix with the black.)[108] Ellington's later comments in Music Is My Mistress are testimony to this early instruction in race pride and black history. That Miss Boston's teachings made a lasting impression is evident throughout his autobiography, not least in its impeccable display of "good manners" and, in particular, its repeated references to "commanding respect."[109] Of trumpeter Arthur Whetsol, for example, he writes "he would speak up in a minute on the subject of propriety . . . . He was aware of all the Negro individuals who were contributing to the cause by *commanding respect.*"[110] Later, recounting that trumpeter Rex Stewart "had been taught the responsibility of commanding respect for his race," Ellington adds: "Since I refer to it often, I should say that commanding respect, in my view, is a social credit that will never become outdated."[111] That Whetsol had doubts about the "propriety" of playing in the Cotton Club (and indeed of playing jazz per se) is implied by Ellington's dry comment: "He left us to go back to Howard University to study medicine. Although he loved the music, I think he felt called upon to pursue a career that was considered, in those days, more respectable."[112] (In fact, Whetsol soon returned to the Ellington orchestra and remained a regular member until 1937.)

If, as I have suggested, Ellington looked askance at the Cotton Club's depictions of black history, it seems he also tried to ease the whites-only entrance policy. According to Cotton Club historian Jim Haskins:

> Within a year Ellington had become such a prize property that the Cotton Club agreed to his request to relax the "whites only" policy. This is not to say that Ellington pushed for complete integration of the clientele, or that the club suddenly welcomed black patrons. But Ellington had hinted that it was a shame some of his friends could not enter the club to hear him and that the families of the other performers were not permitted to watch them. The management, aware of its stake in Ellington, had cautiously accepted, at least while he was at the club.[113]

Haskins adds that "black customers were still carefully examined before being admitted" and "were frequently seated at back tables near the kitchen."[114] Nevertheless, this appears to be an early example of Ellington employing his nonconfrontational approach in a difficult situation with at least a measure of success. (It could also be cited as an example of what you could achieve if you were able to "command respect," in this case by virtue of musical excellence.)[115]

If Ellington's feelings about the Cotton Club were necessarily ambivalent, his delight in Harlem was unequivocal. One of the first indications on disc of his race pride was the series of recordings he made that named Harlem in the title, the best-known probably being "Drop Me Off at Harlem," "Jungle Nights in Harlem," and "Echoes of Harlem." It could be argued that such titles were an attempt to cash in on the vogue for Harlem in the 1920s and early 1930s, and it is probable that Irving Mills was not above changing Ellington's titles to something he considered more commercial. However, while commercialism may have played a part in the choice of such titles, the fact remains that Ellington continued to celebrate Harlem in his music long after its vogue had ended and long after he had parted company with Mills. "Harlem Air-Shaft," written in 1940, was one of Ellington's best-known evocations of Harlem life; in 1951 came the fifteen-minute suite *A Tone Parallel to Harlem*, commissioned by Arturo Toscanini for the NBC Symphony Orchestra. And, from 1941, the Ellington orchestra's theme tune, written by Ellington's close collaborator Billy Strayhorn, was "Take the 'A' Train," its destination the subway express stop at 125th Street in the heart of Harlem. It seems Ellington was exaggerating only a little when he claimed in 1933 that "every one of my song titles is taken from . . . the life of Harlem." [116]

Another series of recordings that revealed Ellington's race pride began in 1928 with "Black Beauty." This was his tribute to the singer and dancer Florence Mills, star of *Shuffle Along* and *Blackbirds*, whose unexpected death the previous year occasioned one of the greatest funerals Harlem had ever seen. Ellington's title in particular seems to carry a charge of racial pride since this was an era when blackness was still widely equated with ugliness rather than beauty. For example, the chorus girls at the Cotton Club had to be light-skinned, "nothing darker than a light olive tint," to please the white clientele. [117] But "Black Beauty" was only the first of a series of tributes to black performers that Ellington continued to record throughout his career. Later examples included "Bojangles (A Portrait of Bill Robinson)," "A Portrait of Bert Williams," "A Portrait of the Lion" (a tribute to Ellington's mentor Willie "the Lion" Smith), and, as part of 1970's *New Orleans Suite*, dedications to Louis Armstrong, Sidney Bechet, and Mahalia Jackson. Ellington was also willing to affirm his admiration of such artists in print. Recuperating after a hernia operation in 1938, he wrote this passage in a short piece for the journal *The Negro Actor*:

> The sky-line from my window in the Wickersham hospital is an inspiring sight. . . . I spent some time comparing the marvelous sky-line to our race, likening the Chrysler tower, the Empire State building and other lofty structures to the lives of Bert Williams, Florence Mills and other immortals of the entertainment field. . . .
>
> We are children of the sun and our race has a definite tradition of beauty and glory and vitality that is as rich and powerful as the sun itself. [118]

What emerges here is not only Ellington's pride in his race but, in the comparison of black artists with the Manhattan skyline, his pride in America too—or, at least, the comparison reveals his belief in the essential *Americanness* of African American art. Ellington's patriotism would become more evident later in his life, but even in the 1920s and 1930s I think it is clear from his music that the focus of his interest was black life *in America*. The celebrations of Harlem and the tributes to his fellow black artists were reflections of the greater vision of African American history that was taking shape in his mind.

Musical depictions of black life and black history were by no means uncommon in the New York of the 1920s and 1930s. Mark Tucker has noted: "Historical scenarios . . . figured repeatedly in the black stage shows produced by white impresario Lew Leslie. The first scene of Leslie's revue *Dixie to Broadway* (1924), starring Florence Mills, was titled 'Evolution of the Colored Race.'"[119] Similar South-to-North motifs were staple fare in black revues, including those at the Cotton Club, where the opening sketch of the 1930–31 *Brown Sugar* show (at which the Ellington orchestra performed) was titled "Dixie to Harlem."[120] Two years earlier, W. C. Handy had staged a concert at Carnegie Hall tracing "'the evolution of black music' from spirituals and work songs to more modern forms,"[121] a precursor of John Hammond's "Spirituals to Swing" presentations of the late 1930s. Handy's program included *Yamekraw*, a "Negro Rhapsody," composed by Ellington's good friend James P. Johnson and orchestrated by William Grant Still.

Either of these figures might have spurred Ellington's interest in using extended musical forms to represent black history. Johnson's 1932 *Harlem Symphony* was a portrait of Harlem life comparable in concept (though not in form) to Ellington's 1951 *A Tone Parallel to Harlem*.[122] Later, Johnson went on to write a piano and a clarinet concerto, a second symphony, two ballets, a string quartet, and two operas, one of which, *De Organizer*, with a radical libretto by Langston Hughes about the unionization of sharecroppers in the South, was performed in 1940. (Unfortunately, most of Johnson's orchestral music was never published and much of it now seems to have been lost.)[123] Still's music was even more concerned with African American history. *Levee Land*, first performed in New York in 1926, was actually based on a theme from "Evolution of the Colored Race" from *Dixie to Broadway* (Still had played oboe in the pit orchestra) and depicted life in the Old South. *Darker America*, also premiered in New York in 1926, was, said Still, "representative of the American Negro. His serious side is presented and is intended to suggest the triumph of a people over their sorrows through fervent prayer."[124] The work's four-part program anticipated that of Still's 1931 *Afro-American Symphony*, which traced African American evolution through movements subtitled (1) Longing, (2) Sorrow, (3) Humor, (4) Aspiration.[125] Still's second symphony, *Song of a New Race*, brought black history up to date and, said Still, "represents the American colored man of today, in so many instances a totally new individual produced through the fusion of white, Indian and Negro bloods . . . ."[126] (Ellington's 1943 title *Black, Brown and Beige* would make a similar point about racial mixing, while the work itself followed a historical program similar to Still's two symphonies.) Yet these pieces also saw Still moving closer to European ideas of musical form and high culture. Whereas *Levee Land*, written for Florence Mills, had brought "the world of popular music into the hallowed sanctuary of the concert hall," by the time of the *Afro-American Symphony* Still was no longer seeking to blend the two musical cultures so much as "to *elevate* a musical idiom typical of the American Negro to symphonic level." [127] (This process was, I believe, one that Ellington had duly noted and was keen to avoid, as we will see in chapter 4.)

Ellington's declared ambition in 1930 to write a history of the Negro in music was repeated to journalists several times during that decade. Sometimes he referred to the work as a five-part instrumental suite (the parts approximating the African past, the slave ship, plantation life, Harlem, and a utopian vision of the future), at other times he spoke of working on an opera, which by the early 1940s had acquired the title *Boola*. [128] Reports are contradictory as to whether he ever completed *Boola*—certainly it was never produced or recorded—but in 1943 at Carnegie Hall he did present the world premiere of a three-part suite, *Black, Brown and Beige*, to which he gave the subtitle "A Tone Parallel to the History of the American Negro." It seems that *Black, Brown and Beige* incorporated a good deal of music originally written for *Boola*, [129] but there was another possible source for the suite.

In 1934, Ellington had composed a soundtrack for the short film *Symphony in Black* (released in 1935), which was divided into four main sections: "The Laborers" is a version of a work song; "Triangle" is a tripartite sequence that includes "Dance," the moody "Jealousy," and a vocal "Big City Blues" (sung in the film by Billie Holiday, making her screen debut); "Hymn of Sorrow" is a quasi-spiritual; "Harlem Rhythm" is the upbeat conclusion. [130] Brian Priestley and Alan Cohen have argued that this music "must be regarded as a preliminary sketch for *Black, Brown and Beige* since, in addition to the work song, it contains a slow vocal blues and an instrumental spiritual theme" (all important features of the later suite). [131] Indeed, Priestley and Cohen show that the similarities are not confined to structural principles but extend to actual musical themes, with elements of both the work song theme and the spiritual theme common to both works. [132] *Symphony in Black* also anticipates *Black, Brown and Beige* in being one of the earliest works for which Ellington explicitly claimed a degree of social significance. In a 1935 article in *New Theatre* magazine, writer Edward Morrow asked Ellington: "Would you say that an honest Negro play would have to contain social criticism?" " 'Absolutely,' declared Ellington. 'That is, if it is expected to hold up. In one of my forthcoming movie "shorts" I have an episode which concerns the death of a baby . . . . I put into the dirge all the misery, sorrow and undertones of the conditions that went with the baby's death. It was true to and of the life of the people it depicted.' " [133] This desire, to be true to the life of the people depicted, could be cited as one of the guiding principles of Ellington's music, and it was certainly a major impulse behind *Black, Brown and Beige*.

The January 1943 concert at which Ellington premiered his suite was a glittering social occasion. Officially a charity event, with proceeds going to Russian War Relief, the concert was the climax of a celebratory "Ellington Week" in New York that marked the twentieth anniversary of his arrival in the city. It was also his debut performance at Carnegie Hall and, says Tucker, "the first time a major black composer would present an evening of original music in New York's most prestigious concert hall." [134] During the concert, which featured many of his earlier and shorter works (including the tributes to Florence Mills, Bill Robinson, and Bert Williams), Ellington was presented with a commemorative plaque signed by thirty-two leading musicians— black and white, popular and classical—who included Marian Anderson, Count Basie, Cab Calloway, Aaron Copland, Benny Goodman, Roy Harris, Earl Hines, Jerome Kern, Eugene Ormandy, Paul Robeson, Artie Shaw, William Grant Still, Leopold Stokowski, Kurt Weill, and Paul Whiteman. For this concert Ellington had created, in *Black, Brown and Beige*, a fifty-minute extended suite that was not only his most ambitious composition to date but also his major musical statement about the history of his people, the culmination of the project he had been mulling over for more than a decade.

At the concert, Ellington provided verbal introductions to each of the work's three sections, and these formed the basis for his later account in *Music Is My Mistress*. I quote that book's account, in slightly abbreviated form.

> *Black, Brown and Beige* was planned as a tone parallel to the history of the American Negro, and the first section, "Black," delved deeply into the Negro past. In it, I was concerned to show the close relationship between work songs and spirituals. . . . "Come Sunday," the spiritual theme, was intended to depict the movement inside and outside the church, as seen by workers who stood outside, watched, listened, but were not admitted. This is

developed to the time when the workers have a church of their own. The section ends with promises. I felt that the kind of unfinished ending was in accordance with reality, that it could not be tied, boxed, and stored away when so much else remained to be done.

The second section, "Brown," recognized the contribution made by the Negro to this country in blood. We began with the heroes of the Revolutionary War . . . proceeded to the Civil War, and then to the lighter attitude prevailing after the Proclamation of Emancipation. "Emancipation Celebration" described the mixture of joyfulness on the part of the young people as well as the bewilderment of the old on that "Great gettin' up mornin'". . . . Moving on to the Spanish-American War, we pictured the homecoming of the decorated heroes, and then that offspring of romantic triangles which was and is "The Blues."

At Carnegie Hall, I introduced the third section, "Beige," by referring to the common view of the people of Harlem, and the little Harlems around the U.S.A., as just singing, dancing, and responding to the tom-toms. On closer inspection, it would be found that there were more churches than cabarets, that the people were trying to find a more stable way of living, and that the Negro was rich in experience and education. . . . Coming more up to date, we found the Negroes struggling for solidarity and in the confusion of it all, just as we were beginning to get our teeth into the tissue, we discovered that our country was in big trouble again. So, just as always before, the Black, Brown, and Beige were soon in there for the Red, White, and Blue.[135]

While Ellington does not exactly gloss over the sufferings of African Americans, it is noticeable that his emphasis in the above passages is on their religious feelings, their pursuit of education and dignity, their continuing patriotism. For Ellington, it seems, what mattered in the history of the Negro, as in his own life, was the doing of such deeds as "commanded respect": the fact that, as he told Helen Oakley a few days before the concert, "Without enough food, with no clothes at all, with hardly a roof over his head, even the poorest sharecropper struggles to put his kids through school."[136] Allied to this feeling is his renewed attack, in his remarks on "Beige," on the "common view" of the Negro as "just singing, dancing, and responding to the tom-toms"; that is, precisely the same Hollywood/Broadway/minstrelsy stereotypes he had satirized in *Jump for Joy* and the view of blacks as jungle primitives he had had to endure in the Cotton Club. Such comments suggest that for Ellington *Black, Brown and Beige* was not merely a "tone parallel" but an attempt at a tonal reconstruction of black history that tried both "to be true to the life of the people it depicted" and to function as a corrective to white misrepresentations of that life.

Given that the subject was so close to his heart, Ellington must have been bitterly disappointed by the critical response to the concert. Although the reviews were not uniformly negative, many classical critics saw the suite as a flawed attempt at European symphonic form, while many jazz critics complained that Ellington was abandoning dance floor jazz.[137] The controversy over *Black, Brown and Beige* raged for some time in the pages of the jazz press (a topic to which I return in chapter 4), but, for all the debate, few people appeared to pay much attention to the work's social content. This lack of historical awareness was, Ellington suggested (perhaps somewhat disingenuously), the main reason why the work had been misunderstood. At his second Carnegie Hall concert, in December 1943, Ellington played only two brief extracts from *Black, Brown and Beige,* explaining to the audience: "We thought we wouldn't play it in its entirety tonight because it represents an awfully long and a very important story. And in that I don't think that too many people are familiar with the story, we thought it would be better to wait until that story was a little more familiar before we did the whole thing again."[138] A news report in *Variety* in June 1943 indicated that Ellington himself had already taken steps to ensure that people did become more familiar with the story:

> Duke Ellington is preparing a book explaining the story behind his much-discussed composition "Black, Brown and Beige," which he debuted during his orchestra's recent Carnegie Hall, N.Y., concert. Leader [sic] feels that detailing the thoughts which motivated the work will help toward a better understanding of it: to this end the story will be printed on the upper half of each page in the book, with the music related to each portion below on the same page so that readers with a knowledge of music can follow both at the same time.[139]

This book never appeared, yet a typescript in the Duke Ellington Collection at the Smithsonian Institution suggests that Ellington did get as far as preparing "the story" for publication. Titled "*Black, Brown and Beige* by Duke Ellington," the typescript is a 32-page account of black American history written in a mixture of poetry and declamatory prose. The work is at times strikingly radical in tone, as in this section on the fight against slavery from "Brown":

> Out of this welter of broken bodies . . . blasted hopes
> And shattered dreams . . . Arose mighty men
> Of action! Nat Turner . . . Denmark Vesey . . . .
> The Gabriels . . . The Catos! The Toms!
> The greatest of them all . . .
> A black woman . . . HARRIET TUBMAN! [140]

The opening sections of "Beige" make especially clear Ellington's views on white exploitation and misrepresentation of black life in Harlem in the 1920s. His vehemence here suggests that the years at the Cotton Club, for all the fame they brought him, also took their toll.

> And was the picture true
> Of you. The camera eye in focus . . .
> Or was it all a sorry bit
> Of ofay hocus-pocus?
>
> How then, this picture
> They have drawn?
>
> It can't be true
> That all you do . . .
> Is dance and sing
> And moan!
>
> Harlem! For all her moral lurches
> Has always had
> LESS cabarets than churches!
>
> Who draped those basement dens
> With silk, but knaves and robbers
> And their ilk?
> Who came to prostitute your art
> And gave you pennies
> For your part . . .
> And ill-repute?
>
> Who took your hunger
> And your pain

Outraged your honor
For their gain?

Who put the spotlight
On your soul
And left you rotting
In the hole
These strangers dug! [141]

It may be that Ellington decided to hold back on the publication of this document because of increasing racial tensions that led to riots in several American cities in the summer of 1943.[142] Or perhaps he decided to stick to his policy of "saying it without saying it." For whatever reason, the book did not appear, and following its Carnegie Hall debut on 23 January 1943 Ellington performed the complete version of *Black, Brown and Beige* on only two other occasions, at concerts in Boston on 28 January 1943 and (probably) in Cleveland on 20 February 1943.[143] When he came to make a studio version of the work in 1944, he chose to record an eighteen-minute selection of extracts — "Work Song," "Come Sunday," "The Blues," and "Three Dances" (comprising "West Indian Dance," "Emancipation Celebration," and "Sugar Hill Penthouse")[144] — and subsequent concert performances took a similar, abbreviated form. (We should probably not read too much into the abbreviated recording — Shellac for records was in short supply in 1944 and LPs did not come into commercial use until a half-dozen years later — but the fact that Ellington never performed the work live in its entirety after February 1943 does suggest that the critical response had deeply wounded him.)

Although at his second Carnegie Hall concert Ellington played only two brief extracts from *Black, Brown and Beige* in what was primarily a program of dance music, he did introduce one new extended piece that I think can be seen as a sequel to the "story" of *Black, Brown and Beige.*

As Priestley and Cohen have pointed out, *Black, Brown and Beige* corresponded to the middle three movements of the initial five-part suite Ellington had outlined in the 1930s; omitted was the African past and the utopian future.[145] It may have been no coincidence, then, that the major new work Ellington premiered at his second Carnegie Hall concert was *New World A-Comin'*, for piano and orchestra, which, while not linked musically to *Black, Brown and Beige*, can be seen as its conceptual successor, the evocation of the visionary future that Ellington had long planned as the final section of his musical history of the American Negro. The circumstantial evidence supports this view. Ellington named his piece after the 1943 book *New World A-Coming* by black writer Roi Ottley, which, like *Black, Brown and Beige*, recounted the history of the Negro in America before concluding with a look-forward into the possibilities of a better future for African Americans after World War II. Mercer Ellington noted: "There was nothing in the book that was news to Ellington, but he considered it well researched and capably written . . . [the music] seemed to express the same kind of mood—looking to the future with a bitter knowledge of the past—that Ottley's book did." [146] Indeed, Ottley ends his book with a statement that could be described as Ellingtonian in its blend of religion, patriotism, and optimism.

> The Negro's cause will rise or fall with America. He knows well that his destiny is intimately bound to that of the nation. America stands today as a symbol of freedom! The loss of this symbol will mean the loss of hope for white and black alike. This war, undeniably, belongs to the Negro as well as to the white man. To this extent, it may be called a "People's War"—for in spite of selfish interests a new world is a-coming with the sweep and fury of the Resurrection. [147]

In *Music Is My Mistress*, Ellington quotes the conclusion of this passage, adding: "I visualized this new world as a place in the distant future where there would be no war, no greed, no categorization, no non-believers, where love was unconditional, and no pronoun was good enough for God." [148] The language here suggests that Ellington also had in mind the fact that he incorporated *New World A-Comin'* into his first Sacred Concert of 1965, but the sentiment is not so far removed from the one he voiced in 1933 when, interviewed in the English *Daily Herald*, he said about the fifth movement of his projected suite: "Then I try to go forward a thousand years. I seek to express the future when, emancipated and transformed, the Negro takes his place, a free being, among the peoples of the world." [149]

Despite the critical hostility, Ellington's first Carnegie Hall concert had been a commercial success, and he continued to play annual concerts there throughout the 1940s, referring to them in his autobiography as "a series of social-significance thrusts." [150] Part of this significance presumably derived from the fact that for an African American to perform his own music at one of America's leading concert halls was a public demonstration of that ability to "command respect" that

Ellington considered so important. Another part was that Ellington composed a new extended work for each concert, and several of these works addressed his continuing concern with black history. After *Black, Brown and Beige* and *New World A-Comin'* (both 1943) came *The Deep South Suite* (1946) and *The Liberian Suite* (1947), which was commissioned by the Liberian government to commemorate that country's centenary as a republic. To this series of works we could add *A Tone Parallel to Harlem*, premiered in 1951 at the New York Metropolitan Opera House.[151] Of these, only *Harlem* was as explicitly programmatic as *Black, Brown and Beige*—and similarly designated by Ellington as "a tone parallel"—but all explored the social and racial issues that had now informed his music for more than two decades.

Black, Brown and Beige, in various guises, continued to occupy Ellington through the 1950s and 1960s. In 1956 the *Christian Science Monitor* reported: "A history of the Negro in America will form part of Mr. Ellington's next big project, an expansion of his 'Black, Brown and Beige' from some years ago. This time he expects to add a choir and perhaps dancers to the orchestral performance."[152] Such a work, *My People*, did appear in 1963, but five years earlier, in 1958, Ellington recorded a new version of *Black, Brown and Beige* that featured Mahalia Jackson.[153] In fact, the music was based entirely on the "Black" section, supplemented by rearrangements of "Come Sunday" and a rendition of the Twenty-third Psalm, sung by Jackson to Ellington's newly composed music.[154] Ellington made more extensive use of *Black, Brown and Beige* in *My People*. One of the last major works of "social significance" that he wrote, this was his contribution to the Chicago "A Century of Negro Progress" Exposition, held to mark the hundredth anniversary of the Emancipation Proclamation. Ellington wrote the entire show—music and lyrics—directed it, and appeared as narrator in some performances.[155] Like *Jump for Joy*, *My People* took the form of a musical revue, mixing songs, sketches, and dances, but in every other important respect its precursor was *Black, Brown and Beige*. The work drew on spirituals and blues and incorporated three extracts from *Black, Brown and Beige*: "Come Sunday" was featured both in a new arrangement and in a completely reworked version titled "David Danced (Before the Lord)," which was played much faster and served as a showpiece for tap dancer Bunny Briggs; "Montage" was a slightly revised version of "Light," the third part of "Black"; and "The Blues," from "Brown," was recycled as well.[156] The show also featured an oration by Ellington that not only recapped the sentiments of *Black, Brown and Beige* in its emphasis on the Negro contribution to American history, but it specifically referred to "Brown" in its allusions to the Spanish-American War and the origins of the blues in "romantic triangles." The opening lines of this monologue constitute probably the most eloquent statement of America's debt to African Americans that Ellington ever put on a record, as if momentarily he dispensed with the art of "saying it without saying it" for the pleasure of telling it like it is (though still masking himself as a "character" in a revue):

> My people! My people! Singing, dancing, praying, thinking, talking about freedom. Working, building America into the most powerful nation in the world. Cotton, sugar, indigo, iron, coal, peanuts, steel, the railroad—you name it. The foundation of the United States rests on the sweat of my people. And in addition to workin' and sweatin', don't ever forget that my people fought and died in every war. Every enemy of the USA has had to face my people in the front line. Yes! And when Teddy Roosevelt led his Rough Riders up San Juan Hill in the Spanish-American War, for the first time my people returned home decorated heroes. They had won another war for Uncle Sam.[157]

My People climaxed with two explicitly political songs. "King Fit the Battle of Alabam" was a tribute to Martin Luther King Jr. and the struggle for civil rights taking place in Birmingham, Alabama. Loosely based on the old spiritual "Joshua Fit the Battle of Jericho," Ellington's contemporary freedom song did not mince words, depicting police chief Bull Connor in the refrain "the Bull jumped nasty, ghastly, nasty," and including such exhortatory verses as:

> Freedom rider, ride
> Freedom rider, go to town,
> Y'all and us gonna get on the bus
> Y'all aboard, sit down, sit tight, sit down! [158]

The closing "What Color Is Virtue?" was a more questioning piece, its urgent refrain "What color is virtue? What color is love?" evoking both Ellington's vision of a world in which color had become irrelevant and his realization that such a world was still a long way off.[159] Perhaps, then, the song stands as a utopian coda to My People in the same way that New World A-Comin' can be seen as a utopian coda to Black, Brown and Beige.

My People was Ellington's most explicitly political work since Jump for Joy and, as I intimated, can be seen in part as Ellington newly presenting the sentiments of Black, Brown and Beige in the more populist "revu-sical" format devised for Jump for Joy [160] —black history done in song and dance, but depicted accurately, as opposed to the Cotton Club's exotic skits. Yet from a slightly different perspective, My People is also important as a major link between Black, Brown and Beige, the most ambitious work of Ellington's middle years, and the first of the Sacred Concerts, which became his chief creative focus during the last decade of his life. "Come Sunday" was featured in all three works, and its faster variant "David Danced (Before the Lord)" was also in both My People and the first Sacred Concert. Two other neospirituals from My People, "Will You Be There?" and "Ain't but the One," recurred in the first Sacred Concert, which also included a new version of New World A-Comin' and a gospel rendition of the Lord's Prayer, an idea that was perhaps anticipated by Mahalia Jackson's singing of the Twenty-third Psalm in 1958.[161] Viewed in this context, My People was not only the closest Ellington came in his later years to a direct political statement, but it also marked the point at which his music began to turn decisively away from a concern with politics and history. Religion would now become the focus of his work.

A few months before his first Sacred Concert, however, Ellington recorded a final version of Black, Brown and Beige. Since the mid-1950s he had been financing private recording sessions at which he would try out new ideas or reinterpret older material, and in March and May 1965 he taped almost the complete Black, Brown and Beige.[162] It is tempting to speculate that Ellington, before turning his attention to his religious music, decided to ensure that a full and well-recorded document of his "tone parallel to the history of the American Negro" would be preserved for posterity.[163] In doing so, he kept the promise he had made in the jazz publication Rhythm some thirty years earlier that "an authentic record of my race written by a member of it shall be placed on record."

Ellington's move toward a more overtly religious music can hardly be called surprising—he had been a devout believer and regular Bible reader for most of his life—but it might not be coincidental that this move came at a time of increasingly bitter and confrontational racial politics in the United States (not only black/white confrontations, but dissension within African American circles). Ellington had always disliked confrontation of any kind, and, despite a personal admiration for Martin Luther King Jr., he was apparently reluctant to align himself directly with the tactics of the civil rights movement. According to Don George, "intellectually he didn't agree with the way the civil rights situation was being handled. He didn't really believe in the marching and the suffering and the killing. He watched it on television sometimes and said, 'Those cats are crazy.'"[164] The patriotic tone that pervades even his *My People* oration should be sufficient to indicate Ellington's distance from the separatism of the burgeoning Black Power movement. If not, consider this statement from his program notes to the second Sacred Concert in 1968; referring to the United States as "the promised land of milk and honey," he concluded, "I am sure we appreciate the blessings we enjoy in this country, but it wouldn't hurt if everyone expressed his appreciation more often."[165] This is the Ellington who, in *Music Is My Mistress*, responded to the question, "What does America mean to you?" with the declaration, "it's where I was born. It's *home*."[166]

Yet we should not forget that this patriotism was rooted in racial pride, in Ellington's conviction that this "home" was built on the rock of black achievement. Possibly his most eloquent avowal of this belief came in a talk he gave to black churchgoers in Los Angeles in February 1941. The occasion was a service to mark Lincoln's birthday. With the United States edging closer to war and racial tensions high because of labor segregation in defense industries,[167] Ellington's speech foreshadowed his program for *Black, Brown and Beige*, stressing—as he so often would do later—the value of the black contribution to American history. Taking as his theme Langston Hughes's line, "I, too sing America," he declared:

> We play more than a minority role, in singing "America." . . .
>
> I contend that the Negro is the creative voice of America, is creative America, and it was a happy day in America when the first unhappy slave was landed on its shores.
>
> There, in our tortured induction into this "land of liberty," we built its most graceful civilization. Its wealth, its flowering fields and handsome homes; its pretty traditions; its guarded leisure and its music, were all our creations.
>
> We stirred in our shackles and our unrest awakened Justice in the hearts of a courageous few, and we recreated in America the desire for true democracy, freedom for all, the brotherhood of man, principles on which the country had been founded. . . .
>
> . . . we became more than a part of America! We—this kicking, yelling, touchy, sensitive, scrupulously-demanding minority— are the personification of the ideal begun by the Pilgrims almost 350 years ago.[168]

This America is not only "home"; it is the blueprint for the utopian vision of *New World A-Comin'*. This America is built on black endeavor, graced by black creativity, held to its principles by black aspiration. In its identification of the Negro with the best of America, Ellington's speech recalls the closing pages of *The Souls of Black Folk*, in which DuBois talks of the three gifts that Africans brought to America—a gift of story and song, a gift of sweat and brawn, a gift of the spirit—and also stresses the contributions and struggles of black life in the United States:

> Around us the history of the land has centred for thrice a hundred years; out of the nation's heart we have called all that was best to throttle and subdue all that was worst . . . . Actively we have woven ourselves with the very woof and warp of this nation,— we fought their battles, shared their sorrow, mingled our blood with theirs, and generation after generation have pleaded with a headstrong, careless people to despise not Justice, Mercy, and Truth lest the nation be smitten with a curse. Our song, our toil, our cheer, and warning have been given to this nation in blood-brotherhood. Are not these gifts worth the giving? Is not this work and striving? Would America have been America without her Negro people? [169]

To that last question, Ellington's music, inextricably black *and* American, answers with a resounding "NO!" And if *Black, Brown and Beige* was his designated "tone parallel to the history of the American Negro," nevertheless his entire oeuvre served that same function. As he told Nat Hentoff (probably in the early 1960s): "For a long time, social protest and pride in the Negro have been the most significant themes in what we've done. In that music we have been talking for a long time about what it is to be a Negro in this country." [170]

Zajj: Renegotiating Her Story

The power of the white world is threatened whenever a black man refuses to accept the white world's definitions.

— *James Baldwin* [1]

If with *Black, Brown and Beige* Ellington had hoped finally to rid himself of the minstrel and jungle stereotypes with which white culture continued to frame its representations of blackness, he was quickly disappointed. Ralph Gleason later wrote: "After his first Carnegie Hall concert in the early 40s, one manager dismissed his extended compositions as worthless (as did some critics) and is supposed to have told him to get back to 'nigger music.'" [2] Much of the critical controversy that raged around *Black, Brown and Beige*, though expressed in more circumspect language, came down to the same notion — Ellington should stick to playing dance music. And so he found himself facing a new stereotype that threatened to limit and define his creativity: the successor to the minstrel Sambo and the jungle savage was the hot jazzman.

The opening shots in this particular battle had been fired several years earlier, in 1935, when the release of the twelve-minute "Reminiscing in Tempo" (Ellington's longest composition to that date) occasioned the first really scathing criticisms of his music. [3] Chief among his American detractors was the writer and record producer John Hammond, whose article "The Tragedy of Duke Ellington, the 'Black Prince of Jazz'" appeared in November 1935 in both the *Brooklyn Eagle* and *Down Beat*. [4] The article is worth looking at in detail, not least because certain of its premises were to prove influential in later phases of jazz criticism.

Hammond dismisses "Reminiscing in Tempo" as "formless and shallow," but by far the greater part of his piece is a personal attack on Ellington in the guise of providing "reasons for the complete sterility of his new opus." The first reason cited by Hammond harks back to previous suggestions (by Gama Gilbert, for example) that Ellington had been unduly swayed by the acclaim of English commentators. "Confronted with the indiscriminating praise of critics like Constant Lambert, he felt it necessary to go out and prove that he could write really important music, far removed from the simplicity and charm of his earlier tunes."[5] Here perhaps is the kernel of the later argument that Ellington should get back to "nigger music," which apparently is to be defined by its simplicity and lack of real importance. In fact, Hammond was being disingenuous in referring to the "simplicity" of Ellington's earlier music because, as we have seen in chapter 3, R. D. Darrell had remarked on its sophistication and originality. And, although Ellington did say that he had written "Reminiscing in Tempo" for his English fans, Hammond was also wrong to suggest that it was praise from the English critics that had prompted his desire to write "really important music" (and to use extended forms), since we know that he had had ambitions to write a five-part suite on Negro history at least two and a half years before his first trip to England in June 1933.

Hammond further claimed that Ellington's music was "losing the distinctive flavor it once had, both because of the fact that he has added slick, un-negroid musicians to his band and because he himself is aping Tin Pan Alley composers for commercial reasons."[6] This charge of commercialism sits oddly with the earlier complaint that Ellington was straining to write "important music," but the most curious aspect of Hammond's critique here is his use of the phrase "un-negroid musicians." Since, with the exception of Barney Bigard, a "Creole of color" (who joined the band in 1928), and Puerto Rican Juan Tizol (a member of the band since 1929), Ellington's orchestra comprised only African Americans, Hammond cannot have been using the term "un-negroid" literally; instead, he apparently was suggesting that certain black players did not *sound black*—or, at least, did not conform to the way he thought black musicians *should* sound. This may be the first appearance of a critical gambit that would be brandished with considerable vehemence by black nationalist critics in the 1960s and 1970s.[7] Hammond also anticipated the black nationalists in requiring a high degree of political commitment from black artists, attacking Ellington on the grounds that he "consciously keeps himself from thinking about such problems as those of the southern share croppers, the Scottsboro boys, intolerable working and relief conditions in the North and South . . . [and] he has never shown any desire of aligning himself with the forces that are seeking to remove the causes of these disgraceful conditions." [8]

Hammond must have known these charges were untrue. He later revealed in his autobiography that when he had organized a benefit concert in 1932 for the Scottsboro Boys defense fund, "I got Benny Carter's orchestra and Duke Ellington — solo — and the benefit was a great success." [9] Indeed, Ellington had previously played a benefit for the Scottsboro boys, organized by the NAACP, in 1931, [10] and in the early 1930s his orchestra played several benefits for the NAACP and other community and charity organizations, including concerts for the Urban League (21 January 1931) and the Brooklyn Home for Aged Colored People (22 February 1933). [11] Nevertheless, Hammond asserted that "the real trouble with Ellington's music is the fact that he has purposely kept himself from any contact with the troubles of his people or mankind in general." [12] (This sweeping condemnation also overlooked Ellington's involvement in the film *Symphony in Black*, which was released in the autumn of 1935, several weeks before Hammond's article appeared.) [13]

Whom Hammond had in mind, and what precisely he meant, when he used the phrase "un-negroid musicians" became evident in his autobiography, where he had this to say about the Ellington of the mid-1930s:

> I felt, however, that he had lost contact with his origins, although I certainly understood his desire to succeed in an alien world. As he grew more successful, I missed the beat, the intensity his music had had in the early days. When Lawrence Brown, a most sophisticated trombonist, joined the band and I heard Duke record "Sophisticated Lady" for Victor, I remember thinking that the orchestra was never going to be the same again. But it was Duke's personal expression of his music to choose instrumentalists who suited his concept of the song. A sophisticated trombonist playing the solo on "Sophisticated Lady" made sense to him. [14]

The point that Hammond is trying to make here becomes clearer in his following paragraph, where he extols the soloists in Fletcher Henderson's band, claiming that "as far as pure jazz was concerned Fletcher was much closer to the mark than Duke," the reason being that "he let many a fine player be himself," whereas Ellington's sidemen, "dominated" by his composerly outlook (i.e., his choosing instrumentalists "who suited his concept of the song"), were "not so free and uninhibited." [15] This critical valorization of the "free and uninhibited" comes uncomfortably close to that white demand for "red-hot feeling" from black musicians that Mercer Ellington had detected in the patrons of the Cotton Club. [16] And since the word "sophisticated" appears to be doing much the same work in the extract from Hammond's autobiography as the term "un-negroid" was doing in his 1935 article, it is hard to avoid the inference that for Hammond sophistication *was* un-negroid, which in turn suggests that he had very definite and very narrow ideas of what Negro music was and how it should sound. [17] Barry Ulanov made a similar observation in 1946, noting that with Hammond's dislike of Brown's playing "the base was being laid" for his later attacks on Ellington for being " 'arty,' 'pretentious' and 'not jazz.' " [18]

Indeed, Ulanov points out that as early as 1932 and 1933 Hammond and a few other critics (notably Englishman Spike Hughes)

> began to find records which weren't "the real Duke," though they never defined "the real Duke." Their taste, in general, was expressed by Hughes, who included the recording, Jungle Nights in Harlem "among my favourite examples of Ellington music on account of its general 'low-downness.' "
>
> These well-bred youngsters, very proper in look, manner and dress, wanted jazz to flagellate their sense of propriety. . . . Their taste ran to blues, "low-down" blues, and when Duke escaped from the tyranny of that limited jazz form . . . they beat a quick retreat from their earlier position of fawning admiration of Ellington. [19]

Ulanov's description of these "well-bred youngsters" wanting jazz to "flagellate their sense of propriety" anticipates Anthony Braxton's critique of what he calls "the across the tracks syndrome," which I have previously summarized as the "observation that many white critics adopt 'jazz' as part of a personal rebellion against the stifling respectability of their own mainstream culture and, consequently, value and define the music not on its own terms but in terms of their argument with establishment values: so, they brandish 'jazz' as a *sensual, soulful* and *goodtime* music. . . ." [20] The result being that the music's intellectual and spiritual dimensions are ignored. Braxton's thesis certainly helps to explain why Hughes revels in the "low-downness" of "Jungle Nights in Harlem," a composition that, as we saw in chapter 3, R. D. Darrell had admired for its "amazing piano and orchestral effects (Rimsky-Korsakov would rub his ears on hearing some of the tone colors here!) Note the parabolic flights in particular." [21]

This desire to treat jazz as exotic and primitive may also have been behind Hammond's criticism, quoted earlier, that Ellington had "lost contact with his origins." Hammond was presumably referring to what he called "the beat, the intensity" of the early Ellington band, as exemplified by their "jungle music." But what Hammond had overlooked was that Ellington's *actual* origins were in the relatively sophisticated milieu of black, middle-class Washington, D.C., society. Only if one accepted the Cotton Club's racist framing of blacks as "primitive" could one construe Ellington's sophisticated compositions as "losing contact with his origins" or Lawrence Brown's sophisticated trombone-playing as "un-negroid." [22]

What Ellington himself thought of these white conceptions of negroid and un-negroid musics can be gauged from a story told by Edmond Anderson, a white fan who met Ellington in the mid-1930s and became a lifelong friend. "Once I asked him what he considered a typical Negro piece among his compositions. He paused a moment before he came up with 'In a Sentimental Mood.' I protested a bit and said I thought that was a very sophisticated white kind of song and people were usually surprised when they learned it was by him. 'Ah,' he said, 'that's because you don't know what it's like to be a Negro.' " [23] Some years later Ellington reiterated the point himself, apparently referring back to Hammond's misgivings about Lawrence Brown's arrival in the orchestra: "As far back as 1933, when I said I was playing Negro music, some critics complained 'Sophisticated Lady is not Negro music.' But the fact remains that Sophisticated Lady is Negro music—it's the Negro I know, and my interpretation." [24] These statements make it clear, I think, that Ellington's insistence on the breadth and variety of black experience served not only as a corrective to the minstrel and jungle stereotypes prevalent in American culture, but also provided the basis for his belief that music was "beyond category." I return to this point later in discussing Ellington's dislike of the word "jazz," a dislike, I will argue, that was based precisely on his apprehension that the word was being used not only to proscribe and limit his own activities as a composer, but also to frame the "common view," which he attacked in Black, Brown and Beige, of African Americans as "just singing, dancing, and responding to the tom-toms."

Perhaps not surprisingly, Hammond was one of the more vociferous critics of *Black, Brown and Beige*, his review in *Jazz* magazine appearing under the headline "Is the Duke Deserting Jazz?" [25] Hammond repeated many of the charges he had made in his 1935 critique of "Reminiscing in Tempo," again claiming that the English critics had turned Ellington's head, and he further alleged: "During the last ten years he has been adding men to his once compact group, has introduced complex harmonies for effect and has experimented with material farther and farther away from dance music. . . ." [26] Of *Black, Brown and Beige* itself, Hammond declared that "it was unfortunate that Duke saw fit to tamper with the blues, in order to produce music of greater 'significance'" and "that by becoming more complex he has robbed jazz of most of its basic virtue. . . ." [27] Ellington had his defenders, too, including Barry Ulanov and Leonard Feather, and Feather wrote a vituperative reply to Hammond in *Jazz*. [28] But it was noticeable that when *Jazz* editor Bob Thiele published a further piece, in which he presented himself as a moderate voice refereeing between the extreme opinions of Hammond and Feather, he nevertheless sprinkled his article with sentiments that indicated a basic allegiance to Hammond's stance on Ellington and jazz. For example: "jazz is dance music," "jazz must be free and exciting, spontaneous and spirited," "Duke Ellington is slowly losing contact with the basic fundamentals of hot jazz," "it is music that springs from the *soul* of musicians," and "I feel that jazz must always contain many, if not all, of these fundamentals or it is not real jazz." [29]

Such assertions also demonstrated that the issue at stake was not so much the inherent qualities or deficiencies of *Black, Brown and Beige* as it was a wide-ranging journalistic power struggle about definitions of jazz authenticity. As Thiele asked exasperatedly: "Why is it hard for musicians and critics to grasp the ideas that constitute real jazz?" [30] Bernard Gendron is surely right to suggest that the controversy over *Black, Brown and Beige* can be related to a larger debate between "modernists" and "revivalists" that occupied much of the American jazz press in the early 1940s. [31] Yet his casual labeling of Hammond's *Jazz* article as a "revivalist response" to *Black, Brown and Beige* begs some important questions. As, famously, the "discoverer" and champion of Count Basie and Benny Goodman, Hammond was closely associated with two of the major figures of the "modernist" swing music to which the "revivalists" were opposed. More pertinently, perhaps, Hammond's 1943 attack on Ellington reprised several of the criticisms he had made in his 1935 "The Tragedy of Duke Ellington," a piece that predated not only the articulation of a "revivalist" position but even the appearance of a "revivalist" movement. So it was not the case that Hammond was a "revivalist," more that the "revivalists" later coincidentally adopted certain of Hammond's attitudes toward jazz.[32]

— • • • ———

While critics continued to bicker over what constituted "real jazz," little attention was paid to Ellington's thoughts on the subject. A headline such as "Is the Duke Deserting Jazz?," evidently designed to incite controversy, could have achieved this effect only if readers (and writers) ignored the fact that Ellington had been trying to distance himself from the "jazz" label for the past thirteen years. His most famous statement on the subject—"There are simply two kinds of music, good music and the other kind"—was not made until 1958,[33] but as early as the 1920s Ellington had tried to evade the "jazz" tag, and in the 1930s he had argued both against the categorization of his own music as jazz *and* against the categorization of jazz as dance music only.[34] If his views occasionally seemed contradictory or ambiguous, this was hardly surprising, given that many of his comments were made off-the-cuff in newspaper interviews and that his main concern probably was less to present a carefully argued definition of his music than to resist all attempts at pigeonholing and to leave himself as much creative space as possible. He accomplished this by adroitly sidestepping whichever labels happened to be thrown his way.

This strategy of evasion is the consistent thread that runs through Ellington's various pronouncements on his music in the 1930s; whenever a popular label is offered, he declines it on the grounds that his music is too broad in scope to be so defined. So, in 1930: "I am not playing jazz. I am trying to play the natural feelings of a people." In 1933: "Mine isn't hot music. It is essentially negro music, and the elaborations of self-expression." In 1939: "Our aim has always been the development of an authentic Negro music, of which swing is only one element."[35] And, in 1941: "His band, he claims, 'doesn't make any attempt at playing jazz or swing.' What it plays is 'unadulterated American Negro music.' . . . 'Swing is only an emotional element, not a type of music. The emotional element is a strong part of Negro music, but it isn't Negro music.'"[36] By denying that his music could be circumscribed within labels such as "jazz," "swing," "hot," or "emotional," Ellington was trying to keep open his options as a composer *and* implicitly insisting that black experience—the subject of his music—

was too broad and multifaceted to be confined within a single musical genre.[37] In particular, in arguing against the reductive view of black music as predominantly emotional, Ellington was offering a more comprehensive appreciation of black creativity—one that did not preclude the intellectual—than that discerned by white critics such as Hammond and Hughes, with their focus on the "free and uninhibited" and "general 'low-downness.'"

Ellington's occasional and apparently contradictory defenses of "jazz" and "swing" can also be understood as a strategy of resistance to white culture's demeaning stereotyping of black music. As we saw at the beginning of chapter 3, as early as 1931 Ellington had tried to rescue the word "jazz" from various popular misconceptions: "I have already said that it is my firm belief that what is still known as "jazz" is going to play a considerable part in the serious music of the future. . . . What we know as "jazz" is something more than just dance music."[38] Ellington returned to this theme a dozen years later in responding to an article in the magazine *American Mercury* by white writer Winthrop Sargeant that enumerated jazz's supposed limitations. Sargeant's 1943 piece "Is Jazz Music?" claimed that, compared to classical music, jazz was characterized by "the extremely limited nature of its emotional vocabulary," that it belonged in "the simple sidewalk and dance hall milieu," and that it should not pretend to the status of "a complex, civilized art." Tracing jazz's roots to the "homemade" music of the uneducated Southern Negro, Sargeant concluded: "as his lot improves, and with it his facilities for musical education, he is bound to be attracted by the bigger scope and intricacy of civilized concert music. Give him the chance to study, and the Negro will soon turn from boogie woogie to Beethoven."[39] Ellington's reply, in a letter to the editor, took particular issue with the claims that jazz lacked "intellectual complexities" and was unable to "encompass such emotions as tragedy, romantic nostalgia, wonder, delicate shades of humor, etc." Sargeant, he noted drily, "has evidently not been exposed to some of the more intelligent jazz."[40] Sargeant's subtext was a restatement of the familiar critical view that jazz was simply dance music, whereas the European concert tradition represented the acme of musical excellence. In this context, Ellington's defense of jazz can hardly be counted a surprise. What he was defending was not "jazz" the label, but the potential of African American music (not least his own) to be as civilized, as big in scope and as intricate as classical music. This point is confirmed, I think, by the fact that several months later, in an article for the Canadian publication *New Advance*, Ellington similarly defended *swing* against criticisms of narrowness: "It has been said that [swing] has no future because it's too narrow a form. I don't think that's right. Swing at its best is 'free' within the form itself." [41]

This willingness (at least temporarily) to defend "jazz" and "swing" may have been prompted by feelings of self-preservation on Ellington's part. By 1944 he must have realized that his attempts to disown such labels had had little impact on the white commercial superstructure; as far as press, promoters, and record companies were concerned, he was a part of the world of jazz and swing (and arguments about the shades of meaning in those terms were strictly an internal affair). In such a situation it obviously would be in his interests to claim as much artistic latitude as possible for jazz and swing, while continuing to insist whenever he had the chance that his own music aspired to even broader scope. Ironically, the critical response to *Black, Brown and Beige*, the work with which he must have hoped he would finally transcend such categorizations, may have edged him back toward a no doubt weary acceptance of his "jazz" status. Whereas the jazz critics attacked him for "deserting jazz," many classical critics castigated *Black, Brown and Beige* for its supposed failure to meet the standards of classical European form. [42] Yet conforming to European standards was precisely what Ellington had been determined *not* to do in his extended pieces. As he said in 1941 (talking about his opera, *Boola*): "arrangements of historic American Negro music have been made by conservatory-trained musicians who inevitably handle it with a European technique. It's time a big piece of Negro music was written from the inside by a Negro." [43] The difference that such an approach might entail was indicated by Gunther Schuller in his observation on the critical response to *Black, Brown and Beige*: "The critics unanimously failed to realize that in a work like BBB—a work rooted in jazz tradition—the essence of *performance* was a much more important factor than some of the technical aspects of composition. They seemed to take Johnny Hodges's soulful rendition of *Come Sunday* (or Lawrence Brown's solos) for granted, whilst harping on the awkwardness of some of Ellington's brief transitional passages." [44]

Certainly, Ellington, perhaps stung by the classical critics' response to *Black, Brown and Beige*, seemed at pains to distance his music from the European classical tradition in two articles that appeared in 1944 and 1945. In "Certainly It's Music!," commissioned by the classical publication *Listen: The Guide to Good Music* and written to meet a prescribed brief "to base this article on the relationship between my work and that of the classical composers," Ellington took the chance to play down any such relationship: "Frankly, I prefer to regard my compositions as strictly, 'yours truly,' as does any creative musician. I am not writing classical music, and the musical devices that have been handed down by serious composers have little bearing on modern swing."[45] And, toward the end of the piece, Ellington reiterated that, although jazz and swing are of equal status to classical music, comparisons between the genres deny the former pair's originality:

> If I seem a little shy about being displayed on a critical plat-
> form with the classical big shots, let me also dispel the notion
> that I hesitate to place the jazz medium in a top musical cate-
> gory. . . . Jazz, swing, jive and every other musical phenomenon
> of American musical life are as much an art medium as are the
> most profound works of the famous classical composers. To at-
> tempt to elevate the status of the jazz musician by forcing the
> level of his best work into comparisons with classical music is to
> deny him his rightful share of originality.[46]

Ellington took the same "equal but different" stance in a 1945 interview, "Why Duke Ellington Avoided Music Schools," which appeared
in the New York left-wing periodical PM. Asked to comment on a *New
York Times* review that argued against his music representing "a growing affinity between jazz and serious music," Ellington repeated his
1931 opinion that jazz *was* serious music: " 'I guess *serious* is a confusing
word,' he said. 'We take our American music seriously. If *serious* means
European music, I'm not interested in that. Some people mix up the
words *serious* and *classical*. They're a lot different. Classical music is supposed to be 200 years old. There is no such thing as modern classical
music. There is great, serious music. That is all.' "[47] He also took a
swipe at critics, noting: "All the music critics think jazz musicians are
trying to get into the symphonic field. Ninety-nine per cent of the jazz
people aren't interested in symphony techniques at all."[48]

Much as he chafed at the constrictions that he felt were imposed
by labels such as "jazz" and "swing," Ellington made it abundantly
clear that he was even less interested in being dubbed a "classical"
musician. Unfortunately for him, since cultural discourse at the time
was constructed almost entirely in terms of dichotomies such as high
art/low art and classical/popular, by ruling himself so firmly out of
the "classical" bag, Ellington was willy-nilly ensnaring himself fur-

ther in the "popular." His claims that jazz was an "art medium" and that there could be "serious" music that was not rooted in European classicism would have been seen as self-contradictory. Yet this cultural discourse was not static. World War II and the immediate postwar years brought important changes in American culture, among which were new values, new perspectives, and new dichotomies that challenged the assumptions of the classical/popular divide. When we look at some of the articles he wrote (and the interviews he gave) during this period, we can see Ellington responding to these shifts, especially in his attempts to reposition jazz in a new kind of opposition to European classical music: i.e., not in terms of high art/low art contrast but by an identification of jazz as original, modern, and—crucially—American.

In fact, Ellington's pronouncements on music in the mid-1940s offer fascinating insights into his attempts to deal with the changing currents of cultural debate, while, as ever, resisting racial stereotyping and trying to preserve as much creative space as possible for his own musical endeavors. The picture that emerges is, I think, of Ellington edging toward a new public defense of "jazz," not as dance music, but as American music. Though it means jumping around rather among various mid-1940s articles and interviews, I would like to sketch this picture in a little more detail. In particular, I want to look at Ellington's attempts to link jazz (and swing) with America, first by virtue of its modernity and then by virtue of its democratic nature.

In his 1944 reply to Winthrop Sargeant, we saw Ellington defending jazz and insisting on its intellectual complexity and breadth of emotional expression. Yet in his later *New Advance* article, Ellington affirmed "Swing is my beat. Not jazz, in the popular sense of the word, which usually means a chatty combination of instruments knocking out a tune." [49] Describing swing as "a new brand of jazz," he stressed—separately—swing's modernity and its essential Americanness: "Swing, as I like to make it and play it, is an expression of sentiment and ideas—modern ideas. It's the kind of music that catches the rhythm of the way people feel and live today. It's American music because it grew out of our folk music, picking up a little from every section of the country as it traveled from New Orleans to Chicago to Kansas City to New York." [50] Ellington had previously championed jazz on the grounds of its modernity—in 1933, for example, he argued that "it has to be accepted as serious music because it is the only type which describes this age" [51]— and the musical journey that he outlines, from New Orleans to New York, we recognize today as a classic account of the history of jazz, not of swing. Ellington's curious disavowal of "jazz" in his *New Advance* piece might have been in response to the "revivalist" assertion that traditional New Orleans music was the only real jazz and that swing was something entirely different.[52] Whatever the reason, by the time of his 1945 *PM* interview, he had reverted to using the word "jazz," albeit reluctantly, in reemphasizing the music's links with modernity and America. "Jazz is like the automobile and the airplane. It is modern and it is American. I don't like the word *jazz* but it is the one that is usually used."[53] Toward the end of the *PM* article he again takes the opportunity to underline the music's Americanness, even at the cost of downplaying its African American components: " 'Twenty years ago when jazz was finding an audience, it may have had more of a Negro character. The Negro element is still important. But jazz has become part of America. There are as many white musicians playing it as Negro. . . . We are all working along more or less the same lines. We learn from each other. Jazz is American now. *American* is the big word.' "[54]

It may be that Ellington simply saw this "Americanization" of jazz as the best way to escape the racial stereotyping and low status that had accompanied its previous designation as black music (as in Sargeant's article, for example). But the focus on the interracial nature of jazz can also be seen in the context of a new move toward integration that characterized black political struggle in the war years and immediately thereafter. During World War II the issue of racial discrimination in the United States took on a fresh urgency, not least because the ideology of fascism was being denounced, partly because of its racial discrimination in the form of anti-Semitism. If many African Americans resented having to fight in a war in which, as far as they were concerned, no difference existed in the racial attitudes of the combatants,[55] others saw an opportunity to push even harder for the integration policies that the federal government upheld in principle but did little to enforce. In 1941 A. Philip Randolph had proposed the Negro March on Washington to protest discrimination in defense industries. In the event, the threat of action was enough to push President Franklin D. Roosevelt into signing Executive Order 8802, which set up the Committee on Fair Employment and committed the government to "opposing racial discrimination in jobs."[56] In 1942 the NAACP began a campaign to persuade Hollywood studios to eliminate old racial stereotypes from the cinema.[57] After some success, the campaign ran into problems, not least of which was white recalcitrance.[58] Nevertheless, the thrust of these initiatives was toward integration, which was the desired goal of the black cultural and political establishment. Black leaders argued that if blacks could fight and die as Americans abroad, they deserved to be treated as Americans at home.

One result of these campaigns was that jazz began to be touted as a symbol of interracial cooperation, even of a potentially harmonious America. In 1945, for example, the African American writer and poet Sterling A. Brown traced the history of black music through the spirituals and blues to jazz, which he claimed was "now an American musical language" and the epitome of democracy:

> Of all the arts, jazz music is probably the most democratic. Mixed units of Negroes and whites have recorded for well over a decade, and most of their records are jazz classics. . . . The mixed band meets up with difficulties, especially in the South. But completely democratic are the jam sessions, both public and private, where Negro and white musicians meet as equals to improvise collectively and create the kind of music they love. Here the performer's color does not matter; the quality of the music he makes is the basis for camradery and respect.[59]

Ellington would have had no problem with this last proposition—it was one of the reasons he gave for his involvement with the 1947 interracial musical *Beggar's Holiday*. Nor would he, as a sincere patriot, proudly aware of the black contribution to American history, have felt any misgivings about calling jazz American music. Yet precisely because he was so aware of the black contribution to jazz, I think we can reasonably assume that Ellington must have had mixed feelings about deemphasizing the African American elements in the music even as he realized that it was a necessary price to pay to establish jazz's contemporary status as an *American* art form.

Certainly it is noticeable that when Ellington addressed the issue of the music's black origins—in a 1947 interview in *Etude* magazine—he did not discard the black roots of jazz so much as disown the previous racial stereotyping of the music by white audiences: "Jazz today is no longer the jazz of twenty years ago. When I began my work, jazz was a stunt, something different. Not everybody cared for jazz and those who did felt it wasn't the real thing unless they were given a shock sensation of loudness or unpredictability along with the music."[60] And, later in the piece, when ostensibly downplaying "the Negro element" in jazz, Ellington manages to turn his argument into a subtle critique of false representations of blackness, so that whereas he begins the article by appearing to agree with the notion that early jazz required "a shock sensation of loudness or unpredictability," he concludes by rephrasing this as "the unbridled, noisy confusion of the Harlem cabaret" and links it specifically to the "supposed-to-be-Negro" of white fantasy:

> Even the Negroid element in jazz turns out to be less African than American. Actually, there is no more of an essentially African strain in the typical American Negro than there is an essentially French or Italian strain in the American of those ancestries. The pure African beat of rhythm and line of melody have become absorbed in its [sic] American environment. It is this that I have tried to emphasize in my own writings. In *Black, Brown and Beige*, I have tried to show the development of the Negro in America; I have shown him as he is supposed to be—and as he is. The opening themes of the third movement reflect the supposed-to-be-Negro—the unbridled, noisy confusion of the Harlem cabaret which must have plenty of "atmosphere" if it is to live up to the tourist's expectation. But—there are, by numerical count, more churches than cabarets in Harlem, there are more well-educated and ambitious Negroes than wastrels. And my fantasy gradually changes its character to introduce the Negro as he is—part of America, with the hopes and dreams and love of freedom that have made America for all of us.[61]

— • • • ———

We have seen Ellington identify jazz with America, and in the last sentence of the quotation above we see him identify America with a "love of freedom." Back in his 1945 PM interview Ellington had also identified jazz with freedom. "Jazz is freedom. Jazz is the freedom to play anything whether it has been done before or not. It gives you freedom."[62] Though Ellington seems here to be using "freedom" in a purely musical context, contrasting jazz's encouragement of originality with the formal constraints of the classical tradition, his later linking in *Etude* of America with freedom was clearly a political statement, and all the more potent for being made in 1947, in the new climate of cold war confrontation that rapidly sprang up in the mid-1940s. Assuming I am right to see Ellington as trying to effect a new perception of jazz in the public eye, redefining its status from "dancefloor music" to "American music," then it was obviously a useful strategy to associate jazz with such supposedly quintessential American values as democracy (as Sterling A. Brown had done) and love of freedom.[63] Yet for Ellington this was a problematic move since certain notions of freedom, in the sense of being "uninhibited" and "spontaneous," were also crucially implicated in the racial stereotyping of black music that he was constantly fighting against.

One result was that his discussions of jazz could become particularly fraught at times. In the 1945 PM article, for example, after stating that "jazz is freedom," Ellington goes on to extol his own unschooled musical background. But in contrasting this with conservatory-taught European technique, he also comes close to endorsing the notion of "spontaneous" jazz held by critics such as Hammond and Hughes. The PM writers then confront him with a contradiction, his reply to which relies too much on special pleading to be entirely convincing:

> "I'm not the offspring of a conservatory. I've avoided music schools and conservatories. I didn't want to be influenced away from what I felt inside. . . .
>
> "I wouldn't have been a good musician if I'd gone to a conservatory and studied the usual way. I haven't the discipline."
>
> In that case, we said, why had he recently established three scholarships for graduates of New York high schools at the Juilliard School of Music?
>
> "Things are different now," he said. "A musician coming along today has to learn a lot. Even if he has loads of natural ability, he has to develop good skills to be eligible for a good job. If he goes about it the way I did, it will take him much too long. Juilliard is a fine school. The people there are aware of American music. They won't hold anyone back. I developed the helter-skelter way. I don't think everyone should be allowed to do that. Most people learn faster and more at school."[64]

The contradiction that Ellington found himself caught in here was the result of wanting to promote jazz as "free" in contrast to the formal restraints of European classicism, while also promoting its status as "serious" music by insisting on the skill and study required to play it.[65]

By the time of his 1947 Etude interview Ellington had adjusted and honed his argument, playing down references to his own unschooled past, reaffirming the hard work needed to play jazz, and adroitly associating its "free" qualities with modernity and America. He again makes the point that things are different now—"Jazz today is no longer the jazz of twenty years ago"—but rather than present his self-taught prowess as a source of pride, he paints a picture of someone muddling through. "I relied on instinct rather than knowledge to guide me, and had to develop many techniques in spotlight positions." He then dismisses (the common perception of) early jazz in order to stress the discipline and intellectual effort required of contemporary players:

> Jazz today is by no means the formless, chancey [sic], irresponsible medium it was around 1920. It is impossible to stress this sufficiently. A certain psychological element enters into jazz which can work great harm to the chances of the enthusiastic young player; there is a vague feeling that "classical" music means hard work while jazz represents the livelier aspects of pure fun. Well, that may be so—to the listener! It certainly is *not* the case as far as the performer is concerned. The jazz musician today needs the most thorough musical background he can possibly get. He needs to be more than moderately expert on his instrument, whatever that may be; he needs to have the kind of theoretic mastery that can solve all sorts of harmonic and arrangement problems without a moment's hesitation; most of all, he needs to be acutely aware of musical history and the position of jazz in that history.[66]

It is only then, after he has firmly established the *discipline* that jazz requires, that Ellington proceeds to make links between jazz, *freedom*, and America. First, he associates jazz with freedom by contrasting it to the "fixed forms" of earlier European music and locating it as the contemporary phase of an evolutionary movement toward freedom of expression:

> Just as the classical form represents strict adherence to a structural standard, just as romantic music represents a rebellion against fixed forms in favor of more personal utterance, so jazz continues the pattern of barrier-breaking and emerges as the freest musical expression we have yet seen. To me, then, jazz simply means freedom of musical speech! And it is precisely because of this freedom that so many varied forms of jazz exist. The important thing to remember, however, is that not one of these forms represents jazz by itself. Jazz means simply the freedom to have many forms.[67]

Ellington then uses this notion of freedom to identify jazz as *the* definitively American music:

> Let us go a step further. In its opening the way for many kinds of free musical expression jazz is peculiarly American. Thus, the American character of jazz derives simply from its freedom rather than from any specifically American line of musical descent. In the case of other lands, we say their music is typically French, Italian, or English, if it follows a traditional pattern (whether of melodic line, harmonization, arrangement, rhythm, or anything at all). We say that music is typically jazz, or typically American, if it follows no pattern at all![68]

This is Ellington at his most astute. Not only has he stretched the definition of jazz to mean the freedom to play virtually anything you want to play, he has used this "freedom of expression" to characterize it as a great American innovation, a breaking free from the traditional patterns of European music, thus flying the flag for democracy and freedom in the midst of cold war hostilities.

In the conclusion to the *Etude* piece, Ellington reprises points he had made earlier about jazz's originality and modernity, and he reaffirms its equal status with classical music. But his focus is again the "scholarship" that playing jazz now requires.

> It becomes increasingly difficult to say just where "good music" leaves off and jazz begins. Jazz is good music—when it sets itself, as earnestly as any other form, to explore and to express the feelings and the conditions of its time. There is good and worthless jazz just as there is good and bad music in the purely classical and romantic styles. But for good jazz, the hit-or-miss days of making a noise and being "different" are gone. Expressive jazz requires as much scholarship, as much musicianship, as any other kind of music. In addition, it requires a peculiar awareness of form and of the human thoughts and feelings those forms express.[69]

Mark Tucker, in his introduction to the *Etude* article, speculates that Ellington's emphasis on the study and discipline which jazz involves may have been in response to the circumstance that he was addressing "an audience that might have misunderstood the role of spontaneity in jazz."[70] (He notes that *Etude* was "read by music teachers and students across America.") While this may certainly have been a contributory factor, I think I have produced sufficient evidence to indicate that

Ellington considered many jazz critics to have misunderstood the role of spontaneity, too, and it is entirely possible that his remarks were directed as much at a jazz audience as at a classically oriented readership. This point is borne out by the later comments on spontaneity and improvisation that Ellington made in his 1958 program note, "The Future of Jazz," where he referred to his recent composition, *The Night Creature* (written for his orchestra and the classical Symphony of the Air), as:

> a new argument, on a much larger scale than ever before, against the theory that jazz cannot be written. There are still a few diehards around who believe in this; in fact, not long ago I made up a little story to interpret their attitude. There was a little raggedy boy out in the middle of a field. He was wandering through the grass and stumbled over what appeared to be a black stick. He picked it up and sat down under a weeping willow tree. We, of course, know that it was a clarinet he was holding; but he didn't know what it was. But somehow or other, intuition told him to just blow on it—and when he blew, out came jazz. And that's the way jazz is supposed to be, according to those diehards—it's not supposed to be prepared or planned in any way.
>
> Another theory they hold is that there is such a thing as unadulterated improvisation without any preparation or anticipation. It is my firm belief that there has never been anybody who has blown even two bars worth listening to who didn't have some idea about what he was going to play, before he started.[71]

Ellington's insistence that *The Night Creature* exemplified written jazz was no doubt related to both Capitol's and Columbia's refusal to record the piece on the grounds that it *wasn't* jazz (and thus was outside Ellington's normal marketing category).[72] Nevertheless, his unequivocal downplaying of spontaneity also supports my argument that his postwar reconstruction of "jazz" was shaped, at least in part, by a reaction to racial stereotyping that placed paramount importance on this element of black music, and against which he had to take special guard in his formulation of "freedom" as a defining quality of the music and its Americanness. Indeed, it is worth noting that nowhere does Ellington equate freedom with improvisation per se (an association made by Hammond and Hughes and one that became a staple of jazz commentary during and after the "free jazz" movement of the 1960s).[73] Freedom for him seems to refer primarily to the freedom of the *composer* to create new forms—freedom, that is, both from the formal constraints of earlier European musics *and* from the tradition of racial stereotyping that restricted African Americans to playing blues or dance music or "low-down" or spontaneous feelings. Both of these traditions he saw as inadequate and inappropriate to convey the rich variety, the full "sepia panorama," of African American experience in the twentieth century.[74]

— • • • ———

I would like to conclude this chapter with a brief look at two Ellington suites that relate to, and are illuminated by, some of the issues raised here. In a January 1951 concert at New York's Metropolitan Opera House, Ellington premiered not only his *A Tone Parallel to Harlem* but also the shorter, two-part *The Controversial Suite*, which was later recorded and released on the *Uptown* LP. In his notes to the CD reissue, Stanley Dance writes that *The Controversial Suite* "is unlike any other Ellington composition in that it looks askance at contemporary jazz movements. 'Before My Time' is an amused and even contemptuous reference to the prevalence of Dixieland at that time. . . . 'Later' reflects the heavy Teutonisms of the Stan Kenton orchestra, then also inexplicably enjoying considerable popularity."[75] James Lincoln Collier also hears the suite's two sections as parodies and suggests a racial motive in that the musical groupings ridiculed were predominantly white movements — "and there is in Duke's send-up of both groups a certain amused attitude that these white styles were only imitations of the real thing."[76] Given that the financial situation of his own band was precarious at the time, one can well imagine Ellington looking askance at the popularity of both Dixieland—a white offshoot of a revival of early black New Orleans jazz—and Kenton's often bombastic and pretentious compositions (especially after the critics' attacks on *Black, Brown and Beige*). One can also imagine Ellington's exasperation at ongoing critical controversy over which of these two forms of white pastiche best represented "real jazz." Yet Ellington does not mention the suite in *Music Is My Mistress*; neither does Mercer Ellington in his memoir; nor do Jewell or Hasse in their biographies. In short, there is little reason to suppose that Ellington considered *The Controversial Suite* as anything other than a minor parody, to which we should probably not attach too much significance.

Ellington provoked a good deal more controversy with the 1957 *A Drum Is a Woman*, which he described in *Music Is My Mistress* as a "musical fantasy or allegory [that] told the story of jazz in terms of the adventures of Madam Zajj and Carribee Joe, from the Caribbean to the moon, via Congo Square and 52nd Street."[77] First released in February 1957 as an LP, *A Drum Is a Woman* was also presented on television the following May, "one of American television's first programs performed exclusively by African-Americans," according to Hasse.[78] Mercer Ellington, Derek Jewell, and the record's producer, Irving Townsend, have all testified to the pleasure and satisfaction that Ellington felt with the piece. Jewell quotes him as saying it was one of his works in which "you feel the weight of the joy,"[79] while Mercer notes that he "packed a lot of color, humor, and fantasy into *Drum*, and it contained several of his basic beliefs about jazz."[80] In 1960 Townsend thought it "the most complex, probably least understood of all Ellington's major recordings," and he further stated: "I think he is still more proud of this work than any other and I think I know why, for it not only combines every talent he possesses on one record, but it contains much of his sense of humour and many of his personal opinions, properly attired in a confounding array of fiction and musicianship."[81] Townsend maintained this view of *Drum*, writing in 1976 that "*A Drum Is a Woman* is one of Ellington's most complicated fantasies. It is also one of his most self-revealing works." And: "*A Drum Is a Woman* is Ellington's 'parallel' of jazz, written, composed, narrated, and performed by a man who saw himself as the one 'Joe' that Madam Zajj could not leave behind. To the end of his life he though[t] of *Drum* as one of his supreme achievements."[82]

The work is certainly sui generis. Divided into four parts, it begins with Carribee Joe in his West Indian jungle, finding "an elaborately fabricated drum," which turns into a woman, Madam Zajj. Zajj tries to entice Joe to accompany her, but he refuses to leave the jungle. So she takes off to seek "other Joes," arriving first in Barbados and then, in part 2, in New Orleans, where she meets Buddy Bolden and dances in Congo Square. Part 3 describes her fame spreading around the globe as she travels "out of New Orleans to the cities of the world, always gathering new acclaim and new Joes as she goes, yet remembering only her original Carribee Joe."[83] She even travels to the moon, returning in a flying saucer to yet greater ovations. In the final part, Zajj dreams that Carribee Joe comes to 52nd Street in New York City and hears bebop, the influence of which he takes back with him to the jungle. But the dream ends, leaving Zajj with her worldly success and her succession of Joes, while her original Carribee Joe continues to make drums in the jungle.

Ellington's affection for *A Drum Is a Woman* was not shared by many of the critics, whose reactions ranged from puzzlement to outright hostility; words such as "naive," "banal," and "self-indulgent" jostled in the reviews alongside "pretentious" and "disjointed."[84] This difference of opinion was set out in stark detail in the pages of the English jazz press. In an interview in *Jazz Journal International* Ellington attributed the work's bad press to the "school of thought that jazz can't be written, and then when you combine it with voices, and you make a fanfare like Madame [sic] Zajj coming out of the flying saucer, well they don't think this is jazz."[85] He then recounted the story of the raggedy boy finding the clarinet, making it clear that he saw criticism of the piece as stemming from the same narrow and restrictive view of African American creativity that he had been battling throughout his career. "They think that Louis Armstrong should always have his handkerchief and Cab Calloway should always sing hi-de-ho, and the minute they do anything new, they're out of character. They think that nobody grows up, everybody stays a child."[86]

Coincidentally, an example of just such an attitude had appeared in another English jazz publication seven months earlier. Edward Towler's *Jazz Monthly* article, "Reflections on Hearing 'A Drum Is a Woman,'" took Ellington to task for letting down both jazz and the African American people: "A major creative composer of Ellington's stature and reputation is in a position not only to further the interests of the music he represents but also to enhance considerably the prestige of his race. I feel that this rather abortive venture of Ellington's into the realm of the imagination will do little for either."[87] One can hear an echo of John Hammond here, castigating Ellington back in 1935 for his supposed lack of race consciousness. Towler adds a further Hammond-esque touch by suggesting that this new Ellington music is a major disappointment compared to his past achievements: "The writing too is . . . strangely nondescript. . . . It possesses none of the charm and subtlety . . . that one associates with Ellington's earlier works."[88] And later: "It is a denial, almost a negation, of nearly everything that Ellington has stood for."[89] But it is the conclusion to Towler's critique that is most likely to have caused Ellington a wry smile: "To call this hybrid a folk opera would be an injustice. Indeed, I find it difficult to categorise a work which at one end of the scale degenerates into a conception of jazz such as one might hear at the local music hall, and which at the other makes a self-conscious attempt to emulate writing more fitted for the concert platform."[90] "Difficult to categorise." Could it be that this point is actually *the* point, and one which Towler seems spectacularly to have missed? I suspect *A Drum Is a Woman* may have been

Ellington's tongue-in-cheek riposte to all such purist notions of categorization. If so, then this was actually a potent *affirmation* of "nearly everything" that he had stood for.

A Drum is undeniably a hybrid. The recording comprises instrumental passages, songs, and a narration spoken by Ellington himself. The music includes calypso ("What Else Can You Do with a Drum"), New Orleans parade music ("Hey, Buddy Bolden"), and Latin-inflected bebop ("Rhumbop"). Ellington also employed the classical soprano Margaret Tynes together with jazz singers Joya Sherrill and Ozzie Bailey. There could hardly be a better demonstration of the point he had made in *Etude* in 1947: "Jazz means simply the freedom to have many forms." Ellington's own views on the historically important influences on jazz can probably be discerned in the emphasis he gives to the Caribbean and to New Orleans, while "Ballet of the Flying Saucers" perhaps reflects and extends a little his belief in jazz's modernity (and his appropriation of the word "ballet" is possibly intended to signify its equal status to European classical forms). Moreover, "You Better Know It," sung by one of the many Joes with whom Madam Zajj associates in her travels, can be read as Ellington's satire on the attitudes of those critics and fans who try to "own" jazz by confining it within *their* categories.

> Zajj, darling, we're in love it appears
> And I surely want to thank you
> But if you get ideas
> I'll surely have to spank you
> I belong to you
> And now I know I show it
> You belong to me
> And you'd better know it.[91]

John Hammond could not have put it plainer. Nor James Lincoln Collier, who on the last page of his Ellington biography cannot resist administering a final spank to Madam Zajj for getting ideas: "When jazz becomes confounded with art, passion flies out and pretension flies in."[92]

Collier had earlier concluded of *A Drum Is a Woman*: "In fact, it has little to do with the history of jazz."[93] This opinion brings to mind Sun Ra's declaration that "history is only his story. You haven't heard my story yet."[94] As Irving Townsend noted, *A Drum Is a Woman* was a "parallel," Ellington's "my story" of the black-based music he had always regarded as more protean than the categories that its white critics and fans alike had devised for it. If *Black, Brown and Beige* had been his musical rewrite of the history of the American Negro, *A Drum Is a Woman* was his "parallel" to the history of American Negro music, his heroine's name signifying on white attempts to write that history (and getting it back to front). These revisions not only provided a corrective to white misrepresentations of the black past, but they also proposed a vision of the future in which such stereotyping no longer had a place. A new world where there would be no racism, no categorization—and jazz, the erstwhile "low-down" sound of the Harlem dive, could encompass a ballet for flying saucers in transit from the moon.

Part III *Anthony Braxton:*

Crossroad Axiums

One must cultivate the art of recognizing

significant communications, knowing what is

truth and what is falsehood, or else the lessons

of the crossroads—the point where doors open

or close, where persons have to make decisions

that may forever after affect their lives—will be

lost.—*Robert Farris Thompson*, Flash of the Spirit

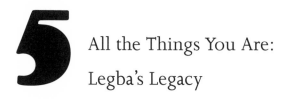

All the Things You Are:
Legba's Legacy

Everything I've lived I am in my music. — *Cecil Taylor* [1]

In a 1977 liner-note musician and author Leo Smith describes his AACM colleague Anthony Braxton as "an enigmatic figure . . . whose music has too often been criticized unjustly and praised for the wrong reasons." This state of affairs Smith blames on "the ill-informed and un-educated 'critics' who parade as authorities on creative music." [2] Smith goes on to address four specific areas of Braxton's musical oeuvre. He cites the music for solo saxophone and Braxton's experiments with "a field of new rhythmic elements" as his chief contributions to creative music; he decries the "fuss" that has been made over Braxton's acknowledgment of white influences (particularly composers from the Western art music tradition); and he defends Braxton's use of codes and diagrams to title his compositions, arguing that titles are important signifiers of the artist's "poetic intent" and noting that "the code and symbolism" which Braxton employs are "primarily mystical." [3]

In this chapter I would like to follow Leo Smith's lead and discuss in turn these four aspects of Braxton's work, with particular reference to how and why they have been "criticized unjustly" by jazz writers. This approach not only will allow us an entry into Braxton's multifaceted soundworld, but it will, I hope, serve to introduce his own thinking on these topics, not least the comprehensive critique of jazz journalism in his *Tri-axium Writings Volume 3* (hereafter *T-a W 3*), which, much like Ellington's rejection of the "primitive," "minstrel," and "hot jazzman" stereotypes, can be seen as a repudiation of white misrepresentations of black cultural history. In chapter 6 I look at Braxton's *Trillium* operas, which illustrate some of the more abstract philosophical ideas he puts forward in the *Tri-axium Writings* and which can, I think, be read, at least in part, as indictments of what he has called "Western ideas and life values,"[4] particularly as they appertain to African Americans and other disempowered groups within Western society.

— • • • ———

Braxton's debut release as leader, the trio/quartet set *3 Compositions of New Jazz*, was recorded early in 1968. Later that year the 23-year-old Chicagoan began to record a series of works for solo saxophone that were eventually released in 1971 as the double album *For Alto*.[5] There had been occasional recordings and performances on solo saxophone before, notably by Coleman Hawkins, Sonny Rollins, Eric Dolphy, and Braxton's AACM colleague Roscoe Mitchell, but *For Alto* was the first-ever release devoted entirely to solo saxophone music, the first recorded example of an extensive musical language developed specifically for and on solo saxophone. It was to prove a highly influential step—soon solo concerts on single-line instruments were commonplace in creative music—and many musicians have since credited the record (and Braxton's contemporaneous solo concerts) as a primary influence.[6]

At the time of its release, however, *For Alto* had a muted and mixed reception. Of the English-language jazz press, only *Down Beat* paid it any attention.[7] In the 24 June 1971 issue, reviewer Joe H. Klee called it a "revolutionary" recording and awarded it the maximum five stars.[8] And in a "Blindfold Test" in the same issue, saxophonist Harold Land, responding to the track "To Artist Murray De Pillars," remarked that "I think that he's a very good saxophonist. . . . I have great respect for his technique and his control of the instrument."[9] But in the issue of 14 October 1971, journalist Leonard Feather, who contributed the "Blindfold Test" column, played the same track to saxophonist Phil Woods and this time elicited an extremely vituperative response:

> That was terrible. I can't imagine the ego of a person thinking they can sustain a whole performance by themselves, when they can't really play the saxophone well.
>
> (L.F.: This is part of a two-LP album in which he plays solo all the way.)
>
> Yeah, well, he should learn to play the saxophone first. It should be called "the trill is gone." If you're going to try and play—and it's a classically-oriented way of playing, that kind of sound he's

trying to get—you should have the training to carry it off. It's not jazzy, it's not classical . . . it's dull . . . it's not well done, he doesn't breathe properly. . . .

No stars. I don't like it at all. I wouldn't even want to guess who it is, because I might hate him.[10]

What I would like to consider here is not so much the fact that a piece of music can spark such wildly different responses—where Woods hears someone who "can't really play," Harold Land has "great respect for his technique and his control of the instrument"—as that such allegations of incompetence recur throughout the history of jazz commentary. Charlie Parker's "Now's the Time" and "Billie's Bounce," now widely regarded as classic bebop recordings, were dismissed in a 1946 *Down Beat* review that claimed Parker's playing was "off form—a bad reed and inexcusable fluffs do not add up to great jazz." [11] Parker's record, too, was awarded no stars. Similar charges of musical ineptitude have been leveled at, among others, Thelonious Monk, Ornette Coleman, Cecil Taylor, and, perhaps most famously (or infamously), John Coltrane. Indeed, Ira Gitler's 1962 *Down Beat* review of "Chasin' the Trane," from the *"Live" at the Village Vanguard* LP,[12] is similar both in tone and outlook to Woods's attack on Braxton.

> Coltrane may be searching for new avenues of expression, but if it is going to take this form of yawps, squawks, and countless repetitive runs, then it should be confined to the woodshed. Whether or not it is "far out" is not the question. Whatever it is, it is monotonous, a treadmill to the Kingdom of Boredom. There are places where his horn actually sounds as if it is in need of repair. In fact, this solo could be described as one big air-leak. . . .[13]

Braxton presumably had this kind of critical abuse in mind when, working on *T-a W 3* in the mid-1970s, he complained:

> master musicians of black creativity are not viewed from the concept of what they have offered the music—in terms of the whole of their output—but instead every participation is viewed from the context of "accountability"—and this is both dangerous and sickening. For example, when John Coltrane began to change the functionalism of his music . . . the thrust of negative journalism that surrounded Coltrane's activity challenged him as if he were a student without any pre-established qualifications.[14]

To write in such derogatory terms and with so little recognition of a musician's achievements—what Braxton calls "the concept of non-sequenced credibility"—is, he suggests, a form of racism that relates back to a slave-owning mentality. "Black artists of the highest caliber— people who have undoubtedly contributed to the composite reality of black creativity—are daily written of as if they are 'on the auction block' or something."[15]

The underlying assumption in both the Gitler and Woods reviews is that there is a "correct" way to play an instrument, a common standard to which all players should adhere. As Braxton notes in T-a W 3, this is one example of the way in which white commentators attempt to impose on black music values that actually originate in Western classical music, a context in which, he says, "a given musician is expected to eventually arrive at producing a 'particular' sound out of his or her instrument."[16] But, he argues, the opposite is true in the tradition of what he terms "creative music from the black aesthetic": "An instrument in this context is viewed as nothing more than a vehicle to establish the musician's spiritual and vibrational reality. Creative musicians are expected to extend the very nature of their activity—including even the sound of the instrument—until that activity affirms the whole of their 'life position.' Even the sound of the instrument is not viewed as existing in a fixed state. . . ."[17] Obviously, Braxton is not saying that players do not need to learn or practice their instruments, but that technical correctness in creative music is not an absolute value because the music is not *about* the "execution of the particulars," and there can be no standard notion of correctness because "strict imitation runs counter to the aesthetic basis of the music."[18]

This distinction between art and technique can also be found in African music,[19] and it is not entirely new to jazz either. Back in the 1940s critic Paul Bacon was suggesting that Thelonious Monk's expressive needs might not be best served by "classical technique": "I believe his style has cost him 50 per cent of his technique. He relies so much on absolute musical reflex that Horovitz's style might be unequal to the job. . . ."[20] Bacon was, writes Martin Williams, "The only American critic who understood Monk in the forties," and well into the 1950s some writers claimed that Monk played the piano "wrong," or they criticized his supposed lack of technique.[21] (Monk played the piano with his fingers flat, which led to the accusations of poor technique. Bacon's point was that Monk had developed the style specifically to meet the needs of his music, not because he couldn't play "properly.")

As Braxton notes in *T-a W 3*, "There has long been an inability on the part of western culture to deal with the realness of 'form' in non-western creativity and the actualness of what that form celebrates." [22]

This continuing inability was demonstrated again as recently as November 1995 by *New York Times* critic Peter Watrous. Reviewing a Braxton solo saxophone concert, Watrous claimed that Braxton "veered between technical sloppiness and conceptual brilliance," adding: "At times, Mr. Braxton seemed barely in control of his instrument, his vibrato wobbled, ideas sounded as if they had been lifted from classical exercise books and then barely executed, notes slipped out of tune." [23] More than twenty-five years after he recorded the groundbreaking *For Alto*, it seems that Anthony Braxton still hasn't learned to play the saxophone "properly"! The serious point here is that Watrous appears to ascribe "technical sloppiness" to any sounds that fall outside a European-derived notion of "correctness." It does not seem to occur to him, for example, that Braxton's "vibrato wobbled" because he *meant* it to wobble; yet such bending of sound has long been a feature of Braxton's solo music, and it has sometimes been among the main characteristics of a work as in, for instance, *Composition 77E* and *Composition 106B*. Referring to the former piece, Braxton writes in his *Composition Notes Book D* that the performer is expected "*to establish a vibrato emphasis section* (that gives fresh insight into what this consideration could mean from 'another mentality')." [24] The problem for Braxton is that such attempts to explore creative music from "another mentality" have often been, and continue to be, misjudged and misdocumented by journalists whose "critical mentality" remains steeped in the values of the European classical tradition.

— • • • ——

Critical misconceptions about Braxton's solo music are as nothing compared to the disputation that has dogged his work in what Leo Smith called "the field of new rhythmic elements." Smith was, I think, referring primarily to the rhythmic components of Braxton's *compositions* (and this is a point to which I return in the next section), but the rhythmic quality of his *playing* was also questioned by several critics, who complained of a failure to "swing." Roland Baggenaes, for example, reviewing a 1972 Braxton recording that included a version of Charlie Parker's "Donna Lee," noted a deficiency of "swing, ease, jazz phrasing"; [25] the irony here is that Parker himself had been criticized in the 1940s for supposedly lacking those very same qualities. Indeed, lack of swing has long been regarded as a cardinal sin by jazz commentators, and its deployment as a criticism of original and/or innovatory music has, like accusations of lack of technique, become a journalistic cliché. Ross Russell noted of the critics' response to bebop that "they took to calling [it] 'non-jazz' or 'anti-jazz' " and "complained that the new music 'didn't swing.' "[26] Some fifteen years later, in a now notorious *Down Beat* column, critic John Tynan labeled the music of John Coltrane and Eric Dolphy "anti-jazz" and, with regard to swing, claimed that they "seem intent on deliberately destroying this essence, this vital ingredient."[27] In a later *Down Beat* interview Coltrane tried to answer the charge that his music didn't swing: "There are various types of swing. . . . In fact, every group of individuals assembled has a different feeling—a different swing."[28] This is a point that Braxton also made repeatedly in the 1970s and 1980s when his playing was criticized on the same grounds:

> How many articles have I read about the fact that my music doesn't "swing"? Yet all of the masters have developed their own relationship to forming, to rhythmic contours, etc. The situation is now designed so that jazz is framed in a little box and if you don't follow in someone else's footsteps, someone who is so-called "jazz," then you're automatically excommunicated. But all the masters followed their own steps, so it's a contradiction in terms.[29]

For Braxton and Coltrane, swing, like instrumental technique, is part of a player's personal language and as such cannot be standardized. Critical attempts to do so are part of what Braxton refers to in *T-a W 3* as "the present distortions surrounding black creativity and the concept of rhythm," in which commentators isolate a particular player's rhythmic expression and try to use this "as a measuring tool for the composite reality of the projection."[30] This represents a profound misunderstanding of the aesthetic basis of the music, Braxton says, "because no matter whether the notes of a given player could be reduced for analysis (and then labeled swinging or 'not swinging') the essence factor that determined the meta-reality of the music was not about focusing in on a moment to determine whether it is valid or not."[31]

The contradiction in terms that Braxton referred to above is especially evident in the matter of swing. The critical community, while generally agreeing with Tynan that swing is the "essence" of jazz, still has no commonly accepted definition of what swing is; in the words of John Gennari, "arriving at such a definition has been one of the great unanswered challenges in the history of jazz criticism."[32] Gunther Schuller, in his epic study *The Swing Era*, defines swing thus in his glossary: "A rhythmic element and a manner of playing (inflecting) peculiar to jazz."[33] Yet even a definition this vague is open to question since the concept of swing and its association with black music appears to predate jazz.

In his preface to *The Book of American Negro Spirituals*, first published in 1926, James Weldon Johnson discusses swing in connection with earlier forms of black music, including spirituals and work songs, and suggests that the rhythmic characteristics of each genre are related to its function. For example: "The 'swing' of the Spirituals is an altogether subtle and elusive thing. It is subtle and elusive because it is in perfect unison with the religious ecstacy that manifests itself in the swaying bodies of a whole congregation."[34] Here, I think, is an example of what Braxton means by the "meta-reality" of the music, a point further elucidated in Johnson's discussion of whether white singers can sing spirituals: "I think white singers, concert singers, *can* sing Spirituals—if they *feel* them. But to feel them it is necessary to know the truth about their origin and history, to get in touch with the association of ideas that surround them, and to realize something of what they have meant in the experiences of the people who created them."[35] What Johnson is saying is that feeling is more vital to the expression of the music than the application of "correct" technique (which would have been de rigeur for white concert singers). But I think it is important to stress that for Johnson *feeling* here emphatically does *not* refer to displays of blatant emoting, but to a kind of sympathetic identification that derives from a knowledge of the music's history and an understanding of its significance in terms of black experience (factors that help to constitute the music's "meta-reality").

I doubt whether anyone, even Braxton himself, could fully explicate the meta-reality nuances of his swing. But I would like to suggest a context in which we can hear Braxton's swing as something more than personal style. That context is the black tradition of "telling inarticulacy" outlined by Nathaniel Mackey in his book *Discrepant Engagement*. In the chapter "Sound and Sentiment, Sound and Symbol," a brilliant account of the relationships between music, language, and transcendence, Mackey notes in several recent texts of (mostly) American fiction the recurring trope of "the travestied, fractured foot," a figure he traces back to "the Fon-Yoruba orisha of the crossroads, the lame dancer Legba."[36] This trope of limping can, he argues, also be associated both with what Robert Farris Thompson has called African music's characteristic *"suspended accentuation patterning* (off-beat phrasing of melodic and choreographic accents)" and with stammering, a speech im-*pedi*-ment equivalent to Legba's limp.[37]

> With the advent of bebop . . . black musicians began to assume a more explicit sense of themselves as artists, conscious creators, thinkers. Dizzy Gillespie would don a beret and a goatee, as would, among others, Yusef Lateef, who would record an album called *Jazz for the Thinker*. Anthony Braxton's pipe, wire-rim glasses, cardigan sweater, and diagrammatic titles are among the present-day descendants of such gestures. The aural equivalent of this more explicit reflexivity would come at times to resemble a stutter, conveying senses of apprehension and self-conscious duress by way of dislocated phrasings in which virtuosity mimes its opposite. Thelonious Monk's mock-awkward hesitancies evoke an experience of impediment or impairment, as do Sonny Rollins even more stutter-like teasings of a tune. . . .[38]

Mackey goes on to suggest that "the black musician's stutter is an introspective gesture that arises from and reflects critically upon an experience of isolation or exclusion," an outsider's ordeal: "it symbolizes a refusal to forget damage done, a critique and a partial rejection of an available but biased coherence. Part of the genius of black music is the room it allows for a telling 'inarticulacy,' a feature consistent with its critique of a predatory coherence . . . and the articulacy that upholds it."[39]

I will return to the topic of Braxton's visual "gestures"; what I would like to propose here is that his perceived lack of swing can be heard as his stammer, a *stagger*-ly (!) rejection of the "biased" and "predatory coherence" of a stereotyped version of jazz tradition that excludes as much as it allows. Certainly, several critics have heard Braxton's playing as stammer-like; Michael Ullman actually uses the phrase "stutter on an alto saxophone."[40] Ullman intends the analogy descriptively rather than derogatorily, but critics who dislike Braxton's playing often claim that they do so because he is not, as it were, a smooth talker. Leonard Feather, for example, complains of "a lack of swing and flow in his phrasing"; Gary Giddins diagnoses "an inability to relax—absolutely essential for the purpose of 'swinging' "; and Phil

Woods, as we have seen, even claims that Braxton "doesn't breathe properly."[41] (As a stammerer myself I can attest that two methods used for treating a stammer are relaxation techniques and breathing exercises.)[42] Where these white listeners seem to want to hear a "natural" swing, Mackey offers a context in which we can hear Braxton's playing as *reflexive* swing, a signifying stutter on a view of black creativity that excludes the thinker, the intellectual. Or as Braxton remarked (in a comment that is appropriately inarticulate and telling): "Man, you spend ten years trying to figure out how not to swing, but to swing."[43]

And if Legba's limp is attributable to his liminal status—his role as a mediator between different realms (with one foot in each)—then perhaps Braxton's swing is shaped by his particular position on several thresholds—tradition and futurity, Africa and Europe, emotion and intellect, real and meta-real (with one foot in each)—by his insistence on the heterogeneity of black creativity. Legba, says Mackey:

> suffers not from deformity but multiformity, a "defective" capacity in a homogenous order given over to uniform rule. Legba's limp is an emblem of heterogenous wholeness, the image and outcome of a peculiar remediation. *Lame* or *limping* . . . cuts with a revitalizing edge to unveil impairment's power, as though the syncopated accent were an unsuspected blessing offering anomalous, unpredictable support. Impairment taken to higher ground, remediated, translates damage and disarray into a dance.[44]

Marilyn Crispell, pianist in Braxton's quartet for a dozen years, noted in 1985 that "those fast complicated compositions of his, they really swing—you have to *listen* to hear it, but there are all kinds of figures in there, jagged, accented, off-the-beat phrases that swing like crazy."[45] Or as Braxton himself once remarked, albeit somewhat enigmatically: "It's just a question of gravitational intrigue."[46]

— · · · ——

But I am tripping over myself, stumbling with that Crispell quotation away from the realm of improvisation and into the realm of Braxton's compositions. So perhaps we should backtrack to consider the role of notation and its relationship to swing. In *The Book of American Negro Spirituals*, James Weldon Johnson makes the point that European bands which attempt to play jazz are often unable to do so satisfactorily because of problems "getting into the 'swing' of it . . . they play the notes too correctly; and do not play what is not written down."[47] In his 1936 auto-biography *Swing That Music*, Louis Armstrong also identifies swing with improvisation, claiming that a swing band never plays a tune the same way twice, because "the boys are 'swinging' around, and away from, the regular beat and melody you are used to, following the scoring very loosely and improvising as they go, by ear and free musical feeling."[48]

For both Johnson and Armstrong, then, swing involves a departure from the notation, which is seen as a guideline rather than something to be strictly adhered to. Braxton elaborates on this idea in *T-a W 3*, arguing that notation in black creative music actually serves a different function than it does in Western classical music.

> Notation as practiced in black improvised creativity is not viewed as a factor that only involves the duplication of a given piece of music—and as such an end in itself. Rather this consideration has been utilized as both a recall-factor as well as a generating factor to establish improvisational co-ordinates. In this context notation is utilized as a ritual consideration and this difference is important for what it signifies about extended functionalism. . . . Notation in this context invariably becomes a stabilizing factor that functions with the total scheme of the music rather than a dominant factor at the expense of the music.[49]

However, many jazz writers, because they retain the traditional European view of notation as something that is supposed to be followed with precision and accuracy, tend to view its presence in jazz with suspicion. A player seen with a score is presumed not to swing. In the words of percussionist Gerry Hemingway, "immediately they see notation up there they make the assumption the music couldn't possibly come out of somewhere soulful and warm . . . it's a cultural judgement."[50]

It is the same cultural judgment that we saw in press reactions to Ellington's *Black, Brown and Beige*, and it is rooted in a racial stereotyping that is at least as old as jazz itself. In *Terrible Honesty*, Ann Douglas relates that in the early 1920s the members of the all-black pit orchestra for the show *Shuffle Along*, although they were all proficient readers of music, "memorized the score and played it without sheet music as if they were improvising on the spot." She quotes Eubie Blake's explanation that "it was expected of us. People didn't believe that black people could read music—they wanted to think that our ability was just natural talent."[51] In more recent jazz commentary this denial of black intellect is evident in the phenomenon that, according to Braxton, "nothing is worse to white critics than the possibility of black music having anything to do with Western art music," a prejudice that he attributes not only to racial stereotyping but also to the "fact" that "nine tenths" of jazz writers have been attracted to the music "as a reaction to the dictates of Western art music" and European high culture.[52] Nevertheless, these writers, consciously or not, still apply European standards to the music; that is, they are less concerned with understanding black music on its own terms than in using it as a weapon in their quarrel with the values of their own cultural milieu.

One might want to dispute Braxton's figure of "nine tenths" as excessive, but the hostility toward anything resembling Western art music that he describes is certainly not unfamiliar in jazz commentary. His own debut LP, *3 Compositions of New Jazz*, drew a bemused response from the critics. *Coda*'s Brian Blevins was unhappy that the opening *Composition 6E* was "fragmented" and resembled "Webern-esque pointillisme,"[53] while Will Smith in *Jazz and Pop* declared that "the failure of Braxton's own album is that it lacks a rhythm section and thus has little impetus. The music is rather like the wanderings of contemporary 'serious composers'—cold, detached, and somewhat static."[54] In fact, the absence of a rhythm section was not necessarily a "failure," but, at least in the case of *Composition 6D*, a major part of the *point*. Braxton writes in CN-A that the piano's role in 6D "would supply alternatives to the traditional (or what we have come to think of as traditional) rhythm section implications of the music. This is so because in Composition No. 6D the pianist functions as soloist as well as 'total rhythm section.' The implications of this difference would move to open up the instrumental dynamics of creative music to other focuses and approaches."[55] Critics can perhaps be excused for not immediately understanding what is happening in a piece of music, especially if something new is being tried, but it is the limited concept of jazz implicit in these critiques (as well as their sweeping and blanket hostility to contemporary composition) that is significant. As Braxton later observed drily, "At that time . . . it was against the law to have an ensemble without bass and drums."[56]

To digress. When Braxton later did employ bass and drums, he continued to explore "other focuses and approaches" to rhythm. These tended to vary from composition to composition, but one virtually consistent factor was that, although his notated themes were often reminiscent of bebop phraseology, he did not use the harmonic frameworks characteristic of bebop. This allowed the rhythm section greater flexibility (the bassist, for instance, no longer had to play "inside" the chords) and enabled Braxton to experiment with bass/drum roles. In *Composition 23G*, for example, the horns play "linear post-bebop phrases," but with "no real harmonic system" overstructure, while the musicians in the rhythm section play what Braxton calls "irregular time pulse patterns," creating a "time shifting" effect that is intended to make the music sound "slightly off center." (Or *limping*, perhaps?) How this works is that the bass and drums come together at irregular notated points, later called "sound attacks," between which they can improvise. *Composition 23G*, notes Braxton, is "in the tradition of Trans African pedagogy," yet the mix of traditional components with the additional "time shifting rhythm tracks" gives the work "a special focus and environment that is very separate from post-Coleman/Ayler functionalism."[57] This perception of a composition being both in the tradition *and* extending it (one foot in either realm) is characteristic of how Braxton sees much of his work.[58] I mention 23G in particular because it is the composition that Braxton has credited with inspiring his later development of "pulse track structures," which became a major feature of his music in the 1980s and which arguably represent his most radical contribution to date to what Leo Smith called the "field of new rhythmic elements" explored in his music.

I do not want to get sidetracked into a technical discussion of pulse tracks, but that they promote what Nathaniel Mackey termed "multiformity" is evident, I think, in the following quotation from Gerry Hemingway, drummer in Braxton's quartet from 1983 to 1993.[59] (He describes playing the pulse track to *Composition 105A* with John Lindberg and Mark Dresser, bassists in the Braxton quartet from 1983–85 and 1985–93, respectively.)

> What John and I did right away was to extend the dynamics of the time, stretch it out a little longer than was actually written. . . .
>
> . . . but since Mark and I got into it, we've tried different approaches—we've sped it up terrifically faster than it's supposed to go and just kept rushing through it, very accurately but real quick; or we change the tempo constantly, speeding it up and slowing it down in the course of doing it. . . .
>
> . . . It's not a given parameter but it's a factor that Mark and

I particularly go for—we share an interest in the concept of changing the tempo all the time, so you don't get locked into one tempo.[60]

It is not hard to imagine how this stretching, rushing, and shifting of tempo could be construed as "deformity" by those who prefer the "homogenous order" of, say, a smooth, regular pulse. But such "uniform rule" is not for Braxton. As he said in 1968, prophetically setting out a credo for his multiformity: "Tempo is a limited use of time. I think of time as *all* time."[61] This embrace of time includes not only changing tempos but extremes of tempo, too, from impossibly fast to virtually standstill. All commonly occur in Braxton's compositions, and all can be seen as evidence of a failure to "swing," of a rhythmic "deformity," that, from a different perspective (Mackey's "higher ground"), translates into an exhilarating dance with the infinite possibilities of time.

Critics Blevins and Smith both took issue with Braxton's rhythmic approach in terms of compositional rather than playing criteria. Indeed, as Robert Palmer pointed out in 1975, it was precisely Braxton's declared interest in composition and structure that had led some commentators to question his "authenticity as a jazzman."[62] Though Braxton was also a student of Indian and Far Eastern musics, his experiments with structure were generally attributed by the press to "European influences." Moreover, writers who disliked these more composed pieces often based their judgments on criteria that suggested their own indebtedness to Europe. Thus, critic Chip Stern, who acknowledged that Braxton's *playing* "does indeed *swing*," could, in the very same article, still dismiss one of Braxton's compositions as "stark, cold, and completely devoid of rhythm, melody, and development."[63] What such a critique fails to address is the possibility that the work in question—*Composition 76*, released on record as *For Trio*[64]—is not concerned with conforming to such Eurocentric (or, at least, Euro-derived) formal values. Yet Braxton makes clear in his liner notes to the LP that *76* has little to do with conventional ideas either of jazz or of Western art music, and in his *Composition Notes* he specifically states: "There is no development at all in Composition No. 76," and each performer "takes on a different role from that of the classical or improvising tradition."[65] (In fact, the work seems inspired less by any specific kind of music than by Braxton's ideas on ritual and spirituality—though he also mentions Japanese painting as an influence.)[66]

The approximately contemporaneous *Composition 82*, released on record as *For Four Orchestras*,[67] an exploration of spatial music, does draw on a variety of precedents in both Western art music and jazz, from Renaissance polyphony to New Orleans parade music, yet still ends up sounding sui generis.[68] As Peter Niklas Wilson has observed in his astute analysis of the much later *Composition 151*, Braxton often creates compositions that contain "traditional references without traditional definitions."[69] There are parallels here with Duke Ellington's extended forms, which, as we have seen, were criticized by jazz writers for "deserting jazz" and by classical critics for not adhering to European notions of correct form. Braxton's similar attempts to create a music that goes beyond "traditional definitions" have been met with cries of "no swing" and with what he has termed the "what makes you think you can play classical music, *nigger*" syndrome.[70] Recalling again Nathaniel Mackey's discussion of Legba's limp, perhaps we can see Braxton's, and Ellington's, compositions not as "deformities" of jazz or Western classical music, but as evidence of multiformity, of a heterogenous creative spirit that cannot be confined within a "homogenous order given over to uniform rule,"[71] which seems to be how jazz and classical critics prefer to view their respective traditions.

Indeed, Braxton's creative spirit is evident not only in his finished pieces but in his very method of working, which further subverts attempts to see improvisation and composition as essentially different homogenous orders. In his *Composition Notes*, Braxton reports that he wrote numerous compositions "in moment time," i.e., as he heard them in his head. To quote Kevin Whitehead: "The composer is always being put down for being overly analytical, but the Braxton who emerges from the *Notes* is an intuitive cat, repeatedly stressing that he writes it down as he hears it in his head, without knowing exactly where it's going, without attempting to conform to some overall structural plan."[72] Much of Braxton's music, then, as with much of Ellington's, could be said to take place in that ambivalent, elusive, and volatile area where composed improvisation mingles with improvised composition and hard, fast "uniform rule" does not exist.

Braxton's reworkings of African American and European (and other) references can also be viewed from the perspective of cultural hybridity, a concept recently reassessed by Homi Bhabha, whose arguments have been summarized by Paul A. Anderson as follows:

> Excessively unified or totalized notions of authentic cultural identity depend on an avoidance of the facts of social heterogeneity.

If its political uses can be and have sometimes been extremely radical, cultural authenticity remains a romantic and conservative concept, leading one toward assertion of relative social unanimity and holism rather than hybridity and internal difference or contestation.[73]

This perspective offers a useful context in which to briefly consider Braxton's relationship with African American jazz writers. The desire for "homogenous order" was not confined to white journalists; black nationalist critics had their own agendas for wanting to keep black music separate from European influences. If the rhetoric of "cultural authenticity" arguably played a radical political role in the 1960s with the debate over a Black Aesthetic, its continuing espousal by writers such as Amiri Baraka and Stanley Crouch has indeed shown it to be "a romantic and conservative concept." (In very different ways, I should add. Baraka seems to view black music as a history of political struggle, whereas Crouch presents it as a history of aesthetic triumphalism. But both are conservative in proposing a narrow view of tradition — Mackey's "biased coherence" — that ruthlessly excludes "internal difference or contestation.")[74]

Baraka and Crouch attacked Braxton's work in the 1970s and 1980s chiefly on account of his declared interest in white composers such as Stockhausen and Cage; yet the most viciously personal criticism probably came from Ted Joans, who in 1975 denounced Braxton as an "Oreo" for the heinous crime of recording with Dave Brubeck.[75] One of the main reasons for such abuse was undoubtedly the relative degree of commercial and critical success that Braxton enjoyed in the mid-1970s. Signed to a major American label, Arista, and hailed by several white critics as the latest inheritor of an exalted lineage that ran back through Coltrane, Parker, and Hodges,[76] Braxton was viewed with suspicion by black critics for his admiration both of white composers and of white jazz players such as Paul Desmond and Warne Marsh. Certainly this is how he sees the situation in retrospect:

> they felt, for whatever reason, that I wasn't a guy who was really "jazz," and that I was in . . . the wrong position. I know Stanley Crouch said something like that to me in that period, that it wasn't that he disliked me but I was in this position that could be potentially influential on some level and that I wasn't really from the right cloth as far as the aesthetics of the music went. I was not "black" enough, as such.[77]

Braxton does not directly address the question of these black critical perspectives in T-a W 3, partly because his chief argument is with the dominant tradition of Eurocentric commentary, partly because there were—and are—so few black critics writing about the music. This absence was for him a more urgent issue than his disagreements with the few black writers who were able to get into print. In T-a W 3, Braxton posits a need for more nonwhite and women writers, but he suggests what really has to change are "the affinity alignment dynamics that Western culture utilizes," not merely "the so-called skin color of the person using the technique."[78]

There is an irony here in that Baraka, perhaps the black critic who has most persistently attacked Braxton (amongst others) for being influenced by Europe, is also the writer whose view of the histories of both African American music and jazz journalism accords most closely with Braxton's arguments in the Tri-axium Writings.[79] It is not my intention to map out in detail the similarities in their thought, but I do want to make the point that Baraka has, in my view, greatly exaggerated the European influence on Braxton's music and I suspect that he has done this for political reasons. He includes Braxton in what he terms the "Tail Europe school of negro musicians who, while presumably playing jazz, really seek to make African-American music a banal appendage of European concert music! Their entire musical mission seems to be to prove to white people that they have heard Webern, Berg, or John Cage."[80] This is a gross misrepresentation of Braxton's music; a quick glance through his Composition Notes will reveal many more references to the likes of Ellington, Monk, Parker, Coltrane, Mingus, Coleman, Ayler, and the AACM than to Schoenberg, Webern, Stockhausen, and Cage. Braxton also has recorded numerous pieces by the first group (including tribute discs to Monk and Parker, with future tributes to Mingus and Wayne Shorter planned), nothing by the second group.

What lies behind this misrepresentation is, I think, Baraka's continuing advocacy of "cultural authenticity" as a radical political position. It was this belief that Ralph Ellison criticized in his review of Blues People: "It is unfortunate that Jones [i.e., Baraka] thought it necessary to ignore the aesthetic nature of the blues in order to make his ideological point, for he might have come much closer had he considered the blues not as politics but as art."[81] This line of criticism also prompted what has been called Ellison's "classic signifyin' parry" of Baraka:[82] "The horrendous burden of sociology which Jones would place upon this body of music is enough to give even the blues the blues."[83] It is this burden of *representing blackness* (or, more specifically, *working-class blackness*) that Baraka continues to impose on the music and which provokes his cultural paranoia about European influences. In his "excessively total-ized notion of authentic cultural identity" (to quote Paul Anderson), an interest in Europe is tantamount to betraying blackness.[84]

This paranoia evidently does not extend into the field of politics, since Baraka has long been happy to call himself a Marxist-Leninist, a coupling for which not even J. A. Rogers was able to adduce an African ancestry! Yet if what Baraka calls "Tail Europe" musicians can be cas-tigated for reflecting "a sector of the black middle class . . . that needs Europe as their ultimate legitimizer,"[85] just how proclaiming yourself a Marxist-Leninist *doesn't* make you a "Tail Europe" political thinker and *doesn't* imply an appeal to European legitimacy is hard to fathom. A rich irony here is that in *T-a W* 2, Braxton criticizes African Ameri-can Marxists on precisely these grounds, namely, that "Marxism—like Capitalism—is the affirmation of European and Euro-American meth-odological perception dynamics," whereas "the seeds underlying black creativity show there are other ways to establish culture."[86] The final twist of irony is that Braxton here is echoing Baraka's own view of Marxism *before* he became a Marxist: "white boys always come out and say, 'Oh, don't you think there'll be a socialistic solution to the world's problems?' Well, you know, that's irrelevant bullshit. It'll be a Black solution to the world's problems."[87]

Where Baraka and Braxton do appear to be in near-total accord is in their belief in black music's potential for effecting both social and spiritual change and the consequent inevitability of attempts to sup-press it and/or misdocument it by the white cultural establishment. Here is Baraka:

> Let the children hear our history, our traditions, the history of revolutionary democratic struggle—whether black, brown, or beige, or "God Bless the Child" or "Impressions," and watch the radical change. There are progressive ideas in that music. Ideas the keepers of the status quo cannot allow to spread through society at large, especially not to the people on the bottom, the African-Americans.[88]

And here is Braxton:

> The distortions that surround the meta-reality of black creativity are directly related to the potential of the music to serve as a fac-

tor for transformation . . . . This is so because it is not to the advantage of western culture to have poor and white people cognizant of alternative options for establishing both functional and vibrational change.[89]

— . . . ———

Nathaniel Mackey has cited Braxton's "pipe, wire-rim glasses, cardigan sweater, and diagrammatic titles" as visual evidence of black musicians' "more explicit sense of themselves as artists, conscious creators, thinkers."[90] This is true, but it is only half the story. As Braxton's titling system gradually evolved, the changes revealed him as a very different kind of thinker than the jazz press had initially assumed. Certainly, in his early years Braxton was keen to emphasize the science and intellectual content of his music, partly because of his genuine interest in those areas, partly in response to what he saw as white culture's denial of such qualities in black creativity: "Charlie Parker's music is separated from his actual thoughts. It's as if the notion they're trying to perpetuate . . . is that this man is sticking all of this dope into his arm and just playing, without making any kind of intelligent decisions about the music."[91] One of Braxton's tactics for combating such a perspective was, as Val Wilmer noted in 1971, by "puffing solemnly on his pipe and trying hard, at the age of 25, to cultivate the demeanour of an elderly professor (his own tongue-in-cheek admission)."[92] One influence here may have been Gigi Gryce and the Jazz Lab Quintet, a late-1950s group whose "very serious, very intellectual" image impressed the teenage Braxton. "For me, as a young African-American guy, growing up and reacting against the notion of 'primitive' that the jazz business complex uses—the 'exotic' African jazzman—to suddenly be exposed to Gigi Gryce and the dedication and profound intellectual dynamic that the group brought to their music was very important to me."[93] Certainly, Braxton did not have to try very hard to cultivate an intellectual image: he had been fascinated by science since childhood; he had studied philosophy at Roosevelt University; he was an expert chess player and briefly made a living playing chess in 1970. Plus, he *really* wore glasses, liked cardigans, and smoked a pipe!

Braxton's tactic was partially successful. Many subsequent pieces on him noted that he was serious, intelligent, intellectual. But the same qualities were used against him by his critics. Gary Giddins, for example, claimed that "his biggest failing, for me, is that he allows his ideas to obstruct spontaneous reactions . . . much of his music remains bloodless and intellectualized," and Giddins concluded by pronouncing that ultimate in condemnations: "At worst, he's an academic."[94] Science imagery began to percolate through the critiques of his music, Giddins complaining that he "frequently plays jazz as though he was a chemist studying it through a microscope," while Chip Stern labeled him "the Buckminster Fuller of jazz" and dismissed *Composition 82* as "interstellar background music, a science of communication without emotion—computers in various star systems exchanging radio waves after all the people have perished."[95] So in trying to avoid the "primitive" label, Braxton instead found himself called cold and cerebral, escaping one kind of "exoticism" only to fall foul of another. What is interesting here, too, is the implicitly negative view of science apparently held by jazz critics. (For example, in the middle of a complimentary review of a Braxton LP, *Coda* writer Kevin Lynch makes the analogy, not with Braxton as scientist, but with Braxton as *mad* scientist!)[96] An irony here is that Braxton partly shares this negative view of science—or, at least, of what he regards as the excessive empiricism of Western science. For him, science also has a "vibrational" level, which includes disciplines such as astrology, numerology, magic, philosophy, and parapsychology,[97] and it is these aspects of science that have often played a major role in his music. In *Composition 82*, for instance, he uses color as part of the notation system in the belief that "each color can then be viewed with respect to both its musical (or note) equivalent as well as its astrological and numerological equivalent."[98] To liken a piece that employs such mystical correspondences to computers communicating by radio waves is, I think, to seriously misrepresent the kind of science that Braxton is using to shape his compositions. And where Giddins sees a chemist, the more resonant analogy, given Braxton's belief in the transformative power of music, might be of Braxton the alchemist, or, to use Mircea Eliade's phrase, the "technician of the sacred."[99]

Similar misunderstandings attended the critical commentary on Braxton's diagrammatic titles—at least in the early stages. What were seen by many as algebraic formulae and mathematical codes—and thus further evidence of a damningly cerebral and esoteric pretension— were actually a far more personal, whimsical (at times), and exploratory venture into the ineffable. As he told Kenneth Ansell in 1977: "Initially, in about '65/66, I ran into the problem of language as a factor that obstructed what I wanted to say. . . . That was the beginning of it.

The fact that if I write a composition and call it 'Brackie's Blues—The Sun Comes Over The Mountain' it really had nothing to do with what I was really doing. It might be something that you could refer to as a title but it wasn't really anything to do with the actual music." [100]

Braxton has said that in the beginning he had no particular system or goal in mind regarding his titles. But as his music evolved, so did the diagrams. By the mid-1970s the mystical—always a factor in his compositions—began to assume increasing prominence. The early "formula" and "alternative coding" titles, which had encoded structural calibrations as well as personal references such as chess moves and friends' initials, gave way to "dimensional drawing" and later to color and shape diagrams that resembled Braxton's use of color and shape in his scores (as graphic notation, for example, and for designating certain kinds of improvisation), a development that drew in turn on his research into astrology, numerology, and systems of correspondence that he traced back to "the ancients" and in particular to ancient Egypt. He revealed to Ansell some of the thinking that went into his titles:

> Now I'm interested in hieroglyphics. It's a symbolic factor to comment on the spiritual and vibrational implications and secrets of a given structural alignment. Every sound, every structure, on top of its functional usefulness also has a spiritual and vibrational significance. And every structure also has a mystical potential or ritual factor. So all these elements are among the considerations I have been dealing with in my titles. [101]

By the early 1980s the titles were changing again, becoming more figurative at times; the central shape of Composition 95, for example, resembles a nuclear reactor, while that for Composition 98 is definitely a telescope. In 1983's Composition 105A the first human figure appears (see Appendix: A). As Braxton's thinking moved, as he put it, "from the abstract to the concrete," [102] the titles followed suit, becoming more like images of activity; by the late 1980s they included landscapes, too. Compositions 110C and 110D also introduced words into the diagrams, and similar subtitles or snatches of dialogue began to appear occasionally (e.g., Compositions 123, 125, 132, 147, 164). The most recent change—as of June 1999—is the appearance of photographs in titles (e.g., Compositions 185, 186, and 193). In addition, several of the more recent compositions have been accompanied by stories, to be read with the CD notes (e.g., Compositions 147, 151, 165), while other pieces have entailed performers singing, speaking, and enacting dialogue (e.g., *Compositions 171, 173, 174, 175*); indeed, Braxton describes *Composition 173* as a one-act play for four actors, albeit with music featured throughout.[103]

In the early 1990s Braxton began to talk of his music system as analogous to a place, an imaginary world that provided locations for his stories. Thus, narrative becomes commingled with a kind of musical reflexivity that also serves as a mapping device. For example, the story that accompanies *Composition 151* involves a car chase through a city, which, in this fantasy world, also *is* the composition.

> "It's now or never!" shouts Jason as he pushes the officer into the sand. "Get in the car and drive, man!" he yells. The first car then pulls out into the highway. "They'll never catch us now, Harvey! I know *Composition 151* forward and backwards. I could drive these lanes with one hand," he chuckles. "The race is on!" And with that remark, he pushes the gas pedal down to the floor. Now both cars are on the highway, traveling at 70 miles an hour. From the police car a megaphone appears as the unnamed second policemen yells from the window: "You'll never get away with this one, guys. *Composition 151* is not a monophonic structure that only addresses the needs of extended improvisation, as defined by the post-Ayler, Cage or AACM (for that matter) structural prototypes, but rather, this is a tri-metric architectural reality that points to a breakthrough in form building and structural categories. This is a transparent terrain of sound beam constructions that define a way of thinking and reacting. Pull over or else!"[104]

The diagram titles for *Composition 151* and other of the "story" pieces each appear to comprise a scene from the story—a scene that features the *location* of the story, as if the titles were a "window" into the composition's imagined topography. Perhaps, if the earlier diagram titles could be read as a geometry of the meta-real, these later landscape titles begin to sketch out its geography.

We will return to this fantasy world in chapter 6. For now, I would like to conclude this section by looking at some of the possible sources on which Braxton may have drawn in creating his titles. While he has intimated that his research into the mystical has taken him back to *The Egyptian Book of the Dead* and the early Egyptian mystery system teachings at Luxor—like Sun Ra, he upholds ancient Egypt as a symbol of great black civilization—it is also possible to find more recent artistic symbologies that are similar to his titles. John F. Szwed has noted correspondences between Braxton's later, figurative titles and the symbology of African American yard art:

> All of these elements seen in yard art are also found in Braxton's titles: *containment* (markers, boundaries, and wires); *figuration* (toy-like objects, simplified animals); *medicine* (plants); and, most persistently, *motion* (ladders, wheels, tires, boats, bicycles, cars and trucks, highways and railroads). To these one might add . . . *flash* (searchlights and spotlights) and *enthronement* (chairs, seats). Yet this break from the European tradition of yard and garden is often read by whites as being no art at all, merely the untidy accumulation of junk.[105]

Szwed further points to a little-remarked tradition of esoteric black jazz titles that resist easy interpretation; these include the "arcane and extremely local names" given to many early jazz records, Charlie Parker's sound-based "Klactoveesedstene" and Monk's ambivalent-about-naming "Let's Call This."[106] To these we could add the use of in-joke black vernacular, as in Ellington's "Skrontch" (slang for the female genitalia), and the diasporal mythologies alluded to in many of Cecil Taylor's titles, as, for instance, *Erzulie Maketh Scent* and *Legba Crossing*. Braxton's titles certainly partake of this tradition of black otherness; they offer a constant visual reminder of Sun Ra's message that "There Are Other Worlds (They Have Not Told You Of)."[107] And if we want to fix Braxton's titles even more firmly within the context of a black aesthetic, we could quote Zora Neale Hurston's crudely essentialist contention that "the white man thinks in a written language and the Negro thinks in hieroglyphics."[108]

Braxton's remark that he "sees" his music as if it were "a three dimensional painting" appears to confirm this point.[109] Yet synesthesia, if this is what he has, is not race-specific; Messiaen and Scriabin were also well-known for their "seeing" of sounds. A 1995 article by the Belgian writer Hugo de Craen argues persuasively that numerous resemblances exist between Braxton's musical and visual art and the spiritual symbology of Wassily Kandinsky—and Braxton has twice used Kandinsky paintings as cover art for his recordings.[110] What links Braxton, Kandinsky, and African American yard art is a shared belief in the mystical power of color, shape, and sound; perhaps Braxton's mysticism, like his music, is a personal synthesis of African and European (and other) sources. What I am trying to suggest is that his titles are not simply badges of racial difference; there is more to them than that. His refusal to discuss the "meaning" of the titles on the grounds that they refer to mystical areas that he cannot understand or articulate should be taken seriously, as should his insistence that they are an integral and vital part of his work. He has said that although he might work on a title for longer than he works on the composition, this work is largely intuitive—that is, the title does not "represent" the music empirically so much as it represents in a different form the same things or forces that the music represents.[111] In his music, too, there are certain areas that he prefers *not* to understand:

> in academia you're constantly talking about your music and that is very dangerous. You're constantly talking about the science of the music, in a two-dimensional way. So I started to move the ray of focus in my model into the poetic logics, as a way to *not know* what I'm doing. Because I'm not interested in a music that's two-dimensional, that I can talk about as being the "it" of the music. By that I'm only saying that I want the undefined component of my music to be on a par with the defined components.[112]

Is this another example of black music allowing for a "telling inarticulacy"? It seems that for Braxton creativity has to do with the unknown, the ineffable, what goes beyond the "homogenous order" of language itself. Perhaps one could relate such a belief to African American traditions of being open to the spirit, as manifested, for example, in the phenomenon of talking in tongues,[113] or, to return to the field of African American art, in the spirit-writing of J. B. Murray and the visionary paintings of James Phillips and John Biggers.[114] And if, like his fellow improviser Legba, Braxton can be said to have a foot in either realm—the mundane and the spiritual—then perhaps his titles are simply footprints, the one tangible trace of his forays into the meta-reality of music.[115]

— • • • ———

As a prelude to a closer look at the *Tri-axium Writings'* critique of Western jazz journalism, I would like to speculate a little more on the links between Braxton's music, his writing, and his attraction to the visual. I believe these connections may help to illuminate the perceived difficulties of his writing, or at least they might offer a new perspective on this contentious issue. That he sees his music, sees sounds, is evident from the *Composition Notes*. Each volume includes in its opening pages a list of nearly a hundred "sound classifications," which represent the basic pool of sounds from which Braxton constructs his musical languages; each sound is given a name and accompanied by its own specific visual designation. His descriptions of the compositions themselves also have frequent recourse to vivid visual imagery—Composition 101, for example, is likened to "a field of tall long trees (of glass)."[116]

Color and space also play important roles in the *Tri-axium Writings*.[117] Braxton in his Introduction appears to imply that he sees the books, like his compositions, much like a three-dimensional painting. Each chapter, he says, is divided into "three levels," the first of which can incorporate up to "four approaches." Each level and each approach also are color-coded.[118] In addition, Braxton highlights crucial sections of the text in bold type, and he scatters throughout the books "integration schematics" that encode in diagram form the relationships between the concepts he is discussing. Altogether, he suggests, these various focuses offer the reader at least six different ways of reading the books, the advantage of such an interactive approach being that "the reader will be able to view a given concept from as many standpoints as possible," an important consideration, he reckons, because "the realness of what I am really trying to communicate is not about 'only one point of view'—or one level of transference."[119] Claiming that "the traditional use of so-called deductive logic has been greatly violated in this time period," Braxton offers the *Tri-axium Writings* as "a bridge for re-information designation," based on his fundamental belief that "the reality of creativity is not limited to only how a given phenomenon works but also involves the meta-reality context from which that phenomenon takes its laws."[120] It is the *Tri-axium Writings'* liminal status, then, as a text that tries to move between the real and the meta-real, that requires the expansion of the linear into the multilevel, a three-dimensional model of narrativity signaled by Braxton's use of color codes and spatial metaphors.

Given this visual dimension to Braxton's texts, might there be musical analogies, too? Certainly, similarities can be found between the criticisms of his music noted earlier and criticisms of his writing. For example, some journalists have taken what could be called the Phil Woods position regarding a lack of technical correctness in Braxton's prose, a point to which he responded rather vehemently in a 1984 *Cadence* interview:

I have found, for instance, five million different levels of criticism of my liner notes, "Did I have a comma in the right place?" "What does he mean by this particular term?" Cries of pseudo-intellectualism, etc. But in the fifteen, twenty years that I've been documenting my music, I've never heard anyone challenge some of the liner notes which have been on my own records or on the records of musicians, so-called "Jazz" musicians for the last fifty years. You know, liner notes written in the most beautiful English, where the Queen herself would have approved of the structure. But articles which didn't know what the fuck they were talking about. And so there's very little tolerance for someone like myself defining my own terms. But there's a lot of tolerance for a so-called "Jazz journalist" who might not know anything about what they're talking about, but who can write very eloquently . . . it's acceptable. In fact, that's the standard of the day.[121]

Talking of eloquence, several journalists have also taken what could be termed the Leonard Feather position regarding Braxton's phraseology, i.e., they complain it does not swing or flow. Kevin Whitehead, in a review of the *Composition Notes*, makes the astute observation that a particular kind of reiteration is characteristic of Braxton's prose style: "He attacks [each composition] from numerous angles—which is good, because sometimes you have to read several explanations before you understand what he's getting at. . . . Sometimes you can wade through a dozen pages only to find that his latest pass at the material is the clearest." [122] I wonder if these repetitions, these several passes at explication, can be heard as an echo of the Braxton alto's signifying stammer, if his insistence on viewing a composition from "numerous angles," like his structuring of the *Tri-axium Writings* to offer the reader "as many different standpoints as possible," are examples in the textual realm of Braxton's multiformity, his resistance to "homogenous order," whether that order be deductive logic, European music theory, or indeed the single-viewpoint linear narrative?

It is Braxton's language, his choice of vocabulary, that is arguably the most intriguing and "difficult" facet of his writing: "he makes Herman Melville read like haiku," complained one disgruntled critic.[123] One of the six ways that Braxton invites us to read the *Tri-axium Writings* is by "translat[ing] my terminology—from both the glossary and throughout the whole book—as a means to view each focus in one's own terms: in other words, I am saying, 'this is my viewpoint in this context and these are my terms, but what do you think? . . .'" [124] Such an invitation, which insists on the equivocal status of the text, implicitly calls into question the authority claimed by other versions of jazz history.[125] This point is underlined by Braxton's subjective choice of terminology, which serves to mark the extent of his distance—and difference—from traditional, more Eurocentric narratives of black cultural history.

To pursue a little further the musical analogies of his writing, I would like to point to the provocative coincidence (?) that the solo saxophone music, which provides the basis for his entire musical oeuvre, is called by Braxton "Language Music." [126] Early examples of his solo work focused on particular instances of what he called "vocabulary strategies," that is, groups of similar kinds of sounds. Later works began to incorporate several "vocabularies" within a single composition, a phase of his music he has described as "like talking in tongues." [127] It seems to me that different "tongues" or "vocabulary strategies" can also be discerned in Braxton's writings, and these can be fitted, for our purposes, into three broad levels of language (between which Braxton is apt to flit, in a Legba-like dance).

One is the concrete or poetic level, exemplified in the *Composition Notes* by the visual images and by terse, descriptive phrases (petal sounds, squeak vapors, dog bark logics), and in the *Tri-axium Writings* by imagistic phrases, such as "the reality of the sweating brow," which name a specific critical mind-set in vivid and precise terminology. This, I think, is the least problematic of Braxton's vocabulary strategies.

The second level involves a more abstract language but one that refers to the mundane—as opposed to the metaphysical—realm. In the *Composition Notes* this is the language of Braxton's music-science (pulse track structures, phrase grouping formings, sound particles, event flow); in the *Tri-axium Writings*, it is the language that describes political/social/cultural processes and phenomena (spectacle diversion syndrome, progressionalism, perception dynamics, gradualism). It is here that Braxton's language begins to seem unwieldy, yet his fondness for compound phraseology at least ensures that the requisite information is included. For example, he often refers to "trans-African functionalism" where others might simply write "jazz." Yet "trans-African functionalism" at least makes clear that he is referring to a way of making music that is rooted in African methodologies, whereas "jazz" conveys little except perhaps a putative association with illicit sexuality, for which it has long been regarded by many African American musicians as a derogatory term. As Braxton himself said in 1979, "I don't know what they mean by 'jazz' with the exception of saying 'nigger.' " [128]

The third level or tongue is completely abstract and is the language in which Braxton clothes his spiritual beliefs. This is the realm of the meta-real and the vibrational, of transformation, cosmic zones, and the higher forces. For those of us raised in the tradition of Western rationalist discourse, this level is probably the most problematic and may require a suspension of disbelief.[129] Braxton has been reluctant to elucidate his mystical leanings, so attempts to clarify this "tongue" have met with little success. For example, in 1985 I asked him if he made distinctions in his use of the words spiritual, vibrational, and mystical:

> B: I make distinctions. By spiritual, I'm talking with respect to God; but for the person who'd say, "wait a minute, I don't believe in God," then it's OK to say vibrational—it serves the same purpose (laughs). What was the other word?
>
> L: Mystical.
>
> B: Well, mystical would have to do with the same area, but by mystical I'd be talking more in terms of forces, spiritual forces at work, when you're asleep (laughs). And when you're awake! (Laughs.) [130]

Of these terms, vibrational seems to be the one that Braxton uses most frequently. And if the *Tri-axium Writings* are located at the crossroads of the real and the meta-real, then vibrational is suitably liminal, a word that presents one face to the realm of cosmic forces and a second to the scientific world of sound waves, electromagnetic waves, and the dance of subatomic particles. Vibrational is the mediating word that enables Braxton to link music to ancient creation myths to the New Physics,[131] the sonic to the visual (as expressions of the same phenomena at different frequencies), his music-science to his music-magic. Vibrational is also a slippery word, impossible to confine within a fixed meaning; it is a trickster word that is always in motion between the real and the meta-real.

We may seem to be wandering away from the notion of musical equivalents to Braxton's textual practices, but I will return to that question in a moment. First, let me draw attention to Winston Smith's remarks on what he calls Braxton's "abstractions of language" and "linguistic interventions," and particularly Smith's assertion that "much seems tied to his need to escape the critical presuppositions of historical categorizations. All notions of history must be reworded." [132] Keeping this quotation in mind, I now want to turn briefly to Nathaniel Mackey's epistolary novel, *Bedouin Hornbook*. In a letter dated 29.V.80, the musician N. responds to an essay he has received in the post from his regular correspondent, Angel of Dust. The essay is titled "Towards a Theory of the Falsetto in New World African Musics," and I would like to quote a few of N.'s comments on it:

> One point I think could bear more insistent mention: What you term "the dislocated African's pursuit of a meta-voice" bears the weight of gnostic, transformative desire to be done with the world. By this I mean the deliberately forced, deliberately "false" voice we get from someone like Al Green creatively hallucinates a "new world," indicts the more insidious falseness of the world as we know it. . . . What is it in the falsetto that thins and threatens to abolish the voice but the wear of so much reaching for heaven? [133]

Later, N. suggests that "the falsetto serves the same alchemical function in nonvocal music" and cites as examples a number of saxophone solos, including Braxton's alto solo on "Howling in the Silence," a track from a 1969 LP by Archie Shepp and Philly Joe Jones.[134] N. concludes: "Which reminds me. I had an odd dream about Braxton the other night . . . [he] talked about 'Braxton' as though he were someone else. Badmouthed him in fact. Told me he couldn't be trusted and called him unreal. 'That Braxton's real slick,' he said. 'Can't trust him. Unreal to the bone. Your basic trickster. A little bit false.' A little bit false as in 'falsetto' perhaps?" [135]

If Braxton's "abstractions of language," his trickster words, strike our Western rationalist/skeptical ears as "a little bit false," perhaps it's because they sound the falsetto notes in the music of his text. And if those vocabulary strategies, those "linguistic interventions," sound deliberately forced or unreal, perhaps it is the result of their "reaching for heaven," their attempt to "reword history" in order to indict the "more insidious falseness" of Western criticism's presuppositions and categorizations. This linking of the upper registers and what Braxton calls "the upper partials," [136] this "pursuit of a meta-voice," may seem a touch fanciful, but Braxton would certainly agree that music has "an alchemical function," and he would not, I think, dispute that the language he uses to address this "transformative desire" is similarly alchemical in its volatile mix of the scientific and the mystical, its talking in tongues.

Near the end of Ishmael Reed's novel *Mumbo Jumbo*, PaPa LaBas (another of Legba's representatives) lectures on "the indefinable quality" in black music that James Weldon Johnson had dubbed "Jes Grew":

> Jes Grew, the Something or Other, that led Charlie Parker to scale the Everest of the Chord . . . that touched John Coltrane's tenor, that tinged the voice of Otis Redding. . . . Jes Grew was the manic in the artist who would rather do glossolalia than be "neat clean or lucid." . . . Jes Grew is the last liturgy seeking its litany. . . . Jes Grew was an influence which sought its text. . . . If it could not find its text then it would be mistaken for entertainment.[137]

Could Jes Grew have found its text in the Tri-axium Writings, with their glossolalia, their rewording of history as litany, their vehement insistence that black creativity should not be mistaken for mere entertainment? At the least, we can perhaps recognize Braxton in PaPa LaBas's description of himself as "a jacklegged detective of the metaphysical," and it is this acknowledgment of the meta-real that sets writers such as Braxton (and Mackey and Reed) apart from the majority of Western commentators on black music. Certainly it was Western journalism's misrepresentations of black music that prompted Braxton to begin work on the Tri-axium Writings in 1973: "it was only after reading 50,000 dumb reviews that I found myself thinking, hmmm . . . I disagree with the critics who even like my music!" [138]

It is to his critique of the critiquers that I would now like to turn. But to set the context, it is necessary first to outline—in extremely simplified and attenuated form—what Braxton calls his "underlying philosophical bases," that is, his concept of creativity as it pertains to what he regards as the three fundamental categories of music: world group musics, Western art musics, and trans-African musics. (I should warn readers who still equate profundity with basso that this is one of the more falsetto zones in the Tri-axium soundworld.)

— • • • ———

Tri-axium Writings, a text at the junction of real and meta-real, is also a dance at the crossroads of time. Braxton defines "Tri-axium" as "having to do with an attempt to gather axium tenets from the past and present —to get to the future," [139] a notion that makes clear the necessity of revising misrepresentations of the black past as a prerequisite for envisioning the future. In particular, an appreciation of the vibrational dimension of creativity is very important. Creativity, says Braxton, "has to do with 'doing' as a means to celebrate and 'affirm' the vibrational forms that dictate 'living.' "[140] Thus, music is not *about* music: "rather music, sculpture, dance, painting are connected to 'cosmic zones' ";[141] so, form and elements of form such as harmony and rhythm are linked to cosmic correspondences and what Braxton calls "the higher forces."[142] Such an understanding of creativity has, he says, long been a part of what he calls world culture groups, by which he appears to mean all cultures except the post-Enlightenment West. In the West, however, a despiritualization of society and the breakdown of traditional cultural verities during the last three hundred years have meant that Western music has become separate from world group music values and has developed according to purely intellectual, or what Braxton terms "existential," criteria—such as the expansion of its inner logic systems—rather than with regard to spiritual or "essence" factors.[143] This empiricism, which goes hand in glove with materialism and mechanistic science and which is part of the overall direction of Western civilization, has resulted in separation and specialization, in the elevation of the composer over the performer, and in an emphasis on technique and "correct" playing at the expense of creativity and improvisation.

The third category in Braxton's musical equation is trans-African musics. He argues that one consequence of slavery was that African musics transported to the United States found themselves in the anomalous position of being spiritually based musics aligned to world group values, but musics forced to exist within the confines of a materialistic Western society. For Braxton, it is this unique position from which African American music both derives its great potential (as an agent for the respiritualization of Western culture) and faces its greatest danger, because, he says, the music is (a) misdocumented by the Western media, which misjudge and misdefine it, using inappropriate Western aesthetic standards; and (b) misunderstood by the commercial sectors of Western society, which overlook its spiritual essence, distort its reality by appropriating its surface features as "style" and "spectacle," and try to make it conform to mainstream white cultural values, a process that Braxton calls "source transfer."

In T-*a* W 2 Braxton considers the relationship between creative music and what he names "the spectacle diversion syndrome," or "what America has rather than culture."[144] He argues that because of various historical factors, notably slavery and the virtual annihilation of Native Americans, the United States has developed a mainstream culture that is implicitly racist and peculiarly hostile to alternative value systems, especially those from within its own world culture minority groups. Mainstream culture, he says, values spectacle—what is of *interest*—over substance—what is of *use* for living; that is, it values entertainment rather than creativity. The spectacle diversion syndrome also interferes with what Braxton calls "affinity dynamics"; that is, the ways in which particular people and groups of people are aligned (or attracted) to different "principle information lines" (loosely translatable as ways of living and the knowledge encoded in such ways).[145] Because Western culture views itself as superior to other world cultures and because of the West's currently dominant position in global politics, it is both keen and able to distort and suppress world group information lines, subjecting them to the spectacle diversion syndrome (turning them into entertainment) and trying to realign their affinity dynamics, largely through control of the media and the power to "define terms." Since Western society is basically controlled by a small number of very rich white men, it is their value systems, their affinity dynamics, their concept of reality, that is considered the norm. This means that all other groupings—women, the poor, African Americans, white mystics, etc.—are constantly under threat; in particular, they have to struggle to affirm their histories, their terminologies, their very perception of themselves against the appropriation strategies of the dominant culture.

In the case of African Americans, their affinity dynamics are particularly under threat from two processes, one of which Braxton calls "gradualism," and the other of which he terms "the grand trade-off." Gradualism refers to the redefining of information in the interests of the redefiner (and thus is one of the chief means by which "source transfer" is effected). Braxton gives as examples the way that Egypt has been written out of the histories of classical Greece, and the white "takeovers" of ragtime, big band swing, and rock 'n' roll.[146] (By takeover here, he is referring to the way in which, for example, Benny Goodman rather than Count Basie or Duke Ellington, became known as "the King of Swing," how Elvis Presley rather than Chuck Berry or Little Richard was crowned "King of Rock 'n' Roll.")

"The grand trade-off" is Braxton's term for a particular mind-set prevalent in postslavery Western society:

> The "grand trade-off" is this: slowly but surely the collected
> forces of western culture have moved to solidify a viewpoint

concerning humanity that has nothing to do with anything but maintaining the present social and political "state of things." In this concept, black people are vibrationally viewed as being great tap dancers—natural improvisors, great rhythm, etc., etc., etc.— but not great thinkers, or not capable of contributing to the dynamic wellspring of world information. White people under this viewpoint have come to be viewed as great thinkers, responsible for all of the profound philosophical and technological achievements that humanity has benefitted from—but somehow not as "natural" as those naturally talented black folks.[147]

The grand trade-off is, says Braxton, one of the most ubiquitous underpinnings of white critical representations of black music. We saw evidence earlier of the grand trade-off in the fact that the *Shuffle Along* orchestra had to mimic improvisation. To recall Eubie Blake's explanation: "People didn't want to believe that black people could read music —they wanted to think that our ability was just natural talent."[148] A more sophisticated variation of the grand trade-off might be the belief that while black people *can* read music, their doing so somehow interferes with or negates their "natural talent." Such thinking is, I think, discernible in an article on the 1993 London Jazz Festival by *Financial Times* critic Garry Booth.[149] Booth sets up an opposition between a duo concert by Braxton and pianist Marilyn Crispell and a later gospel concert by the Five Blind Boys of Alabama. In the space of two short paragraphs, Booth twice pointedly links Braxton's music to mathematics (which I take as a means of signifying its "intellectual" content; on the second occasion, the phrase Booth uses is "mathematical *calculation*"—my emphasis), and each time he follows this reference with an image of musical disorder: scores spilling to the floor, the music "tumbl[ing] out in a great snowstorm of notes." Booth then alludes to mathematics a third time, calling the performance "as evocative as a book of logarithms," before concluding that Braxton's "abstract jazz," these "manic exchanges," "had no heart and did not swing." In contrast, Booth praises the Five Blind Boys' "combination of belief, unashamed sentimentality and showmanship" as "irresistible." One song, he writes, "left bottom lips trembling," another "had them dancing in the aisles"; this, he concludes is "what music ought to do."[150]

There could hardly be a more blatant statement of the grand trade-off belief that black music is all about dancing and feeling, while attempts to move into the more "abstract" areas represented by Braxton's presumed use of "mathematics" are portrayed as transgressive, as leading to mania and chaos, thus reinforcing a political "state of things" (the grand trade-off) that tries to portray itself as self-evidently true.[151] (Or, to recall Nathaniel Mackey's musings on Legba, this review can be seen as another example of Braxton's multiformity—his insistence on the heterogeneity of black culture—being misrepresented as deformity because it challenges the "biased coherence" of a "homogenous order given over to uniform rule" in which black performers are allowed to feel but not to count.)[152]

The result of the grand trade-off—that black creativity is permitted only within sanctioned "low culture zones"—has been engineered, says Braxton, so that Western society can avoid facing the full implications of slavery and the pillage of Africa: "Europeans have historically been interested in keeping black people in the 'exotica zone' as a means to not deal with the significance of Africa. It is important to understand that the mantle of 'black exotica' is not separate from the notion that black people are not thinking human beings and, as such, the raping of Africa was not a negative act toward a civilized people."[153] In this scenario white critics take on the role of guards patrolling the perimeter of black culture. Even Phil Woods's response to *For Alto* can be read as an instance of white outrage at black transgression.[154] Although Woods couches his criticisms chiefly in terms of Braxton's supposedly poor technique, what really seems to bother him is the audacity of the solo concept—as if the development of a solo saxophone music threatens to take the music out of the sanctioned zone: "I'm sure he hasn't studied the saxophone. This doesn't bother me, there's a lot of primitives that play and get a lot of exciting music; but this is such an ego trip that you think you're that much of a bitch that you can do a solo album."[155] Again, the implication could not be clearer: know your place. Either stay in the "primitive"/"exotic" zone or face the full fury of Eurocentric prejudice.

Braxton argues that the concept of "black exotica" can be traced back to the writings of Herodotus, though it was only with the Atlantic slave trade that such a notion became ubiquitous in Western culture. Once established, however, the concept, he says, has served to attract white people for a variety of reasons:

> Every period of black creativity has been used to outline some aspect of western spectacle diversion particulars—which is to say, western culture has long utilized black creativity as a lever

to invoke some aspect of its own desires—either with respect to spiritualism, sexuality, rebellion or to get individually or collectively rich. But, in every case, there has been no attempt by the western establishment to view black creativity, and/or its related information, on its own terms.[156]

Various other concepts that relate to the grand trade-off and to black exotica, Braxton claims, have been operating throughout the history of jazz journalism. The "across the tracks syndrome" he defines as being "the use of black creativity as a means to 'have a good time,' while also suppressing the dynamic implications of the music to accomplish that 'good time.' In this context black creativity is viewed as related to prostitution or the life of sensuality, and western culture is viewed as its opposite—that is, of high information and ethics."[157] The rich white socialites who flocked to the Cotton Club in the 1920s and 1930s exemplify the across-the-tracks syndrome, as do a host of later white critics and performers who viewed jazz as essentially good-time music and not only overlooked what Braxton calls its "vibrational dimension" but even remained unaware of its musical sophistication. I have cited Spike Hughes's celebration of Ellington's supposedly "lowdown" music as one instance of this syndrome; a more recent example would be George Melly's threat to "shit . . . from a great height" on people who take jazz too seriously.[158]

The across-the-tracks syndrome appertains most frequently to white perceptions of black music as representing sexuality and the physical. But, as Braxton notes, there are many varieties of "black exotica." The notion that free jazz can be equated with black political rage is, I think, another example of a similarly reductive stereotyping that fails to acknowledge the breadth and variety of both black experience and black expression. This mind-set, though most evident in the 1960s, persisted long enough to produce one extremely bizarre account of Braxton's music.

In 1977, at a time when Braxton's work had been variously attacked in the jazz press as being overintellectual and insufficiently "black," *Newsweek* reporter Hubert Saal declared of his compositions: "They speak of ghettos, humiliation and pride—in a language as ham-fisted as a street brawl."[159] The stereotyping here—Braxton equals black equals ghetto equals violence—seems so thoughtless as to vindicate Malcolm X's famous jibe about white racists: "Do you know what they call a black man with a PhD? *Nigger!*" Yet Saal's article is generally very complimentary in tone; the strange thing is he seems unable to express his liking for Braxton's music except in terminology that reflects the racial stereotyping of the grand trade-off and the across-the-tracks syndrome. Unlike the Booth article, in which the Five Blind Boys of Alabama were portrayed as representing the black exotica zone of feeling and Braxton's heartless "mathematical" music was seen as transgressive, Saal's "Two Free Spirits" piece contrasts Braxton's music with that of white pianist Keith Jarrett. Although a similar type of racial stereotyping is at work in both articles, Saal's piece portrays Braxton (and his "visceral sounds") in the black exotica role, while Jarrett (and his "melodic music") is discussed in terms uncannily reminiscent of those in which Braxton's music was being condemned by jazz critics at the time! (Saal, a Newsweek reporter, was possibly unacquainted with the details of the "internal debate" about Braxton in the specialist jazz press.) So it is Jarrett whose European influences are noted here (Scriabin and Schumann), whose music is characterized as "a cool world where no one laughs or cries," and aspects of whose work are variously described as "remote," "attenuated," and "arcane." In contrast, Saal hears no European traits in Braxton's music, only a tough-talking black vernacular. His compositions, says Saal: "speak of precursive black musicians such as John Coltrane and Ornette Coleman and black musical forms such as the blues and ragtime. They speak of ghettos, humiliation and pride—in a language as ham-fisted as a street brawl." [160] Saal is right to point out these black music influences, but his abrupt transformation of the bespectacled, pipe-smoking Braxton into this street-fighting Stagolee of the saxophone seems a mite excessive, to say the least.

Saal continues his article with another extraordinary description, this time of Braxton's playing:

> Braxton is a virtuoso on the saxophone, and the instrument has never been subject to such an assault. He squeezes out bizarre sounds and clashing, hitherto unheard tonal colors. He plays like a man possessed in a paroxysm of animalistic grunts, honks, rasps and hollers. He rends the fabric of conventional musical language as he reaches into himself—and back into prehistory—for some primordial means of communication. [161]

At first glance, this might seem like a more extreme and articulate version of Phil Woods's account of "primitives" who play "a lot of exciting music," itself an echo of Romantic and Modernist fascination with the primitive. Yet Saal does not simply label Braxton primitive; indeed, he begins the paragraph by stressing that Braxton is "a virtuoso on the saxophone." It is as if the culturally pervasive mind-set of the grand trade-off somehow prevents him from hearing this virtuosity as, say, an *advance on* or an *evolution of* (or even an *alternative to*) conventional musical language; instead, he can conceive of Braxton's playing only in the violent, primordial imagery appropriate to the "black exotica" zone. Despite this (or because of it—the across-the-tracks syndrome), Saal appears to prefer Braxton's music to Jarrett's, whose "musical results," he avers, "are limited." In contrast, Saal hails Braxton as "the most innovative force in the world of jazz." [162] The problem, it seems, is that in the "low culture zone" of jazz, this innovative force can only move "back into prehistory."

Saal's vivid and approving account of the physical intensity of Braxton's performance also partakes of another critical syndrome identified by Braxton. "The reality of the sweating brow" is his term for the critical prejudice that judges the worth and authenticity of black musical performances by assessing the display of effort and emotion involved. This viewpoint, he argues, is indicative of the mistaken Western emphasis on *how* something is played rather than on *what* is played, a focus linked in turn to the spectacle diversion syndrome and its obsession with surface particulars such as physicality and overt emotional intensity. These criteria, Braxton says, are rarely employed to the same degree when white music is under scrutiny; in such cases, while every performer is expected to have some degree of emotional involvement, "white people recognize that there is no one way to be emotional. . . . Some people are naturally demonstrative in their way of being, and other people are emotional in more subtle ways." [163] However, almost from the outset, jazz commentary has asserted a different line regarding black emotional dynamics:

> the idea that there is only one level of "involvement" by black people. . . .
>
> Jazz musicians are simply supposed to sweat—if they are serious, and this is especially the case after bebop solidified. Ensembles like the Modern Jazz Quartet have long been viewed from a distance—not because of the validity and beauty of their music, but because the dynamics of their involvement challenged the most sacred observation position that has emerged in black music commentary—that being the reality of the sweating brow. [164]

This "observation position" echoes the plantation viewpoint that blacks had to be seen to be working. I am reminded, too, of Roland Barthes's essay on the Joseph L. Mankiewicz film of *Julius Caesar* (1953), in which Barthes points out that the characters are always depicted as sweating as a sign of mental turmoil.[165] Such a sign, he argues, is duplicitous since "it presents itself at once as intentional and irrepressible, artificial and natural, manufactured and discovered."[166] What Braxton claims is that the process can be reversed, that jazz critics can *demand* sweat as proof of authenticity, and they can even define authenticity in terms of sweat. (Barthes also notes that "it is both reprehensible and deceitful to confuse the sign with what is signified.")[167]

The reality of the sweating brow, or rather the lack of it in Braxton's performances, is a subtext that runs through the comments above of Giddins, Stern, and Booth; perhaps it was expressed most unequivocally by Scott Albin in a 1976 *Down Beat* review of a Braxton quartet concert in New York City:

> Braxton is a studied player who always seems to be self-consciously holding back. He is a great technician, as eager to display his virtuosity as he is loathe [*sic*] to reveal—and therefore include—his deepest emotions in his playing . . . one must respect his musicianship, but his rhythmically stunted, introspective, impersonal, and uninspiring playing is altogether unsatisfying. Except for two sopranino solos . . . during which he showed off his formidable technique, *as well as* some inner, human feeling, Braxton's playing was less than good.[168]

Is it little wonder that Braxton regards jazz journalism as a farce? Criticized by Woods and Watrous for being technically inept, here he is criticized by Albin for displaying *nothing* but his "virtuosity" and "formidable technique"! And where Saal heard a player reaching inside himself in animalistic paroxysms to rend the fabric of convention, Albin portrays a performer so studied and introspective that he seems unlikely even to snag his cardigan. In all of these cases, adjectives and prejudices are scattered like confetti, with virtually no attempt to address Braxton's music on its own terms or even to consider what those terms might be.

Braxton identifies two further critical concepts that he says are widely misapplied to black music: "the concept of the good night" and "the concept of non-sequenced credibility." Both are examples of the Western practice of analyzing and judging aspects of music in isolation. Focusing on a player's good or bad night, or even a good or bad solo, is, says Braxton, "an observation criterion that dismisses the composite reality of [the] music" of the performer in question: "'the concept of the good night' is really a way to keep from acknowledging the wholeness of a given individual's offering, as well as a means to keep black musicians (or anyone functioning in that medium) in the position of being 'boys' whose viewpoints and contributions can continually be subjected to either harassment or unnecessary challenges—even by seventeen to thirty year old white jazz critics."[169] "The concept of non-sequenced credibility" refers to the critical expectation that a jazz musician has to prove his or her credentials at every performance, irrespective of past achievements or peer status. I mentioned this concept when discussing Ira Gitler's attacks on Coltrane's 1961 "Chasin' the Trane" recording, and I quoted Braxton's conclusion that "Black artists of the highest order—people who have undoubtedly contributed to the composite reality of black creativity—are daily written of as if they are 'on the auction block' or something."[170]

Mention of the auction block makes explicit the references to slavery hinted at in Braxton's description of black musicians being treated like "boys" and his use of terms such as "the sweating brow." It is as if he is evoking an image of black creative music as a plantation, with the critics as overseers who lay down the rules, make sure people work and sweat, and (verbally) lash anyone who transgresses, especially those caught reading (scores). This may seem an extreme metaphor for a history of jazz journalism, but I think it is fair to say that Braxton does see current critical definitions of jazz as enslaving the creative imagination. As he told me in 1985, "they're defining jazz in such a way that *you cannot do your best* . . . . They have it defined now where, if you think of writing a piece for 500 saxophones, you're looked at as having nothing to do with jazz."[171] Further decrying the way that jazz had been "framed in a little box" and how the idea of tradition had become so rigidified that "if you don't follow in someone else's footsteps . . . then you're automatically excommunicated," he proceeded to underline the Tri-axium Writings argument that critical definitions of jazz are a form of bondage fueled by racial—and racist—considerations:

> "jazz" is the word that's used to delineate the parameters that African-Americans are allowed to function in, a "sanctioned" zone. That's what "jazz" is. "Jazz" is the name of the political system that controls and dictates African-American information

dynamics (and also the European or trans-European information dynamics that come in that particular zone). . . .

But the whole thing is . . . I mean, it's taken for granted that a European or European-American jazz musician has borrowed some aspects of African-American language: why should it be such a big thing that I've learned from Europe? I'm a human being, just like Ronnie Scott or Derek Bailey. Why is it so natural for Evan Parker, say, to have an appreciation of Coltrane, but for me to have an appreciation of Stockhausen is somehow out of the natural order of human experience? I see it as racist.[172]

The critics' reductive and exclusionary view of "jazz" is totally opposed to the openness that Braxton sees as characteristic of trans-African musics, an openness that encompasses individual expression, the exigencies of the moment, and, not least, outside influences. "You can assimilate other cultures freely; that's always been a part of trans-African musics, the ability to assimilate anything that happens around you and put it in your music. If we lose that, we lose a very important component."[173] If this notion of an essential antiessentialism strikes us as paradoxical, it also places Braxton's view of black music in close proximity to that of Ellington ("Jazz means simply the freedom to have many forms"), to Paul Gilroy's idea of an anti-antiessentialism, and to Amiri Baraka's concept of a "changing same."[174] Braxton's resistance to any kind of putative closure, even that of an affirmative "authenticity," is perhaps best summed up in his *T-a W 3* statement that "jazz criticism can be reduced to attempts to make a reality out of a process that has to do with 'becoming.' "[175]

Against this fixative reality—what Nathaniel Mackey called "biased coherence" and "homogenous order" and Sun Ra dismissed as a "manufactured past"—Braxton posits a black creative tradition that is multiform, heterogenous, and open-ended. As are the *Tri-axium Writings*, with their various languages, perspectives, and colors. As, too, is Braxton's music, with its different kinds of structures, its varieties of tempo and timbre, its embrace of registers from contrabass to sopranino. The African American composer Olly Wilson has argued that one of the "underlying conceptions that defines African-American music" is what he calls "the heterogenous sound ideal": "By this term, I mean there exists a common approach to music making in which a kaleidoscopic range of dramatically contrasting qualities of sound (timbre) is sought after in both vocal and instrumental music. The desirable musical sound texture is one that contains a combination of diverse timbres."[176] Wilson adds that this heterogeneity is observable both in the "sound textures of musical ensembles" and in the use of "a wide range of timbres within a single line," especially when that line is a vocal or instrumental solo.[177] I think Braxton's music clearly embraces this ideal and, characteristically, *extends* its celebration of the heterogenous into all facets of music-making.[178]

In his notes to *Composition 82* for four orchestras, Braxton relates his interest in multiorchestra pieces to a childhood love of parade musics, particularly the sounds heard at those events where several bands would march along all playing different tunes: "It is as if the whole of the universe were swallowed up—leaving us in a sea of music and color."[179] Braxton hopes to effect this phenomenon literally—he has already mapped out a series of compositions to be played by orchestras on different planets and in different galaxies. Meanwhile, the image of the universe as a sea of music and color informs "the heterogenous sound ideal" of his own music—he writes in the Introduction to his *Catalogue of Works* that all of his compositions can be performed together at the same time, "as one state of being. . . . This option is the aesthetic/conceptual/vibrational fulfillment of my music."[180]

This image also represents his vision of the transformative potential of trans-African music—a force able to swallow the universe. No wonder, then, he repudiates the critics' view of this tradition as something to be "framed in a little box" and merely replicated. In his eyes, in his performances, the tradition is still in the process of becoming, is a dance between the moment and the stars.

More than that, it is a place to address the "challenge of tomorrow," which, for Braxton, "is directly related to whether all of the children of this planet can realize their potential." Music, with its entries into the meta-real, is the ideal site for these children to dream the "'great dreams' that motivate dynamic participation," and to seize the opportunity offered by Legba, "the ultimate master of potentiality," to be all the things you are.[181]

6 Going to the Territory: Sound Maps of the Meta-Real

As slaves they had long been aware that for themselves, as for most of their countrymen, geography was fate. —*Ralph Ellison*[1]

I noted earlier that Braxton defines "Tri-axium" as "having to do with attempts to gather axium tenets from the past and present—to get to the future."[2] The urgency of this project is underlined by *T-a W 3*'s closing chapter, which concerns "transformation" and sets out Braxton's belief that Western civilization's period of global dominance, which began with the rise of ancient Greece, is now coming to an end (the beginning of this end signaled by the West's post-Enlightenment loss of a spiritual center).[3] Whether this transformation happens sooner or later, whether it is a time of hope and celebration or of cataclysmic disaster, is, says Braxton, partly to do with "cosmic forces," but it may also be affected by how well-prepared and responsible humanity proves to be. Consequently, much of his later music—notably the "ritual and ceremonial" series of compositions—addresses the issue of preparing for the future.

In his notes to 1980's *Composition 95*, the first of the ritual and ceremonial works, he explains:

> By the terms ritual and ceremonial music, I am saying that the meta-reality dynamics of Composition No. 95 were conceived with extra-vibrational intentions—having to do with my belief that the challenge of transformational creativity in this time cycle must involve "postulation" as related to both world culture and its extended "all spiritual" dictates . . . . My original intention when composing this work was that I sensed and felt that the next

immediate cycle in social reality promises to be extremely difficult — *and there is danger in the air* for all people and forces concerned about Humanity and positive participation. Composition No. 95 is composed as a vehicle to alert the spirit about serious change.[4]

For Braxton, postulation as related to world culture and its spiritual dictates involves the reintegration of music with other facets of creativity, including color and shape as part of the notation along with gesture, dance, costume, and "constructed environments" (stage sets, lighting, etc.) as elements of the performance. In some recent compositions, storytelling, too, has become an integral aspect of the work, either in the form of a written story printed with the CD insert notes (as with *Compositions 147, 151,* and *165*) or as a vocal component of the music itself, either sung and/or spoken (as with *Compositions 171, 173, 174,* and *175*). As I mentioned in chapter 5, a particularly intriguing twist to these stories is that Braxton locates them within his music system, which since the late 1980s he has been talking of in spatial terms, as a fantasy world comprising twelve "city-state" regions.[5] Each region is named after one of the twelve major characters in the *Trillium* operas (Alva, Ashmenton, Bubba John Jack, David, Helena, Joreo, Kim, Ntzockie, Ojuwain, Shala, Sundance, Zackko), each of whom in turn "corresponds" to one of the twelve major "Language Types" that make up the foundation of Braxton's music.[6] But the story-compositions are also populated by "local characters." In *165*, for example, two boys, Ben and Johnathon, lose their way in a forest and consult the score of the composition, which they call a "sound map," in order to find their bearings.

In 1993 Braxton explained the idea:

> In the city-state analogy, then, using my tri-partial model, I will build — as far as the stable logics are concerned — a system of tracks, like a giant choo-choo train system that will show the connections, so where a soloist is moving along a track, that will connect to duo logics, trio logics, quartet logics. So, for instance, if you're travelling from "Composition 47," which is a small town, to a city like "Composition 96," the model will demonstrate the nature of combinations and connections in between systems. The mutable logics manifestation of this same construct will involve improvisation, moving through the hills in a mutable way as opposed to the fixed paths of the stable logics. And the synthesis logics will be those points of connection between

mutable and stable logics, based on the identity and particulars of the terrain or composition. As such, a given sonic occurrence will be . . . there'll be local events, territorial events, national events and there'll be individual events. In the same way that New York State has its own laws, Texas has its own laws, but there are highways connecting them. And meanwhile the individual living in Texas has his or her own life. . . .

There are local characters, who inhabit the particular regions. It's like being in the state of Illinois and meeting some of the people in that region. We have to respect the local inhabitants.[7]

By 1995, what began as a geographical analogy had expanded into something like an interactive virtual reality:

I've begun to think more in terms of spatial dimension as a context that can be mapped.

There are several aspects to it. Mapping in the sense of compositions that can help me begin to map the parameters of local space environments, to city-state environments, to continental mappings, to planet mappings. So, for instance, Composition 174 is the beginning of mapping of gradient logics, the mapping of a mountain. My hope is—whether or not it's ever realized, I may not have the money to really do it—I am going to build a three-dimensional tricentric world experience that will be manifested on many levels. For one, I'd like to have a kind of park community, like Disneyland, for the family, for the individual experiencer . . . who wants to get away from work for a couple of days . . . and have some fun in a three-dimensional domain where there will be different kinds of experience; maybe go with three or four friends to Garthstone Castle.[8]

Garthstone Castle is the location for Composition 175, which exemplifies in a small way (it "maps" the interior of a castle) the spatial dimension into which Braxton's work is expanding. The characters Kim and Helena, fleeing from "the evil Count Zargon," stumble into Garthstone Castle and proceed to explore its various rooms, finally uncovering its "secret treasure" of gold.[9] During the course of the composition, they are beset by "images of ghosts and dragons," the "sounds of chains rattling," dancing suits of armor, and voices that shout "BOO! BOO! BOO! BOO! BOO! BOO!" Other voices guide them through the music system/castle, while the two women discuss (in song) the likely whereabouts of the canteen, the possibility of buying souvenirs, and the similarities between certain of the rooms and scenes from old horror films: " 'I've seen those sets before in a Boris Karloff movie,' said Helena." Braxton's gleeful parodies of popular culture are also a feature of *Trillium E*, where his well-known enthusiasm for science fiction and monster films is put to sharp satirical use; in *175* the humor seems less pointed, more a way of showing that moving through a musical structure can, like exploring an old castle, be fun, even (or especially) if there are a few frights along the way. As Kim says at the outset: "There's nothing like a scary castle story to demonstrate the dynamic possibilities of tri-centric modelling."

Such spatialization and narrative have long been present as metaphor in Braxton's music. In *Composition 3* "the listener is asked to journey through the music in the sense of a trip in time or space."[10] Section A of *Composition 23N* "was conceived as a fairy tale type sound environment";[11] *Composition 40L* "is an idea that materialized — 'so that one can literally walk through the rooms of the music' ";[12] *Composition 69(O)* "is a universe of different music types that come together like a 'suite' of interrelated 'stories.' "[13] What is new about the more recent story-compositions is simply the degree to which metaphor has been actualized and integrated into the music, part of that process "from the abstract to the concrete" that Braxton says characterizes his work of the last decade or so. What has also become more concrete, or at least more evident, is the paradox implicit in Braxton's repeated references to his compositions as both "vehicles" *and* "territories," as if, like cyberspace, you create the soundscape by moving through it — an echo of Sidney Bechet's notion that the music creates a "place" that exists for as long as the music is being played.[14] (These changes can be seen as part of the ritualization of the music: ideas previously left implicit are now "enacted.")[15] Another new facet, however, is the mapping that has accompanied this spatialization — a mapping that is as much a representation of Braxton's music system as it is of his compositions' imaginary geography — and the numerous "map references" that occur in the more recent stories and music-texts seem to work as coded directions on how to move through the music. As Kim says in *175*: "Gee, it's great to have G compass series strategies for fresh navigation routes into the system of the music."

The most extensive example of this mapping to date is probably *Composition 171*, which is subtitled "Forest Ranger Crumpton Maps the Tri-

State Region," and which includes four large maps as part of its "constructed environment." (These maps, in color, are also included in the score; see Appendix: B.)[16] The composition—"for solo pianist/actor, 1/4 prompters, four actors, and constructed environment"—takes the form of a press conference at which Forest Ranger Crumpton (the solo pianist/actor) talks about "the southwest national park systems" as they relate to the "tri-state region" comprising Joreo Land, Shala Land, and Ashmenton Land. The onstage maps represent these three areas (a fourth map covers the composite region), with various routes detailed in different colors. During the course of the press conference, as Forest Ranger Crumpton refers to the various routes, these are indicated on the maps by the prompter, using a long pointer. The following two extracts from the libretto show how closely Braxton interweaves his music system with his imagined geography and how well he grounds this fantasy world in mundane and often humorous detail. (The speaker is Forest Ranger Crumpton.)

> Traveling on the roads can be rough if the truck drivers are out—especially at night. A trajectory in this context could outline the nature of interaction dynamics—depending on the feature of the country or region. With the right composition a given traveler can have a great time—that's why the maps are so important! Why, with very little effort, the seasoned traveller can conduct a tour/trajectory experience that might conclude at the wine-tasting vineyards near the coast. Try routes 3k, 7p, and 7s and bend to the left at the double FF Junctions. The construction teams working on paths 23 and 52 should be finished by next month with a little luck. . . .
>
> Swimming in the central district has always been a source of great fun and beauty. Mutable logics in this context involve the nature of blending and apparent transformation—from one identity to the next. I hear that the Olympics are considering the northern sector of the state for the next time cycle—after all we do have four gold medal winners here. Follow paths 6c, 50, 3a to the combination junctures and move on out past the manufacturing districts (near McDonald's) and pull on out towards the garment district. Principle [sic] correspondence points in this region can be located at the triangle sign points—when construction is completed in May our highway system will be the best—believe me, you'll love the beaches in this area.

Composition *171* is also the first piece to use what Braxton calls "three dimensional notation," in which a tripartite system of signs (rect-angles, circles, triangles) is added to the regular score.[17] These signs each indicate a variety of options that the performer can take, includ-ing, for example, changes of tempo, timbre, body position, lighting, or the act of pausing to drink a glass of water. The triangles can also denote the possibility of switching to a different composition, or even the option that "you might want to have five days by yourself."[18] Brax-ton certainly tries to ensure that the "friendly experiencer" who enters his music system is able to move freely in any direction and exit vir-tually at will.

Though the *171* libretto hints at corruption within the park admin-istration, the basically utopian impulse behind Braxton's fantasy world is suggested by his comments.

> Of course, in every experience, I'm not talking of anything dan-gerous or negative that would involve hurting people. I'm not interested in that. It's not that I want to disrespect that, but if I'm going to build me an imaginary space, I want to build one that would be consistent with what I've learned from people like Buckminster Fuller or Walt Disney.[19] Something for men and women and children, where they can go and have a positive, ex-citing experience and no one will get hurt. And where certain qualities will be asked for, before the person can have the defined experience; qualities involving just principal constructs, kind of like the Negative Confessions.[20]

(According to African American writer Yosef ben-Jochannan, the Neg-ative Confessions were an ancient Egyptian code of ethics that pre-figured the Ten Commandments.)[21] This reference to a kind of ethical screening brings to mind the world of the spirituals, with their evo-cations of heaven and frequent admonitions that sinners will not be allowed entry. There are similarities too between Braxton's "imaginary space" and what we might call the symbolic geography and architec-ture of the slaves' sacred realm. Braxton's twelve-state fantasy world could be said to have "12 gates" and certainly has "many mansions";[22] it may not be too fanciful to hear in *174*'s "mapping of a mountain" a distant echo of the spiritual "We Are Climbing the Hills of Zion."[23]

At least one instance of a striking resemblance between a Braxton composition and a particular spiritual goes beyond a shared symbolic geography. This resemblance can be seen in the story that accompanies *Composition 165* and the spiritual "Down in the Valley." Especially intriguing is that Braxton's story, with its sequence of sin, repentance, divine grace, and redemption, could almost be read as a Baptist conversion testimony. First, though, here are the relevant lines from "Down in the Valley":

De lightin' and de flashin' [x3]
    Jesus set poor sinners free

I can't stand the fire [x3]
    Jesus set poor sinners free

De green trees a-flamin' [x3]
    Jesus set poor sinners free

    Way down in the valley
        Who will rise and go with me?
    You've been heern talk of Jesus
        Who set poor sinners free.[24]

In the *165* story, set in "the great valley conclave in Norfolk,"[25] two teenage boys, Ben and Johnathon, ignore the calls of Ben's mother and run off into the forest for the day. As evening draws in, a great storm blows up, "accompanied by patches of lightning" and the boys lose their way. The text then appears to hint at the possibility of their going to Hell as they arrive at an unfamiliar crossroads: "'I think it's this way,' said Ben—'but I don't remember that fork in the road!' 'Come on, man,' said Johnathon, 'you know what the legend says about this forest at night—let's not play around with this.'" As "the trees are now on fire" and as the ground threatens to open up beneath them—"poooooooooooooooooooooow!—(a side of the mountain has crashed to the ground)"—Ben gives voice to feelings of repentance and what could be read as a desire to be "born again": "'Maybe we should have done our share of the work, Johnathon, instead of running off like this—maybe this is what happens when you get off the correct path—(which for us was path 37 moving into corridors A and MM respectively) if only we could start over, if only we could begin anew.'" Though the forest "is now filled with smoke and fire," Ben reaffirms his faith—"'there's something out there, I tell you'"—and Johnathon reiterates his friend's "born-again" sentiment: "'if only I could start over again.'" Moments later, the two boys are given a sign of divine grace, which appears in the heavens: "as the banks of the river begin to give, a sonic cloud formation opens up a 'light' in the forest." Though initially struck by terror—"'What does this mean?' cried Ben, 'maybe it's over for us. Head for the hills . . . run for your life!'"—Ben begins to realize what is happening and, in a moment of illumination (the flash, perhaps, of spiritual rebirth?), he finds his way again. "Ben suddenly pulls out the score of Composition No. 165 and turns on his flashlight. 'Here we are on the "sound map," Johnathon,' said Ben." With divine grace now guiding them—"Suddenly, the cloud configuration has lighted the only path back home for our heroes"[26]—the boys head out of the valley toward their waiting friends and the story closes on a note of "hope and redemption": "As the two boys climbed back into the PRINCIPLE SONIC LANES, it was still possible to hear Ben talking— 'Thanks to the cosmics for the experience of living and for the ability to make a mistake and be forgiven—and even helped! Thank heaven for hope and redemption. The phenomenon of manifestation is the greatest gift of all.'"

While there is humor in this story, it does not have the parodic tone of 175, and the sentiments that Ben expresses at the end are, I think, meant to be taken at face value. Composition 165 is a Braxtonian redemption song. Braxton is not a Christian—which is why the boys are saved by "the cosmics" rather than by Jesus—but he did attend a Baptist church as a child (and sang in the choir), so he does have some knowledge of Baptist theology and symbolism. He has also said: "My mother didn't go to church that much but she was a real Christian kind of person and I was grounded in that way of looking at things."[27] Nevertheless, he writes in T-a W 2 that "I am not much in agreement with the religious particulars of the last two thousand five hundred years," argues in T-a W 3 that "transformation involves not only a re-examination of our relationship with the spiritual aspects of existence but also the formulation of 'new gods,'" and suggests in a 1995 interview that the world is in desperate need of "a theology for the third millennium."[28] It appears that for Braxton, as for Sun Ra, the Christian church and Christian values are limited and inadequate in the face of the changes and challenges of contemporary life. Yet his concern with spiritual issues, evident in 165, suggests that Braxton's work (like Sun Ra's) is fundamentally in accord with the black musical continuum initiated by the spirituals—a continuum in which the music, to recall Sidney Bechet's striking metaphor, creates *a place*, where "My people . . . can be people."[29]

Perhaps the most resonant general similarity between Braxton's imagined space and the slaves' sacred realm is the metaphor of travel or motion. I referred in chapter 5 to John F. Szwed's comparison of figures of motion in Braxton's diagram titles and those present in African American yard art; to Szwed's list of ladders, wheels, tires, boats, bicycles, cars and trucks, highways and railroads in Braxton's titles, we can add skis, water skis, horses, helicopters, and airplanes. The importance of this travel theme in Braxton's work is confirmed by the settings and stories of his compositions: 113 takes place on a railway station and on a train; 132 involves two ships; 151 takes the form of a car chase; 173 is set in an airport; 174 is about climbing a mountain.[30] To the slaves, a people initially displaced and then confined, freedom of movement had a particularly powerful attraction, so much so that the spirituals speak not only of traveling to heaven but then of traveling *around* in it: "When I get to heaven, goin' to put on my shoes, goin' to walk all over God's heaven."[31] Compare as well the figures of motion in Braxton's titles with those found traversing the spirituals' sacred landscapes: Jacob's ladder, Ezekiel's wheel, golden slippers, angels' wings, ships of Zion, trains to glory, chariots flying through the air.[32] The ring shout itself, central arena for the performance of the spirituals, may at times have been a symbolic march to freedom, the slaves enacting "the children of Israel following Moses out of Egypt" and into the Promised Land.[33] (This perhaps brings a new resonance to Braxton's well-known love of marches, particularly in view of a comment such as: "Too often, we tend to wrongly perceive of march music as a negative projection that must necessarily be associated with militarism or disturbance—rather than as a positive spirit indicator that has the power to motivate involvement.")[34]

The wider historical context for African American concern with movement, and the importance of a knowledge of geography, has been outlined by Ralph Ellison in his essay "Going to the Territory":

> As slaves they had long been aware that for themselves, as for most of their countrymen, geography was fate. Not only had they observed the transformation of individual fortune made possible by westward movement along the frontier, but the Mason-Dixon line had taught them the relationship between geography and freedom. They knew that to be sold down the Mississippi River usually meant that they would suffer a harsher form of slavery. And they knew that to escape across the Mason-Dixon line northward was to move in the direction of a greater freedom. But

freedom was also to be found in the West of the old Indian Territory. Bessie Smith gave voice to this knowledge when she sang of "Goin' to the Nation, Going to the Terr'tor'," and it is no accident that much of the symbolism of our folklore is rooted in the imagery of geography. For the slaves had learned through the repetition of group experience that freedom was to be obtained through geographical movement, and that freedom required one to risk his life against the unknown. And geography as a symbol of the unknown included not only places, but conditions relating to their racially defined status and the complex mystery of a society from which they'd been excluded.[35]

If the chariot had once been the favored mode of transport through the slaves' sacred realm, it seems later to have been replaced by the more mundane but tangible train. Railroads had a double metaphorical significance for the slaves: as a means of transport to heaven, and, underground, as a way to freedom in Canada and the North. Szwed has noted the train's importance as an icon in African American and American cultures, where "railroads bring Euro-American and Anglo-Christian symbolism (think of country music's hellbound trains or Nathaniel Hawthorne's 'Celestial Railway' [sic]) into conjunction with African-American images of optimism and earthly escape. (Black railroads, however, run underground, as well as on the surface and elevated to the skies.)"[36] Both Szwed and Heffley have remarked on Braxton's childhood attraction to trains—model and real (his father Clarence worked in Chicago's railroad yards)[37]—and in recent years Braxton has often employed railway metaphors to describe aspects of his music—individual scores, his quartet music's coordinate scheme, the "stable logics" component of his total music system.[38] What Braxton tends to emphasize in using these metaphors are the *connections*, the chances to *switch tracks*, reminding us that Legba is a god of the railway intersection no less than a god of the crossroads.

This context—a black mythology of crossroads and freedom trains —helps us to understand Braxton's obsessive crisscrossing of his imaginary space with metaphorical routes, paths, and highways, and to see it in a positive light, as a way of opening up his sonic universe to an unrestricted freedom of movement and, route-wise, of offering a proliferation of directions and options that can be seen as representing a multiform, heterogenous order of travel—because who knows in which direction, or how far, you might need to travel before you find your freedom or realize your potential. (On the importance of planning your route, and the need for new metaphysical maps, see Charles Mingus's advice to Fats Navarro on how to find God:

> "*All right, Fats.* If you're going to California from New York and you know California exists, you don't guess all over the place. You look up what direction it's in and then you find where it is on the map."
>
> "They got road maps to Heaven?"
>
> "I got one, but you gotta make your own. Unless you get out a pencil and pick what you think is the best route you're not about to get there from looking at New York City and jumping your eyes to California, no matter what kind of imagination you got. And as for the place you're talking about, the few maps available are so old and strangely translated that you can't expect intelligent human beings to try to use the kind they been selling.")[39]

I began this chapter by looking at Braxton's notion of "transformation" and his attempts to prepare people for this change with the ritual and ceremonial series of compositions. Any "tool for transformation," he writes in T-a W 3, must function "in accordance with the cosmic and vibrational principles of justice (not just the word),"[40] and "cosmic justice," he avers in T-a W 2, lies "at the heart of transformation."[41] This appeal to justice allied to transformation suggests a final echo of the spirituals, namely, the evocation of Judgment Day in a work such as "My Lord, What a Morning."[42] Indeed, Braxton's uncertainty as to whether transformation heralds triumph or tragedy is reflected in the alternative spelling of the spiritual's title, "My Lord, What a Mourning" (though the implication in both Tri-axium and the spiritual is that those who adhere to cosmic justice are likely to fare better than those who flout it). Such ethical concerns are part of the "meta-reality dimension" that Braxton sees as characteristic of black (and world) musics and they represent another reason why he views Western criticism's emphasis on the technical as so mistaken.

These issues were given voice on his debut recording, 3 Compositions of New Jazz, the notes to which open with a Braxton quotation to the effect: "We're on the eve of the complete fall of Western ideas and life-values. We're in the process of developing more meaningful values and our music is a direct extension of this." The same notes close with another Braxton quotation: "You are your music. If you try to vibrate towards the good, that's where your music will come from."[43] Braxton later extended this sentiment to include music's ethical influence over the listener, too: "What you hear and how you organise and unify, in terms of how you hear, is very important to who you are."[44]

It is no surprise, then, that Braxton has said one intention behind his use of collage forms is "to aid understanding and unification,"[45] the idea being that people learn how to listen to, and share the space with, others, while maintaining their independence. Braxton is making no special claims for his music: he sees such concerns as characteristic of the African American tradition. "Black music is a spiritual music," he states in T-a W 3, and its place at the center of black culture "has to do with how a given form transmits the moral and ethical implications that it celebrates — either through 'doing' or 'experiencing.' "[46] I guess that the best-known example of this assertion is what we might call black music's exploration of democratic form — from call-and-response to the heterophony of free jazz. The history of jazz in particular is the history of continuing attempts to effect and negotiate (in response to social change) an equable balance between the individual and the collective, freedom of expression and responsibility to the group. One reason why Braxton's work embraces so many different structural forms is because he is keen to explore every facet of such relationships (and, perhaps, to demonstrate in a variety of contexts that people working together, supporting each other, can be both effective and fun). As bassist Mark Dresser has said about performing Braxton's music: "There are a lot of beautiful implications to it. People being independent but working together. I mean, it's a wonderful formula, it has social ramifications that are very beautiful."[47]

— • • • ———

That the spirituals anticipate Judgment Day or that Braxton's music looks toward the "cosmic justice" of transformation can hardly be counted a surprise, given the conspicuous lack of earthly justice in so much of African American history. (Indeed, Braxton once explained his attraction to chess by declaring that, for him, the chessboard represented "a just universe.")[48] The materialism of a Western society that has lost its spiritual center and is blind to the requirements of cosmic justice is a topic that Braxton addresses at length on a philosophical level in the Tri-axium Writings, but for a more graphic and savagely satirical portrayal of "Western ideas and life-values" we must turn to the Trillium operas. Of crucial importance in Braxton's oeuvre, the Trillium operas are both a culmination of the ritual and ceremonial works and an integral link between the story-compositions (whose city-state regions are named after the twelve major *Trillium* characters) and the *Tri-axium Writings*, whose abstract arguments they concretize in a series of "fantasy" scenarios.

Before looking more closely at these fantasies, we need to briefly consider the inception and development of the operas in order to understand the particular forms they have taken. Braxton initially planned *Trillium* as a series of thirty-six one-act operas that could be re-shuffled in any order to comprise twelve three-act opera performances (his hope being that one three-act performance would cap each day of a twelve-day festival of world culture). The first two operas that he wrote adhered to this scheme: both *Trillium—Dialogues A* (1984) and *Trillium—Dialogues M* (1986) are one-act operas, each divided into four scenes.[49] With the subsequent two operas, however, the plan began to go awry. *Trillium R* (1991) and *Trillium E* (1997) followed the same four-part format, but they turned out to be so long that Braxton decided to redesignate each scene as an act—so, technically, *Trillium R* and *Trillium E* each comprise four one-act operas.[50] Despite this anomaly, all four *Trillium* librettos to date have been written according to the same conceptual framework. That is, *Trillium A, M, R,* and *E* each address a specific concept taken from the *Tri-axium Writings* (*A*: transformation; M: value systems; R: attraction; E: principle information), and each is divided into four parts (whether regarded as scenes or acts), each part in turn being intended to illustrate a particular schematic from the *Tri-axium Writings* that relates to the main topic of the opera. (The schematics, liberally scattered through the *Tri-axium Writings*, are graphic diagrams that aim to depict how the concepts discussed in the text relate to each other.)[51] For example, the schematic for act 1 of *Trillium E* appears in the libretto as the coded abbreviation (R)PRI-INFO———INFO.DY.[52] Checking in the *Tri-axium Writings'* glossary of abbreviations, we can decode this phrase as indicating that the act has to do with the reality of principle information—(R)PRI-INFO—as it relates to information dynamics—INFO.DY. Similarly, the schematic for scene 2 of *Trillium M* reads V-SY———POL-DY, which, decoded, indicates that the scene is about the relationship between value systems and political dynamics.

The schematics, then, act as philosophical blueprints for the *Trillium* operas: they lay out the particular sets of abstract ideas that Braxton then attempts to make concrete by dressing each schematic in the clothes of a "fantasy" story. My concern here, however, is not with the schematics, but with the fantasies that Braxton has chosen to illustrate them and enact them, since I believe this level is the one on which his views about Western society are most clearly discernible. In the account of the operas that follows, I attempt a broad overview rather than a detailed analysis of individual librettos, and I focus on similarities rather than differences, a perspective that inevitably results in oversimplification.[53]

One final point requires clarification. Braxton's concept of characterization is unusual:

> Trillium is not a platform for conventional storytelling in the classic sense of Italian and German opera. Rather, the work is constructed as a series of dialogues . . . [that comprise] four (or more) scenes in which the characters act out a series of skits or situation particulars. Each skit serves as a vehicle to elaborate on the variables of given philosophical associations. What this means is that a given character in Trillium will be called upon to portray the "forces" of a given "setting" as opposed to functioning as a separate entity (with his or her own separate identity). As such, in one scene a given character might have the role of a positive character (of whatever persuasion) and in the next scene that same character may portray something completely different. . . . What this means is that the reality of storytelling in Trillium transcends any one focus or plane of definitions. To experience this effort is to enter into a multiple universe of feelings and particulars.[54]

The character that Shala represents in Trillium M, then, is not the same character that Shala represents in Trillium R, and the Shala in Trillium R, act 1, is not the same Shala who appears in Trillium R, act 3 (and both are different from the Shala in act 4). Individual psychology is clearly not a primary focus in Trillium; the "forces" that Braxton asks his characters to portray are in the social domain—ethical, political, spiritual—and the "situation particulars" that his characters enact are largely to do with the interplay of these forces in given fantasy contexts. To these fantasies I would now like to turn.

Trillium M has the subtitle "Joreo's Vision of Forward Motion," and its diagram title shows a figure barring the way of two other figures at what looks like a border checkpoint.[55] The theme of exclusion is introduced in the opening lines of the libretto in this exchange between Joreo and Ashmenton:

> Joreo: I'm sorry, sir! You are not qualified to enter here. There are
> no records of your history that we can find or support. This
> has always been the case with you people.
>
> Ashmenton: My history is documented for all to see—in fact you
> have greatly benefitted from our relationship.[56]

The implicit racial connotations of this exchange—I read it as a dialogue between mainstream White America and marginalized Black
America—are expanded later in the scene, notably when David, one
of Joreo's allies, speaks to Ashmenton and refers to what sounds very
much like the histories of jazz and jazz journalism as detailed in the
Tri-axium Writings: "I understand now how it works, and I've duplicated
every note you've ever created, I play your solos better than you ever
could—taken from your own vocabulary. All of the magazines have
said that I am the best and they're right. I've been to the best schools
and got the best education available. How could someone as poor as
you challenge me? Still there's no respect from you people."[57] A short
time later, David and Shala harangue Ashmenton in terms that recall
Braxton's description of "the grand trade-off" (and that also anticipate
the current backlash against affirmative action):

> David: In our books you will be portrayed as a continuum of buf-
> foons—background players who have never contributed to the
> thrust of positive world inventions.
>
> Shala: No one will know or care about your past, fool. Even among
> yourselves you will fight.
>
> David: Why should you be given special treatment, sir? Do you
> have any idea of who we are?

This racial dynamic continues to resonate through the libretto. In scene
3, Joreo's attempts to buy off Ashmenton evoke arguments about the
role of the black middle class in American society;[58] and in scene
4, discussions among David, Shala, and others about keeping "the
people" unaware of the origins of important information echo Braxton's notion of "source transfer," particularly the debate about Egyptian sources of Greek philosophy and science.

Nevertheless, when I suggested to Braxton that Trillium M was "about
race in the United States," he demurred, insisting that the opera's real
focus was "value systems" (as indicated by the schematics that head
each scene): "It does kind of sound like race relations, but in fact I'm
not interested so much in making a story out of race relations as in cre-

ating a context where I work out a realization of a Tri-*axium* schematic and in fulfilling the possibilities of the philosophical system."[59] What I take Braxton to be saying is that while *Trillium M*'s "situation particulars"—what he calls "the apparent story"—may seem to touch on race relations, the underlying theme of the opera is value systems. And a different story, having nothing to do with race, could have been used equally well to "work out a realization" of the schematic. (Though I think it is not without significance that he chose the story he did.) Certainly, the characters do not directly address the subject of race, while they repeatedly give voice to their thoughts on value systems. These value systems fall broadly into two categories. Spiritual values are espoused by Ashmenton in scenes 1 and 3 ("There can be no value systems unless spirituality is acknowledged, unless there is belief") and by Alva and Ntzockie in scene 2 ("the concept of GOD is the greatest value of all"). And materialistic, or self-serving, values are espoused by various other characters throughout the opera. For example, Joreo in scene 1: "Take your concerns for the poor away from me, friend—I have no need of those who have not proved themselves. . . . What we call value systems in many cases is an excuse for incompetence." Or Ojuwain in scene 4: "There are two sets of standards available to us. One that we use for ourselves and one that we use for our enemies. Value systems in this context seek to preserve our position on this planet. We learned this trick many years ago."

These two sets of values resemble those that Braxton, in the *Tri-axium Writings*, sees as characterizing African American and world group cultures, with their spiritual dimension, and Western culture, with its empiricist tendencies. Yet, as he emphasized above, it is ultimately an ethical rather than a racial conflict that he depicts (both in the opera and in the *Tri-axium Writings*), and a conflict in which those individuals in the white population who are not part of the politically dominant group are likely to suffer, too. *Trillium M*'s subtitle, "Joreo's Vision of Forward Motion," is doubly ironic; not only is this a vision of forward motion that entails leaving many (perhaps most) people behind, but it is also a vision that seeks to move forward by going backward. As Joreo declares in scene 1: "I have a vision about this period of time that concerns all of us. But we must first return to the traditions that allowed for my ascendancy." I am reminded here of a conversation I had with Braxton in 1985, and which I recorded in *Forces in Motion*. Lamenting the decline of the Welfare State under Thatcherism, I remarked: "We're back to the days when education and health-care were privileges for the rich, and the poor just got shafted." " 'It's the same in America,' Braxton sighs. 'When Ronald Reagan was elected, white America thought he was gonna *get those niggers*—and, of course, he got 'em! But they didn't realize he was gonna get them too, if they weren't born with a lot of money. I think America now could be moving towards the Dark Ages.' "[60]

Those "Dark Ages" are portrayed in all their bleak inhumanity in Trillium R, the subtitle of which—"Shala Fears for the Poor"—is another example of deep-dyed irony. "Shala fears the rich forces of the planet are destroying the common people, the poor," Braxton has explained, "but in the fourth act Shala fears for the poor because she knows what she's capable of doing to them if she gets into power."[61] The schematics indicate that "attraction" is the chief focus of these dialogues, though as in Trillium M it is the desire for wealth and power that dominates the "situation particulars" of the stories. The first act presents a board meeting of a large corporation—perhaps a tobacco company or an arms manufacturer. One by one, the characters attest to their determination to maximize profits irrespective of the cost to others or to the environment. Only Shala voices any objections, and these are immediately dismissed by Zackko. "Don't cry to me about the suffering of our citizens when your efforts created their misery. Profit is a fact that can be measured—poverty is a concept and nothing more." The materialistic values previously aired in Trillium M are taken to extremes here. Motivated by greed, the characters drive the logic of capitalism to horrific conclusions:

> David: Certainly many people will be destroyed by our products but this has always been the case. In the past and in the future. I say cut the labor force and let them suffer. Profits are all that interest me.
>
> . . .
>
> Ojuwain: Even as this body meets, the culture is slowly crumbling. All over there are lines of homeless people who have no work or food. And there's no hope in sight. I say let them suffer even more! I have needs, people.

"Attraction" in this act refers not only to the characters' lust for profit but, in particular, to their use of media images to manipulate and control "attraction" to their products. Alva notes that "the image of success is a commodity," while Kim argues that "the reality of attraction on the physical universe levels is not separate from how images are portrayed and documented. What you want is what you'll get." Shala's is the dissenting voice throughout the act, advocating compassion for the poor on the grounds of common humanity—"These people are us! These people are us!"[62]—and proposing that the fact of attraction is a power that could be used for the general good:

> The reality of attraction involves what zones one is taught to turn towards in times of input and fulfilment. We can influence a being on many different levels. This is why we must re-evaluate our purposes and decisions whenever possible. The fact of role models is no light matter when one comprehends the importance of influence and belief. Our company will flourish when we promote the general welfare of the people—over individual gain. The reality of attraction involves whether or not one is taught to realize the evolutionary end of the spectrum as a point of definition for potential and beauty.

Shala's sentiments in this act echo those of Alva and Ntzockie in scene 2 of Trillium M ("We have come to value only money and false images—at the expense of inner peace and purpose"), and her statement that "we have allowed ourselves to ignore spiritual values for commodities!" also makes common ground with the viewpoints expressed by Ashmenton in Trillium M, scenes 1 and 3. Nevertheless, Shala is outvoted by the rest of the board, whose members approve new measures to secure their profits.

Act 2 of Trillium R proffers an affecting counterpoint to the naked self-interest shown in act 1. A middle-aged couple (Ashmenton and Ntzockie) say goodbye to their son, who is leaving home for the first time; they then reflect on their life together. The couple are poor, and there is perhaps a hint that they belong to a minority ethnic group when Ntzockie says of her son: "somehow he became strong enough to weather the misdocumentation that surrounds our people. The reality of attraction in this context involves gaining correct information about the historical complexities of our situation and balancing that knowledge with present-day political decisions."[63] Much of the couple's conversation has to do with reaffirming their love for one another—in a formal language that is oddly touching—and attesting to the happiness of the times they have spent together: "the passing of time can be so beautiful and real." But they also share Shala's concern with the "misuse of attraction." As Ntzockie says: "Attraction on this level is political manipulation, but no one seems to care any more. We must seek to install evolutionary images in the media that can positively motivate all of our people." And Ashmenton assents: "People are going crazy in our culture. The lure of desire has been elevated to restructural levels. Count me out!"

This brief interlude illustrating the attraction of love and respect gives way to further instances of inhumanity in acts 3 and 4. Act 3 takes place in "the Old West" and concerns a crowd of villagers who are alarmed at rumors of a plague ravaging the surrounding countryside. Two strangers, Kim and Zackko, arrive with their young child and ask for refuge, only to be met by a barrage of hatred and fear:

> Ntzockie: Go back to where you came from, people. We cannot help you now. You people have so much nerve. It makes me sick.
>
> . . .
>
> Alva: You people are attracted to our town because it's safe and decent. I could kill you myself. . . . There can be no room in our village for the likes of your kind.
>
> . . .
>
> Shala: How dare you put us in this position—what insensitivity! Sure it's true that your people have always supported our position in times of need, sure it's true that your children have fought side by side with our people.[64] To protect our interests, if you know what I mean. This is simply how a culture works. There were never any guarantees in our union. If one of us must die, let it be you!

As the villagers debate whether to turn the couple away or kill them on the spot, Zackko reveals that he has information which could save them from the plague. Suddenly, two villagers fall to the ground in agony, and, despite threats and entreaties, Zackko declares that it is too late: "Now that you are infected, there's no reason to help you. It's really only a matter of time at this point." As other villagers are stricken by the plague, Zackko and Kim head on out toward the "beautiful gardens just over the north ridge," with Zackko concluding: "I feel good about life, my dear, there's always something fresh to experience. Let's move on into the country."

This morality play, with its sledgehammer irony, is perhaps intended as an example of cosmic justice at its most grimly humorous. No such sense of retribution leavens the horrors of act 4, in which Shala applies to join a small in-group of influential power brokers (akin to the Mafia, the CIA, or the Gestapo): "I could become a hero to millions!

I could have the power to destroy my colleagues. I could fashion an image that the public would kill for! Admit me into the inner circle and I will prove my loyalty." The members of the group reveal that on this very night in order to secure the group's position of power they have planned a terrorist attack on their own society that will be blamed on "the outsiders." Shala is initially appalled: "But you are the privileged people, how can you think of such things?" Given the choice of participating in the terror or being refused entry to the group, however, her response is "Count me in!" As details of the planned attack are recounted in increasingly bloodthirsty terms—"I can't wait to burn the schools, or kill the animals"—Shala twice more voices her doubts, but on each occasion she still opts to join the group. Finally, in a chilling counterpoint to the familial affection displayed in act 2, she even agrees to the likely murder of her parents: "It's true that my parents are visiting the target area during our point of attack. But it can't be helped. Their sacrifice will show once and for all how serious I am about dedication." This ending underlines the dark irony of the subtitle, "Shala Fears for the Poor." And Shala's determination to be "in" at all costs recalls, by way of contrast, the father's emphatic "Count me out!" in act 2, as well as Ashmenton's refusal to betray his friends by joining Joreo's power group in Trillium M, scene 3, and especially his comment: "There will always be someone outside of the circle, Joreo. This is not a recipe for real change or security."

The Trillium E librettos show Braxton's growing assurance as a dramatist. Compared to their predecessors, these operas are fast-paced, action-packed and often very funny.[65] Yet beneath the humor we find the same savagely critical depictions of "Western ideas and life-values." I see the first act as a satire on consumerism and its destructive effect on the imagination. On a family outing to the beach, the father, Herald (Bubba John Jack), finds a lamp half-buried in the sand.[66] On rubbing it, he unleashes the genie, Arfthro (Zackko), who announces: "Your wish is my command." Herald's response suggests that he is an experienced shopper:

> There are wishes and there are wishes. For myself, I'll need 5.3 (five point three) wishes or nothing—(not including the use of relevant catalogues for price comparison and management protection bonuses—or the complexities of state and federal applicable tax structures, which must be viewed as an independent category in itself—separate from the specifics of my designated

choice selections, or the differences between follow-up back-up structures that monitor all supporting systems relative to my gifts, as required by FDA standards—not including Canada). . . .

Herald's first wish is for "thirty eight million, two hundred thousand, fifty-seven dollars and thirty-eight cents," and when the money arrives, he insists on counting it, much to Arfthro's astonishment. "You can't be serious. My firm's respected all over the planet! We haven't made a mistake in this area in over five hundred thousand years!" Arfthro's astonishment hits new heights when Herald and his wife, Effee (Sundance), request a yacht, a car, and clothes, but, rather than let him create "the best yacht ever made," "the car of your dreams," "the best suits in the history of fashion," or setting out the specifications themselves, they insist on ordering the items out of catalogs, which they peruse intently to find the best bargains. Imagination, it seems, has been stunted by the "images" of a consumer society; not only are Herald's wishes spent on icons of consumer culture, but his creativity has been so stymied that he cannot even dream his own dream car but has to select it from a catalog. Turning down Arfthro's offers of international travel or the chance to own a Brazilian soccer team, Herald's last wish is for a set of vintage baseball cards. "This way I'll be prepared for the Wednesday night sports panel questions on channel four." The arrival of the cards prompts Herald into a speech that momentarily echoes the concerns over media and information control aired in both Trillium M and Trillium R: "The concept of history has been made into new TV docu-dramas that bring forth love and excitement—even on cable television (which was supposed to be cheaper in the beginning). Either way, what's the difference? The truth belongs to the group that defines the terms of 'experience.' This has always been the case." I noted earlier that the main focus of the Trillium E operas was "principle information." Act 1 perhaps suggests that Herald and his family have been so shaped by the principle information of Western consumerism that they are unable to step outside these "terms of 'experience,'" even when they are offered the chance to do so by Arfthro, who, identified with the power of the imagination, possibly represents a different order of "information dynamics," an alternative "truth."

Act 2 comprises three short scenes, the first and last of which have to do with cloning. They are separated by a curious episode in which a well-to-do "socialite" keeps changing her mind about which of her two suitors she loves. I must admit I remain somewhat mystified as to what point Braxton is making in this act, although the third scene, featuring Joreo as "the man who has it all" and his five clone wives, could be taken as a critique of sexist "misuse" of cloning. (Certainly it gives a new twist to "cosi fan tutti.") The dialogue in these three scenes, however, is frequently hilarious:

> Suitor No. 1: Oh my darling, what a wonderful day to go flying in our private jet. I can see you now, in that new green hat of yours from Gimbel's.
>
> Suitor No. 2: I cannot agree with his concept of hats. If you want the truth, the red hat would be much better on a day like this one.[67]

This comic vein continues through acts 3 and 4, which find Braxton gleefully parodying popular culture forms as a means of reflecting on imperialisms, past and future. Act 3 is a skit on *Star Trek*, with Captain Zackko of the Starcraft Explorer beaming down to planet Delta r2m to check reports of alien life there. As his "space rangers" start shooting at some moving rocks, Zackko cries: "People of Delta r2m—we have come in peace. Put down your arms and surrender your weapons of hate and destruction." The ironies soon become even more barbed. Revisiting the planet, Zackko encounters the Fish People and suggests their culture should be "reabsorbed into the greater whole of composite existence. Sure it's rough—but these are the threads of documented history. Let's just say, it's nothing personal." When the Fish People appear reluctant to give up their planet to "the federation," reminding him by way of a chant that "WE ARE HERE AND YOU ARE NOT," Zackko reflects: "Maybe this planet should be blown up!" Later, as the crew members beam down again to take souvenir photographs and "sample" the planet's mineral wealth, they grow increasingly hostile to the planet's inhabitants:

> Ojuwain: Your citizens ask for too much, sir. (Talking to an alien.)
>
> Kim: As far as I'm concerned, you people have too many needs for your own good.
>
> Ntzockie: You think the world owes you something.
>
> Ashmenton: You feel superior to the rest of us!
>
> Kim: You feel your planet's so special!
>
> . . .
>
> Ojuwain: Why for a moment I felt these people understood us— but now I feel used and ashamed.
>
> Ntzockie: We can't let these foreigners get away with this.

Zackko, pondering on the fact that "they are aliens and they will always be aliens—and this is what concerns me," leads the crew back to the spaceship and gives the order to destroy the planet, adding the excuse favored by imperialist invaders from Africa to Vietnam: "Prepare to detonate four hundred nuclear bombs on Delta r2m. It's for their own good—not ours." [68] The Starcraft Explorer then sets a new course for the Andromeda star belt, with Captain Zackko musing: "Life in space is rough but life 'not in space' is even rougher."

Act 4 pokes fun at the explorer/adventure film genre, its *Indiana Jones*-style scenario further embellished by the addition of dinosaurs. Set in 1904, it follows a team of archaeologists on an expedition "through the jungle to search for the secret Pyramid Ghara 4." Speculating on what riches they might discover, the archaeologists concur that "whatever we find here is ours!" They are attacked by seven giants, twenty feet tall, who guard the pyramid, and their leader, Dr. Wallingford (Ashmenton), dies, but not until he has reminded them of "the curse of the golden seal" that also protects the pyramid. Later, inside the pyramid, as they break into the king's burial chamber, they are attacked by a gang of mummies, but, regrouping, they continue into the chamber and find untold treasures. Suddenly, the "Guardian angel of the tomb" appears and pronounces the curse, but very politely! "Disrespect us if you will but please know you have been forewarned about the future." The archaeologists are not impressed; representatives of the modern West, they are confident the age of materialism has replaced the age of the sacred:

> *Joreo:* Hear us, Goddess from the past, for our time has come.
> *Zackko:* We're in business to stay.
> *Bubba John Jack:* And we've got the goods to prove it!
> *Sundance:* Nobody can tell us what to do at this point in time, people.
> *Bubba John Jack:* Your influence belongs to another time and place. This landscape is a merchandiser's fantasy and I say—roll out the new strategies!

The archaeologists are temporarily inconvenienced by an attack of "giant dinosaurs," but the opera ends with the pyramid plundered, statues being defaced, and the team planning to turn the sacred site into a money-spinning theme park. [69] As Joreo remarks: "What a life!"

Whether we view the operas from Braxton's perspective as dialogues about value systems, attraction, and principle information, or whether we focus on their "apparent stories," which suggest to me critiques of racism, capitalism, and imperialism, it is fair to say that a common theme which emerges repeatedly from the librettos is Braxton's concern with *disrespect for the other*—other people, other values, other cultures—a disrespect that he portrays, paradoxically, as a denial of *common* humanity for the sake of self-interest, whether that interest is power, wealth, or self-preservation. I think it is also clear that Braxton sees this disrespect for the other as linked to what he regards as the breakdown of spiritual values in the West and the subsequent rise of creeds based on individual and material considerations. Disregarding cosmic justice, post-Enlightenment Western society was built on what Braxton has called "the raping of Africa" and the institution of slavery.[70] The *Trillium* operas argue that the values and attitudes which underpinned those events are still with us and are still dominant, and that continuing to pursue them is likely to result in social collapse, perhaps even global destruction.

In 1985 Braxton explained to me that his work was dedicated to the ideal of "synthesis":

> I know one thing: either human beings are going to establish some understanding of unification or. . . . Well, if we blow up the planet, it would be a tragedy for sure and it seems we're moving towards that. World unification must be, on some level, world tolerance. That must be the objective—understanding, forgiveness, the concept of love; these are not just words. I've been fortunate to travel around the planet and see how other people live and think; I've come to see the beauty in all the differences and I've also come to see that there are no differences.[71]

The contrary Western viewpoint is to insist on difference and to deny its beauty, unless that beauty can be translated into exotica or spectacle and represented (i.e., misrepresented) within a Western frame of reference. This is the process of appropriation with which African American music has had to contend and which Sun Ra, Duke Ellington, and Anthony Braxton, in their various ways, have tried to expose and resist. If the *Tri-axium Writings*, like *Black, Brown and Beige*, offer a counterhistory to the dominant culture's distortions of black life and black culture, the *Trillium* operas focus more on "Western ideas and life-values" per se, providing a parodic antithesis to the West's heroic narratives of the explorer, the political leader, the captain of industry. And, like Sun Ra's occasional intimations of apocalypse, their often dystopian scenarios sound the warning note within the overall uto-pian project of Braxton's music.

Together with the revision of history, this utopian impulse is a major thread that links the music of Ra, Ellington, and Braxton, evident in Ra's space visions, Ellington's hope of a New World, Braxton's deline-ations of the meta-real. These projects may seem impossibly opti-mistic, but, as Sun Ra has noted, "The impossible attracts me because everything possible has been done and the world didn't change."[72] He also declared: "Yet the impossible is a thought / And every thought is real."[73] Braxton, too, has said much the same: "The challenge of cre-ativity . . . is to move towards the greatest thought that you can think of." And: "Whatever you think can be manifested. And whatever that is can be regenerated."[74] For Braxton, the creative urge is a defining quality of humanity. As the father puts it in *Trillium R*, act 2: "The thrust of our species involves transcending what is possible, and raising the challenge of the moment." The history of African American music is, I think, the history of one such form of transcendence. To paraphrase Sun Ra, the impossible is in the music and the music is real.

Coda: House of Voices, Sea of Music

"My people," wrote Sidney Bechet, "all they want is a place where they can be people." [1] He understood the crucial role that music plays in the creation of these imagined spaces, these visions of a future Promised Land. "The man singing it, the man playing it, he makes a place. For as long as the song is being played, *that's* the place he's looking for." [2] Bechet knew, too, that this utopia could not escape its past, that the music which shaped the future was also history in code. "The blues, and the spirituals, and the remembering, and the waiting, and the suffering, and the looking at the sky watching the dark come down—that's all inside the music." [3]

This sense of history, of music as the "remembering song," certainly pervades the work of Sun Ra, Duke Ellington, and Anthony Braxton. Much of their time is spent revising white distortions of that history, not least because they realize that a better future for black people cannot be attained until the old stereotypes have been thrown aside. Yet the "places" they create in their musics keep the hope of utopia alive, are big enough to keep the remembering in perspective (were perhaps created to put it into perspective). So their awareness of "the dark come down" does not extinguish the light of their optimism but instead makes it all the more credible. They know they are playing—literally—against the odds.

Trying to reconcile the imperatives of the utopian impulse with those of the remembering song is no easy task. Those who straddle this crossroads can so easily become mired in contradiction. [4] Yet Ra, Ellington, and Braxton have not been alone in the attempt. While I make no claims for its ubiquity, I think a Blutopian resonance can be heard in much African American music. Like a chord voiced differently by different artists, a changing same, it sounds through the century, now loud, now faint, echoing from Scott Joplin's *Treemonisha* to the work of contemporary masters like Bill Dixon, Joe McPhee, Cecil Taylor, and Wadada Leo Smith. Many people have heard it, too. Consider, for example, the response of European painter Jimmy Ernst to the 1938 "Spirituals to Swing" concert he attended at Carnegie Hall:

> Until this particular evening the histories of lynchings and segregation that I had been all too familiar with before coming here had existed only as exaggerated European notions of some dim post-colonial past. There was something in the music that was trying to reach my sensibilities. There was the fleeting thought, at some point in the night, that, hidden in the intricate structures of boogie-woogie, Kansas City, New Orleans and, yes, the blues, was the image of an architecture. I recall fantasizing the picture of a man, both hands tied, trying to build a house with his voice while sitting on a cot in his jail cell.[5]

My aim in this book has been to illuminate certain aspects of the work of Sun Ra, Duke Ellington, and Anthony Braxton. With explication done, I would like to close on an upbeat, a brief rhetorical flourish that celebrates these artists and the imaginative power of the tradition they represent. The places they conjure in their musics—"impossible" alternative universes shaped by black mythology, black history, black metaphysics—could yet turn out to be black holes, in which our little local universe of Western materialism will be "swallowed up—leaving us in a sea of music and color."[6] Perhaps at that moment Blutopia will be able to forget its history, cast off its blues, and fulfill Albert Ayler's gentle prophecy: "One day, everything will be as it should be."[7]

Appendix

A. Examples of Anthony Braxton's diagram titles, showing the evolution from the early coding, dimensional drawing, and hieroglyphic titles, through the introduction of human figures, subtitles, and snatches of dialogue, to the more recent titles that feature landscapes and scenes from the composition's "story."

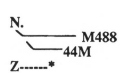

Composition 6D (late 1960s)

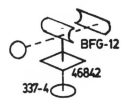

Composition 40K (mid 1970s)

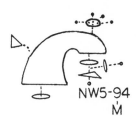

Composition 76 (1977)

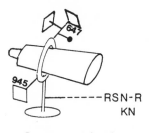

Composition 98 (1981)

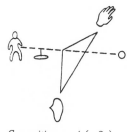

Composition 105A (1983)

Composition 110D (1984)

Composition 125 (1986)

Composition 132 (1986)

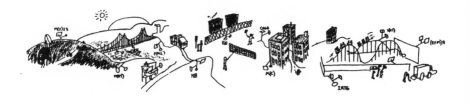

Composition 142 (1988)

Composition 151 (1991)

B. Maps of Ashmenton Land (top) and the South West Tri-State Region, from Anthony Braxton's *Composition 171*. (Ashmenton Land is in the top northwest corner of the Tri-State Region.)

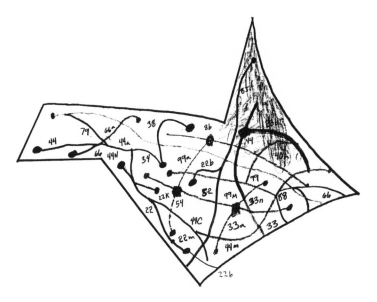

Ashmenton Land

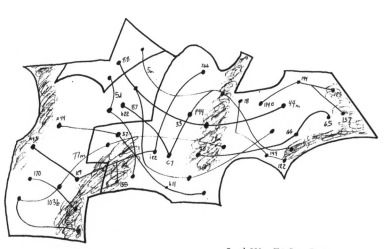

South West Tri-State Region

Notes

Introduction

1 Sidney Bechet, *Treat It Gentle: An Autobiography* (1960; New York: Da Capo, 1978) 202–03.

2 James Baldwin, "Of the Sorrow Songs: The Cross of Redemption," 1979, *The Picador Book of Blues and Jazz*, ed. James Campbell (London: Picador, 1996) 329.

3 Meinrad Buholzer, "Cecil Taylor: Interview," *Cadence* Dec. 1984: 6. At first glance, the word "breath" in Taylor's penultimate sentence appears to be a misprint for "breadth." However, Taylor's use of "breath" elsewhere suggests that it may be correct. See, for example, Cecil Taylor, "Sound Structure of Subculture Becoming Major Breath/Naked Fire Gesture," CD insert notes to *Unit Structures* by Cecil Taylor, rec. 1966, Blue Note CDP 7 84237 2, 1987.

4 The "politics of transfiguration" is a phrase used by Paul Gilroy in his discussion of the "utopian desires" voiced by black music. See Gilroy, *The Black Atlantic: Modernity and Double Consciousness* (London: Verso, 1993) 37. It could be argued that Ellington's work inclines more toward what Gilroy describes as a complementary "politics of fulfilment," but this particular distinction is not one that I intend to pursue here.

5 Duke Ellington, "Blutopia," *The Duke Ellington Carnegie Hall Concerts: December 1944* by Duke Ellington and His Orchestra, Prestige 2PCD-24073-2, 1991. (N.B. In referring to recordings, I have tried whenever possible to list the most recent issue.)

6 Given that this is a book in which I repeatedly criticize white misrepresentations of black music, it is a piquant irony that my title requires what is almost certainly a misreading of its creator's intention. Blue was Ellington's favorite color, so if "Blutopia" was any more than a piece of humorous wordplay, it was probably intended to convey the blissful state described by Don George: "When Duke was surrounded by blue, he knew that God was in His heaven, all was well with the world." George, *The Real Duke Ellington* (London: Robson, 1981) 69. I had not been aware of Ellington's predilection for blue when I first came across "Blutopia."

7 Victor Schonfield, ed., *Sun Ra: Intergalactic Research Arkestra*, concert program (London: Music Now, 1970) 2.

8 Mark Sinker, untitled essay on Anthony Braxton, *Mixtery: A Festschrift for Anthony Braxton*, ed. Graham Lock (Exeter: Stride, 1995) 235–36.

9 Duke Ellington, *Music Is My Mistress* (1973; London: Quartet, 1977) 183. *New World A-Comin'* is the title of a 1943 Ellington composition, which I discuss in more detail in chapter 3.

10 Duke Ellington, "Heaven" and "Almighty God," *Second Sacred Concert* by Duke Ellington, rec. 1968, Prestige PCD 34045-2, 1990.

11 John Edward Hasse, *Beyond Category: The Life and Genius of Duke Ellington* (New York: Simon & Schuster, 1993) 254. This information makes nonsense of James Lincoln Collier's claim that, after leaving school, Ellington "seems not to have read much literature of any kind." Collier, *Duke Ellington* (1987; London: Pan, 1989) 295.

12 "Ko-Ko," originally part of Ellington's unfinished opera *Boola*, "supposedly represented the frenzied dancing of the slaves in New Orleans' Congo Square." Mark Tucker, "Duke Ellington, 1940–42," CD insert notes, *The Blanton-Webster Band* by Duke Ellington, rec. 1940–42, Bluebird-BMG 74321 13181 2, 1986. (Since the pages of so many CD inserts are unnumbered, I have not indicated "n.p." each time this occurs. However, where page numbers are available, I have included them in the reference.)

13 He calls them "mighty men of action" in an unpublished poem he wrote to accompany *Black, Brown and Beige*. See chap. 3.

14 For example, Ellington tried to avoid calling his music "jazz" because "the word never lost its association with those New Orleans bordellos. In the 1920's I used to try to convince Fletcher Henderson that we ought to call what we were doing 'Negro music.'" Qtd. in Nat Hentoff, *Jazz Is* (1975; London: W. H. Allen, 1978) 30.

15 Anthony Braxton, *Tri-axium Writings 3* (N.p.: Synthesis Music, 1985) 288. Cf. Cecil Taylor's comments on Africa quoted at the beginning of this introduction.

16 Graham Lock, *Forces in Motion: Anthony Braxton and the Meta-reality of Creative Music* (London: Quartet, 1988) 209.

17 From the spiritual, "My Lord, What a Mornin,'" *The Book of American Negro Spirituals*, ed. James Weldon Johnson (London: Chapman & Hall, 1926) 162. Hereafter cited as J. W. Johnson, *Book*.

18 One nonacademic model whose influence I would like to acknowledge is Val Wilmer's *As Serious as Your Life: The Story of the New Music* (1977; London: Pluto, 1987), particularly for her insistence on taking seriously what the musicians have to say about their work. Two important reference books that I found especially useful are Robert L. Campbell, *The Earthly Recordings of Sun Ra* (Redwood, N.Y.: Cadence Jazz, 1994), and *The Duke Ellington Reader*, edited by Mark Tucker (New York: Oxford UP, 1993).

19 See, for example, Sun Ra's assertion that the word "Negro" was deliberately derived from "necro," meaning "dead," as a kind of psychological trap to prevent black people from functioning. Graham Lock, *Chasing the*

Vibration: Meetings with Creative Musicians (Exeter: Stride, 1994) 160. Cf. Braxton's claim: "One of the most sophisticated weapons that white people have come up with would be language—words—a mono-dimensional language used to evaluate and distort a multi-dimensional music." Qtd. in Brian Case, LP liner notes to B-X⁰ / NO-1-47ᴬ by Anthony Braxton, Affinity AFF 15, n.d. Cf. also Ellington's typically terse appraisal: "You can say anything you want on the trombone, but you gotta be careful with words." Qtd. in Richard O. Boyer, "The Hot Bach," 1944; rpt. in Tucker, *Duke Ellington Reader*, 238.

20 See, for example, Henry Louis Gates Jr., *The Signifying Monkey: A Theory of African-American Literary Criticism* (1988; New York: Oxford UP, 1989) Part One.

21 Gilroy, *Black Atlantic*, 37. In chapter 5 I will argue that sometimes this politics can also be heard on a *higher* frequency!

22 Which is what I think happens, to a degree, in Samuel A. Floyd Jr.'s attempt to adapt Gatesian literary theory to African American music. See Floyd, *The Power of Black Music: Interpreting Its History from Africa to the United States* (New York: Oxford UP, 1995).

23 For an excellent critique of this new "narrow history" of jazz, see Andrew W. Bartlett, "Cecil Taylor, Identity Energy, and the Avant-Garde African-American Body," *Perspectives of New Music* 33 (1995): 274–93. For the benefit of nonacademic readers, I should explain that "signifying" is the term given to various kinds of indirect commentary that are common in African American vernacular speech. The black literary critic Henry Louis Gates Jr. has argued that such signifying (which he reinscribes as "Signifyin[g]") is not only characteristic of black culture but one of its major rhetorical strategies, a ubiquitous presence in both the literature and the music of African Americans. Though Gates lists many different kinds of signifying, I think all of them involve the notion of *indirect reference*, and in many cases this reference occurs by means of *repetition with a difference*, the nature of the difference indicating the signifier's attitude to what he or she is signifying on. So parody, for example, is a negative form of signifying—something (a text or a song) is repeated but altered in such a way as to poke fun at the original. In the context of music, a player who parodies or pastiches, alludes or refers to, or quotes from another work or player (or even his or her own earlier playing) can be said to be signifying. Though Gates's book is certainly the best introduction to the theory of signifying, his focus is almost exclusively on literature. Various attempts to apply the theory to music have, in my view, been only partially successful. But this is potentially a huge field of enquiry that musicologists are only beginning to explore.

24 Braxton says he uses "axium" because he considers "axiom" too "mono-dimensional" for what he wishes to convey. I will discuss his "axiums" in chapter 5.

25 See Ingrid Monson, *Saying Something: Jazz Improvisation and Interaction* (Chicago: U of Chicago P, 1996) 199–213. Cf. Cornel West's comment, while discuss-

ing whether bebop is best categorized as modernist or postmodernist, that "there is a much deeper question as to whether these terms *modernist/postmodernist* relate to Afro-American cultural practices in any illuminating way at all." Braxton has made it clear that he thinks not, that his music is best viewed in terms of its own cultural and philosophical traditions: "I don't see my work as 'modernist' or as 'postmodernist,' I'm not interested in those labels. I see it more as relating to that Old Time Religion. [*Smiles*.]" Qtd. in Graham Lock, "*Composition 192: Like a Never Ending Song*," CD insert notes to *Composition 192* by Anthony Braxton and Lauren Newton, rec. 1996, Leo Records CDLR 251, 1998, 4. The West quotation is from Cornel West, *Prophetic Reflections: Notes on Race and Power in America* (Monroe, Maine: Common Courage, 1993) 93.

26 Krin Gabbard, "Introduction: The Jazz Canon and Its Consequences," *Jazz Among the Discourses*, ed. Gabbard (Durham, N.C.: Duke UP, 1995).

Chapter 1   Astro Black: Mythic Future, Mythic Past

1 Ralph Ellison, *Shadow and Act* (1964; New York: Vintage/Random House, 1972) 115.

2 John Corbett, *Extended Play: Sounding Off from John Cage to Dr. Funkenstein* (Durham, N.C.: Duke UP, 1994) 172.

3 Benny Green, "Angel in a Noddy Bonnet Wanted to Save the Planet," *Daily Mail* 2 June 1993: 39.

4 Steve Voce, "Sun Ra," *Independent* 1 June 1993: 20. This piece elicited at least one stinging riposte; see Val Wilmer, "Sun Ra," *Independent* 1 July 1993: 26.

5 Allan S. Chase, "Sun Ra: Musical Change and Musical Meaning in the Life and Work of a Jazz Composer," diss., Tufts U, 1992, 248. Chase also points out the inability of such notions to account for Sun Ra's many musical accomplishments over a period of nearly forty years.

6 Qtd. in Schonfield, 9.

7 Robert L. Campbell, "Sun Ra: Super Sonic Sounds from Saturn," *Goldmine* 23 Jan. 1993: 42; Wilmer, *As Serious*, 90.

8 Wilmer, *As Serious*, 96. A quick survey of the Arkestra's headgear alone will make the point. At various times they have been reported as wearing fezes, propellers, pyramids, and flashing lights; there is even a photograph of Sun Ra sporting a model of the solar system on his head. See the CD insert notes to *Other Planes of There* by Sun Ra and His Solar Arkestra, Evidence ECD 22037-2, 1992. The Arkestra members wore a lot of other kinds of costume, too. For a full discussion of Sun Ra's attire, see John F. Szwed, *Space Is the Place: The Lives and Times of Sun Ra* (New York: Pantheon, 1997) 172–76. Clothing has played an important and often provocative role in African American history; see, for example, Shane White and Graham White, "Slave Clothing and African-American Culture in the Eighteenth and Nineteenth Centuries," *Past and Present* 148 (1995): 149–86, and Robin D. G. Kelley, "The Riddle of the Zoot," in his *Race Rebels: Culture, Politics, and the Black Working Class* (New York: Free Press, 1996) 161–81.

9   Sun Ra, "Astro Black," *Astro Black*, Impulse-ABC AS 9255, 1973.

10 Lock, *Forces*, 23.

11 For an indication of the scope of Sun Ra's interests, see John F. Szwed, CD insert notes to *Soundtrack to the Film Space Is the Place* by Sun Ra and His Intergalactic Solar Arkestra, Evidence ECD 22070-2, 1993, in particular his description of the course Sun Ra taught at the University of California at Berkeley in 1971. The course, "The Black Man in the Cosmos," came with a reading list that included "*The Egyptian Book of the Dead*, the *Radix* (a 19th century astrology journal), Alexander Hislop's *Two Babylons*, books on etymology, hieroglyphics, color therapy, Afro-American folklore, ex-slaves' writings, the theosophical works of Madam Blavatsky, spiritually-channelled tomes like *The Book of Oahspe*, Henry Dumas' poetry and short stories, Dr. Livingstone's travels in Africa, the Bible, and accounts of the origins of the Rosicrucians." Szwed reports: "When distressed students told Sun Ra that the books were either missing from the library or had never been there in the first place, he merely smiled knowingly."

12 Norman C. Weinstein, *A Night in Tunisia: Imaginings of Africa in Jazz* (New York: Limelight, 1993) 21–36; Frank Kofsky, *Black Nationalism and the Revolution in Music* (1970; New York: Pathfinder, 1978) 48–50.

13 See Wilmer, *As Serious*, 81.

14 Wilmer, *As Serious*, 80.

15 Chase, 130. Chris Trent has pointed out that many of Ra's arrangements for Red Saunders, for whom he worked in the late 1940s and early 1950s, are very much in the same "Latin/exotic" vein. Personal correspondence, Feb. 1998.

16 *The Nubians of Plutonia* by Sun Ra and His Myth Science Arkestra was re-issued on CD in 1993, Evidence ECD 22066-2. Though the LP had one side of "space" songs and one side of "Africa" songs, as if to signal very clearly Ra's major areas of interest, its original title was *The Lady with the Golden Stockings*. It was not until 1969 that it was retitled. "Ancient Aiethopia" is from *Jazz in Silhouette* by Sun Ra and His Arkestra, reissued on CD in 1991, Evidence ECD 22012.

17 Thoth can be seen as the mythological precursor to the West African gods Esu (Yoruba) and Legba (Fon), who crossed the Atlantic in the slave ships and survive as Papa Legba in Haitian voodoo mythology and as Papa La Bas in the hoodoo mythology of the United States. See Lock, *Forces*, 21n. Thoth is also one of the Egyptian gods who accompany Sun Ra in the film *Space Is the Place*. I discuss this film, and the issue of Sun Ra's name, in chapter 2. Pictures depicting aspects of ancient Egyptian mythology can be seen, for example, on the jackets of the LPs *Horizon* and *Cosmo-Earth Fantasy* (or at least on some issues, since Sun Ra often issued a recording in a variety of liner jacket designs, some of which were individually hand-drawn). These two LPs were also issued, or at least distributed (since distributors sometimes assigned titles to LPs that Ra had left untitled), under various alternative titles. For full discographical details, see Campbell, *Earthly Recordings*.

18 Sun Ra, "Blackman," *Soundtrack to the Film Space Is the Place*.

19 Lock, *Chasing*, 150. A fuller account of this interview with Tyrone Hill appears in Graham Lock, "'Tell 'em About It, Tyrone': An Interview with Arkestra Trombonist Tyrone Hill," *Stride Magazine* 37 (1995): n.p. MFSB was the name of the house band on Kenny Gamble and Leon Huff's Philadelphia International label, home in the 1970s to such outstanding soul artists as Harold Melvin and the Blue Notes and the O'Jays.

20 Ancient Egyptian imagery later became more prevalent in black music, especially when used on LP jackets by popular groups such as Earth, Wind & Fire. See also Paul Gilroy, *Small Acts: Thoughts on the Politics of Black Cultures* (London: Serpent's Tail, 1993) 237–57.

21 For example, see W. E. B. DuBois, *The World and Africa: An Inquiry into the Part Which Africa Has Played in World History* (1947; New York: International, 1992) 98–114.

22 Cf. the early writings of the Senegalese author Cheikh Anta Diop, whose arguments are similar to those of James. See Diop, *The African Origin of Civilization: Myth or Reality* (1955, 1967; Westport, Conn.: Lawrence Hill, 1974).

23 James's work was continued by a small group of African American scholars, including his student Yosef ben-Jochannan, whose writings Anthony Braxton has cited as a major influence on his view of black history. See Lock, *Forces*, 277.

24 Martin Bernal, *Black Athena: The Afroasiatic Roots of Classical Civilization*, vol. 1 (1987; London: Vintage, 1991) 30.

25 DuBois, *World*, 99. Cf. Anthony Braxton's concept of "the grand trade-off," discussed in chap. 5.

26 See John Gilmore's comments in Lock, *Chasing*, 158–59, and the essay on Sun Ra in Corbett, *Extended Play*, 163–77, which reproduces the official document by which Herman Blount changed his name to Le Sony'r Ra on 20 October 1952.

27 Chase, 82; Graham Lock, unpublished interview with Sun Ra, London, 10 June 1990.

28 Sun Ra, CD insert notes to *Sun Song*, Delmark DD-411, 1990. Reissue of *Jazz by Sun Ra*, Transition TRLP J-10, 1957.

29 George G. M. James, *Stolen Legacy: Greek Philosophy Is Stolen from Egyptian Philosophy* (Trenton, N.J.: Africa World, 1992) 27–31. Rpt. of *Stolen Legacy, the Greeks Were Not the Authors of Greek Philosophy but the People of North Africa, Commonly Called the Egyptians*. 1954.

30 See Campbell, *Earthly Recordings*, 234–35, for a complete listing of the "Discipline" compositions known to exist on tape. Examples of Ra referring to discipline in interviews include Tam Fiofori, "Sun Ra's African Roots," *Melody Maker*, 12 Feb. 1972: 32; Cole Gagne, *Soundpieces 2: Interviews with American Composers* (Metuchen, N.J.: Scarecrow, 1993) 370; Len Lyons, *The Great Jazz Pianists: Speaking of Their Lives and Music* (1983; New York: Da Capo, n.d.) 88; Rich Theis, "Sun Ra," OP, Sept./Oct. 1983: 48–51.

31 James, 139–51. Sun Ra also had a penchant for covering compositions with "sun" references in the title, e.g., "East of the Sun," "Keep Your

Sunnyside Up," "On the Sunny Side of the Street." For full recording details, see Campbell, *Earthly Recordings*.

32   Lock, unpublished interview, 1990.

33   James, 153.

34   James, 155.

35   James, 157.

36   James, 158.

37   James, 161.

38   Wilmer, *As Serious*, 81. Later research has shown that Sun Ra's grandmother was the main religious influence in his childhood; see Chase, 38–40, and Szwed, *Space*, 9. Ra himself said: "My mother didn't go to church. She said you make your own heaven and hell." Francis Davis, unpublished interview with Sun Ra, Philadelphia, Jan. 1990.

39   For an example of such a pamphlet, see Cuthbert Ormond Simpkins, *Coltrane: A Biography* (Perth Amboy, N.J.: Herndon House, 1975) 99–100, and Szwed, *Space*, 76–78. John Gilmore also mentions these pamphlets in Lock, *Chasing*, 159.

40   For examples of the "equations" that Ra sometimes performed in interviews, see Chase 250–53, and Szwed, *Space*, 304–08. However, the most extensive example of Ra's equations I have seen to date occurs in an unpublished interview with Charles Blass, Copenhagen, 21 Mar. 1992. Victor Schonfield also has a series of equations that Sun Ra wrote down for him in 1991 (not 1970, as incorrectly captioned in Szwed, *Space*).

41   Szwed, notes to *Soundtrack*.

42   Zora Neale Hurston, *Mules and Men* (1935; New York: Harper & Row, 1990) 125. Victor Schonfield has suggested that Sun Ra's "equations" may have been related to his study of music, in that "music is full of things which are the same only different, like chord inversions, where one note is transposed down an octave: it's still B, but now has a completely different relationship to the other notes, and the chord is still what it was, but also a new chord if you simply read it from the bottom up. Sonny's madness was to think that you can do this to language and actually learn something, doubly mad since he added numerology into the pot." Personal correspondence, 9 June 1994.

43   Sun Ra, "To the Peoples of Earth," *Black Fire: An Anthology of African-American Writing*, ed. LeRoi Jones and Larry Neal (New York: William Morrow, 1968) 217. Cf. his statement to Phil Schaap in 1987: "This planet's really trapped by words . . . words are trapping people and destroying them." Schaap, "An Interview with Sun Ra," *WKCR Program Guide* Jan./Feb. 1989: 30.

44   Graham Lock, unpublished interview with Sun Ra, London, Oct. 1983. It is possible that Ra's criticisms were aimed in part at the Nation of Islam, whose members "do not sing or use any kind of music at religious meetings." E. U. Essien-Udom, *Black Nationalism: The Rise of the Black Muslims in the U.S.A.* (1962; Harmondsworth, Middlesex: Penguin, 1966) 167. I look more closely at Sun Ra's relationship with the Nation of Islam in chapter 2.

45 Lock, unpublished interview, 1990. Sun Ra referred to several biblical stories to substantiate his accusations against Moses. He also insisted that his antipathy to Moses was not fueled by anti-Semitism. This position will, I think, become clear below.

46 Albert Raboteau, *Slave Religion: The "Invisible Institution" in the Antebellum South* (1978; New York: Oxford UP, 1980) 311.

47 Qtd. in Raboteau, 311–12.

48 The last quotation is from Raboteau, 319. The others are from J. W. Johnson, *Book*, 51, 60, and 70; and Thomas Wentworth Higginson, "Negro Spirituals," 1867, *The Social Implications of Early Negro Music in the United States*, ed. Bernard Katz (New York: Arno and New York Times, 1969) 13, 14.

49 Raboteau, 320.

50 Jon Michael Spencer, *Blues and Evil* (Knoxville: U of Tennessee P, 1993) 105.

51 Spencer, 106. *The Chicago Defender*'s twenty-fifth anniversary issue was published on 3 May 1930.

52 Szwed, *Space*, 51–52.

53 Corbett, *Extended Play*, 176.

54 Szwed, notes to *Soundtrack*.

55 Martin Luther King Jr., "I See the Promised Land," *The Eyes on the Prize Civil Rights Reader: Documents, Speeches, and Firsthand Accounts from the Black Freedom Struggle, 1954–1990*, ed. Clayborne Carson, David J. Garrow, Gerald Gill, Vincent Harding, and Darlene Clark Hine (New York: Penguin, 1991) 411.

56 King, 418–19.

57 Sun Ra, "There Is Change in the Air," *The Antique Blacks*, Saturn 81774, 1974. A shorter version of this composition, retitled "Everything Is Space," later appeared on the CD *Somewhere Else*, Rounder 3036, 1995.

58 Lock, unpublished interview, 1983. Ra's views here on the importance of beauty and culture echo almost exactly the sentiments he had expressed more than twenty-five years earlier in his notes to *Sun Song*: "it is not possible to substitute anything for ART and CULTURE. They are inseparable. *The well being of every person on this planet depends upon the survival and growth of civilization; every civilization is determined, to great extent, by the scope and development of its ART FORMS*." Sun Ra, notes to *Sun Song*. These views also echo the high value placed on art by the leaders of the Harlem Renaissance—for example, James Weldon Johnson's 1922 statement: "The final measure of the greatness of all peoples is the amount and standard of the literature and art that they have produced." Quoted in Guthrie P. Ramsey Jr., "Cosmopolitan or Provincial?: Ideology in Early Black Music Historiography, 1867–1940," *Black Music Research Journal* 16 (1996): 25. The difference is that the leaders of the Harlem Renaissance, unlike Sun Ra, did not regard jazz as art. See chap. 3.

59 Sun Ra, "I, Pharaoh," *A Quiet Place in the Universe*, Leo CD LR 198, 1994.

60 Sun Ra, "Your Only Hope Now Is a Lie," *Hambone* 2 (Fall 1982): 112. A fuller version of this talk was also issued under its original title, "The Possibility of Altered Destiny," as a limited-edition CD, *Live from Soundscape* by the Sun Ra Arkestra, DIW 388B, 1994.

61 Davis, unpublished interview. Compare, however, Paul Gilroy's contrasting opinion: "Blacks today appear to identify far more readily with the glamorous pharaohs than with the abject plight of those they held in bondage." Gilroy, *Black Atlantic*, 207.

62 Chase, 285. I have added "Slumming on Park Avenue" to this list; I saw the Arkestra perform this Irving Berlin piece in London in 1990. Henderson recorded it in 1937. Some commentators have suggested that Ra's extensive use of Ellington and Henderson material may have been triggered, at least in part, by Ellington's death in 1974.

63 Tam Fiofori, "Sun Ra's Space Odyssey," *Down Beat* 14 May 1970: 14.

64 Phil Schaap, "Sun Ra: The Sequel," *WKCR Program Guide* Mar. 1989: 28.

65 See John C. Reid, "It's After the End of the World," *Coda* Apr./May 1990: 30.

66 Robert D. Rusch, *Jazztalk: The Cadence Interviews* (Secaucus, N.J.: Lyle Stuart, 1984) 67. Cf. Lock, *Forces*, 17–18.

67 Lock, unpublished interview, 1990.

68 This chant closes the *Live at "Praxis '84" Volume III* LP by the Sun Ra Arkestra, Praxis CM 110, 1984. The tracks on the recording are untitled. Campbell, *Earthly Recordings*, 120, does not list this chant separately but treats it as a part of the preceding "Strange Mathematics." According to my own concert notes, Sun Ra also performed this chant, again seguing from "Strange Mathematics," at a London concert on 12 October 1983. Incidentally, Ra's occasional references to mathematics, as in "Strange Mathematics" or his remark to me in 1990 that mathematics provided "the key to immortality," begin to make a lot more sense once you discover the word's derivation from the ancient Egyptian concept of Ma'at, which referred to (among other things) the cosmic principle of balance and harmony. See Molefi Kete Asente, *Kemet, Afrocentricity and Knowledge* (Trenton, N.J.: Africa World, 1991) 80–92.

69 Mark Sinker, "Sun Ra," *Stride Magazine* 37 1995: n.p. In fact, Ra had already featured the music of these and other white composers in the early 1960s on LPs such as *Holiday for Soul Dance*, *The Invisible Shield*, and *What's New*.

70 Sinker, "Sun Ra." Presumably the title of *The Invisible Shield* LP, released in 1974 but including tracks from the early 1960s (see n. 69), refers to this "shield of beauty."

71 Sun Ra, "Out Beyond the Kingdom of," *Out Beyond the Kingdom of*, Saturn 61674, 1974.

72 Qtd. in Schonfield, 2. Cf. the 1968 French students' slogan: "Be realistic — demand the impossible." Qtd. in Lock, *Forces*, 15.

73 Sun Ra, qtd. in CD insert notes to *Interstellar Low Ways*, Evidence ECD 22039-2, 1992. The quotation appears on the jacket of my 1967 copy of the LP, but I do not know if it was on the original ca. 1966 issue, which was titled *Rocket Number Nine Take Off for the Planet Venus* by Sun Ra and His Myth-Science Arkestra, Saturn 9956-2-MIN.

74 Lock, "Tell 'em."

75 "Celestial Road," which includes the chant "Travelin' / Strange celestial road / To endless heaven," is a track from *Strange Celestial Road* by Sun Ra,

Rounder CD 3035, 1987; DuBois closed *The Souls of Black Folk* by quoting from a nineteenth-century spiritual, "Let us cheer the weary traveller / Along the heavenly way." W. E. B. DuBois, *The Souls of Black Folk* (1903; New York: Bantam Classics, 1989) 188.

76　Sun Ra, "New Horizons," notes to *Sun Song*.

77　Sun Ra, notes to *Sun Song*.

78　For a more detailed account of Ra's musical development, see Chase, esp. 88–105, 129–45, 154–60, and 182–97. Chris Cutler has written of Ra: "There's no doubt at all in my mind that nobody has made such a definitive contribution to the vocabulary and grammar of electronic keyboards. Almost everyone doing anything of interest seems to have been influenced directly or indirectly by Ra." Chris Cutler, *File Under Popular: Theoretical and Critical Writings on Music* (London: November, 1985) 76.

79　Sun Ra, notes to *Sun Song*.

80　Sun Ra, notes to *Sun Song*. The track was originally called "Brainville, Uranus," but it was never recorded under that title.

81　This observation gels with Campbell's comment that "1959 was the year that the Arkestra began to perform space chants." Campbell, *Earthly Recordings*, 18. I should point out, however, that at this point the "chants" were still individual songs; judging from the set lists in Campbell, it seems to have been only in the mid-1970s that Ra began to sequence these songs into the chant medleys that later became such a prominent part of his repertoire.

82　See Campbell, *Earthly Recordings*, for full discographical details.

83　Sun Ra, "On Jupiter," *On Jupiter*, El Saturn 101679, 1979.

84　Sun Ra, "Space Is the Place," *Space Is the Place*, Impulse 12492, 1998. This song also appears on numerous other Sun Ra recordings; see Campbell, *Earthly Recordings*, for details.

85　Wilmer, *As Serious*, 81.

86　Lock, *Chasing*, 160.

87　Qtd. in Simpkins, 96–97. Parentheses and ellipsis in original.

88　Sun Ra, notes to *Sun Song*.

89　Sun Ra, "Enticement," notes to *Sun Song*. The power of the imagination and of dreaming was a recurring theme in Ra's music. Also in 1957 he recorded "Dreams Come True," reissued on *Sound Sun Pleasure!!* by Sun Ra and His Astro Infinity Arkestra, Evidence ECD 22014, 1992, and two pieces he later chose to perform frequently were the Ellington/Strayhorn "Day Dream" and Jerome Kern's "I Dream Too Much."

90　Sun Ra, notes to *Sun Song*.

91　Sun Ra, "New Horizons," notes to *Sun Song*.

92　Sun Ra, "Sun Song," notes to *Sun Song*.

93　One plausible source for Sun Ra's interest in outer space is Ray Bradbury's 1951 story "Way in the Middle of the Air," which depicts the black population of the U.S. South emigrating to Mars in spaceships. I look at this story more closely in chap. 2. Bradbury, *The Martian Chronicles* (London: Granada, 1980) 141–55. Rpt. of *The Silver Locusts*. 1951. Since I first wrote this section, a 1954 Sun Ra composition titled "Spaceship Lullaby" has been discovered in the Library of Congress, but as far as I am aware it remains exceptional in the early Ra oeuvre for its specific reference to a spaceship.

94 Ira Gitler, LP liner notes to *Martians Stay Home* by Shorty Rogers and His Giants, Atlantic Records K50714, 1980.

95 The situation in Little Rock provoked a furious, and widely reported, attack on President Eisenhower's "lack of guts" by the normally tight-lipped Louis Armstrong. See Ralph J. Gleason, *Celebrating the Duke: And Louis, Bessie, Billie, Carmen, Miles, Dizzy and Other Heroes* (New York: Delta, 1975) 34.

96 Duke Ellington, "The Race for Space," *The Duke Ellington Reader*, ed. Mark Tucker (New York: Oxford UP, 1993) 295. Another point of interest in this article, written in late 1957, is that Ellington compares "the inhumanity" involved in building the pyramids of the pharaohs, a task that he assumes required "thousands and thousands of slaves," to the "brutal subjugation of the individual" in the Soviet Union. Ibid., 294.

97 James Weldon Johnson, *The Autobiography of an Ex-Colored Man* (1912; London: X, 1995) 152–53. It is possible that the figure of John Brown was drawn from the famously charismatic Southern preacher John Jasper (d. 1893), who also spoke of celestial matters: "His celebrated sermon 'De Sun Do Move an' De Earth Am Square' was delivered with such power and conviction that it swayed even those who came to laugh." Paul Oliver, *Songsters and Saints: Vocal Traditions in Race Records* (Cambridge: Cambridge UP, 1984) 141.

98 Rev. A. W. Nix, "The White Flyer to Heaven—Part One," *Complete Recorded Works in Chronological Order, Volume 1: 23 April 1927 to 26 October 1928*, Document DOCD 5328, 1995. The information regarding Nix comes from Oliver, 150–53. Sun Ra appears to acknowledge this traditional image of the gospel train in his poem "The Cosmo Man": "Get on the Cosmo train / Run while you can / The Cosmo-train is a word-express / Get on the Cosmo train." Sun Ra, "The Cosmo Man," *Extension Out: The Immeasurable Equation Volume II* (Chicago: Ihnfinity/Saturn Research, 1972) 52.

99 Sun Ra, "Space Chants—A Medley," *Live in London 1990*, Blast First BFFP60CD, 1996. I wonder if that "Pluto too" isn't a sly dig, if not at Nix directly, then at the sermon tradition he represented and which did not include Pluto, since it was not discovered until 1930. It is as if Ra is signaling that his cosmology is more scientifically accurate and up-to-date than the Christian cosmology of the sermons—but I may be reading too much into this. It was in my notes to this CD that I first remarked on the similarities between the Nix sermon and Sun Ra's space chants. See Graham Lock, "Cosmos Songs: Sun Ra's Alternative Spirituals," CD insert notes to *Live in London 1990* by Sun Ra and His Year 2000 Myth Science Arkestra, Blast First BFFP60CD, 1996.

100 The London concert may be unusual in that not all of Ra's space chants followed the sermon narrative so closely in taking the audience from planet to planet through the solar system. However, another Sun Ra space chant, "Third Heaven," not only traverses the solar system but echoes Nix's ref-

erences to a First and Second Heaven: "Mercury is the first heaven, Venus is the second heaven." Sun Ra, "Third Heaven," *The Soul Vibrations of Man*, El Saturn 771, 1976. ("Third Heaven" is actually Campbell's title. The track is untitled on the LP.)

101 Rev. J. M. Gates, "The Eagle Stirs Her Nest," *Complete Recorded Works in Chronological Order, Volume 6: 20 February 1928 to 18 March 1929*, Document DOCD 5457, 1996. Qtd. in Oliver, 157.

102 Sun Ra, "Sun Song," notes to *Sun Song*.

103 "I Believe This Is Jesus," qtd. in John W. Work, *American Negro Songs and Spirituals* (New York: Bonanza, 1940) 147; "In Bright Mansions Above," qtd. in J. B. T. Marsh, *The Story of the Jubilee Singers, Including Their Songs* (London: Hodder and Stoughton, 1898) 232. Cf. also the title of a 1980 Sun Ra LP, *The Rose Hued Mansions of the Sun*.

104 After "Sun Song," the only plausible Ra allusion to the eagle tradition I have been able to trace on record is the 1970 title "A Bird's Eye View of Man's World," an instrumental track on the LP *The Night of the Purple Moon*, though there is a fleeting reference to "the eagle flying high" in the chant "Lost Horizon," which Ra performed in the 1980s but which has yet to appear on record. However, Ra did persist with bird imagery in his poems; see, for example, "Birds Without Wings" and "Everytime a Bird Goes By" in Sun Ra, *The Immeasurable Equation* (Philadelphia: Sun Ra, 1980) 48, 68. "Birds Without Wings" is also the title of an unreleased Ra composition, deposited with the Library of Congress on 27 December 1962. (Thanks to Chris Trent for this information.)

105 Qtd. in Schonfield, 3. Note, too, that Ra sometimes invited fans to join his "Ra legion." The wordplay is humorous but also makes a point.

106 Mark Sinker, "The Brother from Another Planet," *The Face* Sept. 1989: 44.

107 Spencer, 117–18. Similar pleas were voiced in white society, too, of course, especially after the much-publicized Scopes trial in 1925.

108 Barney E. Page, "Joshua Fit de Battle of Jericho," letter, *Chicago Defender* 16 Apr. 1932: editorial page.

109 Lawrence W. Levine, *Black Culture and Black Consciousness: Afro-American Folk Thought from Slavery to Freedom* (1977; Oxford: Oxford UP, 1978) 31–32.

110 Levine, 32–33.

111 Apart from cover versions of standards by other composers, the Arkestra's vocal repertoire consisted almost entirely of space chants and the half-chanted, half-declaimed Ra monologues that Campbell pointedly describes as "sermons." So Ra could be said to have fashioned his own spirituals and sermons, deliberate alternatives to those of the African American Christian tradition. In performance, the chants and sermons were often mixed together, recalling the way in which recorded sermons such as the Rev. A. W. Nix's "White Flyer to Heaven" were punctuated by snatches of spirituals. As noted, Ra's earliest space chants date from 1959. If I am right in supposing they were intended as science fiction alternatives to the spirituals, it is possible that the idea may have been prompted in part by the tremendous impact made in the mid-1950s by Ray Charles

and, a short time later, by Sam Cooke, with their secular R&B versions of gospel songs, an area of music previously considered sacrosanct within the black community. See Peter Guralnick, *Sweet Soul Music: Rhythm and Blues and the Southern Dream of Freedom* (1986; London: Penguin, 1991) 34–37, 50–51, 63–64.

112 Sun Ra, "Children of the Sun," *Live at "Praxis '84" Volume I*, Praxis CM 108, 1984; "He's Jus' de Same Today," J. W. Johnson, *Book*, 80–81. The only other performance of "Children of the Sun" that has been released on disc does not contain these lines (*When Spaceships Appear aka Children of the Sun aka Cosmo-Party Blues*, Saturn Sun Ra 101485, 1985), but an extended version of the chant, with these lines included, can be heard on a concert tape broadcast by New York's WKCR radio station in 1987. See Campbell, *Earthly Recordings*, 94.

113 Sun Ra, "I Am the Brother of the Wind," *Soundtrack to the Film Space Is the Place*; "Hold the Wind," *Work*, 159.

114 Of these, Campbell (*Earthly Recordings*) indexes only "Motherless Child" and "This World," the second of which he mistakenly identifies as a Sun Ra composition. "Swing Low" can be heard on audience tapes of concerts at the Newport Festival (3 July 1969), where it is used as a countermelody to the chant "Prepare for the Journey to Other Worlds," and Frankfurt (16 Aug. 1984), where it is included in a chant that also features "This World" and "Motherless Child." Special thanks to Chris Trent for this information and for supplying the relevant tapes. Examples of recordings of the other spirituals I listed are discussed in the text.

115 Sun Ra, "U.F.O.," *On Jupiter*.

116 Sun Ra, "Rocket Number Nine," *Beyond the Purple Star Zone*, El Saturn 123180, 1981.

117 Versions of "No Hiding Place" appear in J. W. Johnson, *Book*, 74, and *Work*, 149.

118 I think much of Ra's work, chiefly his space chants and "sermons," could be approached as examples of signifying. I have not done so here, however, since I believe the more detailed stylistic analysis required would be a diversion from my main areas of interest. For more on signifying, see Gates, esp. 44–124.

119 Sun Ra, "Third Heaven," *The Soul Vibrations of Man*. Versions of "All God's Chillun Got Wings" appear in J. W. Johnson, *Book*, 71, and *Work*, 180.

120 Sun Ra, "Space Chants — A Medley," *Live in London 1990*.

121 "The Old Ship of Zion," qtd. in William E. Barton, "Hymns of the Slave and the Freedman," Katz 96. There are many different versions of this spiritual; see also Katz, 18, for three others. Similar references to captains and tickets are commonly found in spirituals that feature a gospel ship or a gospel train.

122 "The Downward Road Is Crowded," *Work*, 163; "Hail! Hail!," Marsh, 295.

123 Sun Ra, "Space Chants — A Medley," *Live in London 1990*; "Good News," Higginson, 18.

124 Sun Ra, "21st Century" (my title), included in the space chant medleys

listed under the titles "We Travel the Spaceways" and "They'll Come Back," *Live at the Hackney Empire*, Leo CD LR 214/15, 1994; "Somebody Knocking at Your Door," Work, 192. The way in which the same few lines can recur in different chants resembles the way in which the spirituals, too, seem to have been put together; so, for example, the lines "I looked over Jordan and what did I see / A band of angels coming after me" occur in both "Swing Low, Sweet Chariot" and "Wade in the Water." Various Artists, *African-American Spirituals: The Concert Tradition*, Wade in the Water Volume I, Smithsonian Folkways CD SF 40072, 1994. Many blues songs also share this characteristic.

125 Sun Ra, "Face the Music," *Live at the Hackney Empire*; "Got to Go to Judgment," Work, 91.

126 Sun Ra, *The Night of the Purple Moon*, El Saturn IR 1972, 1974; "Didn't My Lord Deliver Daniel," J. W. Johnson, *Book*, 149–50. This may also account for Ra's CD title *Purple Night*, A&M 395 342-2, 1990.

127 Sun Ra, *Monorails and Satellites*, Evidence ECD 22013-2, 1991; Derek Lee Ragin, "Ev'ry Time I Feel the Spirit," *Ev'ry Time I Feel the Spirit: Spirituals*, Channel Classics CCS 2991, 1991.

128 Sun Ra, "Down Here on the Ground," *Live in London 1990*; "O Mary Don't You Weep Don't You Mourn," Work, 176. Cf. "Plenty Good Room," Work 188, and "Ev'ry Day'll Be Sunday," Work, 213, both of which include almost identical lines.

129 Chase, 237.

130 See DuBois, *Souls*, 177–88.

131 Sun Ra, "Satellites Are Spinning," *Soundtrack to the Film Space Is the Place*; Sun Ra, "Enlightment," *Nuits de la Fondation Maeght Volume I*, Recommended RR11, 1981.

132 Schaap, "Sun Ra," 28. Cf. Gagne, 371–72, where Ra again attacks church music and church services, claiming that God's response is "I don't like what you're doing. Don't sing those songs to me. I hate your solemn assemblies. I don't wanna hear them sad songs. Don't sing nothing like that to me."

133 Levine has argued that, far from being "sorrow songs," the spirituals were in fact "pervaded by a sense of change, transcendence, ultimate justice and personal worth." Levine, 39. Much the same could be said of Sun Ra's music.

134 This may be another reason for his attraction to "sun"-related songs, like "Keep Your Sunnyside Up."

135 Sun Ra, notes to *Sun Song*; Jim Macnie, "Sun Ra Is the Heaviest Man in This Galaxy . . . but He's Just Passing Through," *Musician* Jan. 1987: 60.

136 Chase, 238.

137 Lock, *Chasing*, 151. Ra sounds particularly bitter in a 1990 conversation with Chris Capers, John Hinds, and Peter Hinds, in which he claims he would rather destroy his music than publish it: "I don't want it out there. I don't want nobody to hear it . . . I don't want to help this planet. I want to forget I ever knew about it." Qtd. in Peter Hinds, ed., *Sun Ra Research* 8 Sept. 1996: 1–2.

138 Levine, 37.

139 In 1983 Sun Ra explained, "they do say Lucifer was the top musician in heaven. And I have to deal with that." Lock, unpublished interview, 1983. He also told me he was planning to release an LP called *Music from the Private Library of God*, which consisted of music "I composed and played for God alone" because "I felt that God should have something he couldn't get anywhere else." Though he mentioned this recording to several other interviewers, no LP of that title was ever released. (Szwed suggests that Ra regarded his entire oeuvre as being composed for "the private library of God"; see *Space*, 122–23.) The only version of "A Fireside Chat with Lucifer" on record is an instrumental, on *A Fireside Chat with Lucifer*, Saturn 198459-9, 1982, but a 1987 radio broadcast, which exists on tape, includes a track with this title that features a rap by Ra, in the role of an emissary from Lucifer, in which he repeatedly informs his audience, "God says, he don't want you no more."

140 Qtd. in Oliver, 152.

141 "Religion Is a Fortune," Work, 172. Cf. "Going to talk to the Father, talk to the Son," "Tell All the World, John," Work, 171.

142 Qtd. in Chase, 258. See also Chase, 261–63, for a discussion of Sun Ra's confusing and often contradictory statements about various "deities and supernatural beings."

143 Schaap, "An Interview," 28.

144 Francis Davis, "Philadelphia Stories," *The Wire* Sept. 1991: 12.

145 For more on the importance of the ring shout in African American slave culture, see Levine, 30–55, 165–66; Raboteau, 66–73; and, esp. Sterling Stuckey, *Slave Culture: Nationalist Theory and the Foundations of Black America* (1987; New York: Oxford UP, 1988) 3–97. Ring shouts have persisted in African American religious practice; examples of contemporary ring shouts can be heard on Various Artists, *African-American Congregational Singing: Nineteenth Century Roots*, Wade in the Water Volume II, Smithsonian Folkways CD SF 40073, 1994.

146 The Arkestra can be seen circling counterclockwise at the end of Robert Mugge's 1980 film *Sun Ra: A Joyful Noise*, Rhapsody Films, 1993. They can also be seen dancing in counterclockwise circles on collectors' videos of televised concerts in Chicago (1981) and Spain (1985) and in an audience video of a concert in Liverpool (1990). (Special thanks again to Chris Trent for sending me the relevant videotapes.) One piece of apparently contradictory visual evidence proved to be misleading. The photograph on the insert cover to the *Live at the Hackney Empire* CD shows the Arkestra circling in a clockwise direction. However, when I contacted label owner Leo Feigin, he explained that the photo had been printed left-for-right (i.e., as a mirror-image of the original shot) because it had been taken from a video, a process that gives you a left-for-right image. The usual practice is then to reprocess the image to return it to its original state, but because this procedure involves additional expense and because he thought "it didn't make

any difference," Feigin decided to forgo the reprocessing in this instance (and for all the other photographs used in the booklet and packaging).

147 Levine, 37–38.

148 The quotations are from the chants "We Travel the Spaceways," "Enlightment" (aka "Enlightenment"), and "Outer Spaceways Incorporated," all of which Sun Ra performed and recorded many times. Examples can be heard on, respectively, *We Travel the Spaceways*, Evidence ECD 22038-2, 1992, *Nuits de la Fondation Maeght Volume I*, and *Live at "Praxis '84" Volume I*.

149 John Corbett, "Anthony Braxton's *Bildungsmusik*: Thoughts on 'Composition 171,' " Lock, *Mixtery*, 185.

150 Qtd. in Corbett, "Anthony Braxton's *Bildungsmusik*," 185.

151 Oliver, 153. Cf. James Cone's argument that the image of heaven in the spirituals represented a "Transcendent Present": "The only requirement for acceptance on the 'gospel train' was the willingness to *move*, to step into the future. . . . Blacks were able, through song, to transcend the enslavement of the present and to live *as if the future had already come*." (Second emphasis mine.) James Cone, *The Spirituals and the Blues: An Interpretation* (New York: Seabury, 1972) 94–95.

152 Qtd. in Raboteau, 68.

153 Qtd. in Schonfield, 9.

154 It is possible that Ra was also signaling the music's black roots, as represented by the ring shout. Later performances of spirituals, as popularized by the Fisk Jubilee Singers in the 1870s and eulogized by W. E. B. DuBois in 1903, were concert presentations, often with more Europeanized harmonies and less rhythmic power—in short, dignified and mellifluous expressions of "sorrow" delivered statically onstage rather than in the participatory ring shout. In 1934 Zora Neale Hurston referred to these songs as "neo-spirituals" and regarded this new manner of performance as inauthentically black: "Glee clubs and concert singers put on their tuxedos, bow prettily to the audience, get the pitch and burst into magnificent song—but not *Negro* song." Zora Neale Hurston, "Spirituals and Neo-Spirituals," *Negro*, ed. Nancy Cunard (1934; New York: Frederick Ungar, 1979) 224. By presenting his space chants as ring shouts, Ra could perhaps be said to be reaffirming their (and the spirituals') status as "*Negro* song."

155 In Gilroy, *Small Acts*, 224. A few lines later, talking about different versions of African American history, and expressing regret that so many African Americans "are embracing an ideology of victimization," hooks remarks that if it has to come down to a choice "between identifying either with slaves or with pharaohs . . . then we must identify with the pharaohs." Ibid., 224–25.

156 Sun Ra, "Your Only Hope," 106.

157 Sun Ra, notes to *Sun Song*.

158 See, for example, "Didn't My Lord Deliver Daniel," "My Lord, What a Mornin,' " and "O Rocks Don't Fall on Me," J. W. Johnson, *Book*, 148, 162, 164.

159 Sun Ra, "Nuclear War," *A Fireside Chat with Lucifer*.

160 See, for example, the interviews with Gagne, Macnie, and Reid.

161 Lock, unpublished interview, 1983.

162 Sun Ra, notes to *Sun Song*.

163 Chase, 258n.

164 See Cone, 88–90; Levine, 51–52; Miles Mark Fisher, *Negro Slave Songs in the United States* (Ithaca, N.Y.: Cornell UP, 1953) 41.

165 Sometimes he said he had been there (Davis, unpublished interview); sometimes he said he hadn't (Sun Ra, "Your Only Hope," 99).

166 Lock, *Chasing*, 149. The main evidence that Ra advanced for this feeling was his belief that in various ancient mythologies Saturn had been associated with the color black: "There were black kings and Babylon was a black nation, and they built a temple to Saturn, but, of course, religions came and obliterated it." Ibid.

167 Fiofori, "Sun Ra's African Roots," 32.

168 Sun Ra, "Journey to Saturn," *Out Beyond the Kingdom of.*

169 Corbett, *Extended Play*, 171.

170 Szwed, *Space*, 381–82. (I assumed "Le Son'y Ra" was a misprint for "Le Sony'r Ra," but John Szwed has told me that, according to his informant, the former is the spelling on the headstone.) He reports, too, that at the graveside ceremony, the Baptist preacher, the Rev. Pherelle Fowler, "called on those assembled to ask the Lord that Sun Ra be raised on eagle wings and taken on high where he might shine like the sun" (*Space*, 381). It is ironic, to say the least, that Ra's departure should have been evoked in the imagery of the very Baptist sermon tradition from which he had emerged (in "Sun Song") and had consequently spent so much of his time trying to subvert and transform.

171 The quotations are from "All God's Chillun Got Wings," J. W. Johnson, *Book*, 71; "The Angels Changed My Name," Marsh, 261.

172 "The Angels Changed My Name," Marsh, 261.

Chapter 2 Of Aliens and Angels: Mythic Identity

1 Untitled spiritual, qtd. in Cone, 105.

2 Lock, *Forces*, 12. The description is of the opening moments of a concert in Brixton, London, on 11 November 1985.

3 Now renamed Alabama A&M University. Chase, 48. I cannot resist pointing out that Ra left Normal in 1936 and never went back!

4 For a detailed and moving account of this period in Ra's life, see Szwed, *Space*, 39–46. Ra's health problems involved a hernia condition that had developed in adolescence and that may have been a contributory cause of his death; see Corbett, *Extended Play*, 174.

5 A copy of the document legalizing Ra's change of name is reproduced in Corbett, *Extended Play*, 175.

6 For full biographical details, see Szwed, *Space*.

7 Ellison, *Shadow*, 148. See also Kimberly W. Benston, "I Yam What I Yam: The Topos of Un(naming) in Afro-American Literature," *Black Literature and*

Literary Theory, ed. Henry Louis Gates Jr. (1984; New York: Routledge, 1990) 151–72.

8 See, for example, bassist Hakim Jami's comments: "I mean Duke Ellington wasn't the 'King of Jazz,' Paul Whiteman was. And if that's the case, then I don't consider Duke Ellington a *jazz* musician. Whatever he's playing, he's the best I've heard, so I've got to call him the King of that." Wilmer, *As Serious,* 23–24. This quotation illustrates how debate over who names the musicians leads to debate over who has the authority to define and name the music, an issue to which we will return in the chapters on Duke Ellington and Anthony Braxton.

9 Though, in fact, Ellington acquired his name "Duke" while still at school. D. Ellington, *Music Is,* 20.

10 Julio Finn, *The Bluesman: The Musical Heritage of Black Men and Women in the Americas* (London: Quartet, 1986) 195–96. Other "black names" in the blues tradition would include, for example, Muddy Waters, Howlin' Wolf, Leadbelly, Lightnin' Hopkins, and Magic Sam. Many of these artists were either based, or recorded, in Chicago during the period that Sun Ra was resident there.

11 Noble Drew Ali, for example, proposed that African Americans should retitle themselves Moorish-Americans and claimed they were descended from the Moors of Morocco. See Essien-Udom, 46. For more on Elijah Muhammad's beliefs, see below.

12 Sara Harris, *Father Divine: Holy Husband* (New York: Doubleday, 1953) 12.

13 Qtd. in Chase, 258n. And: " 'The Magic City' was a promotional slogan for Birmingham. . . . Sun Ra was born and raised close to the railroad station where every day he would have seen the huge sign which welcomed visitors to the city with those very words." John F. Szwed, CD insert notes to *The Magic City* by Sun Ra and His Solar Arkestra, Evidence ECD 22069-2, 1993. The insert booklet includes a photograph of this sign.

14 Bret Primack, "Captain Angelic: Sun Ra," *Down Beat* 4 May 1978: 14.

15 Rusch, 65.

16 Schaap, "Sun Ra," 28. At a 1985 concert in Chicago, Ra announced he had been here for five thousand years (thanks to Chris Trent for this information). Both Father Divine and Sun Ra were mere starchildren, however, compared to bassist Maghustut Malachi Favors of the Art Ensemble of Chicago, whose biographical entry on a press release, ca. 1969, began: "Into being in this universe some 43,000 years ago." Qtd. in John Litweiler, *The Freedom Principle: Jazz After 1958* (1984; Poole, Dorset: Blandford, 1985) 176.

17 Corbett, *Extended Play,* 222; Lock, *Chasing,* 159–60. The only example Gilmore gives of the Muslims stealing from Ra is the idea of "a Negro being a dead body." The Muslims indeed referred to unconverted blacks as "dead," but Essien-Udom suggests that the idea originated with Noble Ali Drew. Essien-Udom, 46. For more on Ra's early contacts with the Nation of Islam, see Szwed, *Space,* 105–06.

18 Elijah Muhammad, "What Do the Muslims Want?" *Black Nationalism in*

America, ed. John H. Bracey Jr., August Meier, and Elliott Rudwick (Indianapolis: Bobbs-Merrill, 1970) 406.

19 Essien-Udom, 121–22.

20 Essien-Udom, 130.

21 Sun Ra, "Satellites Are Spinning," *Soundtrack to the Film Space Is the Place.*

22 The "shield of beauty," which I mentioned in chap. 1, comes from Sinker, "Sun Ra."

23 Essien-Udom, 179. Cf. Ra's various references to black people being asleep (Wilmer, *As Serious*, 81; Sinker, "Sun Ra"), living "lies" (Schonfield, 10), and being stuck in "a past that somebody manufactured for 'em" (Lock, unpublished interview, 1983).

24 Essien-Udom, 179.

25 Stuckey, 195.

26 Ibid.

27 James Olney, "'I Was Born': Slave Narratives, Their Status as Autobiography and as Literature," *The Slave's Narrative*, ed. Charles T. Davis and Henry Louis Gates Jr. (Oxford: Oxford UP, 1985) 153.

28 Stuckey, 194–95. Perhaps, too, Sojourner Truth's declaration that "I am not going to die, I am going home like a shooting star" sheds light on Ra's various statements about leaving the planet—but *not* by dying. (See, for example, Lock, *Chasing*, 144.) The Sojourner Truth statement appears in Venice Johnson, ed., *Voices of the Dream: African-American Women Speak* (San Francisco: Chronicle, 1995) 5. (Thanks to Jack Collier for drawing my attention to this book.)

29 Ra's statement to me that "I gave up my life by never living it" can perhaps be taken as referring to the life of Herman Poole Blount. Lock, *Chasing*, 153.

30 Ira Steingroot, "Sun Ra's Magical Kingdom," *Reality Hackers*, Winter 1988: 50. Peter Watrous, in his liner notes to the *Reflections in Blue* LP by the Sun Ra Arkestra, Black Saint BSR 0101, 1987, says that Ra's mother knew Black Herman, but in the interviews I have seen where Ra talks about Black Herman, he makes no mention of this.

31 Ishmael Reed, *Mumbo Jumbo* (1972; London: Alison & Busby, 1988) 32.

32 See Robert Farris Thompson, *Flash of the Spirit: African and Afro-American Art and Philosophy* (1983; New York: Vintage/Random House, 1984) 19.

33 Rusch, 68. Chris Trent has suggested in conversation that Ra may have said "Amon," which certainly comes from ancient Egypt, as in Amon-Ra. However, Ra also told Ira Steingroot that both Herman and Arman, read backward, meant "name Ra." Steingroot, 50.

34 Lock, *Chasing*, 158–59. Slightly different versions appear in Campbell, "Sun Ra," 24, and Corbett, *Extended Play*, 219.

35 Steingroot, 50.

36 For example, Schaap, "Sun Ra," 9.

37 Qtd. in Schonfield, 2.

38 Corbett, *Extended Play*, 316. For more on Ra's wordplay with names, see Szwed, *Space*, 79–87.

39 Olney, 155.

40 Lock, *Chasing*, 156. Cf. the lines from the spiritual "Sometimes I Feel Like a Motherless Child": "Sometimes I feel like I'd never been borned." Qtd. in Barton, 91.

41 Ra also did the following "equation" on the word "birth": "This birth thing is very bad for people. The word should be abolished. Supreme beings have trapped humans with words and one of the words is birth. You see, birth is also spelled berth, which means a bed, and when they bury a person that's their berth because they're placed in a berth. So the day they're dead becomes their berthday. Berthday also has the phonetic word for earth in it—erth—so you could also say be-earth day." Sun Ra, untitled quotation in *Sun Ra* (Milbrae, Calif.: Omni Press, 1989) n.p.

42 Qtd. in Schonfield, 9.

43 Olney, 152.

44 Zora Neale Hurston, "Conversions and Visions," *Negro*, ed. Cunard, 32–34.

45 Clifton H. Johnson, ed., *God Struck Me Dead: Religious Conversion Experiences and Autobiographies of Ex Slaves* (Philadelphia: Pilgrim, 1969).

46 See Andrew P. Watson, "Negro Primitive Religious Services," C. H. Johnson, 1–2.

47 See, for example, C. H. Johnson, 19, 58, 64, 165.

48 Schaap, "An Interview," 31.

49 Schaap, "An Interview," 32.

50 C. H. Johnson, 146. See also 9, 66, 171.

51 C. H. Johnson, 145.

52 C. H. Johnson, 165, 143.

53 Qtd. in Work, 148.

54 Sinker, "Sun Ra." This 1989 interview and that with Francis Davis (1990) contain Sun Ra's most detailed accounts of his abduction experience. The two accounts are virtually identical, though in the one with Davis, he states that "I landed on a planet that I identified as Saturn" and adds: "First thing I saw was something like the rail—long rail—of a railroad track comin' down out of the sky." (Davis, unpublished interview, 1990.) If this image recalls the title *Monorails and Satellites* and the lines "Ain't but one train on this track / Runs to heaven and runs right back" (from "Ev'ry Time I Feel the Spirit"), it also recalls the image of Jacob's Ladder, as figured in at least one of the conversion visions in *God Struck Me Dead*: "I saw, as it were, a ladder. It was more like a pole with rungs on it let down from heaven, and it reached from heaven to earth." C. H. Johnson, 147. A "pole with rungs on it" looks very much like a rail as well as a ladder.

55 C. H. Johnson, 61.

56 "Free at Last," Work, 197.

57 Sinker, "Sun Ra."

58 C. H. Johnson, 151.

59 C. H. Johnson, 91.

60 C. H. Johnson, 100. It is possible that Ra was comparing himself to this

"little man" as a fellow divine messenger as well as making a timely joke in his 1984 chant, "I'm Big Brother's Little Brother." This title is not listed in Campbell, *Earthly Recordings*, but I heard Ra perform it in London in 1984. Gates notes that two of the characteristics of the West African trickster god Esu, also a divine messenger, are his small size and penetrating eyes. (Gates, 17–18.) That the little man of the slave testimonies is often described as pale perhaps reflects the "whitening" of this mythology as it became absorbed into Christian myth. Esu, in contrast, is very dark and also limps, two characteristics he retains in his other Christian mythological incarnation, demonized as the Devil.

61 Sinker, "Sun Ra."

62 Ibid.

63 C. H. Johnson, 94.

64 C. H. Johnson, 171. Cf. also 59–60, 67.

65 C. H. Johnson, 123–24. Cf. also 111. John Corbett has kindly drawn my attention to a little-known record from 1956 called *Authentic Music from Another Planet* (State Records 211), which, he says, "recounts an abduction story in which the narrator, Howard Menger, was driving home one evening and had control of his car seized by a force which led him into the countryside. He reports being led into a house where some music was being performed by a 'man from Saturn' who played in an unusual way on a 'Saturnian instrument very much like our piano.' After this encounter, Menger, who had never had any instruction, could play piano guided by unseen forces. Bizarre coincidence, no?" Indeed! Personal correspondence, 2 Feb. 1998.

66 For reports of comparable nineteenth-century testimonies and experiences, and contemporary white commentators' belief in their "unmistakable sincerity," see Levine, 36.

67 The Rev. Jessie Jefferson, qtd. in Hurston, "Conversions," 33. For an account of more recent abduction experiences, see John E. Mack, *Abduction: Human Encounters with Aliens* (London: Simon & Schuster, 1994).

68 Thomas S. Szasz, "The Sane Slave: An Historical Note on the Use of Medical Diagnosis as Justificatory Rhetoric," *American Journal of Psychotherapy* 25 (1971): 228–29.

69 Szasz, 230.

70 All the more so since many white doctors continue to diagnose cultural difference as evidence of insanity. See Roland Littlewood and Maurice Lipsedge, *Aliens and Alienists: Ethnic Minorities and Psychiatry*, 2nd ed. (London: Unwin Hyman, 1989). Special thanks to Jack Collier for this reference. For a modern equivalent to drapetomania, try this statement: "In 1957 psychiatrists suggested that mental illness among blacks in the USA was due to an interest in politics: the black was 'constantly stirred up by his needs, as well as by the propaganda of his leaders and by the communists.'" Qtd. in Littlewood and Lipsedge, 38.

71 Baldwin, "Of the Sorrow Songs," 326.

72 Lock, *Chasing*, 150–51.

73 C. Vann Woodward, *The Strange Career of Jim Crow*, 3rd rev. ed. (New York: Oxford UP, 1974) 114.

74 Woodward, 114–15.

75 Woodward, 115.

76 Woodward, 116.

77 Woodward, 117. Sun Ra's wordplay occasionally hints at the influence of Southern politics. For example, his declaration that it was better to be a "superior" being than a "supreme" being could perhaps be seen as a sideswipe at the notion of white supremacy. Qtd. in Graham Lock, "Wavelength Infinity," CD insert notes to *Friendly Galaxy* by the Sun Ra Arkestra, Leo CD LR 188, 1993.

78 Corbett, *Extended Play*, 7–24.

79 Corbett, *Extended Play*, 15.

80 Corbett, *Extended Play*, 15–17.

81 Levine, 33.

82 Paul Radin, "Status, Fantasy, and the Christian Dogma: A Note about the Conversion Experiences of Negro Ex-Slaves," Foreword, C. H. Johnson, viii.

83 In the film *Sun Ra: A Joyful Noise*.

84 Radin, ix.

85 Albert Ayler, "Music Is the Healing Force of the Universe," *Music Is the Healing Force of the Universe*, Impulse!-ABC AS 9191, 1970. Ra also told Phast Phreddie in 1990 that his music "can heal people too." Phast Phreddie, "Sun Ra Has a Master Plan," *Contrasts* Mar. or Apr. 1990: 44.

86 Corbett, *Extended Play*, 8–9.

87 Lee "Scratch" Perry, "I Am a Madman," *Battle of Armagideon* (Millionaire Liquidator) by Mr. Lee "Scratch" Perry and the Upsetters, Trojan TRLS 227, 1986. I had better make clear that I am not suggesting Ra never said anything that sounded "mad." His use of humor often involved making the most outrageous (and wickedly funny) proposals in a totally deadpan manner, leaving the audience/interviewer utterly confused as to how seriously he intended his statements to be taken. (For some examples, see Chase, 266.) But, at the risk of sounding like a nose-grinding pedant, what I am trying to do here is to let the humor speak for itself and look at what else might be going on. And it is at this point that it does make a difference whether Ra represented himself as insane or, as I will argue below, as alien.

88 Sun Ra, "Somebody Else's World," *My Brother the Wind Volume II*, Evidence ECD 22040-2, 1992.

89 Steingroot, 50. Ellipsis in original.

90 *Space Is the Place*, prod. Jim Newman, dir. John Coney, performed by Sun Ra and His Intergalactic Solar Arkestra, Rhapsody Films, 1993.

91 Cf. his declamation that opens "Of Invisible Them": "Are you so wilfully ignorant of what you should be / That you think you are only what others say you are?" From *Purple Night*.

92 Lock, *Chasing*, 153.

93 John F. Szwed, "Sun Ra, 1914–1993," *Village Voice* 15 June 1993: 70.

94 Lock, *Chasing*, 148. Ra said much the same to Francis Davis: "Anything before history is a myth. That's where black people are." Davis, unpublished interview, 1990.

95 Qtd. in Chase, 271–72. Original interview by Jean-Louis Noames in *Jazz Magazine*, Dec. 1965.

96 Sun Ra, "Your Only Hope," 113. Cf. his statements in the film *Sun Ra: A Joyful Noise*: "Those of the reality have lost their way. Now they have to listen to what myth has to say. . . . They can judge whether I'm really telling a lie or whether I'm telling the truth, and if I'm telling a lie they have to judge whether the lie is more profitable to them than the truth that they know. So therefore I'm paving the way for humanity to recognize the myth and become part of my mythocracy instead of their theocracies and democracies . . . ." Ra often criticized democracy because he thought the premise that everybody was equal was "a fantasy." See Gagne, 369.

97 Remembering his statement, "The impossible attracts me because everything possible has been done and the world didn't change." Qtd. in Schonfield, 2. Remembering, too, that African Americans would refer to their folk tales and myths as "lies"; see Hurston, *Mules*, 8.

98 Qtd. in Woodward, 113.

99 Muddy Waters, "Mannish Boy," *They Call Me Muddy Waters*, Instant-Charly Records CD INS 5036, 1990.

100 Chase, 260. Another reason why Ra might have had ambivalent feelings about the word "man" concerned the hernia problem I mentioned earlier, which was related to the retraction of one of his testicles. This condition caused Sun Ra both physical pain and mental anguish; see, in particular, the letters he wrote in 1942–43 concerning his claim to be a conscientious objector. Szwed, *Space*, 41–45.

101 Reported in *Jazz FM* magazine, issue 2 1990: 8.

102 Mark Sinker, unpublished interview with Sun Ra, Philadelphia, Spring 1989.

103 Theis, 49.

104 Corbett, *Extended Play*, 17.

105 Qtd. in Cone, 105.

106 Primack, 41. However, on other occasions, he claimed to be a demon!

107 Primack, 41.

108 Qtd. in *Jazz FM*, issue 2 1990: 9.

109 Houston A. Baker Jr., *Modernism and the Harlem Renaissance* (1987; Chicago: U of Chicago P, 1989) 51.

110 Baker, 50.

111 Baker, 51.

112 Qtd. in *Mothership Connection*, prod. Avril Johnson, dir. John Akumfrah, Black Audio Film Collective Production for Channel 4, 1995.

113 Qtd. in Shamoon Zamir, *Dark Voices: W. E. B. DuBois and American Thought, 1888–1903* (Chicago: U of Chicago P, 1995) 55. See Zamir, 46–60, for a full discussion of this story.

114 Richard Wright, *The Outsider* (New York: Harper & Row, 1953) 26–27.

115 The famous "Roswell incident," when the U.S. military initially announced that a flying saucer had crash-landed in the New Mexico desert and then immediately denied it, took place in 1947, i.e., *after* the scene in the café (though it is possible that Wright may have had this incident in mind when he wrote the book).

116 See Corbett, *Extended Play*, 7–24.

117 Qtd. in Arthur Taylor, *Notes and Tones: Musician to Musician Interviews* (1982; London: Quartet, 1983) 69–70.

118 Qtd. in the *Mothership Connection* television film. After I had written this section, I was intrigued to read that Sun Ra told the audience at a 1988 New York concert that the word "nigger" was derived from the Hebrew word "ger," meaning "stranger" or "alien." Szwed, *Space*, 313.

119 Dumas was the Hank Dumas who wrote the LP liner notes reprinted in the CD insert notes to *Cosmic Tones for Mental Therapy* and *Art Forms of Dimensions Tomorrow* by Sun Ra and His Myth Science Arkestra, Evidence ECD 22036-2, 1992. These were first published on the sleeve of *Cosmic Tones*, which was issued on LP in 1967. Henry Dumas was shot dead in mysterious circumstances by a New York City Transit policeman on 23 May 1968. John Szwed told me that he had heard Dumas had been returning home from a visit to Sun Ra when he was killed. Given the date, it is possible that Dumas had been returning from a birthday celebration (though Ra would not have called it that). This would perhaps help to account for Ra's extreme fury on hearing of Dumas's death. See Szwed, *Space*, 223.

120 Henry Dumas, "Outer Space Blues," *Knees of a Natural Man: The Selected Poetry of Henry Dumas*, ed. Eugene B. Redmond (New York: Thunder's Mouth, 1989) 66–67.

121 Szwed, notes to *Soundtrack*.

122 Ibid.

123 Ibid.

124 Olney, 153.

125 Frederick Douglass, *Narrative of the Life of Frederick Douglass, an American Slave* (1845; New York: Penguin, 1986) 113.

126 Although Covey in the Douglass narrative is white, overseers were sometimes black, as is the Overseer in *Space Is the Place*. See William Kauffman Scarborough, *The Overseer: Plantation Management in the Old South* (Baton Rouge: Louisiana State UP, 1966) 16–19.

127 There may also be a jazz in-joke involved here, the coupling of chariot and Cadillac a humorous reference to (or perhaps inspired by?) Dizzy Gillespie's 1967 LP *Swing Low, Sweet Cadillac*, the title track of which is a witty updating of the spiritual that Gillespie had featured in concert for many years. The recording was reissued on CD in 1996, Impulse! 11782.

128 M. R. Delany and Robert Campbell, *Search for a Place: Black Separatism and Africa, 1860* (Ann Arbor: U of Michigan P, 1969). Rpt. of *Official Report of the Niger Valley Exploring Party* by M. R. Delany, and *A Pilgrimage to My Motherland:*

An *Account of a Journey Among the Egbas and Yorubas of Central Africa, in 1859–60* by Robert Campbell.

129 The earliest listed performance of the Sun Ra song "Space Is the Place" is October 1971 (Campbell, *Earthly*, 55). Another song, "Outer Space," which Campbell describes as "a precursor" to "Space Is the Place," is first listed in 1969, but it does not include the phrase "space is the place."

130 Qtd. in Langston Hughes, *Not Without Laughter* (1930; New York: Alfred A. Knopf, 1971) 214. Sun Ra may have had this spiritual in mind when he titled a 1981 composition "Journey Stars Beyond." See Sun Ra, *Journey Stars Beyond*, aka *Oblique Parallax*, Saturn SR 72881, 1981.

131 Bradbury, *Martian*, 147.

132 Essien-Udom, 49.

133 Bradbury, *Martian*, 145.

134 Bradbury, *Martian*, 152.

135 Marsh, 170.

136 Bradbury, *Martian*, 154.

137 He confirmed this to me in 1983.

138 " 'Way in the Middle of the Air' may be the single most incisive episode of black and white relations in science fiction by a white writer. But its very rarity demonstrates how alien the territory of American science fiction in its so-called golden age after the second world war was for black readers . . . ." Robert Crossley, Introduction, *Kindred* by Octavia E. Butler (Boston: Beacon, 1988) xv.

139 In light of the earlier discussion of Ra's claims of extraterrestrial origins and subsequent labeling as a "nutter," another Bradbury story makes interesting reading. In "The Earth Men," a four-man space crew from Earth lands on Mars, only to be met by complete indifference on the part of the Martians, who, assuming the men are insane, direct them to the local lunatic asylum, which turns out to be full of Martians who claim to be from Earth. The psychiatrist, Mr Xxx, thinks the crew and the rocket ship (which they take him to see) are telepathic hallucinations created by the supposedly mad captain of the crew. Mr Xxx congratulates him on being "a psychotic genius" before shooting him to put him out of his supposed misery. When, to his surprise, the other three crew men fail to disappear—"You continue to exist? This is superb! Hallucinations with time and spatial persistence!"—he shoots them, too. But although the bodies and the spaceship itself continue to "persist," Mr Xxx still refuses to believe they are real. Instead, he fears he has been "contaminated" by the captain's "insanity" and so shoots himself. Ray Bradbury, "The Earth Men," *The Stories of Ray Bradbury* (London: Granada, 1981) 102–14.

140 Woodward, 11.

141 For example, Woodward, 6, 18, 92.

142 Hans Nathan, *Dan Emmett and the Rise of Early Negro Minstrelsy* (Norman: U of Oklahoma P, 1962) 245. Relatively recent research has thrown doubt on Emmett's authorship, and it now seems likely that "Dixie" actually origi-

nated with the Snowdens, a musical family of African Americans who had moved from the South in the early 1800s and settled near Emmett's home in Mount Vernon, Knox County, Ohio. See Howard I. Sacks and Judith Rose Sacks, *Way Up North in Dixie: A Black Family's Claim to the Confederate Anthem* (Washington, D.C.: Smithsonian Institution, 1993).

143 Anonymous ex-slave, qtd. in B. A. Botkin, *Lay My Burden Down: A Folk History of Slavery* (1945; Chicago: U of Chicago P, 1969) 193.

144 Sacks and Sacks, 4.

145 See Booker T. Washington, *Up from Slavery* (1901; New York: Penguin, 1986) 239.

146 See Sacks and Sacks, 4.

147 Sun Ra, "Space Is the Place," Soundtrack.

148 Chase has outlined some resemblances between Ra's beliefs and those of Madam Blavatsky: 261–62. See also Szwed, *Space*, 107–08.

149 Sinker, unpublished interview, 1989. Ellipsis in original.

150 For Legba and the blues, see Finn; for Esu and literature, see Gates; for further discussion of the origins and influence of these related gods, see Thompson, *Flash*, 18–33.

151 Ra at various times claimed to be the ambassador or servant of the Creator, Lucifer, Satan, and Death.

152 For more on the importance of the crossroads in blues mythology, see Finn, especially his discussion of the well-known story that Robert Johnson went to the crossroads at midnight to sell his soul to the devil (i.e., Legba, as demonized by the Christian church). Finn, 210–23. A wry resonance of this tale was told to me by Paul Smith of Blast First Records, who, for his first business meeting with Sun Ra, was instructed to be at a certain New York City intersection at midnight with a bagful of cash.

153 Sun Ra, "Spiral Outwardly," poem included in CD insert notes to *Other Planes of There*.

Chapter 3   In the Jungles of America: History Without Saying It

1 Arthur A. Schomburg, "The Negro Digs Up His Past," *The New Negro*, ed. Alain Locke (1925; New York: Atheneum, 1969) 231.

2 Janet Mabie, "Ellington's 'Mood in Indigo': Harlem's 'Duke' Seeks to Express His Race," *Christian Science Monitor* 13 Dec. 1930. Rpt. in Tucker, *Duke Ellington Reader*, 43. In subsequent references to this anthology, I use the abbreviation DER.

3 Florence Zunser, "'Opera Must Die,' Says Galli-Curci! Long Live the Blues!" *New York Evening Graphic Magazine* 27 Dec. 1930. Rpt. in Tucker, DER, 45. The mention of Egypt suggests that Ellington, like Ra, was impressed by the ancient black civilization of the Nile Valley, though this was not a theme he developed in his work; indeed, as we saw in chapter 1 (n. 96), in 1957 Ellington was comparing the rule of the pharaohs to the inhumanity of Soviet dictatorship.

4 Duke Ellington, "The Duke Steps Out," *Rhythm* Mar. 1931. Rpt. in Tucker, *DER*, 49–50.

5 See Mark Tucker, *Ellington: The Early Years* (Urbana: U of Illinois P, 1991), esp. 3–15.

6 Qtd. in Steven Lasker, CD insert notes to *Jungle Nights in Harlem* (1927–1932) by Duke Ellington and His Cotton Club Orchestra, Bluebird-BMG ND82499, 1991.

7 James de Jongh, *Vicious Modernism: Black Harlem and the Literary Imagination* (Cambridge: Cambridge UP, 1990) 5.

8 De Jongh, 9.

9 Marshall W. Stearns, *The Story of Jazz* (1956; New York: Oxford UP, 1970) 184. Stearns must have seen this sketch between December 1927, when Ellington's orchestra moved into the Cotton Club, and February 1929, when Bubber Miley left the band. Norman Weinstein has suggested that the subject of this skit was "Colonel Hubert Fauntleroy Julian, the first black aviation hero. Who could forget that day he parachuted over Harlem, saxophone in hand, playing ragged choruses of 'Runnin' Wild' during his descent" (Weinstein, 40). There are two problems with this suggestion. Julian's saxophone-toting descent had taken place more than four years earlier, in 1923, so it was hardly topical material for a sketch. Nor does Weinstein explain why a sketch written by white writers for an all-white audience should feature a black character who, if Stearns's response was typical, seems to have been unknown to that audience. And Weinstein is surely mistaken in his subsequent claim that the 1941 track "Menelik (The Lion of Judah)," recorded by an Ellington small group under the nominal leadership of trumpeter Rex Stewart, was a tribute to Julian. According to William R. Scott, in his *Sons of Sheba's Race: African-Americans and the Italo-Ethiopian War, 1935–1941* (Bloomington: Indiana UP, 1993), by 1936 Julian had become "easily the most detested man in black America" because of what was perceived as his cowardly conduct in Ethiopia after the Italian invasion (Scott, 81). It seems much more likely that Stewart's track, recorded in July 1941, commemorated the liberation of Addis Ababa the previous May and that the title saluted Emperor Haile Selassie, "the Lion of Judah," by comparing him to Menelik II, the nineteenth-century Ethiopian emperor who was famous for defeating the Italians at the battle of Adwa in 1896. Rex Stewart, "Menelik (The Lion of Judah)," rec. 1941, *The Great Ellington Units* by Johnny Hodges/Rex Stewart/Barney Bigard, Bluebird-BMG ND86751, 1988.

10 Robert C. Toll, *Blacking Up: The Minstrel Show in Nineteenth-Century America* (New York: Oxford UP, 1974) 34.

11 See Mark Tucker, "Ellington's 'Jungle Music,'" *Duke Ellington and New Orleans: A 90th Birthday Tribute*, ed. Caroline Richmond (Lugano: Festa New Orleans Music Production, 1989) 13.

12 Thomas Cripps, *Slow Fade to Black: The Negro in American Film, 1900–1942* (New York: Oxford UP, 1977) 254–55.

13 Tucker, "Ellington's 'Jungle Music,'" 13.

14 De Jongh, 24.

15 Alain Locke, "The Negro Spirituals," Locke, *New Negro*, 199.

16 J. A. Rogers, "Jazz at Home," Locke, *New Negro*, 221. Rogers noted jazz's roots in Africa, but he also made a point of differentiating it from Africa, writing that "it bears all the marks of a nerve-strung, strident, mechanized civilization. It is a thing of the jungles—modern man-made jungles" (Rogers, 218).

17 Cf. John Gennari's comment: "it is a shortcoming of the Harlem Renaissance intelligentsia that they failed to appreciate fully the cultural importance of Armstrong, Ellington, Bessie Smith, Fletcher Henderson, and other jazz and blues artists—in retrospect the most significant artists of their time." He goes on to quote Nathan Huggins's explanation that none of the Harlem intellectuals took jazz seriously because they viewed it as a folk art, whereas they were fixated on creating high culture. John Gennari, "Jazz Criticism: Its Development and Ideologies," *Black American Literature Forum* 25 (1991): 471. The spirituals, in contrast, though originally a folk art, had undergone a process of Europeanization that began in the 1870s with the first performances of the Fisk Jubilee Singers, and by the 1920s they could be, and were, presented in concert as high art. See Hurston, "Spirituals," 223–25.

18 Qtd. in Leonard Feather, "Duke Ellington," *The Jazz Makers: Essays on the Greats of Jazz*, ed. Nat Shapiro and Nat Hentoff (1957; New York: Da Capo, 1988) 192. Ruth Ellington claims to have been "about eight years old" when she heard this broadcast, which would date it to 1923. This is presumably a case of faulty memory, since Ellington is not known to have broadcast nationally until 1928, nor was his music known as "jungle music" until that time.

19 D. Ellington, *Music Is*, 419–20. Ellington's men were not the first or only players to use mutes, of course. But Ellington, greatly helped by Miley, was the first band leader to meld such effects into a distinctive and identifiable group style. See Gunther Schuller, *Early Jazz: Its Roots and Musical Development* (1968; New York: Oxford UP, 1986) 320–32.

20 Collier, 43.

21 Weinstein, 38–39.

22 The various names were necessary for contractual reasons. The band needed a different name for each label it recorded for.

23 See Brian Rust, *Jazz Records 1897–1941*, vol. 1 (New Rochelle, N.Y.: Arlington House, 1978) 474–84. "Jungle Jamboree" was actually written by Fats Waller. One other "jungle" title, "Echoes of the Jungle," was recorded in June 1931, a few months after Ellington left the Cotton Club.

24 During this same period of Ellington's Cotton Club residency, December 1927 to February 1931, I have been able to find only two other Ellington recordings that refer explicitly to Africa: "Hottentot" (1928) and the mock-primitivist "Diga Diga Doo" (also 1928), which Ellington did not write.

25 It is worth noting that whereas Ellington's titles from 1927 until 1931 con-

tain just a handful of "jungle" references, they frequently allude to places in the United States. These include several titles that mention Harlem (more on this later), plus, for example, "East St. Louis Toodle-Oo," "Louisiana," "Memphis Wail," "Mississippi Moan," "Swanee Shuffle," "Rocky Mountain Blues," and "Wall Street Wail." Many other titles refer to aspects of African American life or incorporate African American slang: "Black and Tan Fantasy," "Saturday Night Function," "Jubilee Stomp," "Rent Party Blues," "The Mooche," "The Dicty Glide," "Stack O'Lee Blues." Ellington did not write all of these songs, but he did record them. See Rust 474–84. See also Duke Ellington, "My Hunt for Song Titles," *Rhythm* Aug. 1933, rpt. in Tucker, DER, 87–99, in which Ellington claimed his titles were inspired primarily by black urban life in Harlem. Many of these titles can be found on the CDs *Early Ellington* (1927–1934) by Duke Ellington and His Orchestra, Bluebird-BMG ND86852, 1989; *Jubilee Stomp* by Duke Ellington and His Orchestra, Bluebird-BMG 74321101532, 1992; and *The Okeh Ellington* by Duke Ellington, Columbia Jazz Masterpieces 466964-2, 1991.

26 Langston Hughes, *The Big Sea* (New York: Alfred A. Knopf, 1940) 258. Hughes recounts the incident in order to show the folly of trying to foist high art onto people. Marshall Stearns uses the same quotation to make the point that "the citizens of Harlem neither knew nor cared about any jungle, and they didn't identify themselves with Africa either" (Stearns, 183). Jerome Kern and Oscar Hammerstein II drew a similar conclusion in *Showboat* (1927), when in one scene they have a group of "Dahomey Villagers" sing "In Dahomey—let the Africans stay / In Dahomey—Gimme Avenue A / Back in old New York." EMI CDS T 49108 2, 1988, libretto p. 100.

27 Derek Jewell, *Duke: A Portrait of Duke Ellington* (London: Sphere, 1978) 80.

28 Barry Ulanov, *Duke Ellington* (1946; London: Musicians Press, 1947) 242. Ulanov gives no date for this work, which as far as I have been able to determine was never performed, published, or recorded. However, an instrumental track called "Air Conditioned Jungle" was played at Ellington's January 1946 Carnegie Hall concert; it featured clarinetist Jimmy Hamilton, who is credited as co-composer. *The Duke Ellington Carnegie Hall Concerts: January 1946*, Prestige 2PCD-24074-2, 1991. And an echo of the original idea turns up in Ellington's late comic opera *Queenie Pie*, scene 7 of which includes the lines:

> A native runs in shouting:
> > Boat's Coming, Boat Coming off-shore!!!
> *King*: (Jumping up) Everybody turn off the air-conditioning.
> Take off all those pretty silk clothes. Don skins and feathers.
> Get yo' drums and get yo' spears.

Duke Ellington, *Queenie Pie: An Opera Buffa in Seven Scenes*, unpublished 1973 typescript, McGettigan Collection, Archives Center, National Museum of American History, Smithsonian Institution, Washington, D.C., scene 7, p. 7. For a contemporary variation on the same theme, cf. "Quick, hide the computer and the VCR, the anthropologists are coming!" George Lewis, "Airplane," *Changing with the Times*, New World 80434-2, 1993.

29 Don George (p. 103) tells a story about the time that Ellington trumpeter Cootie Williams used his mute on *The Dick Cavett Show*:

> At the end of the number, Dick asked, "Mr. Ellington, wasn't that a toilet plunger he used?"
>
> Duke said, "Well, yes, it was a toilet plunger, but you see, it was made for the trumpet first and since then they've found other uses for it."

30 Cotton Club programs during Ellington's residency there from 1927 until 1931 included the sketches "The Splendor of Arabia" (March 1929), "L'Argentine" (March 1930), "Andalusian Nights" and "Fantasie de Paris" (September 1930), as well as the more predictable "Congo Jamboree" (billed as "An exhibition of unrestrained Nubian abandon," September 1929) and numerous sketches with either Harlem or minstrelsy settings. See Klaus Stratemann, *Duke Ellington Day by Day and Film by Film* (Copenhagen: Jazz-Media, 1992) 687–93.

31 Cf. John Gennari's observation: "When Picasso incorporated African-influenced plastic forms into his work, he was celebrated for infusing core European art with the more organic, more natural, vitally 'primitive' impulses of peripheral (to European) culture. But when Louis Armstrong incorporated African-influenced tonality and syncopation into his work, if he was celebrated at all—and mostly he was ignored or demeaned—, it was for *being* a 'primitive,' a creature of instinct, who was struggling nobly to incorporate European rationalism." Gennari, 465.

32 Qtd. in Hasse, 112.

33 Ibid.

34 Tucker, "Ellington's 'Jungle Music,'" 15. I should make clear that I am not saying that Ellington never deliberately created music which he knew would be perceived as "dirty" or "low-down." I am saying such implicitly pejorative terms are a hopelessly inadequate and inappropriate means of conveying the tremendous excitement and creativity of this music. They also reflect and reinforce Eurocentric divisions of art into "high" and "low," "modern" and "primitive," even when it is the second quality in each pairing that is being praised. Anthony Braxton refers to this approach as the "across the tracks syndrome," a concept I discuss in chap. 5.

35 R. D. Darrell, *Phonograph Monthly Review* July 1927. Rpt. in Tucker, *DER*, 33–34.

36 Darrell, *Phonograph*, 38.

37 Darrell, *Phonograph*, 39.

38 R. D. Darrell, "Black Beauty," *disques* June 1932. Rpt. in Tucker, *DER*, 58.

39 Gennari, 468–69.

40 At least, in the United States. European critics were often closer to Darrell's viewpoint. I look in more detail at critical responses to Ellington's music in chapter 4.

41 Vic Bellerby, "Analysis of Genius," *Duke Ellington: His Life and Music*, ed. Peter

Gammond (London: Phoenix House, 1958) 162. Yet the critical outrage occasioned by some of Ellington's later, extended-form works (see chapter 4), when many writers complained bitterly that he was "deserting jazz," suggests how useful the "jungle" label may have been in masking this early sophistication.

42 George Wein, CD insert notes to *Money Jungle* by Duke Ellington, Blue Note CDP 7 46398 2, 1987. Mingus biographer Brian Priestley has suggested to me that the title might in fact have originated with Mingus, who is known to have performed a piece called "The Jungle with Money" at least a month before the *Money Jungle* recording sessions. However, Max Roach's account of the recording session makes it clear that the idea of the money jungle was Ellington's. See Keith Shadwick, "Talking Drums," *Jazz FM* 2, n.d., 29.

43 D. Ellington, *Music Is*, 447. Cf. Barry Ulanov's remark: "The real jungle wasn't the African jungle . . . it was the business jungle." Qtd. in *Duke Ellington: Reminiscin' in Tempo*, prod. and dir. Robert S. Levi, Omnibus, BBC1, 1994.

44 Qtd. in Lasker, n.p. Ellipsis in original.

45 Mercer Ellington with Stanley Dance, *Duke Ellington in Person: An Intimate Memoir* (London: Hutchinson, 1978) 44. The street entrance to the Cotton Club was also made up to look like a log cabin; see the photograph in Hasse, 99.

46 Cab Calloway, *Of Minnie the Moocher and Me* (New York: Thomas Y. Crowell, 1976) 88.

47 Lewis A. Erenberg, *Steppin' Out: New York Nightlife and the Transformation of American Culture, 1890–1930* (Chicago: U of Chicago P, 1984) 254.

48 See Toll, chaps. 2 and 8, esp. 52 and 262–63.

49 Joseph Boskin, *Sambo: The Rise and Demise of an American Jester* (New York: Oxford UP, 1986) 86–88.

50 Boskin, 167. Characters based on minstrel stereotypes persist in the media today—e.g., the Cat in the BBC TV series *Red Dwarf*.

51 This notion was often perpetrated by the performers. So, like their nineteenth-century minstrel predecessors, Charles J. Correll and Freeman J. Gosden, who created Amos 'n' Andy, claimed that their characters were "true to life." Boskin, 172.

52 Qtd. in Boskin, 158–59.

53 Stratemann, 691.

54 The band had appeared in the 1929 short *Black and Tan*, which, together with a few brief extracts from *Check and Double Check* (plus other material), can be seen in the video *Duke Ellington and His Orchestra* (1929–1943), Storyville, 1991.

55 Hasse, 129. Hasse adds: "History does not record what Tizol, Bigard—or Ellington—thought of this affront." Not at the time, perhaps, but I think the 1941 *Jump for Joy*, which I discuss below, makes absolutely clear what Ellington thought of such affronts.

56 Cripps, 269.

57 Hasse, 129. Since Mills was nominally the lyricist, it seems likely the title would be his. However, Mills claimed coauthorship of numerous Ellington compositions—such manager's perks being standard practice at the time—so we cannot be sure.

58 Dan Morgenstern, CD insert notes to *Early Ellington* (1927–1934).

59 This was true of the first film version, made by Universal in 1929. In the original 1927 Broadway stage production, however, the part of Queenie was played by the Italian actress Tess Gardella, "who always appeared in blackface in her characterization of Aunt Jemima. It was the character of Aunt Jemima, not Miss Gardella, who was credited in the program for the role of Queenie." Miles Kreuger, *Showboat: The Story of a Classical American Musical* (New York: Oxford UP, 1977) 54.

60 "He followed instructions. He did what I wanted . . . this kind of a tune or that kind of a tune." Mills on Ellington, qtd. in Collier, 69.

61 Boskin, 85.

62 Billie Holiday with William Dufty, *Lady Sings the Blues*, rev. ed. (1956; London: Abacus, 1975) 60.

63 The article's undertow of hostility toward the English, with their intellectual affectations, also has precedents in antebellum working-class theater, where a tradition sprang up of "arrogant" English actors being chased offstage with a bombardment of "rotten eggs, vegetables, and chairs" hurled by fiercely patriotic and determinedly lowbrow audiences. See Toll, 16–18.

64 Gama Gilbert, "'Hot Damn!' Says Ellington When Ranked with Bach," *Philadelphia Record* 17 May 1935. Rpt. in Tucker, DER, 112.

65 Gilbert, 112–13.

66 Gilbert, 113–14.

67 Mark Tucker favors the first of these options (DER, 112). My thanks to Victor Schonfield for suggesting the second.

68 John Pittman, "The Duke Will Stay on Top," unidentified clipping, probably from a San Francisco newspaper, August or September 1941. Rpt. in Tucker, DER, 149.

69 D. Ellington, *Music Is*, 175.

70 Ibid. Ellington's concern with the Uncle Tom stereotype is more easily appreciated if one bears in mind not only the continuing popularity of the "Uncle Tom" shows mentioned above but also, for example, the fact that four film versions of *Uncle Tom's Cabin* had been made before 1930.

71 Patricia Willard, LP booklet notes, *Jump for Joy* by Duke Ellington and His Orchestra, Smithsonian Collection of Recordings R037 DMM 1-0722, 1988, 23. The project with Welles fell through after an unrelated dispute between the director and RKO.

72 D. Ellington, *Music Is*, 175–76.

73 Willard, 17.

74 D. Ellington, *Music Is*, 180.

75 Willard, 22.

76 Cf. his 1944 statement: "You can say anything you want on the trombone, but you gotta be careful with words." Boyer, 238.

77 Or so Ellington claimed in 1942. Qtd. in Hasse 247. For a description of the sketch on which Ellington based his claim, see Willard, 16–17. Willard (p. 31) also suggests this sketch was the origin of the phrase "zoot suit."

78 A notion fostered, for example, in *The Green Pastures* and *Gone with the Wind*, two films tweaked in *Jump for Joy*. *Green Pastures* establishes its sensitivity to racial stereotypes in an opening scene that depicts the black vision of Paradise as "a grand fishfry." Cripps, 260.

79 Qtd. in Willard, 13.

80 Ellington, Sid Kuller, Paul Francis Webster, "Jump for Joy," *The Blanton-Webster Band* by Duke Ellington, Bluebird-BMG 74321 131812, 1986. This three-CD set also includes "I've Got It Bad and That Ain't Good" plus a handful of other songs from *Jump for Joy*.

81 Paul Francis Webster and O. Rene, "Uncle Tom's Cabin Is a Drive-In Now," qtd. in Willard, 16.

82 Willard, 19.

83 Hal Borne, Paul Francis Webster, and Ray Golden, "I've Got a Passport from Georgia," qtd. in Willard, 15. She notes that "Fiorello H. La Guardia was the popular mayor of New York City from 1934 to 1946."

84 Qtd. in Willard, 31.

85 D. Ellington, *Music Is*, 184. When writing *The Deep South Suite*, Ellington may have had in mind Billie Holiday's famous recording of "Strange Fruit," made in 1939, which in Lewis Allen's lyrics drew similar contrasts between the "dream picture" and the reality of life (and death) in the South: "Pastoral scene of the gallant South / The bulging eyes / And the twisted mouth / Scent of magnolia / Sweet and fresh / Then the sudden smell of burning flesh." *The Complete Commodore Recordings* GRP CMD 24012, 1997. Ellington may also have been aware of William Grant Still's 1940 choral piece, *And They Lynched Him on a Tree*, based on an actual lynching in Mississippi in the 1920s. See Still, *Witness*, vol. 2, Collins Classics 1454-2, 1995. Another possible influence may have been Aaron Douglas's ironically titled 1934 mural panel, "An Idyll of the Deep South," which depicts a lynching. See Amy Helene Kirschke, *Aaron Douglas: Art, Race, and the Harlem Renaissance* (Jackson: UP of Mississippi, 1995) 123.

86 M. Ellington, 96.

87 Collier, 281.

88 These quotations occur in both of the only two performances of "Magnolias Just Dripping with Molasses" that have appeared on record, which suggests that they were an integral, preplanned part of the composition rather than something that Lawrence Brown improvised on the spur of the moment. The performances on disc, both from 1946, are the Carnegie Hall concert of 23 Nov., on Queen 018 (LP), and a 10 Nov. concert at Chicago's Civic Opera House, released on Limelight 844 401-2, 1994, as part of the two-CD set *The Great Chicago Concerts* by Duke Ellington.

89 See my comments on "Dixie" in chap. 2.

90 Stratemann, 277. The several lynchings that happened at this time prompted President Harry S. Truman to set up a Committee on Civil Rights in 1947. The committee's report, *To Secure These Rights*, which called for "the elimination of segregation, based on race, color, creed, or

national origin, from American life" was one of the early harbingers of the greater political changes to come in the 1950s and 1960s. See Woodward, 135–36.

91 D. Ellington, *Music Is*, 184.

92 M. Ellington, 182–83.

93 "The man in the embassy may not have approved of his companion, but he couldn't really express his own feelings because he never knew exactly who was the great influence responsible for sending Ellington into the area and his own head might roll if he didn't act right. Disapproval there may have been, but there was no overt act." M. Ellington, 179–80.

94 M. Ellington, 48.

95 Littlewood and Lipsedge, 42–43. Ellington was well aware of the dangers of racial mixing in public. Don George relates a story (p. 166) concerning the orchestra's engagement at a prestigious fund-raising evening for charity at a plush hotel in Dallas, where the band members were strictly warned *not* to mingle with the guests. Joan Crawford, onstage to hand out prizes, suddenly

> fainted dead away and fell back into the saxophone section between Johnny Hodges and Harold Ashby. Not wanting to violate the rule "No mingling with the guests," they moved their chairs slightly and calmly let her lie there, until eventually one of the hotel people came and picked her up.
>
> Duke was asked, "Why didn't you pick up Joan Crawford?"
>
> He held up his hands, palms out, shaking his head and took a step backward, saying "Not me, I wouldn't lay my hands on a white woman in Texas."

The humorous tone of this story should not obscure the fact that in the South a black man might be lynched for touching a white woman.

96 D. Ellington, *Music Is*, 185. To "say it without saying it" could, I think, be seen as a classic definition of signifying.

97 Qtd. in Tucker, *DER*, 266.

98 Qtd. in Willard, 3. Kuller himself was white.

99 D. Ellington, *Music Is*, 185. Unfortunately, hardly any of Ellington's music for this show has ever appeared on record.

100 M. Ellington, 183.

101 David Meeker, *Jazz in the Movies: A Guide to Jazz Musicians, 1917–1977* (London: Talisman, 1977) entry 339; D. Ellington, *Music Is*, 195–96. For a more detailed account of the film, see Stratemann, 587–90.

102 Don George recounts a conversation in which Ellington humorously discusses the consequences of transplanting a *black* brain into a *white* body. George, 223–24.

103 Tucker, *Ellington*, 12.

104 Qtd. in Tucker, *Ellington*, 7–8.

105 Ibid.

106 For a full account, see Tucker, *Ellington*, chap. 1.

107 D. Ellington, *Music Is*, 17.

108 See Albert Murray, "Storiella Americana as She Is Swyung: Duke Ellington, the Culture of Washington, D.C. and the Blues as Representative Anecdote," *Conjunctions* 16 (1991): 211; and D. Ellington, *Music Is*, 17.

109 Ellington's "good manners" could appear exaggerated to the point of parody, as in his comments that "at dinner I sat next to Mrs. Hubert Humphrey. What a wonderful and charming dinner companion she was! She made so much sense in everything she talked about, and was very informative too." D. Ellington, *Music Is*, 430. That Ellington knew exactly what he was doing is suggested by his remark to Mercer on the book's publication: "We've written the Good Book and now we'll write the Bad Book!" M. Ellington, 172.

110 D. Ellington, *Music Is*, 54.

111 D. Ellington, *Music Is*, 125.

112 D. Ellington, *Music Is*, 54.

113 Jim Haskins, *The Cotton Club* (New York: Random House, 1977) 57.

114 Haskins, 57, 75.

115 That Ellington saw "commanding respect" as akin to a political statement is suggested by his remarks to Nat Hentoff: "From 1934 to 1936 we went touring deep into the South, without the benefit of Federal judges, and we commanded respect. We didn't travel by bus. Instead, we had two Pullman cars and a 70-foot baggage car. We parked them in each station, and lived in them. We had our own water, food, electricity, and sanitary facilities. The natives would come up and say, 'What's that?' 'Well,' we'd say, 'that's the way the President travels.' " "We made our point," the Duke continued. "What else could we have done at that time? In the years since, we've done more benefits for civil-rights groups than anybody, but still the best way for me to be effective is through music." Qtd. in Hentoff, 31.

116 D. Ellington, "My Hunt," 88. The article makes clear that Ellington saw Harlem life as exemplifying urban sophistication rather than "primitivist" retentions.

117 Haskins, 75. Similar attitudes some twenty years earlier had decreed that white singer Sophie Tucker "sang in blackface, largely because she was considered too ugly to perform naturally." Erenberg, 195.

118 Duke Ellington, "From Where I Lie," *The Negro Actor* 15 July 1938. Rpt. in Tucker, *DER*, 131. Sun Ra also used the phrase "children of the sun" to title a composition and an LP. The phrase was not uncommon in black culture. John F. Szwed cites two books about ancient Egypt and published in the early years of the century with that title (*Space*, 67, 69). There was also a 1919 vaudeville show called *The Children of the Sun*; see John Graziano, "Black Musical Theater and the Harlem Renaissance Movement," *Black Music in the Harlem Renaissance: A Collection of Essays*, ed. Samuel A. Floyd Jr. (New York: Greenwood Press, 1990) 90.

119 Mark Tucker, "The Genesis of *Black, Brown and Beige*," *Black Music Research Journal* 13 (1993): 70. Ellington, a keen painter himself, would also have been aware of the work of Harlem Renaissance painters who took their

topics from contemporary black life and black history. Aaron Douglas, in particular, shared Ellington's interest in depicting the African American past. The murals he painted for Fisk University in 1930 traced, he said, "the story of the Negro's progress from central Africa to present day America." (Qtd. in Kirschke, 112.) And the famous four-part mural that Douglas painted for the New York Public Library in 1934, *Aspects of Negro Life*, depicted, much like Ellington's planned epic, scenes from a black history that began in Africa, moved through slavery and Reconstruction, and culminated in the confusions of black urban life, as the glamour and optimism of the Jazz Age gave way to the miseries of the Great Depression. See Kirschke, 121–23. Douglas's murals may also have provided Ellington with a model of extended form that could be both narrational and multisectional, as *Black, Brown and Beige* would later prove.

120 Stratemann, 692.

121 Scott Deveaux, "The Emergence of the Jazz Concert, 1935–1945," *American Music* 7 (1989): 8.

122 James P. Johnson, "Harlem Symphony," *Victory Stride: The Symphonic Music of James P. Johnson*, Music Masters Classics 01612-67140-2, 1994; Duke Ellington, "A Tone Parallel to Harlem (The Harlem Suite)," *Uptown*, CBS Jazz Masterpieces 460830-2, n.d.

123 The two surviving movements of the piano concerto are included on the *Victory Stride* CD; see n. 122. For more on *De Organizer*, see Scott E. Brown, *James P. Johnson: A Case of Mistaken Identity* (Metuchen, N.J.: Scarecrow and the Institute of Jazz Studies, Rutgers University, 1986) 220. "Hungry Blues," the only music from the opera to be recorded, reveals a yearning utopianism that anticipates Ellington's *New World A-Comin'* (see below) in its evocation of "A brand new world / So clean and fine / Nobody's hungry / And there ain't no color line." Langston Hughes, James P. Johnson, "Hungry Blues," rec. 1939, *I Grandi del Jazz: James P. Johnson*, Fabbri Editori GdJ85, 1982.

124 William Grant Still, 1926 program notes to *Darker America*, qtd. in Carol J. Oja, "'New Music' and the 'New Negro': The Background of William Grant Still's *Afro-American Symphony*," *Black Music Research Journal* 12 (1992): 159.

125 Oja, 159–60.

126 William Grant Still, 1937 program notes, qtd. in Michael Fleming, CD insert notes to Symphony No. 2 in G minor, *Song of a New Race*, Chandos CHAN 9226, 1993, 4.

127 William Grant Still, "Notes on: *The Afro-American Symphony*," qtd. in Oja, 155. Emphasis added.

128 Three different newspaper reports from 1933 refer to the five-part suite: see Jewell, 64–65; Tucker, *DER*, 98; Ulanov, 155. References to the opera occur in 1938, 1941, and 1944 and can be found in Tucker, *DER*, 116n., 145, 150, and 218.

129 This was stated at the time by Howard Taubman in the *New York Times Magazine*, Tucker, *DER*, 160, and by Irving Kolodin, in his program notes for the Carnegie Hall concert (presumably based on information from Ellington himself), Tucker, *DER*, 161–64. Cf. also "Ellington intends to perform a jazz

symphony, composed of themes taken from his original and as yet unpro-
duced opera, 'Boola,' " "Ellington on Negro Music," *Variety* 9 Dec. 1942: 37.

130 *Symphony in Black* is available on the video *Duke Ellington and His Orchestra*
(1929–1943), Storyville 1991.

131 Brian Priestley and Alan Cohen, "Black, Brown and Beige," *Composer* 51,
52, 53, 1974–75. Rpt. in Tucker, *DER*, 187n.

132 Priestley and Cohen, 187n.

133 Edward Morrow, "Duke Ellington on Gershwin's 'Porgy,' " *New Theatre* Dec.
1935. Rpt. in Tucker, *DER*, 116–17. The episode that Ellington refers to is
the "Hymn of Sorrow" sequence from *Symphony in Black*.

134 Mark Tucker, editorial introduction to "V. Black, Brown and Beige (1943),"
Tucker, *DER*, 153. Tucker implies that "Ellington Week" was an official tribute from the city of New York; Hasse though, says it was "a publicity
gimmick" (260).

135 D. Ellington, *Music Is*, 181–82.

136 Helen M. Oakley, "Ellington to Offer 'Tone Parallel,' " *Down Beat* 15 Jan.
1943. Rpt. in Tucker, *DER*, 157.

137 For a detailed survey of this critical response, see Scott Deveaux, "*Black,
Brown and Beige* and the Critics," *Black Music Research Journal* 13 (1993): 125–46.

138 Qtd. in Andrew Homzy, "*Black, Brown and Beige* in Duke Ellington's Repertoire, 1943–1973," *Black Music Research Journal* 13 (1993): 89.

139 "Duke's Book Will Explain His Carnegie Hall Symph," *Variety* 9 June 1943: 2.

140 Duke Ellington, "Brown," p. 8, *Black, Brown and Beige*, undated typescript,
Duke Ellington Collection, Smithsonian Institution, Washington, D.C. El-
lipses in original. The typescript appears to be based on an earlier untitled
handwritten manuscript, also in the Duke Ellington Collection, which relates the history of Boola, and thus seems to confirm that *Black, Brown and
Beige* was indeed based on Ellington's planned opera. See Tucker, "Genesis," 76.

141 D. Ellington, "Beige," 3–4, *Black, Brown and Beige* typescript.

142 Referring apparently to the "Boola" manuscript on which the *Black, Brown
and Beige* typescript was based, Ellington said in a 1966 interview that
it was "very strong social comment, which I sometimes look at and say,
'Man, you sure were bitter, weren't you?' Or something like that." Qtd.
in *Tempo — Meet the Duke*, Granada TV, 6 Mar. 1966. The typescript certainly
contains stronger social commentary than anything else Ellington said or
wrote about *Black, Brown and Beige*.

143 Stratemann, 241; Homzy, 88–89. The original Carnegie Hall performance
was recorded by the venue's own sound engineers but did not appear on
record until 1977, three years after Ellington's death. It is now on CD: *The
Duke Ellington Carnegie Hall Concerts: January 1943*, Prestige 2PCD 34004-2, 1991.

144 Duke Ellington, *Black, Brown and Beige (The 1944–1946 Band Recordings)*,
Bluebird-BMG 6641-2-RB, 1988.

145 Priestley and Cohen, 186.

146 M. Ellington, 95–96.

147 Roi Ottley, *New World A-Coming* (Boston: Houghton Mifflin, 1943) 347.

148 D. Ellington, *Music Is*, 183.

149 Qtd. in Jewell, 64–65.

150 D. Ellington, *Music Is*, 183.

151 The occasion was an NAACP benefit concert. Stratemann, 324.

152 R. N., "Ellington Discusses Jazz," *Christian Science Monitor* 2 Apr. 1956: 204.

153 Duke Ellington and His Orchestra, featuring Mahalia Jackson, *Black, Brown and Beige*, Columbia CL 1162, 1958.

154 Homzy, 95.

155 He could only appear in some performances because he was dividing his time between Chicago and Stratford, Ontario, where he was writing the music for a production of *Timon of Athens* at the Shakespeare festival.

156 Homzy, 98–99.

157 Duke Ellington, "My People," *My People*, Red Baron AK 52759, 1992. I have transcribed this quotation from the recording, so the punctuation is mine and I have done scant justice to Ellington's richly declamatory style. Questioned later on a television show about his people, Ellington prevaricated consummately: "Well, I'm in several groups. I'm in the group of the piano players, I'm in the group of the listeners, I'm in the group of those who aspire to be dilettantes. . . . What? Oh yeah, I'm in the group of those who appreciate beaujolais." Qtd. in the *Duke Ellington: Reminiscin' in Tempo* television documentary. Perhaps further light is shed on Ellington's evasive style in interviews by his comment in *Music Is My Mistress*: "The only reason an interviewer sometimes asks the interviewee stupid questions is because the interviewer thinks the interviewee is stupid." D. Ellington, *Music Is*, 472.

158 Duke Ellington, "King Fit the Battle of Alabam," *My People*. Also qtd. in Jewell, 172.

159 Duke Ellington, "What Color Is Virtue?," *My People*.

160 *Jump for Joy* was referred to as a "revu-sical" in the program for the show. See D. Ellington, *Music Is*, 177.

161 Duke Ellington, *Concert of Sacred Music*, rec. 1965, BMG 74321192542, 1994.

162 Duke Ellington, *The Private Collection, Volume Ten — Studio Sessions; New York & Chicago 1965, 1966 and 1971*, SAJA 7 91234-2, 1989. The "Blues" section was not recorded until 1971, and three brief parts of "Beige" were either not recorded or deemed unusable. See Homzy, 99–105, for a detailed analysis of the 1965 sessions.

163 Ellington presumably knew the original 1943 concert had been recorded, and if so he would also have known that the sound quality of the recording was extremely poor.

164 George, 114. George also describes Ellington resisting attempts to persuade him to join King's march on Washington in 1963. He quotes Ellington as saying, "You can do more good for the people if you're the best at what you're doing and you conduct yourself admirably." This sounds like a restatement of his insistence on *commanding* respect by your own actions rather than *demanding* it with, say, marches and protests that involve both

confrontation and the possibility of refusal. Ellington's attitudes may appear patrician at times, but his dislike of outright political protest seems to have been a mixture of sincere belief—specifically his notion that to say it without saying it made for better art than just saying it—and a personal psychology that invariably shied away from confrontation, whether political or emotional. George writes: "He was just completely incapable of existing with turmoil or negativeness or uproar." George, 140. See also Hentoff, 33–35, for Ellington's similarly nonconfrontational relationship with his band.

165 Duke Ellington, CD insert notes, *Second Sacred Concert*, Prestige PCD-24045-2, 1990.

166 D. Ellington, *Music Is*, 464.

167 This was the issue that prompted A. Philip Randolph to propose his All-Negro March on Washington, scheduled for 1 July 1941. See Ottley, 290–91.

168 Duke Ellington, "We, Too, Sing America," published as "Speech of the Week" in the *California Eagle* 13 Feb. 1941. Rpt. in Tucker, *DER*, 147.

169 DuBois, *Souls*, 186–87.

170 Hentoff, 30–31. Hentoff is vague about the date of this statement; writing in the mid-1970s, he simply says it was made "years ago (when the term 'Negro' had not been supplanted by 'black')."

Chapter 4   *Zajj: Renegotiating Her Story*

1 James Baldwin, *The Fire Next Time* (1963; Harmondsworth, Middlesex: Penguin, 1970) 62.

2 Gleason, 157.

3 Duke Ellington, "Reminiscing in Tempo," *Duke Ellington, 1935–1936*, Classics 659CD, 1993.

4 John Hammond, "The Tragedy of Duke Ellington, the 'Black Prince of Jazz,'" *Brooklyn Eagle* 3 Nov. 1935, and *Down Beat* Nov. 1935. Rpt. in Tucker, *DER*, 118–20.

5 Hammond, "Tragedy," 119. One cannot but help noticing a rather proprietary tone in the writings of Hammond and Gilbert (see chap. 3). It is as if they felt outraged that these English critics had been praising one of "their boys" and "putting ideas into his head" (to borrow the terminology of the slave owner).

6 Hammond, "Tragedy," 120.

7 See, e.g., the attacks on Anthony Braxton's music by Amiri Baraka and Ted Joans, which I discuss in chap. 5.

8 Hammond, "Tragedy," 120.

9 John Hammond with Irving Townsend, *John Hammond on Record: An Autobiography* (1977; Harmondsworth, Middlesex: Penguin, 1981) 85.

10 See Hasse, 151.

11 See Stratemann, 45, 52. Ironically, in the 1940s the FBI had both Ellington

and Hammond under investigation for their "left-wing political associations." See David W. Stowe, *Swing Changes: Big Band Jazz in New Deal America* (Cambridge, Mass.: Harvard UP, 1994) 50–51.

12 Hammond, "Tragedy," 120.

13 The film was released on 13 September (Stratemann, 119); Hammond's article appeared in November.

14 Hammond, *John Hammond*, 137. Hammond's memory seems to be at fault here, since Ellington's first recordings of "Sophisticated Lady," made in 1933, the year after Lawrence Brown joined the band, were done for the Brunswick and Columbia labels. The orchestra did not record the piece for Victor until the mid-1940s.

15 Hammond, *John Hammond*, 137.

16 As we will see, Ellington himself frequently criticized what he regarded as the misconception that jazz had to be entirely spontaneous, neither written down nor planned in advance.

17 Hammond's attack on Ellington seems to anticipate elements of the "revivalist" aesthetic that grew up in the late 1930s and early 1940s and that championed "authentic" Dixieland as opposed to "sophisticated" swing. "The revivalist writers were unhesitant, and indeed proud, to admit that the music of Jelly Roll Morton and Louis Armstrong was, in an important sense, a 'vulgar' and 'low' art. Indeed, it was as important for them to oppose Dixieland to high art as well as to the hit parade and to attack swing for its symphonic pretensions as well as for its commercialism." Bernard Gendron, "'Moldy Figs' and Modernists: Jazz at War (1942–1946)," *Jazz Among the Discourses*, ed. Krin Gabbard (Durham, N.C.: Duke UP, 1993) 38–39. I look more closely at this "jazz war" below.

18 Ulanov, *Duke Ellington*, 105.

19 Ulanov, *Duke Ellington*, 104–05.

20 Lock, *Forces*, 116. I discuss "the across the tracks syndrome" in more detail in chap. 5, but perhaps I should make clear that I am not denying that a sensual element to the music does exist and can be hugely enjoyable. The complaint is that many critics have focused solely on this element, to the extent of essentializing it and expecting all black musicians to grant it similar prominence in their work—as in the "hot jazzman" stereotype.

21 Darrell, *Phonograph*, 39. To be fair to Hughes, though he shared John Hammond's dislike of Lawrence Brown's sound, "Sophisticated Lady," and, later, "Reminiscing in Tempo," his appreciation of Ellington's music was more discerning than the remark quoted by Ulanov indicates. He certainly differed from Hammond in his suggestion that listeners could hear in Ellington's work "the music of a race which has suffered, and still suffers, untold hardship and injustice." Spike Hughes, "Meet the Duke," *Daily Herald* 13 June 1933. Rpt. in Tucker, DER, 72–75. In an earlier piece describing a visit to New York City, Hughes also wrote caustically of the racism and vulgarity he encountered at the Cotton Club. Hughes, "Impressions of Ellington in New York," Tucker, DER, 69–72. Rpt. of "The Duke—In Person," *Melody Maker* May 1933.

22 Another possible instance of Hammond's view of black music being shaped by racial stereotyping concerns his alleged sacking of Billie Holiday from the Count Basie band. Hammond always denied that she was fired, but Donald Clarke quotes Basie drummer Jo Jones as saying: "She was fired. John Hammond. But nobody's got guts enough to tell the people that because he's the great white father. Bullshit . . . . He fired her because he wanted her to sing the blues, he wanted her to be a coloured mammy. . . . They love to do that. All they think is, that as a black person you're supposed to sing the blues. Stay in your place, little boy." Qtd. in Donald Clarke, *Wishing on the Moon: The Life and Times of Billie Holiday* (London: Viking, 1994) 134–35. Clarke suggests that Hammond, a self-confessed "vaudeville freak," may also have tried to persuade Holiday to sing vaudeville repertoire from the 1920s. (Clarke, 137–38.)

23 Qtd. in Jewell, 71.

24 Duke Ellington, "The Future of Jazz," program notes to the Ellington orchestra's Great Britain tour, 5–26 Oct. 1958, n. p. (Exeter University Audio Visual Collection.) This article is virtually identical to, and presumably the source for, a piece titled "Where Is Jazz Going?" which appeared in *Music Journal* Mar. 1962 and was reprinted in Tucker, DER, 324–26.

25 John Hammond, "Is the Duke Deserting Jazz?," *Jazz* May 1943. Rpt. in Tucker, DER, 171–73. By this time, too, the acrimony between the two men had been exacerbated by an article Ellington wrote for *Down Beat* in 1939 attacking Hammond, and by subsequent disagreements between them in the recording studio. (In January 1939 Hammond had been appointed head of jazz recording at Columbia, the label to which Ellington was then signed—though he left soon after.)

26 Hammond, "Is the Duke," 172.

27 Hammond, "Is the Duke," 172–73.

28 Leonard Feather, untitled article, *Jazz* May 1943. Rpt. in Tucker, DER, 173–75. Feather describes one of the rows in the recording studio between Ellington and Hammond that I mentioned in n. 25, above.

29 Bob Thiele, "The Case of Jazz Music," *Jazz* July 1943. Rpt. in Tucker, DER, 175–78.

30 Thiele, 177.

31 See Gendron, 31–56.

32 Gendron places the beginning of the New Orleans revival in "the late 30s" and dates "the first shot of the modernist-revivalist war" to a 1942 *Metronome* attack on purist "moldy figs." Gendron, 32. That Hammond cannot be easily situated within the binary opposition that Gendron proposes as the model for this discourse suggests that a more complex model may be needed to fully illuminate the subtleties of the situation.

33 D. Ellington, "Future."

34 "The word 'jazz' has been part of the problem. The word never lost its association with those New Orleans bordellos. In the 1920's I used to try to convince Fletcher Henderson that we ought to call what we were doing

'Negro music.' But it's too late for that now." Duke Ellington, qtd. in Hentoff, 30.

35 Qtd. in Tucker, DER, 45, 81, and 135.

36 Almena Davis, "Duke Ellington Fascinates Interviewer as He Takes 'Downbeat' Writer to Task," *California Eagle* 9 Jan. 1941. Rpt. in Tucker, DER, 145. Ellington's recourse to terms such as "essentially negro," "authentic," and "unadulterated" makes it sound as if he were claiming an impossible racial purity for his music, yet this hardly squares with his integrationist and pro-miscegenation sympathies discussed in chap. 3. What I think is happening here is that Ellington is trapped within the confines of a modernist discourse that designated black art as "primitive." In trying to establish the scope and sophistication of his music, Ellington has also to continue to insist on its blackness or else the former qualities, if acknowledged at all, would almost certainly have been attributed either to white elements perceived as already in the music or to its supposed aspirations toward a European model. Indeed, this is the line that Hammond took in depicting Ellington's move toward sophistication as virtually an act of race betrayal. Yet Ellington's affirmation of his music's blackness should not be seen as only strategic: his racial pride was deep-seated and at times may have run contrary to his integrationist ideals.

37 Note, for example, the varieties of experience (and musical styles) evoked in Ellington titles such as "Jubilee Stomp," "Breakfast Dance," "Ebony Rhapsody," "Bugle Call Rag," "Beggar's Blues," "Mood Indigo," "Black and Tan Fantasy," "Creole Love Call," etc., etc.

38 D. Ellington, "The Duke," 47.

39 Winthrop Sargeant, "Is Jazz Music?," *American Mercury* Oct. 1943. Rpt. in Tucker, DER, 208.

40 Duke Ellington, "Defense of Jazz," letter to the editor, *American Mercury* Jan. 1944. Rpt. in Tucker, DER, 208–09.

41 Duke Ellington, "Swing Is My Beat," *New Advance* Oct. 1946. Rpt. in Tucker, DER, 249. Previously, in 1937, Ellington had defended swing from the accusation that it provoked sex crimes. See Tucker, DER, 128–29.

42 See Mike Levin, "Duke Fuses Classical and Jazz," *Down Beat* 15 Feb. 1943, for a brief survey of classical critics' responses. Rpt. in Tucker, DER, 167. See also Deveaux, "*Black, Brown*," 126–28.

43 Qtd. in Alfred Frankenstein, " 'Hot Is Something About a Tree,' Says the Duke," *San Francisco Chronicle* 9 Nov. 1941: 29. In this article, journalist Frankenstein comments that jazz fans appreciate the niceties of players' personal styles with a passion "that is altogether foreign to the followers of music with three capital Bs." This curious phrase, referring (I assume) to classical music as the music of Bach, Beethoven, and Brahms (the three capital Bs), immediately brings to mind Ellington's music with three capital Bs, *Black, Brown and Beige*, and raises the possibility that Ellington's choice of title might just have been intended in part as a riposte to the classicists, the message being that American Negro music had its own three Bs tradition that was no less important or significant than that of Europe.

44 Gunther Schuller, *The Swing Era: The Development of Jazz, 1930–1945* (1989; New York: Oxford UP, 1991) 142. Albert Murray made a similar point in his delineation of Ellington's music as American vernacular art: "It is not a matter of working folk and pop materials into established or classical European forms but of extending, elaborating and refining (which is to say ragging, jazzing and riffing and even jamming) the idiomatic into fine art. *Skyscrapers, not Gothic cathedrals.*" Murray, 217. There seems to be a bigger issue lurking here, however, that neither Schuller nor Murray addresses directly: if Ellington's extended forms go beyond the traditional limits of "dancefloor jazz" and are also outside the norms of European classical music, then presumably we need a correspondingly new kind of musical analysis that will explicate *how* these forms differ from the traditional models, and we also need to devise the appropriate aesthetic criteria by which to evaluate them.

45 Duke Ellington, "Certainly It's Music!," *Listen* Oct. 1944. Rpt. in Tucker, *DER*, 246.

46 D. Ellington, "Certainly," 247.

47 "Why Duke Ellington Avoided Music Schools," *PM* 9 Dec. 1945. Rpt. in Tucker, *DER*, 253.

48 "Why Duke," 253.

49 D. Ellington, "Swing," 248.

50 D. Ellington, "Swing," 249.

51 D. Ellington, "My Hunt," 87.

52 See Gendron, 35. He also notes that, in a contrary move, "what had previously been called 'jazz' was now being reclassified as 'early swing.'" Gendron, 36. Ellington's reference to "a chatty combination of instruments knocking out a tune" could be interpreted as a dismissive description of Dixieland. See also Stowe, 5–7.

53 Qtd. in "Why Duke," 253.

54 "Why Duke," 254.

55 See Ottley, 307.

56 Ottley, 293.

57 See Cripps, 349–89.

58 For an in-depth discussion of the problems encountered in the making of the 1944 film *Jammin' the Blues*, see Arthur Knight, "*Jammin' the Blues*, or the Sight of Jazz, 1944," *Representing Jazz*, ed. Krin Gabbard (Durham, N.C.: Duke UP, 1995) 11–53.

59 Sterling A. Brown, "Spirituals, Blues and Jazz," *Tricolor* 1945. Rpt. in *Jam Session: A Jazz Anthology*, ed. Ralph J. Gleason (1958; London: Jazz Book Club and Peter Davies, 1961) 24.

60 Gunnar Askland, "Interpretations in Jazz: A Conference with Duke Ellington," *Etude* Mar. 1947. Rpt. in Tucker, *DER*, 255.

61 Askland, 257. Ellington's ploy of depicting the "supposed-to-be-Negro" can be seen as an example of what Houston A. Baker has called "mastery of form." In particular, Ellington's strategy is comparable to that of Booker T. Washington, who, argues Baker, adroitly employed familiar

minstrel stereotypes in *Up from Slavery* to reassure his white readership and thus keep their attention. See Baker, 25–36.

62 "Why Duke," 253.

63 Ellington, as an occasional painter, may have been aware of the way in which abstract expressionist art was being redefined as essentially American since it was "for many the expression of freedom. . . . Expressionism stood for the difference between a free society and a totalitarian one." And against the cold, unfeeling, programmed "totalitarian man," America "offered the exuberant Jackson Pollock, the very image of exaltation and spontaneity." Serge Guilbaut, *How New York Stole the Idea of Modern Art: Abstract Expressionism, Freedom, and the Cold War*, trans. Arthur Goldhammer (1983; Chicago: U of Chicago P, 1985) 201–02. That such thinking could also apply to jazz—and could still be in effect some twenty years later—is suggested by the *New York Times* headline over a report on performances by Ellington and some Soviet poets (including Yevgeni Yevtushenko) at the first World Festival of Negro Arts in Senegal:

> SOVIET POETS FAIL
> TO CAPTURE DAKAR
> Duke Ellington the Winner
> in Propaganda Skirmish

New York Times 30 Apr. 1966. Qtd. in Kofsky, 111. In the 1960s, Ellington officially represented the United States on a number of State Department-sponsored tours. For a description of Ellington's 1963 tour to Asia and the Middle East—and his reasons for refusing to discuss the racial situation in the United States with the foreign press—see Stanley Dance, *The World of Duke Ellington* (1970; New York: Da Capo Press, n.d.) 16–26.

64 "Why Duke," 253. Cripps reports that in an early draft of the screenplay for *Casablanca* (1942), the heroine, Ilse, at one point praises the black pianist Sam on his abilities as "a natural musician." He, however, "will have none of it and reminds her of his twelve years at Juilliard. 'Well,' she smiles, 'all the best theories are going under these days.'" Cripps, 373.

65 There may be a wider cultural contradiction in play here, too, namely the assumption that talent not trained "in the usual way" must be "natural"; the kind of training Ellington had received at the elbow of Willie "The Lion" Smith, for example, would not have been recognized as study. That Ellington's comments here on the importance of schooling were probably strategic—a way of countering the "free" and "uninhibited" hot jazzman stereotype—is made more likely by Mercer Ellington's contention that his father retained a "dislike of formal training." M. Ellington, 158.

66 Askland, 256.

67 Askland, 256–57. While Ellington's penultimate sentence can perhaps be seen as a rebuke to the revivalists for claiming Dixieland as the only "real" jazz or to critics like Hammond who claimed that he was "deserting jazz," his definition here of jazz as "the freedom to have many forms" can also be seen as a formula for reconciliation between jazz's warring factions,

which by this time would have included beboppers as well as swing modernists and Dixieland revivalists.

68 Askland, 257. I think it is clear that Ellington is less concerned here with ethnomusicological accuracy than with a political strategy to redefine jazz. He also appears to shift his ground, from claiming that jazz is "the freedom to have many forms" to suggesting here that "it follows no pattern at all." I assume that Ellington does not mean that jazz literally has *no* form or pattern, but that it does not have to adhere to a traditional, fixed pattern. Ironically, one of Ellington's most eloquent champions, Albert Murray, comes close to contradicting the maestro's viewpoint in his argument that Ellington's major achievement "was a steady flow of incomparable twentieth century American music that is mostly the result of the extension, elaboration and refinement of the traditional twelve bar blues chorus and the standard thirty-two bar pop song form." Murray, 216. One final point: Ellington's notion that the essence of jazz is that it has no essence anticipates both Amiri Baraka's description of the music as a "changing same" and the concept of "anti-anti-essentialism" proposed by Paul Gilroy. See Amiri Baraka (as LeRoi Jones), *Black Music* (London: McGibbon & Kee, 1969) 180–211; Gilroy, *Black Atlantic*, 99–103.

69 Askland, 257–58.

70 Tucker, DER, 255.

71 D. Ellington, "Future," n.p. A few lines later Ellington remarks that "jazz today, *as always in the past*, is a matter of thoughtful creation, not mere unaided instinct." (Emphasis added.) This, I think, tends to confirm my hypothesis that his disparaging comments about early jazz in *Etude* were actually attempts to discredit white misrepresentations of that music.

72 See Hasse, 352, and Jewell, 139. *The Night Creature* was eventually recorded in 1963 and released on the LP *The Symphonic Ellington* by Duke Ellington and His Orchestra, reissued on CD on Discovery 71003, 1992.

73 More recent study of Ellington's scores for *Black, Brown and Beige* has shown that several solo passages which listeners had long assumed to be improvised were in fact composed by Ellington. See Wolfram Knaver, " 'Simulated Improvisation' in Duke Ellington's *Black, Brown and Beige*," *Black Perspective in Music* 18 (1990): 20–38. (That Ellington composed solos that sound not only like improvisations but like improvisations characteristic of specific players raises all kinds of intriguing questions about the relationship between jazz, improvisation, and freedom. But that is for another time.) Mercer Ellington, too, has stated that once a composition had taken shape, Ellington "believed it should hold its dimensions, be heard in an identical form from day to day." M. Ellington, 159.

74 That Ellington's efforts to redefine jazz as an American music met with at least some success was signaled by, for example, a 1956 article in *Good Housekeeping* magazine, "From the Dive to the Dean, Jazz Becomes Respectable," which reported that jazz had become part of mainstream American culture and could now be found "in the nicest homes." Perhaps more pertinently, in that same year the State Department began to sponsor foreign

tours by jazz groups, whose members now were seen as suitable ambassadors for American culture. (Ellington participated in these tours in the 1960s.) See Ronald M. Radano, *New Musical Figurations: Anthony Braxton's Cultural Critique* (Chicago: U of Chicago P, 1993) 15–16. One reason for the new respectability bestowed on jazz was the rise of rock 'n' roll, denounced in 1957 by Frank Sinatra as "the most brutal, ugly, degenerate vicious form of expression it has been my displeasure to hear . . . sung, played, and written for the most part by cretinous goons." Qtd. in Gerald Early, "One Nation Under a Groove," *New Republic* 15 and 22 July 1991: 31.

75 Stanley Dance, CD insert notes to *Uptown* by Duke Ellington, CBS Jazz Masterpieces CBS 460830-2, n.d., 8.

76 Collier, 284.

77 D. Ellington, *Music Is*, 191.

78 Hasse, 330–31.

79 Jewell, 143.

80 M. Ellington, 113.

81 Irving Townsend, "When Duke Records," *Just Jazz* 4, ed. Sinclair Traill and the Hon. Gerald Lascelles (London: Souvenir, 1960). Rpt. in Tucker, *DER*, 320.

82 Irving Townsend, "Ellington in Private," *Jazz Journal International* Oct. 1976: 5, 6.

83 Uncredited CD insert notes, *A Drum Is a Woman* by Duke Ellington and His Orchestra, rec. 1956, Columbia COL 471320 2, n.d.

84 Ellington's work did find a few champions. *Down Beat* ran a favorable response (to the TV show) by Leonard Feather, next to a critical piece by Barry Ulanov. *Down Beat* June 1957: 18. And Peter Gammond defended the LP in "A Drum Is a Woman," Gammond, *Duke Ellington*, 132–37.

85 Charles Melville, interview with Duke Ellington on BBC Network 3. Rpt. in Steve Voce, "Quoth the Duke," *Jazz Journal International* Mar. 1959: 3.

86 Melville, 3.

87 Edward Towler, "Reflections on Hearing 'A Drum Is a Woman,'" *Jazz Monthly* Sept. 1957: 30.

88 Towler, 30.

89 Ibid.

90 Towler, 31.

91 Duke Ellington, "You Better Know It," *A Drum Is a Woman*. This is not the place to launch into a discussion of Ellington's sexual politics. Still, I should point out that the casual attitude to sexual violence here is contradicted by the lyric of an earlier track on the recording, "What Else Can You Do with a Drum?": "It isn't civilized to beat women." On the other hand, Mercer Ellington claimed that his father "had a basic contempt for women . . . basically he hated them." M. Ellington, 128. For a black feminist response to this issue, see Jayne Cortez, "If the Drum Is a Woman," *Coagulations: New and Selected Poems* (London: Pluto, 1985) 57–58.

92 Collier, 307.

93 Collier, 285.

94 Qtd. in the film *Sun Ra: A Joyful Noise*.

Chapter 5 All the Things You Are: Legba's Legacy

1 Qtd. in Hentoff, 30.

2 Leo Smith, "Notes on the Creative Artistry of Anthony Braxton," LP liner notes to *The Complete Braxton 1971* by Anthony Braxton, Arista/Freedom AF 1902, 1977. Subsequent quotations in this paragraph come from the same source. AACM is the common abbreviation for the Association for the Advancement of Creative Musicians, the well-known musicians' organization founded in Chicago in 1965. Like Ellington, these musicians disliked the word "jazz," and many of them, including Braxton and Smith, have preferred to use the term "creative music."

3 In the text I refer to Braxton's compositions by the opus numbers that he assigned them in the early 1980s. Before that time it was not possible to refer to the titles in print except by reproducing the relevant graphics, and, at least in the case of the more complex shapes, it was not possible to refer to them in speech at all. Such "inarticulacy" is a point that I discuss in more detail later.

4 Qtd. in John Litweiler, CD insert notes to *3 Compositions of New Jazz* by Anthony Braxton, rec. 1968, Delmark DD 415, 1991.

5 Anthony Braxton, *For Alto*, Delmark DS 420/1, 1971.

6 See, for example, Steve Lacy, untitled letter to Anthony Braxton, Lock, *Mixtery*, 27; Evan Parker, untitled article on Anthony Braxton, Lock, *Mixtery*, 181–84. See also Graham Lock, "A Vision of Forward Motion: Notes on the Evolution of Anthony Braxton's Solo Music," Lock, *Mixtery*, 48–54.

7 See Hans Wachtmeister, *A Discography and Bibliography of Anthony Braxton* (Stocksund, Sweden: Blue Anchor Jazz Bookshop, 1982) 88.

8 Joe H. Klee, review of *For Alto* by Anthony Braxton, *Down Beat* 24 June 1971: 18.

9 Leonard Feather, "Blindfold Test—Harold Land," *Down Beat* 24 June 1971: 26. Land also commented that he "didn't get any emotional reaction" to the track; in this, he presumably differed from Klee, who thought the LP as a whole showed Braxton "fully exposing his inner emotions." Such divergences of opinion regarding the emotional content of Braxton's music have not been uncommon, as we will see.

10 Leonard Feather, "Blindfold Test—Phil Woods," *Down Beat* 14 Oct. 1971: 33.

11 *Down Beat* 22 Apr. 1946. Qtd. in Ross Russell, *Bird Lives! The High Life and Hard Times of Charlie "Yardbird" Parker* (1973; London: Quartet, 1980) 197.

12 John Coltrane, *"Live" at the Village Vanguard*, rec. 1961, MCA/Impulse! MCAD-39136, n.d.

13 Ira Gitler, review of *"Live" at the Village Vanguard* by John Coltrane, *Down Beat* 26 Apr. 1962: 29. Qtd. in Simpkins, 157.

14 Anthony Braxton, *T-a W 3*, 305. Because Braxton's *Tri-axium Writings* and

Composition Notes were self-published, they were not subject to the usual editing and proofreading processes and the resulting texts include many obvious typographical errors. For the sake of clarity, I have taken the liberty of correcting these in the extracts quoted here.

15 Braxton, *T-a W* 3, 306. Of course, not all negative criticism can be fitted into this model; for example, instances occur of black musicians being highly uncomplimentary in print about other black musicians (see Kenny Dorham's review of *Spiritual Unity* by Albert Ayler, *Down Beat* 15 July 1965: 29–30). Nevertheless, the great bulk of jazz commentary has been written by white critics.

16 Braxton, *T-a W* 3, 249. To be more specific, "Western classical" values such as smoothness of tone evolved from the standardization processes (in instrument design and manufacture, performance practice, etc.) that accompanied the growth of the nineteenth-century symphony orchestra.

17 Braxton, *T-a W* 3, 249. (I will discuss Braxton's use of terms like "vibrational," together with his mystical beliefs, later in this chapter.) Cf. Archie Shepp's statement that "Chasin' the Trane" is important precisely because "in it the saxophone as an instrument is completely redefined in parameters outside the standard occidental context." Archie Shepp, "Innovations in Jazz," *History and Tradition in Afro-American Culture*, ed. Günther H. Lenz (Frankfurt: Campus Verlag, 1984) 258.

18 Braxton, *T-a W* 3, 248–50.

19 See Francis Bebey, *African Music: A People's Art*, trans. Josephine Bennett (London: Harrap, 1975). "In Europe, for example, a technically proficient musician is almost automatically classed as an artist. Technique and art are, however, two entirely different things. . . . In the West, a high level of technical skill is considered essential to the creation of a work of art. Technique should be the handmaiden of art, but all too often works of art are judged by the degree of technique involved; a wrong note, a false step, or a careless brush stroke are judged inadmissible.

"The African musician, on the other hand, is primarily concerned with the *art* of playing an instrument and not with the technique. Technique is an intermediary stage and once he has mastered the rudiments of his instrument, he pays little attention to it. This relatively brief period of apprenticeship explains why the same kind of instrument may be played in a multitude of different ways; technique is very much a matter of individual taste." Bebey, 132.

20 Qtd. in Martin Williams, *The Jazz Tradition*, rev. ed. (Oxford: Oxford UP, 1983) 161.

21 Williams, 161. Cf. Cecil Taylor's comments on Monk and technique in A. B. Spellman, *Four Lives in the Bebop Business* (1966; New York: Limelight, 1985) 31–32, 40–43. For an intriguing essay on how Miles Davis's supposed "lack of technique" was actually an integral part of his creative endeavour, see Robert Walser, " 'Out of Notes': Signification, Interpretation, and the Problem of Miles Davis," Gabbard, *Jazz*, 165–88.

22 Braxton, *T-a W* 3, 257.

23 Peter Watrous, "A Saxophonist Veering between Poles," review of solo saxophone concert by Anthony Braxton, the Knitting Factory, New York, *New York Times* 24 Nov. 1995: C3.

24 Anthony Braxton, *Composition Notes Book D* (hereafter CN-D, etc.) (n.p.: Synthesis Music, 1988) 198. A little later he adds: "The vibrato in this context can be used as a 'cry' that smears from 'thought to thought' or as a 'whining-like' sound attitude . . . or as a 'light' that seeks to remind us of 'back then.' " CN-D, 202. Thanks to Jack Collier for this reference. Recordings of 77E can be heard on *Alto Saxophone Improvisations 1979*, Arista Records A2L 8602, 1979, and *Anthony Braxton / Robert Schumann String Quartet*, rec. 1979, Sound Aspects SAS CD 009, 1989.

25 Roland Baggenaes, review of *Donna Lee* by Anthony Braxton, *Coda* Sept. 1975: 20–21.

26 Russell, 173.

27 John Tynan, "Take 5," *Down Beat* 23 Nov. 1961: 40.

28 *Down Beat* 12 April 1962. Qtd. in Simpkins, 153.

29 Lock, *Forces*, 91.

30 Braxton, *T-a W* 3, 241.

31 Braxton, *T-a W* 3, 242.

32 Gennari, 457. For a minority of commentators, the point of "swing" is that it should be indefinable. They use the word to denote a purported ineffable essence to jazz; that is, as part of what we might call a rhetoric of difference—although in practice usually the only difference denoted is between what they like ("it swings") and what they dislike ("it doesn't swing")!

33 Schuller, 867.

34 J. W. Johnson, *Book*, 28.

35 J. W. Johnson, *Book*, 29.

36 Nathaniel Mackey, *Discrepant Engagement: Dissonance, Cross Culturality, and Experimental Writing* (Cambridge: Cambridge UP, 1994) 243.

37 Mackey, *Discrepant*, 234.

38 Mackey, *Discrepant*, 251.

39 Mackey, *Discrepant*, 252–53.

40 Michael Ullman, *Jazz Lives: Portraits in Words and Pictures* (1980; New York: Perigree, 1982) 214.

41 Leonard Feather, *Encyclopedia of Jazz in the Seventies* (1976; London: Quartet, 1978) 73; Gary Giddins, "Anthony Braxton Marches as to Jazz," *Village Voice* 30 Aug. 1976: 69.

42 Of course, my equation of the stammer and Braxton's swing may be part of the particular "biased coherence" that I am trying to impose on his work, my bias deriving not only from my own history of stammering but also from my need to construct an acceptable academic framework in which to discuss his work.

43 Peter Occhiogrosso, "Anthony Braxton Explains Himself," *Down Beat* 12 Aug. 1976: 15.

44 Mackey, *Discrepant*, 244.

45 Lock, *Forces*, 184.

46 Qtd. in Kenneth Ansell, "Anthony Braxton," *Impetus* 6 (1977): 250.

47 J. W. Johnson, *Book*, 28. Cf. Braxton's advice to students at a workshop in London in 1985: "What you don't play is as important as what you do play." Lock, *Forces*, 291.

48 Louis Armstrong, *Swing That Music* (1936; New York; Da Capo, 1993) 33. It is interesting that Armstrong, writing early in the "Swing Era," does not associate swing exclusively with rhythm, but with improvising around the beat *and* the melody.

49 Braxton, *T-a W* 3, 35–36. Cf. Braxton's remarks on his *Composition* 116: "All of the structures in this category seek to remain open to the challenge of the moment so that the invention and 'spiritual meaning' of a given participation take precedence over any existentially imposed criterion of 'correct.' What this means is that the notated material of Composition No. 116 can be shaped according to the particulars of its interpreters — don't worry about me please!" Braxton, CN-E, 443. For examples of African American musicians urging colleagues to "play it wrong," see Szwed, *Space*, 99, and Lock, *Chasing*, 48.

50 Qtd. in Lock, *Forces*, 252. That some African American musicians (such as Charles Mingus, Cecil Taylor) have preferred players to learn their music *by ear* rather than give them notation to perform — a methodology they believe enables group members to interpret the music in a more personal way — does not alter the point that many critics' reaction to the sight of notation may be rooted in cultural prejudice. I should also add that the presumed emphasis in European music on respecting the score has not prevented numerous debates within that tradition on questions of interpretation and appropriate performance style.

51 Ann Douglas, *Terrible Honesty: Mongrel Manhattan in the 1920s* (New York: Farrar, Straus and Giroux, 1996) 431. Cf. Braxton's 1979 observation that whatever a black person does, "you're a 'jazz musician' or you're a 'great athlete' or you have that 'natural ability'. So you might work for 20 or 30 years and if you're able to master what you're dealing with or become proficient on any level it will be attributed to your 'natural ability.' " Herman Gray and Nathaniel Mackey, untitled 1979 interview with Anthony Braxton, Lock, *Mixtery*, 59.

52 Braxton, *T-a W* 3, 300. Braxton attributes this kind of racial stereotyping to what he calls "the grand trade-off," while the subsequent misunderstanding of black music by even enthusiastic white writers he terms "the across the tracks syndrome." I discuss these concepts in detail below. Another result of this stereotyping is the attempt by white "classical" critics to deny or demote the influence of jazz on contemporary Western musics. As Braxton notes in *T-a W* 1 (366), "In the fifties and sixties the Euro-American and European western art community tried to advance aleatory process as a new compositional technique that had nothing to do with improvisation — which is ridiculous. Both aleatory and indeterminism are words which have been coined . . . to bypass the word improvisa-

tion and as such the influence of any non-white sensibility. . . ." This idea has been discussed in detail by George E. Lewis, who further argues that Euro-derived definitions of improvisation as "pure spontaneity" represent "a notion of spontaneity that excludes history or memory" (and so avoids having to acknowledge an indebtedness to black music), whereas "the African-American improviser, coming from a legacy of slavery and oppression, cannot countenance the erasure of history. The destruction of family and lineage, the rewriting of history and memory in the image of whiteness, is one of the facts with which all people of color must live." George E. Lewis, "Improvised Music After 1950: Afrological and Eurological Perspectives," Black Music Research Journal 16 (1996): 107–09.

53 Brian Blevins, review of 3 Compositions of New Jazz by Anthony Braxton, Coda Aug. 1969: 19. Blevins's antipathy to Western art music is more apparent in his comments about violinist Leroy Jenkins on the LP's closing composition, "The Bell" (by Leo Smith): "Classically grounded, he does much to give the piece the emotional sterility characteristic of much contemporary European music."

54 Will Smith, "Chicago: Winds of Change," Jazz and Pop Apr. 1970, rpt. in Giants of Black Music, ed. Pauline Rivelli and Robert Levin (New York: Da Capo, 1979) 110. Rpt. of The Black Giants, 1970.

55 Braxton, CN-A, 54.

56 Peter Rothbart, " 'Play or Die': Anthony Braxton Interview," Down Beat Feb. 1982: 20.

57 All quotations in this paragraph regarding Composition 23G come from Braxton's notes on the work in CN-B, 63–72. Recordings of 23G can be heard on Five Pieces 1975, Arista AL 4064, 1975; Performance (Quartet) 1979, hat ART CD 6044, 1990; Quartet (Coventry) 1985, Leo CD LR 204/5, 1993; and Willisau (Quartet) 1991, hat ART CD 4-6001/4, 1992. For a comparison of these different performances, see Mike Heffley, The Music of Anthony Braxton (New York: Excelsior Music, 1996) 375–77.

58 And why he describes himself, and certain of his colleagues, as a restructuralist.

59 Briefly, a pulse track comprises repeating sequences of notation that alternate, rapidly and irregularly, with short, five- to ten-second spaces for improvisation. Pulse tracks are usually, but not invariably, played by the bassist and the drummer. See Graham Lock, "Colours of the Spiritway: 25 Years of Anthony Braxton's Compositions for the Creative Ensemble. Stories and Histories," CD insert notes to Willisau (Quartet) 1991 by Anthony Braxton, 4–5. See also Lock, Forces, 195–206.

60 Lock, Forces, 263–64. This quotation confirms Braxton's statement that he is less interested in a "correct" performance of his notated material than that it should remain "open to the challenge of the moment." A performance of Composition 105A with Hemingway and Lindberg can be heard on Four Compositions (Quartet) 1983, Black Saint BSR 0066 CD, n.d.; and a version with Hemingway and Dresser is on Quartet (London) 1985, Leo CD LR 200/1, 1990.

61 Qtd. in Litweiler, CD insert notes to *3 Compositions*.

62 Robert Palmer, LP liner notes to *Five Pieces 1975* by Anthony Braxton.

63 Chip Stern, "Kelvin/*7666* = Blip-Bleep," *Village Voice* 11 June 1979: 61.

64 Anthony Braxton, *For Trio*, Arista AB4181, 1978.

65 Braxton, CN-D, 145, 139.

66 *Composition 76* was composed in what Braxton calls "modular notation," each module being printed on a separate card. The performers can decide in which order to play the cards and also in which direction to perform each module. Improvisation in *76* is regulated by color and shape and occurs in short "sound bursts," an idea that Braxton says was inspired by the quick brush strokes of certain kinds of Japanese painting and that encapsulates much of the overall "feel" of the work. "Moments in Composition No. 76 form and dissipate in brief light flashes that give no sense of linear continuity ('and expectations'). To experience Composition No. 76 is to enter a 'temple of sound' that calls out for our sense of well-being. There is no happiness or sadness in this space—only 'the experience.'" For Braxton's full account of *Composition 76*, see CN-D, 136–54.

67 Anthony Braxton, *For Four Orchestras*, Arista A3L 8900, 1978.

68 For an analysis of *Composition 82*, see Art Lange, "Implications of a Creative Orchestra, 1972–78," Lock, *Mixtery*, 128–30. Braxton's notes on the work are in CN-D, 279–307. Unfortunately, many of 82's spatial features, which involve tiers of players on revolving chairs sending different sounds around the auditorium on a variety of trajectories, do not come across well on a stereo recording.

69 Peter Niklas Wilson, "Firmly Planted in Mid-Air: Notes on the Syntax and Aesthetics of Anthony Braxton's 'Composition 151' (1991)," Lock, *Mixtery*, 144. He is actually quoting the character Jason in the Braxton story that accompanies *Composition 151*. See Anthony Braxton, "Notes to Composition No. 151," CD insert notes to *2 Compositions (Ensemble) 1989/1991*, hat ART CD 6068, 1992. Cf. also Braxton's comments in regard to *Composition 26C* that "the instrumentalist is expected to establish a music with conventional techniques and get unconventional results." CN-B, 205.

70 Qtd. in Graham Lock, "Let 100 Orchestras Blow," *The Wire* June 1985: 19.

71 Mackey, *Discrepant*, 244. Cf. Robert Farris Thompson's description of Eshu-Elegbara (Mackey's Legba) as "the ultimate master of potentiality": "Outwardly mischievous but inwardly full of overflowing creative grace, Eshu-Elegbara eludes the coarse nets of characterization." Thompson, *Flash*, 19. Much the same could be said of Braxton and Ellington (and, in a slightly different context, of Sun Ra).

72 Kevin Whitehead, review of *Composition Notes* by Anthony Braxton, *Cadence* Nov. 1990. Revised rpt. in Lock, *Mixtery*, 156. Cf. Braxton's comment: "Composition's not the big deal they make it at colleges. They paralyse people with rules. I just sit down, write out an idea and work on it." Lock, *Forces*, 97.

73 Paul A. Anderson, "Ellington, Rap Music, and Cultural Difference," *Musi-*

cal Quarterly 79 (1995): 183. For a full discussion of black diasporal creative hybridity, see Gilroy, *Black Atlantic*.

74 For a more detailed discussion of their respective critical stances, see Gennari, esp. 485–86, 506–08.

75 Ted Joans, review of Le Festival Mondial, *Coda* Oct. 1975: 37.

76 See, for example, Bill Smith's declaration: "It doesn't matter if your likes are Johnny Hodges, Lester Young, Bird, Ornette or Trane, for Anthony Braxton is the present account of that lineage. He is THE one. . . ." Bill Smith, review of four LPs by Braxton, *Coda* Apr. 1974: 16. Though I have concentrated in this chapter on negative critical responses to Braxton's work, favorable reviews such as Smith's were in the majority. See Ronald M. Radano, "Braxton's Reputation," *Musical Quarterly* 72 (1986): 503–22. Nevertheless, Radano's claim that a "survey of the literature from 1974 to 1982 shows that only two critics disliked Braxton's music and wrote vituperative commentary about it" (504) is clearly erroneous. See the above quotations from Giddins, Joans, Stern, et al., none of whom are among the two antipathetic critics named by Radano. He does mention Giddins's critiques, but he argues that Giddins "balanced his taunts with praise" (504 n.8). Radano presumably sees this as critical "balance" because he is arguing against the notion that Braxton's work provoked genuine controversy in the press. Yet the fact that his music could draw such contrary responses from a critic seems to me evidence less of balance than of the very controversy that Radano is trying to play down. The chapter "Black Experimentalism as Spectacle" in Radano's book *New Musical Figurations* draws heavily on the material in this essay and in my view seriously misrepresents Braxton's depiction in the jazz press during the mid-1970s. And not only in my view; see Art Lange, review of *New Musical Figurations* by Ronald M. Radano, *Midwest Jazz*, Winter 1994–95: 13–14, 20.

77 Graham Lock, unpublished interview with Anthony Braxton, Middletown, Conn., 1 Dec. 1995. Although he did not mention it, the facts that Braxton's quartet in the mid-1970s often included three white players and that in 1975 he married a white woman, Nickie Singer, probably contributed to his being deemed "not 'black' enough" for some critics. It is richly ironic that Crouch, now a great champion of Ellington's music, should have attacked Braxton on the same grounds that John Hammond used to attack Ellington in the 1930s and 1940s.

78 Braxton, *T-a W* 3, 312–13.

79 Baraka's 1963 essay "Jazz and the White Critic," for example, anticipates several of the points on which Braxton elaborates in his critique of jazz journalism in *T-a W* 3, 235–308. See Baraka, *Black Music*, 11–20. See also Heffley, 150–53, for a discussion of the similarities in Baraka's and Braxton's thinking on the jazz critical establishment.

80 Amiri Baraka, "Blues, Poetry, and the New Music," *The Music: Reflections on Jazz and Blues*, Amiri Baraka and Amina Baraka (New York: William Morrow, 1987) 266. He has named Braxton as being in this "school" (e.g., Baraka and

Baraka, 320), although he more often attacks the group without naming individual players. Baraka's contention that their "mission" is fueled by a desire to assimilate into white middle-class culture seems to me undercut by the fact that white middle-class America has remained distinctly lukewarm about the music of Cage and the serialists. In the mid-1960s Braxton switched from music to philosophy at Roosevelt University because, in the music department "there was no real respect for Stockhausen or John Cage. They were still debating whether or not Schoenberg was valid!" (Lock, *Forces*, 44.) This suggests that Braxton's interest in these composers predates any possibility of his being able to use such an interest to impress white middle-class America, even had he wanted to do so. In fact, the most evident response to Braxton's acknowledgment of an interest in these composers was almost entirely negative—from the white middle-class Americans who reviewed his records!

81 Ellison, *Shadow*, 257.

82 Gennari, 490.

83 Ellison, *Shadow*, 249.

84 See, for example, Amiri Baraka, "Class Struggle in Music," Baraka and Baraka, 317–27.

85 Baraka, "Class Struggle," 319.

86 Braxton, *T-a W* 2, 458.

87 From a 1968 interview with Marvin X, qtd. in Mackey, *Discrepant*, 23.

88 Baraka, "Class Struggle," 327.

89 Braxton, *T-a W* 2, 466.

90 Mackey, *Discrepant*, 251.

91 Lock, *Forces*, 67. Cf. Braxton's 1985 remarks on his outlook in the 1960s: "everywhere I looked I was seeing a profound disrespect in how the music was written about. I reacted against that; I didn't want my music to be perceived as having no thought. I mean, only in jazz is thinking a dirty word!" Lock, *Forces*, 237.

92 Val Wilmer, "Musicians Talking—Anthony Braxton," *Jazz and Blues* May 1971: 27.

93 Graham Lock, "Now's the Time: An Interview with Anthony Braxton," CD insert notes to *Anthony Braxton's Charlie Parker Project 1993*, hat ART CD 2-6160, 1995, 8.

94 Gary Giddins, "Anthony Braxton as Ideas Man," *Village Voice* 28 Apr. 1975: 112.

95 Giddins, "Anthony Braxton Marches," 66; Stern, 61.

96 "If a mad scientist ever drank a potion he had concocted to formulate 'jazz musician,' he would undoubtedly transform into Anthony Braxton." Kevin Lynch, review of *Solo Live at Moers Festival* by Anthony Braxton, *Coda* Feb. 1978: 18. The implication that jazz and (sane) science are somehow incompatible can perhaps be attributed to what Braxton terms "the grand trade-off." I discuss this idea in detail below.

97 See Braxton, *T-a W* 3, 51–87, esp. 54.

98 Braxton, *CN-D*, 305.

99 Nevertheless, Braxton has continued to employ analogies from what could be called orthodox science in talking of his music. He seems especially fond of references to astronomy and genetics. See, for example, Lock, *Forces*, 202.

100 Ansell, 249–50. Braxton's view of language as something that obstructs what he wants to say perhaps allows us to regard his diagram titles as another aspect of black music's capacity for "telling inarticulacy."

101 Ansell, 250.

102 Lock, *Forces*, 170–71.

103 See Anthony Braxton, *Composition No. 173*, Black Saint 120166-2, 1996. These "story" compositions can perhaps be seen as an extension of a familiar jazz tradition. In the words of George E. Lewis: "One important aspect of Afrological improvisation is the notion of the importance of personal narrative, of 'telling your own story.'" Lewis, 117.

104 Braxton, "Notes." So not only do the characters in the story drive through the city/composition, the instrumentalists too "navigate different paths" through the work, guided by symbols in the score such as "'sign posts,' which approximate traffic directions—U-turns, right turn only, etc." Bill Shoemaker, "A Wake-up Call," CD insert notes to *2 Compositions (Ensemble) 1989/1991* by Anthony Braxton. Revised rpt. in Lock, *Mixtery*, 132.

105 John F. Szwed, "The Local and the Express: Anthony Braxton's Title-Drawings," Lock, *Mixtery*, 209.

106 Szwed, "Local," 209. Cf. Winston Smith, "Let's Call This: Race, Writing, and Difference in Jazz," *Public* (Toronto) 4/5 (1990/91): 71–83, for an intriguing discussion of attitudes to language in modern black creativity (Monk, Braxton, Mackey, et al.). Thanks to John Szwed for this reference.

107 Sun Ra, "There Are Other Worlds (They Have Not Told You Of)", *Lanquidity*, Philly Jazz PJ666, 1978.

108 Hurston, "Characteristics of Negro Expression," 24. The context makes it clear that Hurston is using the term "hieroglyphics" to indicate an image-based visual language.

109 Lock, *Forces*, 151–52.

110 Hugo de Craen, "Braxton and Kandinsky: Symbolists of the Spiritual." Lock, *Mixtery*, 212–24. The Kandinsky paintings on Braxton recordings are *Black Relationship* 1924 on *Six Compositions: Quartet*, Antilles 422-848 585-2, 1982, and *Looking Back on the Past*, 1924 on *2 Compositions (Ensemble) 1989/1991*. Braxton has confirmed that the choice of paintings was his.

111 See Lock, *Forces*, 217; Braxton, CN-E, 510–13, 521–22.

112 Graham Lock, "A Highway to the Cosmics," Lock, *Mixtery*, 246. Braxton went into academia in 1985 when he began a full-time teaching job at Mills College in Oakland, California. He has since remained in academia and is now professor of ethnomusicology at Wesleyan University in Middletown, Connecticut.

113 Braxton has used the "talking in tongues" analogy in reference to aspects of his solo music and has also endorsed the notion of his playing being "open to the spirit." See Lock, "Highway," 248–49. His most recent inno-

vatory form, Ghost Trance Music, appears to take a further step into the ineffable: "I try to get into a state of meditation and compose a stream of pitches, and just go with it, . . . like a stream of consciousness . . . this is my trance music." Lock, unpublished interview 1995. Examples of Ghost Trance Musics can be heard on *Sextet (Istanbul) 1996*, Braxton House BH 001, 1996 (comprising *Compositions 185* and *186*) and *Tentet (New York) 1996*, Braxton House BH 004, 1996 (comprising *Composition 193*).

114 See Robert Farris Thompson, "The Song That Named the Land: The Visionary Presence of African-American Art," *Black Art: Ancestral Legacy: The African Impulse in African-American Art*, ed. Robert V. Rozelle, Alvira Wardlaw, Maureen A. McKenna (Dallas: Dallas Museum of Art; New York: Harry W. Abrams, 1990) 97–141, esp. 102–03, 110–13, 117–23. I am reminded, too, of the "personal hieroglyphics" of James Hampton, "a language that apparently originated and died with its author." Hampton, who worked after World War II as a janitor in Washington, D.C., is best known for his single work of art, *The Throne of the Third Heaven of the Nations' Millennium General Assembley*, an astonishing "heavenly vision" that he constructed in his garage from bits of old furniture, planks, cardboard, broken glass, and other "found objects," all covered in gold and silver tinfoil. See Regenia A. Perry, *Free Within Ourselves: African-American Artists in the Collection of the National Museum of American Art* (Washington, D.C.: National Museum of American Art, Smithsonian Institution; San Francisco: Pomegranate, 1992) 80–85.

115 Braxton himself made a similar analogy in a 1982 interview: "I am moving more toward being aware of the mystical and the spiritual aspects of the music and the titles are, among other things, a part of my own vibrational imprints, footpaths, as I'm walking through all this." Joe Carey, "Anthony Braxton: Interview," *Cadence* Mar. 1984: 8.

116 Braxton, CN-E, 142. For a particularly intriguing instance of Braxton's synesthetic approach, listen to *Composition 173*, in which four actors describe various sounds in strikingly visual imagery and then try to vocalize the sounds as the instruments play them. The actors' attempted vocalizing can be seen as another example of "telling inarticulacy," a particular kind of musical "stammering," in which the characters try to enunciate such words/sounds as "NNNEEEETTTTTWWWWWCZZZZZX" and "QQQQQQQQQUUUUUUUIIIIXXXXCCCZZZZZZZIIY." In this case inarticulacy certainly speaks on a higher level, since Braxton has said that 173 explores the vodun concept of spirit possession.

117 Each volume of the Tri-axium *Writings* and of the *Composition Notes* also has its own diagrammatic title.

118 In the event, Braxton could not afford to print the books in color. For the intended color code, see *T-a W* 1, viii–ix.

119 Braxton, *T-a W* 1, vii, x.

120 Braxton, *T-a W* 1, x, xiii, iv.

121 Carey, 6. Cf. Mike Heffley's argument that Braxton's lack of "correct" technique in his writing is because, as in his music, "correctness" is much less a priority for him than creativity. Heffley, 158. He also suggests that Brax-

ton's use of language at times resembles "the process of improvisation" (159).

122 Whitehead, 156.

123 Stern, 61.

124 Braxton, T-a W 1, x.

125 Cf. "I offer nothing in this book as definitively 'true' (because for too long we have been deluged by so-called experts with interpretations that are presented as facts—but aren't—and this misuse of interpretation has moved to damage the whole of this time period)." Braxton, T-a W 1, v. Throughout the books, Braxton frequently reminds the reader that he is only expressing his opinion. Given the scope and complexity of the Tri-axium Writings, this comes over as a fairly authoritative "opinion," though one that paradoxically both aims at totality yet resists closure. As Mark Sinker has noted: "Braxton's worldview seems remarkable in that it's open, equally . . . to everything *and its opposite*." Sinker, untitled essay, 230. In 1985 Braxton characteristically attributed such a perspective to his (and my) star sign: "Anything we can talk about we can also talk about and prove its opposite—as a Gemini you must be aware of that! All of these matters are relative." Lock, *Forces*, 205.

126 See Lock, "Vision," 48–54.

127 Lock, "Vision," 51.

128 Gray and Mackey, 59. Cf. Ellington's complaint, quoted in chapter 4, that the word "jazz" had become too closely identified with the brothels of New Orleans.

129 Or, at least, reflection on Braxton's statement that "one cannot comment on the reality specifics of non-western focuses without making serious adjustments in the vibrational nature of one's use of language." T-a W 1, ii.

130 Lock, *Forces*, 282.

131 For more on this point, see Lock, *Forces*, 294–307.

132 Winston Smith, 72. Smith's notion of Braxton "rewording" history also offers a key, I think, to a better understanding of Braxton's various "in the tradition" and tribute recordings, which can be seen as comparable "retellings" of history in their attempts to explore possibilities ignored or excluded by narrow, more conventional versions of history (both writ-ten and played). Cf. Stuart Broomer's reviews of Braxton's piano quartet discs, which feature "standard" postbop repertoire by such composers as Brubeck, Mingus, and Monk. (Braxton plays piano on these discs.) Com-menting on the *Knitting Factory* CD, Broomer writes: "Braxton creates a kind of dream language, putting together a loose 'Jazz' band that sounds like it might have played in the early sixties, then mounting a furious piano assault on it, counterpointing the classics of modernist repertoire with a general unleashing of harmonic and rhythmic possibility. In a sense it is a reenactment of history, but it's also an act of tremendous inven-tion, an assault of the imagination." (Stuart Broomer, review of *Knitting Factory (Piano/Quartet)* 1994, vol. 1 by Anthony Braxton, *Cadence* Apr. 1996: 94.) And in a later piece on the *Yoshi's* CD, Broomer restates the point in

this way: "[Braxton's] reading in the 'old modern' is broader than any neo-conservative's, his mingling of fixed and free elements immeasurably more significant as he explores ways to hear history." (Broomer, review of *Piano Quartet, Yoshi's 1994* by Anthony Braxton, *Cadence* Nov. 1996: 44.) In this context, Braxton's treatment of older musics resembles the "restructuralist" impulse of his own compositions and exemplifies the philosophical approach that he advocates in the *Tri-axium Writings* of recasting the "axiums" of the past and the present to better meet the challenges of the future.

133 Nathaniel Mackey, *Bedouin Hornbook*, vol. 1 of *From a Broken Bottle Traces of Perfume Still Emanate* (Lexington: UP of Kentucky/Callaloo Fiction Series, 1986) 51–52.

134 Archie Shepp and Philly Joe Jones, *Archie Shepp and Philly Joe Jones*, rec. 1969, Fantasy 86018, n.d.

135 Mackey, *Bedouin*, 53.

136 In musicology, the "upper partials" are the overtones of the fundamental note. Braxton uses this as an analogy for other contexts, so the "upper partials" become the vibrational factors that Western empiricism cannot always "hear." See, for example, Lock, *Forces*, 64, 219–21.

137 Reed, 211.

138 Lock, *Forces*, 284.

139 Braxton, *T-a W* 1, xiii.

140 Braxton, *T-a W* 1, 132.

141 Braxton, *T-a W* 1, 133.

142 For more on the history of such correspondences and their role in ancient belief systems, see Lock, *Forces*, 294–307.

143 In the glossary to the *Tri-axium Writings*, Braxton defines existentialism as "the phenomenon and state of being that arises when spiritualism is subjected to logical analysis without respect for its proper affinity adjustments, which results in despiritualism and emphasis instead on the 'particulars' of a physical universe occurrence—with the understanding being that 'something that happens is really what has happened' as opposed to 'something that happens is an expression of . . . greater forces.'" *T-a W* 1, 508. Ellipsis in original. Braxton's use of the terms "existential" and "essence" suggests an awareness of Sartre's philosophy, just as his notion of the "spectacle diversion syndrome" (see below) implies a possible situationist influence, though in both cases Braxton redefines the terms to give them very much his own meaning and value.

144 Braxton, *T-a W* 2, 26.

145 See *T-a W* 2, 52–95, for Braxton's full account of affinity dynamics.

146 Braxton, *T-a W* 1, 292–94.

147 Braxton, *T-a W* 1, 305.

148 Qtd. in Douglas, 431.

149 Garry Booth, "The Gospel According to the Five Blind Boys," review of London Jazz Festival concerts, *Financial Times*, 25 May 1993: 19d. All subsequent quotations from this review have the same page reference.

150 Just as critics in the 1970s misrepresented Braxton's interest in "vibrational science" as an interest in empirical science (to substantiate their labeling of him as cold, calculating etc.), so Booth here backs up his depiction of Braxton's music as "heartless" by misrepresenting his interest in numerology as an interest in mathematics. But, as Braxton noted in 1977, "I could never learn math in school. They kept telling me that 1 and 1 made 2. But they never told me what 1 was or what 2 was." Qtd. in Hubert Saal, "Two Free Spirits," *Newsweek* 8 Aug. 1977: 41. Curiously, John Coltrane's 1961 London performance was likened to "higher mathematics" and described as "apparent chaos" by a disconcerted *Melody Maker* reviewer, Bob Dawbarn, who was at least honest enough to admit that he had "no idea . . . what it was all about." In this review, the contrasting Five Blind Boys role was assigned to Dizzy Gillespie, whose group played at the same concert, and whom Dawbarn lauded as "a true Jazz Great." Qtd. in Simpkins, 139.

151 Booth's moral imperative about what music "ought to do" recalls James Lincoln Collier's similarly prescriptive—and nonsensical—statement: "When jazz becomes confounded with art, passion flies out and pretension flies in." Collier, 307.

152 One wonders, too, if on some level Braxton was being "punished" for performing onstage with a white woman, a "transgression" that some would see as even more reprehensible than an interest in "mathematics"!

153 Braxton, *T-a W 3*, 288.

154 Of course, the premise of the "Blindfold Test" is that the auditor does not know the identity of the artist on whose work he or she is commenting. I think it is highly likely that Phil Woods did know, or at least suspect, that Braxton was the artist in question, if only because *For Alto* had been out for several months, had already been given a five-star review in *Down Beat*, and had featured in a previous "Blindfold Test." Moreover, Leonard Feather specifically mentions that the track played comes from a double album of solo saxophone music, and *For Alto* was the only record at the time to fit this description. Even if Woods really did not know the artist's identity (and thus his color), I think it is still suggestive that he apparently regarded the very idea of making a solo saxophone record as somehow violating the limits of what was permissible in jazz.

155 Feather, "Blindfold Test—Phil Woods," 33.

156 Braxton, *T-a W 3*, 289–90. Cf., on the individual level, the protagonist of Ralph Ellison's *Invisible Man*: "I am invisible, understand, simply because people refuse to see me. Like the bodiless heads you see sometimes in circus sideshows, it is as though I have been surrounded by mirrors of hard, distorting glass. When they approach me they see only my surroundings, themselves, or figments of their imagination—indeed, everything and anything except me." Ralph Ellison, *Invisible Man* (1952; Harmondsworth, Middlesex: Penguin, 1982) 7.

157 Braxton, *T-a W 3*, 290. Perhaps I should stress that Braxton is not arguing against sensuality per se but against the obsession with this facet of black music demonstrated by many white listeners and critics—an obsession

that leads them to downplay black music's other qualities and construct the kind of false musical categorizations that he describes here.

158 Qtd. in Eddie Prévost, "Withered Jazz," letter, *The Wire* Mar. 1989: 66. The original statement was made in an *Omnibus* TV profile of Courtney Pine, broadcast on BBC 1, 24 Nov. 1988. Contrast Melly's silly pronouncement with McCoy Tyner's belief that "Music's not a plaything—it's *as serious as your life.*" Wilmer, *As Serious*, 258.

159 Saal, 41.

160 Ibid.

161 Ibid. Radano (*New*, 265) argues that this passage "captures the mass of stereotypes" used to depict Braxton's music in the mid-1970s. I see it as more idiosyncratic and better explicated in the context of Braxton's own theoretical framework (the grand trade-off, black exotica, etc.) than in terms of the "primitive/intellectual homology" that Radano proposes as the dominant construct in critical accounts of Braxton's work. I find this last point unconvincing, since Radano, in my opinion, fails to provide sufficient evidence that Braxton was widely portrayed as "primitive."

162 Saal, 41.

163 Braxton, *T-a W 3*, 298.

164 Braxton, *T-a W 3*, 298–99. The "sweating brow" can perhaps be seen as a later version of the "hot jazzman" stereotype, with the flame of critical preconception now turned up a notch to "very hot"!

165 Roland Barthes, *Mythologies*, trans. Annette Lavers (1957; St. Albans, Herts.: Paladin, 1973) 26–28. In the film, says Barthes, "To sweat is to think— which evidently rests on the postulate, appropriate to a nation of businessmen, that thought is a violent, cataclysmic operation, of which sweat is only the most benign symptom." In jazz commentary, to sweat is to *not* think—which evidently rests on the postulate, appropriate to a nation of former slave owners, that thought is a dangerous, subversive activity best prevented by excessive physical labor, of which sweat is only the most reassuring sign. And just as black overseers were sometimes used to enforce sweat on the plantation, so some black writers have valorized the jazzman's sweaty brow. For a thought-provoking discussion of how the fetishization of "swing" by Stanley Crouch and Wynton Marsalis can be read as "a retention of the idea that 'jazz' musicians are . . . 'simply supposed to sweat,'" see Alun Ford, *Anthony Braxton: Creative Music Continuums* (Exeter: Stride, 1997) 57–59. I wonder if there is also an implicit rhetoric of masculinity lurking in the fondness for sweat and swing. David Ake has suggested that the advent of free jazz—specifically Ornette Coleman's 1959 Atlantic LP *The Shape of Jazz to Come*—challenged "accepted codes of jazz masculinity." Ake argues persuasively that bebop and hard bop players saw virtuoso displays of "running the changes" as a means of asserting their masculinity. When Coleman's new music inaugurated a paradigm shift in notions of jazz virtuosity, the boppers were suddenly confronted by a crisis of gender-identity. "For many of the men faced with this new style, it was not simply a matter of not knowing what to

play but who to *be*." See David Ake, "Re-Masculating Jazz: Ornette Coleman, 'Lonely Woman,' and the New York Jazz Scene in the Late 1950s," *American Music* 16.1 (1998): 25–44. With harmonic complexity no longer such a significant presence in our post–free jazz era, perhaps "swing" has now become the last remaining—and desperately defended—arena in which certain—and, some would say, outmoded—codes of jazz masculinity can still be affirmed. (However, to explore this topic in full would require more space than I can spare here.)

166 Barthes, 28.

167 Ibid.

168 Scott Albin, review of concerts by the Anthony Braxton Quartet and Tashi, The Bottom Line, New York City, *Down Beat* 25 Mar. 1976: 41.

169 Braxton, *T-a W* 3, 303.

170 Braxton, *T-a W* 3, 306.

171 Lock, *Forces*, 91.

172 Lock, *Forces*, 92. Cf. Cecil Taylor's 1958 remarks, "Everything I've lived I am in my music" and "I am not afraid of European influences. The point is to use them—as Ellington did—as part of my life as an American Negro." Qtd. in Hentoff, 30, 228. Cf. also Braxton's 1994 complaints about "concepts which said, you can't listen to Schoenberg because it isn't relevant to your experience. Or, you can't listen to George Clinton because you can't like Schoenberg and George Clinton. . . . And I'm saying, wait a minute, this is part of the *baggage of unhappiness* related to this millennium . . . why burden anyone, with these concepts?" Lock, "Highway," 249.

173 Graham Lock, unpublished interview with Anthony Braxton, London 16 May 1994.

174 See Gilroy, *Black Atlantic*, 99–103; Baraka, *Black Music*, 180–211.

175 Braxton, *T-a W* 3, 256.

176 Olly Wilson, "The Heterogenous Sound Ideal in African-American Music," *New Perspectives in Music: Essays in Honor of Eileen Southern*, eds. Josephine Wright with Samuel A. Floyd, Jr. (Warren, Mich.: Harmonie Park, 1992) 329. Examples of such heterogeneity exist in European and Euro-American classical musics, too, of course, although I doubt that any musicologist would claim it as an "underlying conception" in those traditions.

177 O. Wilson, 329.

178 As, for example, in his use of "collage forms" (see Lock, *Forces*, 202–06) and even in his piano playing on standards, in which Bill Shoemaker has noted his "disposition towards the extremes of register . . . dynamics . . . rhythm . . . and duration." Shoemaker, "What It Is: The Reception Dynamics and Information Alignment of Piano Quartet (Yoshi's) 1994," CD insert notes to *Piano Quartet, Yoshi's 1994* by Anthony Braxton, Music & Arts CD 849, 1996, 11.

179 Braxton, *CN-D*, 294.

180 Braxton, *CN-A*, 396. The *Catalogue of Works* is reprinted at the back of each volume of the *Composition Notes*.

181 Braxton, *T-a W* 2, 197; Legba quotation, Thompson, *Flash*, 19.

1 Ralph Ellison, *Going to the Territory* (New York: Vintage/Random House, 1987) 131.

2 Braxton, *T-a W* 1, xiii.

3 Braxton, *T-a W* 3, 428–536. In condensing more than 100 pages of Braxton's text into a single sentence, I am obviously losing a lot of the subtleties of his arguments!

4 Braxton, CN-E, 3.

5 Braxton remains unsure if "city-state" is the most appropriate term to describe his notion of each region being based on a particular "identity." Given that he has cited Plato's *The Republic* as an influence on his conception of a fantasy world, I asked if he had had in mind the ancient Greek form of city-state, but he replied, "no, not consciously." Graham Lock, unpublished interview with Anthony Braxton, London, June 1996. However, since he also refers to his *Trillium* operas as "Dialogues" (and studied Greek philosophy at university), further exploration of Platonic echoes in Braxton's work might prove a fruitful line of enquiry.

6 These are (1) Long Sounds (Static); (2) Accented Long Sounds (Active); (3) Trills; (4) Staccato Line Formings; (5) Intervallic Formings; (6) Multiphonics; (7) Short Attacks; (8) Angular Attacks; (9) Legato Formings; (10) Diatonic Formings; (11) Gradient Formings; and (12) Subidentity Formings. Braxton also gives each of these "Language Types" its own visual designation. See Lock, "Vision," 48–49.

7 Lock, "Highway," 246–47, 248.

8 Lock, unpublished interview, 1995. *Composition* 174 is available on Leo Records CD LR 217, 1994.

9 This quotation and subsequent ones from 175 come from an unpublished manuscript headed "Composition No. 175 (Story)," kindly supplied by Anthony Braxton. *Composition* 175 was performed by Braxton and the Creative Jazz Orchestra at London's Sadler's Wells Theatre on 15 May 1994 as part of the London Jazz Festival. The performance was recorded and later broadcast on BBC Radio 3. Thanks to Derek Drescher of Radio 3 for a copy of this recording. For more on Braxton's 1994 UK tour with the Creative Jazz Orchestra, see Lock, *Mixtery*, 190–96.

10 Braxton, CN-A, 21.

11 Braxton, CN-B, 124.

12 Braxton, CN-C, 119.

13 Braxton, CN-C, 537. See also Graham Lock, "Sound Travel: Braxtonian Adventures in Time and Space," CD insert notes to *11 Compositions (Duo) 1995* by Anthony Braxton and Brett Larner, Leo Records CD LR 244, 1997.

14 I guess this may also be related to Braxton's synesthesia, i.e., that he does "see" the sounds simultaneous to hearing them.

15 John Corbett quotes Braxton's phrase, "Navigation through form," and links it with Mikhail Bakhtin's notion of the "chronotope," defined as "the intrinsic connectedness of temporal and spatial relationships" as ex-

pressed in artistic form. What Braxton's (and Sun Ra's) work offers, says Corbett, is the possibility of "(spatial and spiritual) navigation through (musical and poetic) form." Corbett, "Anthony Braxton's *Bildungsmusik*," 186. The ring shout, another form of ritual music enactment that involved symbolic movement in space, could also be considered a precedent for Braxton's "ritual and ceremonial" musics. (I am thinking in particular of Levine's suggestion that ring shouts manifested the slaves' sense of a "sacred time and space" in which they would enact historical/mythological *stories*, such as Joshua at the battle of Jericho or Moses leading the Children of Israel out of Egypt. See Levine, 37–38.)

16 Both the score and libretto of *Composition 171* remain unpublished in 1999. Subsequent quotations from the libretto come from a private manuscript copy kindly supplied by Anthony Braxton. A "concert" performance of parts of *171* was given by Frederic Rzewski at the CIM Festival in Den Haag, Holland, in November 1993. See Corbett, "Anthony Braxton's *Bildungsmusik*." An instrumental quartet version of parts of *171* can be heard on *12 Compositions: Live at Yoshi's* (July 1993) by Anthony Braxton, Music & Arts CD 835, 1994.

17 See Heffley, 320, for an example of Braxton's use of perspective to suggest three-dimensional notation on the score of the much earlier *Composition 76*.

18 Lock, unpublished interview, 1996.

19 That both Braxton and Sun Ra have been fans of Walt Disney may seem incongruous, given the various racist and imperialist ideologies that some commentators have discerned in Disney's work; see, for example, Ariel Dorfman and Armand Mattelart, *How to Read Donald Duck: Imperialist Ideology in the Disney Comic*, trans. David Kunzle (1971; New York: International General, 1975). However, Braxton's stated liking for *Star Trek* certainly did not prevent him from recognizing and caustically satirizing that show's implicit political premises, as we will see below in discussing *Trillium E*.

20 Lock, unpublished interview, 1996. It is possible the word in the last sentence should be "principle" rather than "principal."

21 See Lock, *Forces*, 280.

22 "12 gates to the city" is a line from the spiritual, "Oh, What a Beautiful City" (the city being Heaven), on the Ragin CD. Numerous spirituals refer to heavenly mansions.

23 Marsh, 234.

24 Qtd. in Higginson, 15.

25 All quotations from *165* come from the untitled story included with the CD *Composition No. 165 (for 18 instruments)* by Anthony Braxton, New Albion NA 050 CD, 1992.

26 I wonder if Braxton's linking of clouds and the meta-real carries an echo of the spiritual "My Way's Cloudy." J. W. Johnson, *Book*, 92–93. Cf. also Braxton's *Composition 110D*, which has the subtitle "Nickie Journeys to the City of Clouds to Make a Decision." Unusually, he provides no commentary on this work in his *Composition Notes*.

27 Lock, unpublished interview, 1994.

28 Braxton, *T-a W* 2, 543; *T-a W* 3, 511; Lock, unpublished interview, 1995.

29 Bechet, 203.

30 *Composition 192*, which he premiered in London on 20 June 1996, is accompanied by the showing of a video of a circuitous car trip around Manhattan, the Outer Boroughs, and New Jersey. Braxton referred to this video showing as the first in a series of "pathway experiences" he was planning to build into future compositions. Qtd. in *Impressions*, interview with Anthony Braxton by Alyn Shipton, BBC Radio 3, 22 Feb. 1997.

31 From the spiritual known as "Heaven" (Ragin CD), "All God's Chillun Got Wings" (J. W. Johnson, *Book*, 77), and various other names.

32 Cf. Chuck Berry's sly 1964 parody of such varieties of transport when he has to switch from bus to train to jet to reach the "Promised Land" of California. Chuck Berry, "The Promised Land," *The Best of Chuck Berry*, Music Club MCCD 019, 1991.

33 Levine, 38.

34 Braxton, *CN-C*, 195. He is writing in reference to *Composition 45*.

35 Ellison, *Going*, 131. For more on the importance of freedom of movement in African American culture, see Levine, 261–67, and Szwed, *Space*, 134–35.

36 Szwed, "The Local," 211. Such trains have remained a powerful symbol in black music. I cite the Impressions' 1965 hit "People Get Ready" as an example because Braxton remembers playing with the Impressions in the mid-1960s, when he was working in the house band at Chicago's Royal Theatre. See Lock, *Forces*, 43–44. The Impressions, "People Get Ready," *Definitive Impressions*, Kent CDKEND 923, 1989.

37 Szwed, "Local," 209–11; Heffley, 212–13.

38 See, respectively, Heffley, 418, 413; Lock, "Highway," 246.

39 Charles Mingus, *Beneath the Underdog: His World as Composed by Mingus*, ed. Nel King (1971; Harmondsworth, Middlesex: Penguin, 1975) 256–57.

40 Braxton, *T-a W* 3, 506.

41 Braxton, *T-a W* 2, 180.

42 J. W. Johnson, *Book*, 162.

43 Qtd. in Litweiler, CD insert notes.

44 Mark Sinker, "Other Voices," *New Musical Express*, 23 July 1988: 45.

45 Qtd. in Lock, "Colours," 5. See also Lock, *Forces*, 203–04.

46 Braxton, *T-a W* 3, 457.

47 Qtd. in Lock, *Forces*, 121.

48 Ullman, 202.

49 For the sake of concision, I refer below to the operas simply by their initial letter, without including the word "Dialogues" each time.

50 Mark Sinker opens his thought-provoking essay on Braxton's work as a form of "Black Science Fiction" by quoting William Blake's dictum: "I must create a system, or be enslaved by another man's." Sinker, untitled essay, 236–37. Braxton, I think, takes this principle a step further and refuses to be constrained even by his own system(s).

51 For an example of a schematic and an account of how to "read" it, see *T-a W* 1, xiv–xv. This example is also reproduced in Lock, *Forces*, 309.

52 All references to the librettos of the Trillium operas are to unpublished manuscript copies kindly supplied by Anthony Braxton.

53 The libretto itself offers only a partial account of the complete performance, which not only includes music but also involves elements such as costume, lighting, and choreography (which are not always indicated in the libretto) as part of the opera's overall "meaning." To date, Trillium R is the only one of Braxton's operas to have been given fully staged performances—at New York's John Jay Theater on 25 and 26 October 1996. Both Trillium A and the first two scenes of Trillium M have received concert performances.

54 From an unpublished manuscript introduction to Trillium. Braxton also likens his use of the twelve principal Trillium characters to the way that, in a troupe of actors, one person may play several roles. This is certainly the case in Trillium E, where the characters have "local" names, even though these roles are "played" by the twelve main Trillium characters (and are sometimes referred to by these main names in the libretto, though this may simply be a mistake).

55 I am unable to include Trillium A in this discussion because my copy of the libretto is not entirely legible. Fortunately, the work is less germane to my interests here than the other operas. Trillium A was Braxton's first opera and is the least dramatic, by which I mean that relatively little occurs onstage and the libretto is the most abstract of the four, with the dialogue often sounding very similar to the prose of the *Tri-axium Writings*. In this respect, Trillium A is perhaps the opera that most resembles the Socratic dialogues that Braxton has cited as an influence. I should also explain that I have not discussed the operas' musical content here because there are no recordings yet of Trillium M, scenes 3 and 4, or Trillium E. The music for Trillium R, which is scheduled for release by Braxton House in the summer of 1999, is a characteristically personal synthesis-cum-transformation of various influences, including the Second Viennese School (Braxton particularly admires the operas of Alban Berg) and African diasporal practices, such as improvisation. For example, each singer is partnered by an instrumental soloist, who improvises around the vocal lines and mediates between the different (notated) realms of singer and orchestra.

56 In my manuscript copy of the Trillium M libretto, Braxton identifies the characters only by number after an initial cast list that indicates to which characters the numbers refer. For the sake of clarity I have included the full names of the speakers here and in subsequent quotations. I have also corrected obvious typing errors and anomalies in the manuscripts of all the librettos.

57 Cf. the discussion of "source transfer" and "gradualism" in chap. 5.

58 There is perhaps a distant echo, too, of Braxton's extremely funny account of how the agent Sid Bernstein tried to persuade him to make his music more commercial. "C'mon, are you gonna let your children starve for the

sake of a few dreams?" Lock, *Forces*, 285. Joreo tells Ashmenton, "Refuse my offer and your children will suffer—refuse my offer and your cities will burn—your lineage will be stopped."

59 Lock, unpublished interview, 1995.

60 Lock, *Forces*, 146.

61 Lock, unpublished interview, 1996.

62 There is perhaps another distant echo here of a dialogue in *Forces in Motion*. Braxton is describing how, when the group Circle (of which he was a member) joined the Scientology movement in the early 1970s, one of the organization's officials tried to persuade him to make his music more commercial: "he took me to the window, high over Central Park, and pointed to all the people walking around below. He said, 'Look! Do you want to be one of them or one of us?' I looked down and I thought, that's not them, that's people. I told him, sir, I want out." Lock, *Forces*, 286.

63 At the opera's premiere, Ntzockie was played by a European-American singer, Ashmenton by an African American singer. See Ben Ratliff, "An Anarchist Visionary's Protest Against Evil," review of *Shala Fears for the Poor* by Anthony Braxton, John Jay Theater, New York, *New York Times* 30 October 1996: C18.

64 I am reminded here of Ellington's point—made in *Black, Brown and Beige* and *My People*—that African Americans have always defended the United States in times of crisis. Braxton, I think, again raises the possibility of a racial "reading" of the situation without ever making it explicit—which leaves room for other interpretations, such as the plague being a metaphor for AIDS, and the "you people" and "your kind" that the villagers refer to as being the gay community.

65 When I originally wrote this chapter, Braxton did not have a subtitle for *Trillium E*. Later, he decided on "Wallingford's Polarity Gambit."

66 In the *Trillium E* librettos, Braxton again indicates characters by numbers. The cast list at the beginning of each act indicates which of the twelve major *Trillium* characters the numbers refer to and the names of the characters they are playing.

67 My copy of the libretto attributes both of these speeches to Suitor No. 1, which must be a mistake.

68 The planet's name is perhaps intended to carry a memory of Vietnam's Mekong Delta.

69 The very end of the opera has the archaeologists briefly discussing the opening of a zoo, too (I think), though it is not clear to me what exactly is going on.

70 Braxton, *T-a W 3*, 288.

71 Lock, *Forces*, 223–24.

72 Qtd. in Schonfield, 2.

73 Sun Ra, "The Potential," poem on the LP liner jacket of *Art Forms of Dimensions Tomorrow* by Sun Ra and His Solar Arkestra, Saturn 9956, 1965. This poem is not included with the Evidence CD reissue.

74 Lock, *Forces*, 211.

Coda

1 Bechet, 208.

2 Ibid.

3 Bechet, 218.

4 I am thinking, for example, of Sun Ra's ever-shifting attitudes to African Americans. In outlining the visions and revisions of Ra, Ellington, and Braxton, I have focused on elucidation because that seemed to me the priority. Nevertheless, in the work of all three I think there are moments of uncertainty, particularly regarding the status of race, that could be explored further. The contrary pull between an insistence on the value of black history and black aesthetics and an imaginary future in which race and color are deemed to be of no significance seems mostly to have generated a creative tension in their musics, but we should not be surprised if the outcome of wrestling with this "impossible" fusion sometimes appears to be contradiction and uncertainty.

5 Qtd. in Mona Hadler, "Jazz and the New York School," *Representing Jazz*, ed. Krin Gabbard (Durham, N.C.: Duke UP, 1995) 254.

6 Braxton, CN-D, 294.

7 Albert Ayler, "Introduction by Albert Ayler," *My Name Is Albert Ayler*, rec. 1963, Black Lion 760211, 1996.

Works Cited

Sound Recordings

Ayler, Albert. *Music Is the Healing Force of the Universe*. Rec. 1969. Impulse!-ABC AS919, 1970.

—————. *My Name Is Albert Ayler*. Rec. 1963. Black Lion 760211, 1996.

Berry, Chuck. *The Best of Chuck Berry*. Rec. 1955–1969. Music Club MCCD 019, 1991.

Braxton, Anthony. *2 Compositions (Ensemble) 1989/1991*. hat ART CD 6086, 1992.

—————. *3 Compositions of New Jazz*. Rec. 1968. Delmark DD 415, 1991.

—————. *12 Compositions: Live at Yoshi's (July 1993)*. Music & Arts CD 835, 1994.

—————. *Alto Saxophone Improvisations 1979*. Arista A2L 8602, 1979.

—————. *Anthony Braxton/Robert Schumann String Quartet*. Rec. 1979. Sound Aspects SAS CD 009, 1989.

—————. *Composition No. 165 (for 18 instruments)*. New Albion NA 050 CD, 1992.

—————. *Composition No. 173*. Black Saint 120166-2, 1996.

—————. *Composition No. 174*. Leo CD LR 217, 1994.

—————. *Composition No. 175*. Live "concert" performance at Sadler's Wells Theatre, London, 15 May 1994. Private recording.

—————. *Five Pieces 1975*. Arista AL 4064, 1975.

—————. *For Alto*. Rec. 1968. Delmark DS 420/21, n.d.

—————. *For Four Orchestras*. Arista A3L 8900, 1978.

—————. *For Trio*. Rec. 1977. Arista AB 4181, 1978.

—————. *Four Compositions (Quartet) 1983*. Black Saint BSR 066 CD, n.d.

—————. *Knitting Factory (Piano/Quartet) 1994*, vol. 1. Leo LR CD 222/23, 1995.

—————. *Performance (Quartet) 1979*. Originally issued as *Performance 9/1/79* Hat Hut 2R19. hat ART CD 6044, 1990.

—————. *Piano Quartet, Yoshi's 1994*. Music & Arts CD 849, 1996.

—————. *Quartet (Coventry) 1985*. Leo CD LR 204/05, 1993.

—————. *Quartet (London) 1985*. Leo CD LR 200/01, 1990.

—————. *Sextet (Istanbul) 1996*. Rec. 1995. Braxton House BH001, 1996.

—————. *Six Compositions: Quartet*. Rec. 1981. Antilles 422-848-585-2, 1982.

—————. *Tentet (New York) 1996*. Braxton House BH004, 1996.

—————. *Trillium—Dialogues M: Joreo's Vision of Forward Motion*. Live "concert" performance of scenes 1 and 2. Sadler's Wells Theatre, London, 15 May 1994. Private recording.

————. Trillium—Dialogues R: Shala Fears for the Poor. Live performance at the John Jay Theater, New York, 25 and 26 October 1996. Private recording. To be released on Braxton House in 1999.

————. Willisau (Quartet) 1991. hat ART CD 4-61001/4, 1992.

Coltrane, John. "Live" at the Village Vanguard. Rec. 1961. Impulse!-MCA MCAD-39136, n.d.

Ellington, Duke. Black, Brown and Beige (The 1944–1946 Band Recordings). Bluebird-BMG 6641-2-RB, 1988.

————, and His Orchestra. Featuring Mahalia Jackson. Black, Brown and Beige. Columbia CL 1162, 1958.

————. The Blanton-Webster Band. Rec. 1940–42. Bluebird-BMG 74321 13181 2, 1986.

————. Concert of Sacred Music. Rec. 1965. BMG 74321192542, 1994.

————, and His Orchestra. A Drum Is a Woman. Rec. 1956. Columbia COL 471320 2, n.d.

————. Duke Ellington, 1935–1936. Classics 659 CD, 1993.

————, and His Orchestra. The Duke Ellington Carnegie Hall Concerts: January 1943. Prestige 2PCD-34004-2, 1991.

————, and His Orchestra. The Duke Ellington Carnegie Hall Concerts: December 1944. Prestige 2PCD-24073-2, 1991.

————, and His Orchestra. The Duke Ellington Carnegie Hall Concerts: January 1946. Prestige 2PCD-24074-2, 1991.

————, and His Orchestra. Early Ellington (1927–1934). Bluebird-BMG ND86852, 1989.

————. The Great Chicago Concerts. Rec. 1946. Limelight 844 401-2, 1994.

————, and His Orchestra. Jubilee Stomp. Rec. 1927–34. Bluebird-BMG 74321101532, 1992.

————, and His Orchestra. Jump for Joy. Rec. 1941. Smithsonian Collection of Recordings R037 DMM 1-0722, 1988.

————, and His Cotton Club Orchestra. Jungle Nights in Harlem (1927–1932). Bluebird-BMG ND82499, 1991.

————. Money Jungle. Rec. 1962. Blue Note CDP 7 46398 2, 1987.

————. My People. Rec. 1963. Red Baron AK 52759, 1992.

————. The Okeh Ellington. Rec. 1927–30. Columbia Jazz Masterpieces 466964-2, 1991.

————. The Private Collection, Volume Ten. Studio Sessions; New York & Chicago 1965, 1966 and 1971. SAJA 7 91234-2, 1989.

————. Second Sacred Concert. Rec. 1968. Prestige PCD-24045-2, 1990.

————, and His Orchestra. The Symphonic Ellington. Rec. 1963. Discovery 71003, 1992.

————. Uptown. Rec. 1951–52. CBS Jazz Masterpieces CBS 460830-2, n.d.

Gates, (Rev.) J. M. Complete Recorded Works in Chronological Order, Volume 6: 20 February 1928 to 18 March 1929. Document DOCD 5457, 1996.

Gillespie, Dizzy. Swing Low, Sweet Cadillac. Rec. 1967. Impulse!-GRP IMP 11782, 1996.

Holiday, Billie. *The Complete Commodore Recordings.* Rec. 1939, 1944. Commodore-GRP CMD 24012, 1997.

Impressions, The. *Definitive Impressions.* Rec. 1961–68. Kent CDKEND 923, 1989.

Johnson, James P. *I Grandi del Jazz: James P. Johnson.* Rec. 1921–1939. Fabbri Editori GdJ85, 1982.

———. *Victory Stride: The Symphonic Music of James P. Johnson.* The Concordia Orch. Cond. Marin Alsop. Music Masters Classics 01612-67140-2, 1994.

Kern, Jerome, and Oscar Hammerstein II. *Showboat.* Perf. Frederica Von Stade, Jerry Hadley, Teresa Stratas. London Sinfonietta. Cond. John McGlinn. EMI CDS 7 49108 2, 1988.

Lewis, George. *Changing with the Times.* New World 80434-2, 1993.

Menger, Howard. *Authentic Music from Another Planet.* State 211, 1956.

Nix, (Rev.) A. W. *Complete Recorded Works in Chronological Order, Volume 1: 23 April 1927 to 26 October 1928.* Document DOCD 5328, 1995.

Perry, Mr. Lee "Scratch," and the Upsetters. *Battle of Armagideon (Millionaire Liquidator).* Trojan TRLS 227, 1986.

Ragin, Derek Lee. *Ev'ry Time I Feel the Spirit: Spirituals.* Channel Classics CCS 2991, 1991.

Shepp, Archie, and Philly Joe Jones. *Archie Shepp and Philly Joe Jones.* Rec. 1969. Fantasy 86018, n.d.

Stewart, Rex. "Menelik (The Lion of Judah)." Rec. 1941. *The Great Ellington Units.* By Johnny Hodges/Rex Stewart/Barney Bigrad. Bluebird-BMG ND86751, 1988.

Still, William Grant. "And They Lynched Him on a Tree." *Witness,* vol. 2. Various artists, Plymouth Music Series Chorus and Orch. Cond. Philip Brunelle. Collins Classics 1454-2, 1995.

———. Symphony No. 2 in G minor, "Song of a New Race." Detroit Symphony Orch. Cond. Neeme Jarvi. Chandos CHAN 9226, 1993.

Sun Ra. *The Antique Blacks aka Interplanetary Concepts aka There Is Change in the Air.* Saturn 81774, 1974.

———. *Astro Black.* Impulse!-ABC AS 9255, 1973.

———, and His Arkestra. *Beyond the Purple Star Zone aka Immortal Being.* El Saturn 123180, 1981.

———, and His Arkestra. *Cosmo Earth Fantasy aka Sub Underground aka Temple U.* Rec. 1974. El Saturn 92074, 1977.

———, and His Outer Space Arkestra. *A Fireside Chat with Lucifer.* Rec. 1982. Saturn 198459-9, 1983.

———, and His Arkestra. *Horizon aka Live in Egypt, vol. 3 aka Starwatchers.* Rec. 1971. Saturn 121771, 1972.

———, and His Solar Arkestra. *Interstellar Low Ways.* Originally issued as *Rocket Number Nine Take Off for the Planet Venus* by Sun Ra and His Myth-Science Arkestra. Saturn 9956-2-MIN. Rec. 1959–61. Evidence ECD 22039-2 (coupled with *Sun Ra Visits Planet Earth*), 1992.

———, and His Arkestra. *Jazz in Silhouette.* Originally issued on Saturn K70P3590/1. Rec. 1958. Evidence ECD 22012-2. 1991.

————. *Journey Stars Beyond* aka *Oblique Parallax*. Saturn SR 72881, 1981.

————. *Lanquidity*. Philly Jazz PJ666, 1978.

————, and the Year 2000 Myth Science Arkestra. *Live at the Hackney Empire*. Rec. 1990. Leo CD LR 214/15, 1994.

———— Arkestra. *Live at "Praxis '84,"* vol. 1. Praxis CM 108, 1984.

———— Arkestra. *Live at "Praxis '84,"* vol. 3. Praxis CM 110, 1984.

———— Arkestra. *Live from Soundscape*. Rec. 1979. DIW 388, 1994. Limited edition two-CD set. Includes the talk "The Possibility of Altered Destiny" aka "Your Only Hope Now Is a Lie."

————, and His Year 2000 Myth Science Arkestra. *Live in London 1990*. Originally issued as a limited edition three 10″ disc box set in 1990. Blast First BFFP60CD, 1996.

————, and His Solar Arkestra. *The Magic City*. Originally issued on Saturn LPB 711. Rec. 1965. Evidence ECD 22069-2, 1993.

————. *Monorails and Satellites*. Originally issued on El Saturn SR 509. Rec. ca. 1966. Evidence ECD 22013-2, 1991.

————, and His Solar Myth Arkestra. *My Brother the Wind*, vol. 2 aka *Otherness*. Originally issued on Saturn 523. Rec. 1969. Evidence ECD 22040-2, 1992.

————, and His Astro Solar Infinity Arkestra. *The Night of the Purple Moon*. Rec. 1970. El Saturn IR 1972, 1974.

————, and His Myth Science Arkestra. *The Nubians of Plutonia*. Originally issued as *The Lady with the Golden Stockings*. Saturn 9956-11E/F. Rec. 1958–59. Evidence ECD 22066-2 (coupled with *Angels and Demons at Play*), 1993.

————. *Nuits de la Fondation Maeght*, vol. 1. Originally issued on Shandar 10.001. Rec. 1970. Recommended RR 11, 1981.

————, and His Arkestra. *On Jupiter* aka *Seductive Fantasy*. Saturn 101679, 1979.

————, and His Solar Arkestra. *Other Planes of There*. Originally issued on Saturn KH98766. Rec. 1964. Evidence ECD 22037-2, 1992.

————, and His Outer Space Arkestra. *Out Beyond the Kingdom of* aka *Discipline 99*. Saturn 61674, 1974.

————. *Purple Night*. Rec. 1989. A&M 395 342-2, 1990.

————, and His Arkestra. *A Quiet Place in the Universe*. Rec. ca. 1976–77. Leo CD LR 198, 1994.

————. *Somewhere Else*. Rec. 1988–89. Rounder 3036, 1993.

————. *The Soul Vibrations of Man*. El Saturn 771, 1976.

————, and His Astro Infinity Arkestra. *Sound Sun Pleasure!!* Originally issued on Saturn SR 512. Rec. 1956–58. Evidence ECD 22014-2, 1992.

————, and His Intergalactic Solar Arkestra. *Soundtrack to the Film Space Is the Place*. Rec. 1972. Evidence ECD 22070-2, 1993.

————. *Space Is the Place*. Originally issued on Blue Thumb BTS 41. Rec. 1972. Impulse! 12492, 1998.

————. *Strange Celestial Road*. Rec. 1979. Rounder CD 3035, 1987.

————. *Sun Song*. Originally issued as *Jazz by Sun Ra*. Transition TRLP J-10. Rec. 1957. Delmark DD-411, 1990.

————, and His Myth Science Arkestra. *We Travel the Spaceways*. Originally issued on Saturn HK 5445. Rec. 1956–61. Evidence ECD 22038-2 (coupled with *Bad & Beautiful*), 1992.

Various. *African American Spirituals: The Concert Tradition.* Wade in the Water, vol. 1. Smithsonian/Folkways CD SF 40072, 1994.

———. *African American Congregational Singing: The Nineteenth-Century Roots.* Wade in the Water, vol. 2. Smithsonian/Folkways CD SF 40073, 1994.

Waters, Muddy. *They Call Me Muddy Waters.* Rec. 1948–55. Instant-Charly CDINS 5036, 1990.

Texts

Ake, David. "Re-Masculating Jazz: Ornette Coleman, 'Lonely Woman,' and the New York Jazz Scene in the Late 1950s." *American Music* 16.1 (1998): 25–44.

Albin, Scott. Review of concerts by the Anthony Braxton Quartet and Tashi. The Bottom Line, New York City. *Down Beat* 25 Mar. 1976: 41, 48.

Anderson, Paul A. "Ellington, Rap Music, and Cultural Difference." *Musical Quarterly* 79 (1995): 172–206.

Ansell, Kenneth. "Anthony Braxton." *Impetus* 6 (1977): 248–52.

Armstrong, Louis. *Swing That Music.* 1936. New York: Da Capo, 1993.

Asante, Molefi Kete. *Kemet, Afrocentricity and Knowledge.* Trenton, N.J.: Africa World, 1991.

Askland, Gunnar. "Interpretations in Jazz: A Conference with Duke Ellington." *Etude* March 1947. In Tucker, DER, 255–58.

Baggenaes, Roland. Review of *Donna Lee* by Anthony Braxton. *Coda* Sept. 1975: 20–21.

Baker, Houston A., Jr. *Modernism and the Harlem Renaissance.* 1987. Chicago: U of Chicago P, 1989.

Baldwin, James. *The Fire Next Time.* 1963. Harmondsworth, Middlesex: Penguin, 1970.

———. "Of the Sorrow Songs: The Cross of Redemption." 1979. In *The Picador Book of Blues and Jazz.* Ed. James Campbell. London: Picador, 1996. 324–31.

Baraka, Amiri [as LeRoi Jones]. *Black Music.* London: MacGibbon & Kee, 1969.

——— [as LeRoi Jones]. *Blues People: Negro Music in White America.* 1963. New York: William Morrow, 1971.

———. "Blues, Poetry, and the New Music." In Baraka and Baraka. 262–67.

———. "Class Struggle in Music." In Baraka and Baraka. 317–27.

Baraka, Amiri, and Amina Baraka. *The Music: Reflections on Jazz and Blues.* New York: William Morrow, 1987.

Barthes, Roland. *Mythologies.* 1957. Trans. Annette Lavers. St. Albans, Herts.: Paladin, 1973.

Bartlett, Andrew W. "Cecil Taylor, Identity Energy, and the Avant-Garde African American Body." *Perspectives of New Music* 33 (1995): 274–93.

Barton, William E. "Hymns of the Slave and the Freeman." In Katz, 90–105.

Bebey, Francis. *African Music: A People's Art.* Trans. Josephine Bennett. London: Harrap, 1975.

Bechet, Sidney. *Treat It Gentle: An Autobiography.* 1960. New York: Da Capo, 1978.

Bellerby, Vic. "Analysis of Genius." In Gammond, *Duke*, 156–69.

Benston, Kimberly W. "I Yam What I Am: The Topos of Un(naming) in Afro-American Literature." 1984. In *Black Literature and Literary Theory.* Ed. Henry Louis Gates Jr. New York: Routledge, 1990. 151–72.

Bernal, Martin. *Black Athena: The Afroasiatic Roots of Classical Civilization,* vol. 1. 1987. London: Vintage, 1991.

Blass, Charles. Unpublished interview with Sun Ra. Copenhagen. 21 Mar. 1992.

Blevins, Brian. Review of *3 Compositions of New Jazz* by Anthony Braxton. *Coda* Aug. 1969: 18–19.

Booth, Garry. "The Gospel According to the Five Blind Boys." Review of London Jazz Festival concerts. *Financial Times* 25 May 1993: 19d.

Boskin, Joseph. *Sambo: The Rise and Demise of an American Jester.* New York: Oxford UP, 1986.

Botkin, B. A. *Lay My Body Down: A Folk History of Slavery.* 1945. Chicago: U of Chicago P, 1969.

Boyer, Richard O. "The Hot Bach." *New Yorker* 24 June, 1 July, 8 July 1944. In Tucker, *DER*, 214–45.

Bradbury, Ray. *The Martian Chronicles.* London: Granada, 1980. Rpt. of *The Silver Locusts.* 1951.

———. *The Stories of Ray Bradbury.* London: Granada, 1981.

Braxton, Anthony. *Composition No. 171: Forest Ranger Crumpton Maps the Tri-State Region.* 1993. Unpublished libretto.

———. *Composition No. 175 (Story).* 1994. Unpublished libretto.

———. *Composition Notes* [CN]. 5 vols., A–E. N.p.: Synthesis Music, 1988.

———. "Notes to Composition No. 151." CD insert notes. *2 Compositions (Ensemble) 1989/1991.* By Anthony Braxton. hat ART CD 6086, 1992.

———. *Tri-axium Writings* [T-a W]. 3 vols. N.p.: Synthesis Music, 1985.

———. *Trillium.* N.d. Introductory statement. Unpublished manuscript.

———. *Trillium — Dialogues E.* 1995. Unpublished opera libretto.

———. *Trillium — Dialogues M: Joreo's Vision of Forward Motion.* 1986. Unpublished opera libretto.

———. *Trillium — Dialogues R: Shala Fears for the Poor.* 1991. Unpublished opera libretto.

———. Untitled story. CD insert notes. *Composition No. 165 (for 18 instruments).* By Anthony Braxton. New Albion NA 050 CD, 1992.

Broomer, Stuart. Review of *Knitting Factory (Piano/Quartet) 1994,* vol. 1 by Anthony Braxton. *Cadence* Apr. 1996: 93–94.

———. Review of *Piano Quartet, Yoshi's 1994* by Anthony Braxton. *Cadence* Nov. 1996: 43–44.

Brown, Scott E. *James P. Johnson: A Case of Mistaken Identity.* Metuchen, N.J.: Scarecrow and the Institute of Jazz Studies, Rutgers University, 1986.

Brown, Sterling A. "Spirituals, Blues and Jazz." *Tricolor,* 1945. In *Jam Session: A Jazz Anthology.* Ed. Ralph J. Gleason. 1958. London: Jazz Book Club and Peter Davies, 1961. 17–24.

Buholzer, Meinrad. "Cecil Taylor: Interview." *Cadence* Dec. 1984: 5–9.

Calloway, Cab. *Of Minnie the Moocher and Me.* New York: Thomas Y. Crowell, 1976.

Campbell, Robert L. *The Earthly Recordings of Sun Ra.* Redwood, N.Y.: Cadence Jazz Books, 1994.

———. "Sun Ra: Super Sonic Sounds from Saturn." *Goldmine* 22 Jan. 1993, 22–42, 104, 124–25, 132–33.

Carey, Joe. "Anthony Braxton: Interview." *Cadence* Mar. 1984: 5–10, 21.

Case, Brian. LP liner notes. *B-A°/NO-1-47ᴬ.* By Anthony Braxton. Affinity 15, n.d.

Chase, Allan S. "Sun Ra: Musical Change and Musical Meaning in the Life and Work of a Jazz Composer." Diss. Tufts U, 1992.

Clarke, Donald. *Wishing on the Moon: The Life and Times of Billie Holiday.* London: Viking, 1994.

Collier, James Lincoln. *Duke Ellington.* 1987. London: Pan, 1989.

Cone, James H. *The Spirituals and the Blues: An Interpretation.* New York: Seabury, 1972.

Corbett, John. "Anthony Braxton's *Bildungsmusik*: Thoughts on 'Composition No. 171.'" In Lock, *Mixtery*, 185–86.

———. *Extended Play: Sounding Off from John Cage to Dr. Funkenstein.* Durham, N.C.: Duke UP, 1994.

Cortez, Jayne. *Coagulations: New and Selected Poems.* London: Pluto, 1985.

Cripps, Thomas. *Slow Fade to Black: The Negro in American Film, 1900–1942.* New York: Oxford UP, 1977.

Crossley, Robert. Introduction. *Kindred.* By Octavia Butler. Boston: Beacon, 1988. ix–xxvii.

Cunard, Nancy. *Negro: An Anthology.* 1934. Abridged ed. New York: Frederick Ungar, 1979.

Cutler, Chris. *File Under Popular: Theoretical and Critical Writings on Music.* London: November Books, 1985.

Dance, Stanley. CD insert notes. *Uptown.* By Duke Ellington. CBS Jazz Masterpieces CBS 460830-2, n.d. 4–8.

———. *The World of Duke Ellington.* 1970. New York: Da Capo, n.d.

Darrell, R. D. "Black Beauty." *disques* June 1932. In Tucker, *DER,* 57–65.

———. "Dance Records." Column. *Phonograph Monthly Review* 1927–1931. In Tucker, *DER,* 33–40.

Davis, Almena. "Duke Ellington Fascinates Interviewer as He Takes 'Downbeat' Writer to Task." *California Eagle* 9 Jan. 1941. In Tucker, *DER,* 143–46.

Davis, Francis. "Philadelphia Stories." *The Wire* Sept. 1991: 12.

———. Unpublished interview with Sun Ra. Philadelphia. Jan. 1990.

de Craen, Hugo. "Braxton and Kandinsky: Symbolists of the Spiritual." In Lock, *Mixtery*, 212–24.

de Jongh, James. *Vicious Modernism: Black Harlem and the Literary Imagination.* Cambridge: Cambridge UP, 1990.

Delany, M. R., and Robert Campbell. *Search for a Place: Black Separatism and Africa, 1860.* Ann Arbor: U of Michigan P, 1969. Rpt. of *Official Report of the Niger Valley Exploring Party* by M. R. Delany, and *A Pilgrimage to My Motherland: An Account of a Journey Among the Egbas and Yorubas of Central Africa, in 1859–60* by Robert Campbell.

Deveaux, Scott. "*Black, Brown and Beige* and the Critics." *Black Music Research Journal* 13 (1993): 125–46.

———. "The Emergence of the Jazz Concert, 1935–1945." *American Music* 7 (1989): 6–29.

Diop, Cheikh Anta. *The African Origins of Civilization: Myth or Reality.* 1954, 1967. Ed. and trans. Mercer Cook. Westport, Conn.: Lawrence Hill, 1974.

Dorfman, Ariel, and Armand Mattelart. *How to Read Donald Duck: Imperialist Ideology in the Disney Comic.* 1971. Trans. David Kunzle. New York: International General, 1975.

Dorham, Kenny. Review of *Spiritual Unity* by Albert Ayler. *Down Beat* 15 July 1965: 29–30.

Douglas, Ann. *Terrible Honesty: Mongrel Manhattan in the 1920s.* New York: Farrar, Straus and Giroux, 1996.

Douglass, Frederick. *Narrative of the Life of Frederick Douglass, an American Slave.* 1845. New York: Penguin, 1986.

DuBois, W. E. B. *The Souls of Black Folk.* 1903. New York: Bantam Classics, 1989.

———. *The World and Africa — An Inquiry Into the Part Which Africa Has Played in World History.* 1947. Enlarged ed. New York: International, 1992.

"Duke's Book Will Explain His Carnegie Hall Symph." Uncredited news story. *Variety* 9 June 1943: 2.

Dumas, Henry. *Knees of a Natural Man: The Selected Poetry of Henry Dumas.* Ed. Eugene B. Redmond. New York: Thunder's Mouth, 1989.

Early, Gerald. "One Nation Under a Groove." *New Republic* 15 and 22 July 1991: 30–41.

Ellington, Duke. *Black, Brown and Beige.* Undated typescript. Duke Ellington Collection, Archives Center, National Museum of American History, Smithsonian Institution, Washington, D.C.

———. CD insert notes. *Second Sacred Concert.* By Duke Ellington. Prestige PCD-24045-2, 1990.

———. "Certainly It's Music." *Listen* Oct. 1944. In Tucker, DER, 246–48.

———. "Defense of Jazz." Letter to the Editor. *American Mercury* Jan. 1944. In Tucker, DER, 208–09.

———. "The Duke Steps Out." *Rhythm* March 1931. In Tucker, DER, 46–50.

———. "From Where I Lie." *The Negro Actor* 15 July 1938. In Tucker, DER, 131.

———. "The Future of Jazz." Program notes for concert tour of Great Britain, 5–26 Oct. 1958.

———. *Music Is My Mistress.* 1973. London: Quartet, 1977.

———. "My Hunt for Song Titles." *Rhythm* Aug. 1933. In Tucker, DER, 87–89.

———. *Queenie Pie: An Opera Buffa in Seven Scenes.* 1973. Typescript. McGettigan Collection, Archives Center, National Museum of American History, Smithsonian Institution, Washington, D.C.

———. "The Race for Space." In Tucker, DER, 293–96.

———. "Swing Is My Beat." *New Advance* Oct. 1944. In Tucker, DER, 248–50.

———. "We, Too, Sing America." "Speech of the Week." *California Eagle* 13 Feb. 1941. In Tucker, DER, 146–48.

Ellington, Mercer, with Stanley Dance. *Duke Ellington in Person: An Intimate Memoir.* London: Hutchinson, 1978.

Ellison, Ralph. *Going to the Territory.* New York: Vintage/Random House, 1987.

———. *Invisible Man.* 1952. Harmondsworth, Middlesex: Penguin, 1982.

———. *Shadow and Act.* 1964. New York: Vintage/Random House, 1972.

Erenberg, Lewis A. *Şteppin' Out: New York Nightlife and the Transformation of American Culture, 1890–1930.* Chicago: U of Chicago P, 1984.

Essien-Udom, E. U. *Black Nationalism: The Rise of the Black Muslims in the U.S.A.* 1962. Harmondsworth, Middlesex: Penguin, 1966.

Feather, Leonard. "Blindfold Test—Harold Land." *Down Beat* 24 June 1971: 26.

———. "Blindfold Test—Phil Woods." *Down Beat* 14 Oct. 1971: 33.

———. "Duke Ellington." 1957. *The Great Jazz Makers: Essays on the Greats of Jazz.* Ed. Nat Shapiro and Nat Hentoff. New York: Da Capo, 1988. 187–201.

———. *Encyclopaedia of Jazz in the Seventies.* 1976. London: Quartet, 1978.

———. Untitled article on Duke Ellington. *Jazz* May 1943. In Tucker, DER, 173–75.

Finn, Julio. *The Bluesman: The Musical Heritage of Black Men and Women in the Americas.* London: Quartet, 1986.

Fiofori, Tam. "Sun Ra's African Roots." *Melody Maker* 12 Feb. 1972: 32.

———. "Sun Ra's Space Odyssey." *Down Beat* 14 May 1970: 14–17.

Fisher, Miles Mark. *Negro Slave Songs in the United States.* Ithaca, N.Y.: Cornell UP, 1953.

Fleming, Michael. CD insert notes. Symphony No. 2 in G minor, "Song of a New Race." By William Grant Still. Detroit Symphony Orch. Cond. Neeme Jarvi. Chandos CHAN 9226, 1993. 4–6.

Floyd, Samuel A., Jr. *The Power of Black Music: Interpreting Its History from Africa to the United States.* New York: Oxford UP, 1995.

Ford, Alun. *Anthony Braxton: Creative Music Continuums.* Exeter: Stride, 1997.

Frankenstein, Alfred. "'Hot Is Something About a Tree,' Says the Duke." *San Francisco Chronicle* 9 Nov. 1941: 29.

Gabbard, Krin. "Introduction: The Jazz Canon and Its Consequences." In Gabbard, *Jazz*, 1–28.

———, ed. *Jazz Among the Discourses.* Durham, N.C.: Duke UP, 1995.

Gagne, Cole. *Soundpieces 2: Interviews with American Composers.* Metuchen, N.J.: Scarecrow, 1993.

Gammond, Peter. "A Drum Is a Woman." In Gammond, *Duke*, 132–37.

———, ed. *Duke Ellington: His Life and Music.* London: Phoenix House, 1958.

Gates, Henry Louis, Jr. *The Signifying Monkey: A Theory of African-American Literary Criticism.* 1988. New York: Oxford UP, 1989.

Gendron, Bernard. "'Moldy Figs' and Modernists: Jazz at War (1942–1946)." In Gabbard, *Jazz*, 31–56.

Gennari, John. "Jazz Criticism: Its Development and Ideologies." *Black American Literature Forum* 25 (1991): 449–523.

George, Don. *The Real Duke Ellington.* London: Robson, 1981.

Giddins, Gary. "Anthony Braxton as Ideas Man." *Village Voice* 28 Apr. 1975: 112.

————. "Anthony Braxton Marches as to Jazz." *Village Voice* 30 Aug. 1976: 66–69.

Gilbert, Gama. "'Hot Damn!' Says Ellington When Ranked with Bach." *Philadelphia Record* 17 May 1935. In Tucker, DER, 112–14.

Gilroy, Paul. *The Black Atlantic: Modernity and Double Consciousness.* London: Verso, 1993.

————. *Small Acts: Thoughts on the Politics of Black Cultures.* London: Serpent's Tail, 1993.

Gitler, Ira. LP liner notes. *Martians Stay Home.* By Shorty Rogers and His Giants. Atlantic K50714, 1980.

————. Review of *"Live" at the Village Vanguard* by John Coltrane. *Down Beat* 26 Apr. 1962: 29.

Gleason, Ralph J. *Celebrating the Duke: And Louis, Bessie, Billie, Bird, Carmen, Miles, Dizzy and Other Heroes.* New York: Delta, 1975.

Gray, Herman, and Nathaniel Mackey. Untitled 1979 interview with Anthony Braxton. In Lock, *Mixtery*, 56–69.

Graziano, John. "Black Musical Theater and the Harlem Renaissance Movement." In *Black Music in the Harlem Renaissance.* Ed. Samuel A. Floyd Jr. New York: Greenwood, 1990. 87–110.

Green, Benny. "Angel in a Noddy Bonnet Wanted to Save the Planet." Sun Ra obituary. *Daily Mail* 2 June 1993: 39.

Guilbaut, Serge. *How New York Stole the Idea of Modern Art: Abstract Impressionism, Freedom, and the Cold War.* 1983. Trans. Arthur Goldhammer. Chicago: U of Chicago P, 1985.

Guralnick, Peter. *Sweet Soul Music: Rhythm and Blues and the Southern Dream of Freedom.* 1986. London: Penguin, 1991.

Hadler, Mona. "Jazz and the New York School." In *Representing Jazz.* Ed. Krin Gabbard. Durham, N.C.: Duke UP, 1995. 247–59.

Hammond, John. "Is the Duke Deserting Jazz?" *Jazz* May 1943. In Tucker, DER, 171–73.

————, with Irving Townsend. *John Hammond on Record: An Autobiography.* 1977. Harmondsworth, Middlesex: Penguin, 1981.

————. "The Tragedy of Duke Ellington, the 'Black Prince of Jazz.'" *Down Beat* Nov. 1935 and *Brooklyn Eagle* 3 Nov. 1935. In Tucker, DER, 118–20.

Harris, Sara. *Father Divine: Holy Husband.* New York: Doubleday, 1953.

Haskins, Jim. *The Cotton Club.* New York: Random House, 1977.

Hasse, John Edward. *Beyond Category: The Life and Genius of Duke Ellington.* New York: Simon & Schuster, 1993.

Heffley, Mike. *The Music of Anthony Braxton.* New York: Excelsior, 1996.

Hentoff, Nat. *Jazz Is.* 1976. London: W. H. Allen, 1978.

Higginson, Thomas Wentworth. "Negro Spirituals." *Atlantic Monthly* 19, June 1867. In Katz, 11–21.

Hinds, Peter, ed. *Sun Ra Research* 8 Sept. 1996.

Holiday, Billie, with William Dufty. *Lady Sings the Blues.* 1956. Rev. ed. London: Abacus, 1975.

Homzy, Andrew. "Black, Brown and Beige in Duke Ellington's Repertoire, 1943–1973." *Black Music Research Journal* 13 (1993): 87–110.

Hughes, Langston. *The Big Sea*. New York: Alfred A. Knopf, 1940.

———. *Not Without Laughter*. 1930. New York: Alfred A. Knopf, 1971.

Hughes, Spike. "Impressions of Ellington in New York." In Tucker, DER, 69–72. Rpt. of "The Duke—in Person." *Melody Maker* May 1933.

———. "Meet the Duke." *Daily Herald* 13 June 1933. In Tucker, DER, 72–75.

Hurston, Zora Neale. "Characteristics of Negro Expression." In Cunard, 24–31.

———. "Conversions and Visions." In Cunard, 32–34.

———. *Mules and Men*. 1935. New York: Harper & Row, 1990.

———. "Spirituals and Neo-Spirituals." In Cunard, 223–25.

James, George G. M. *Stolen Legacy: Greek Philosophy Is Stolen Egyptian Philosophy*. Trenton, N.J.: Africa World, 1992. Rpt. of *Stolen Legacy, the Greeks were not the authors of Greek Philosophy, but the people of North Africa commonly called the Egyptians*. 1954.

Jewell, Derek. *Duke: A Portrait of Duke Ellington*. London: Sphere, 1978.

Joans, Ted. Review of Le Festival Mondial. *Coda* Oct. 1975: 36–38.

Johnson, Clifton H., ed. *God Struck Me Dead: Religious Conversion Experiences and Autobiographies of Ex-Slaves*. Philadelphia: Pilgrim, 1969.

Johnson, James Weldon. *The Autobiography of an Ex-Colored Man*. 1912. London: X, 1995.

———. "O Black and Unknown Bards." Preface. J. W. Johnson, Book, 11–12.

———, ed. *The Book of American Negro Spirituals*. London: Chapman & Hall, 1926.

Johnson, Venice, ed. *Voices of the Dream: African-American Women Speak*. San Francisco: Chronicle, 1995.

Katz, Bernard, ed. *The Social Implications of Early Negro Music in the United States*. New York: Arno and the New York Times, 1969.

Kelley, Robin D. G. *Race Rebels: Culture, Politics, and the Black Working Class*. New York: Free Press, 1996.

King, Martin Luther, Jr. "I See the Promised Land." 1967. In *The Eyes on the Prize Civil Rights Reader: Documents, Speeches, and Firsthand Accounts from the Black Freedom Struggle, 1954–1990*. Ed. Clayborne Carson, David J. Garrow, Gerald Gill, Vincent Harding, Darlene Clark Hine. New York: Penguin, 1991. 409–19.

Kirschke, Amy Helene. *Aaron Douglas: Art, Race, and the Harlem Renaissance*. Jackson: UP of Mississippi, 1995.

Klee, Joe H. Review of For Alto by Anthony Braxton. *Down Beat* 24 June 1971: 18.

Knaver, Wolfram. "'Simulated Improvisation' in Duke Ellington's *Black, Brown and Beige*." *Black Perspective in Music* 18 (1990): 20–38.

Knight, Arthur. "'Jammin' the Blues, or the Sight of Jazz, 1944." In *Representing Jazz*. Ed. Krin Gabbard. Durham, N.C.: Duke UP, 1995. 11–53.

Kofsky, Frank. *Black Nationalism and the Revolution in Music*. 1970. New York: Pathfinder, 1978.

Kreuger, Miles. *Showboat: The Story of a Classical American Musical*. New York: Oxford UP, 1977.

Lacy, Steve. Untitled letter to Anthony Braxton. In Lock, Mixtery, 27.

Lange, Art. "Implications of a Creative Orchestra, 1972–78." In Lock, Mixtery, 122–30.

————. Review of *New Musical Figurations* by Ronald M. Radano. *Midwest Jazz* winter 1994–95: 13–14, 20.

Lasker, Steven. CD insert notes. *Jungle Nights in Harlem (1927–1932)*. By Duke Ellington and His Cotton Club Orchestra. Bluebird-BMG ND82499, 1991.

Levin, Mike. "Duke Fuses Classical and Jazz." *Down Beat* 15 Feb. 1943. In Tucker, DER, 166–70.

Levine, Lawrence W. *Black Culture and Black Consciousness: Afro-American Folk Thought from Slavery to Freedom*. 1977. Oxford: Oxford UP, 1978.

Lewis, George E. "Improvised Music After 1950: Afrological and Eurological Perspectives." *Black Music Research Journal* 16 (1996): 91–122.

Littlewood, Roland, and Maurice Lipsedge. *Aliens and Alienists: Ethnic Minorities and Psychiatry*. 2nd ed. London: Unwin Hyman, 1989.

Litweiler, John. CD insert notes. 1968. *3 Compositions of New Jazz*. By Anthony Braxton. Delmark DD 415, 1991.

————. *The Freedom Principle: Jazz After 1958*. 1984. Poole, Dorset: Blandford, 1985.

Lock, Graham. "Along Came Ra." *The Wire* spring 1984: 2–6.

————. *Chasing the Vibration: Meetings with Creative Musicians*. Exeter: Stride, 1994.

————. "Colours of the Spiritway: 25 Years of Anthony Braxton's Compositions for the Creative Ensemble. Stories and Histories." CD insert notes. *Willisau (Quartet) 1991*. By Anthony Braxton. hat ART CD 4-61001/4, 1992.

————. "Composition 192: Like a Never Ending Song." CD insert notes. *Composition 192*. By Anthony Braxton and Lauren Newton. Leo CD LR 251, 1998.

————. "Cosmos Songs: Sun Ra's Alternative Spirituals." CD insert notes. *Live in London 1990*. By Sun Ra and His Year 2000 Myth Science Arkestra. Blast First BFFP60CD, 1996.

————. *Forces in Motion: Anthony Braxton and the Meta-reality of Creative Music*. London: Quartet, 1988.

————. "A Highway to the Cosmics." In Lock, *Mixtery*, 246–49.

————. "Let 100 Orchestras Blow." *The Wire* June 1985: 19–22.

————. "Now's the Time: An Interview with Anthony Braxton." CD insert notes. *Anthony Braxton's Charlie Parker Project 1993*. By Anthony Braxton. hat ART CD 2-6160, 1995. 2–12.

————. "Sound Travel: Braxtonian Adventures in Time and Space." CD insert notes. *11 Compositions (Duo) 1995*. By Anthony Braxton and Brett Larner. Leo CD LR 244, 1997.

————. " 'Tell 'em About It, Tyrone': An Interview with Arkestra Trombonist Tyrone Hill." *Stride Magazine* 37 (1995): n.p.

————. Unpublished interview with Anthony Braxton. London. 16 May 1994.

————. Unpublished interview with Anthony Braxton. Middletown, Conn. 1 Dec. 1995.

————. Unpublished interview with Anthony Braxton. London. 20 June 1996.

————. Unpublished interview with Sun Ra. London. Oct. 1983.

————. Unpublished interview with Sun Ra. London. 10 June 1990.

————. "A Vision of Forward Motion: Notes on the Evolution of Anthony Braxton's Solo Music." In Lock, *Mixtery*, 48–54.

————. "Wavelength Infinity." CD insert notes. *Friendly Galaxy*. By the Sun Ra Arkestra. Leo CD LR 188, 1993.

————, ed. *Mixtery: A Festschrift for Anthony Braxton*. Exeter: Stride, 1995.

Locke, Alain. "The Negro Spirituals." In Locke, *New Negro*, 119–210.

————, ed. *The New Negro*. 1925. New York: Atheneum, 1969.

Lynch, Kevin. Review of *Solo Live at Moers Festival* by Anthony Braxton. *Coda* Feb. 1978: 18.

Lyons, Len. *The Great Jazz Pianists: Speaking of Their Lives and Music*. 1983. New York: Da Capo, n.d.

Mabie, Janet. "Ellington's 'Mood in Indigo': Harlem's 'Duke' Seeks to Express His Race." *Christian Science Monitor* 13 Dec. 1930. In Tucker, *DER*, 41–44.

Mack, John E. *Abduction: Human Encounters with Aliens*. London: Simon & Schuster, 1994.

Mackey, Nathaniel. *Bedouin Hornbook*. Vol. 1 of *From a Broken Bottle Traces of Perfume Still Emanate*. Lexington: UP of Kentucky/Callaloo Fiction Series, 1986.

————. *Discrepant Engagement: Dissonance, Cross Culturality, and Experimental Writing*. Cambridge: Cambridge UP, 1994.

Macnie, Jim. "Sun Ra Is the Heaviest Man in This Galaxy . . . But He's Just Passing Through." *Musician* Jan. 1987: 60–62, 70.

Marsh, J. B. T. *The Story of the Jubilee Singers, Including Their Songs*. New ed. London: Hodder and Stoughton, 1898.

Meeker, David. *Jazz in the Movies: A Guide to Jazz Musicians, 1917–1977*. London: Talisman, 1977.

Melville, Charles. Interview with Duke Ellington. BBC Network 3. In Steve Voce, "Quoth the Duke," *Jazz Journal International* Mar. 1959: 2–4.

Mingus, Charles. *Beneath the Underdog: His World as Composed by Mingus*. Ed. Nel King. 1971. Harmondsworth, Middlesex: Penguin, 1975.

Monson, Ingrid. *Saying Something: Jazz Improvisation and Interaction*. Chicago: U of Chicago P, 1996.

Morgenstern, Dan. CD insert notes. *Early Ellington (1927–1934)*. By Duke Ellington and His Orchestra. Bluebird-BMG ND86852, 1989.

Morrow, Edward. "Duke Ellington on Gershwin's 'Porgy.'" *New Theatre* Dec. 1935. In Tucker, *DER*, 114–17.

Muhammad, Elijah. "What Do the Muslims Want?" 1962. In *Black Nationalism in America*. Ed. John H. Bracey, Jr., August Meir, and Elliott Rudwick. Indianapolis: Bobbs-Merrill, 1970. 404–07.

Murray, Albert. "Storiella Americana as She Is Swyung: Duke Ellington, the Culture of Washington, D.C. and the Blues as Representative Anecdote." *Conjunctions* 16 (1991): 209–19.

Nathan, Hans. *Dan Emmett and the Rise of Early Negro Minstrelsy*. Norman: U of Oklahoma P, 1962.

Oakley, Helen M. "Ellington to Offer 'Tone Parallel.'" *Down Beat* 15 Jan. 1943. In Tucker, *DER*, 155–58.

Occhiogrosso, Peter. "Anthony Braxton Explains Himself." *Down Beat* 12 Aug. 1976: 15–16, 49.

Oja, Carol J. "'New Music' and the 'New Negro': The Background of William Grant Still's *Afro-American Symphony*." *Black Music Research Journal* 12 (1992): 145–69.

Oliver, Paul. *Songsters and Saints: Vocal Traditions on Race Records*. Cambridge: Cambridge UP, 1984.

Olney, James. "'I Was Born': Slave Narratives, Their Status as Autobiography and as Literature." In *The Slave's Narrative*. Ed. Charles T. Davis and Henry Louis Gates Jr. Oxford: Oxford UP, 1985. 148–75.

Ottley, Roi. *New World A-Coming*. Boston: Houghton Mifflin, 1943.

Page, Barney E. "Joshua Fit de Battle of Jericho." Letter. *Chicago Defender* 16 Apr. 1932: Editorial page.

Palmer, Robert. LP liner notes. *Five Pieces 1975*. By Anthony Braxton. Arista AL4064, 1975.

Parker, Evan. Untitled article on Anthony Braxton. In Lock, Mixtery, 181–84.

Perry, Regenia A. *Free Within Ourselves: African-American Artists in the Collection of the National Museum of American Art*. Washington, D.C.: National Museum of American Art, Smithsonian Institution; San Francisco: Pomegranate, 1992.

Phast Phreddie. "Sun Ra Has a Master Plan." *Contrasts* Mar. or Apr. 1990: 39–44.

Pittman, John. "The Duke Will Stay on Top." Unidentified clipping. 1941. In Tucker, DER, 148–151.

Prévost, Eddie. "Withered Jazz." Letter. *The Wire* Mar. 1989: 66.

Priestley, Brian, and Alan Cohen. "Black, Brown and Beige." *Composer* 51, 52, 53 (1974–75). In Tucker, DER, 185–204.

Primack, Bret. "Captain Angelic: Sun Ra." *Down Beat* 4 May 1978: 14–16, 40–41.

R. N. "Ellington Discusses Jazz." *Christian Science Monitor* 3 Apr. 1956: 204.

Raboteau, Albert J. *Slave Religion: The "Invisible Institution" in the Antebellum South*. 1978. New York: Oxford UP, 1980.

Radano, Ronald M. "Braxton's Reputation." *Musical Quarterly* 72 (1986): 503–22.

———. *New Musical Figurations: Anthony Braxton's Cultural Critique*. Chicago: U of Chicago P, 1993.

Radin, Paul. "Status, Fantasy, and the Christian Dogma: A Note About the Conversion Experiences of Negro Ex-Slaves." Foreword. In Clifton H. Johnson, ed., vii–xiii.

Ramsey, Guthrie P., Jr. "Cosmopolitan or Provincial?: Ideology in Early Black Music Historiography, 1867–1940." *Black Music Research Journal* 16 (1996): 11–42.

Ratliff, Ben. "An Anarchist Visionary's Protest Against Evil." Review of *Shala Fears for the Poor* by Anthony Braxton. Live opera performance. John Jay Theater, New York. *New York Times* 30 Oct. 1996: C18.

Reed. Ishmael. *Mumbo Jumbo*. 1972. London: Alison & Busby, 1988.

Reid, John C. "It's After the End of the World." *Coda* Apr./May 1990: 30–32.

Rogers, J. A. "Jazz at Home." In Locke, New Negro, 216–24.

Rothbart, Peter. "'Play or Die': Anthony Braxton Interview." *Down Beat* Feb. 1982: 20–23.

Rusch, Robert D. *Jazztalk: The Cadence Interviews*. Secaucus, N.J.: Lyle Stuart, 1984.

Russell, Ross. *Bird Lives! The High Life and Hard Times of Charlie "Yardbird" Parker*. 1973. London: Quartet, 1980.

Rust, Brian. *Jazz Records, 1897–1942*. vol. 1. New Rochelle, N.Y.: Arlington House, 1978.

Saal, Hubert. "Two Free Spirits." *Newsweek* 8 Aug. 1977: 40–41.

Sachs, Howard I., and Judith Rose Sachs. *Way Up North in Dixie: A Black Family's Claim to the Confederate Anthem*. Washington, D.C.: Smithsonian Institution, 1993.

Sargeant, Winthrop. "Is Jazz Music?" *American Mercury* Oct. 1943. In Tucker, DER, 207–08.

Scarborough, William Kauffman. *The Overseer: Plantation Management in the Old South*. Baton Rouge: Louisiana State UP, 1966.

Schaap, Phil. "An Interview with Sun Ra." *WKCR Program Guide* Jan./Feb. 1989: 3–8, 25–32.

———. "Sun Ra: The Sequel." *WKCR Program Guide* Mar. 1989: 9–15, 25–29.

Schomburg, Arthur A. "The Negro Digs Up His Past." In Locke, *New Negro*, 231–37.

Schonfield, Victor, ed. *Sun Ra: Intergalactic Research Arkestra*. Concert program. London: Music Now, 1970.

Schuller, Gunther. *Early Jazz: Its Roots and Musical Development*. 1968. New York: Oxford UP, 1986.

Scott, William R. *The Sons of Sheba's Race: African-Americans and the Italo-Ethiopian War, 1935–1941*. Bloomington: Indiana UP, 1993.

Shepp, Archie. "Innovations in Jazz." In *History and Tradition in Afro-American Culture*. Ed. Günther H. Lenz. Frankfurt: Campus Verlag, 1984. 256–61.

Shadwick, Keith. "Talking Drums." *Jazz FM* 2 (n.d.): 20–30.

Shoemaker, Bill. "A Wake-up Call." CD insert notes. *2 Compositions (Ensemble) 1989/1991*. By Anthony Braxton. hat ART CD 6086, 1992. Revised version in Lock, *Mixtery*, 130–32.

———. "What It Is: The Reception Dynamics and Information Alignment of Piano Quintet (Yoshi's) 1994." CD insert notes. *Piano Quintet, Yoshi's 1994*. By Anthony Braxton. Music & Arts CD 849, 1996.

Simpkins, Cuthbert Ormond. *Coltrane: A Biography*. Perth Amboy, N.J.: Herndon House, 1975.

Sinker, Mark. "The Brother from Another Planet." *The Face* Sept. 1989: 42–45.

———. "Other Voices." *New Musical Express* 23 July 1988: 45.

———. "Sun Ra." *Stride Magazine* 37 (1995): n.p.

———. Unpublished interview with Sun Ra. Philadelphia. Spring 1989.

———. Untitled essay on Anthony Braxton. In Lock, *Mixtery*, 226–37.

Smith, Bill. Review of four LPs by Anthony Braxton. *Coda* Apr. 1974: 15–16.

Smith, Leo. "Notes on the Creative Artistry of Anthony Braxton." LP liner notes. *The Complete Braxton 1971*. By Anthony Braxton. Arista/Freedom AF 1902, 1977.

———. *The Swing Era: The Development of Jazz, 1930–1945*. 1989. New York: Oxford UP, 1991.

Smith, Will. "Chicago: Winds of Change." *Jazz and Pop* April 1970. In *Giants of Black Music.* Ed. Pauline Rivelli and Robert Levin. New York: Da Capo, 1979. 108–12. Rpt. of *The Black Giants,* 1970.

Smith, Winston. "Let's Call This: Race, Writing, and Difference in Jazz." *Public* (Toronto) 4/5 (1990/91): 71–83.

Spellman, A. B. *Four Lives in the Bebop Business.* 1966. New York: Limelight, 1985.

Spencer, Jon Michael. *Blues and Evil.* Knoxville: U of Tennessee P, 1993.

Stearns, Marshall W. *The Story of Jazz.* 1956. New York: Oxford UP, 1970.

Steingroot, Ira. "Sun Ra's Magical Kingdom." *Reality Hackers* winter 1988: 46–51.

Stern, Chip. "Kelvin/*7666* = Blip-Bleep." *Village Voice* 11 June 1979: 61.

Stowe, David W. *Swing Changes: Big Band Jazz in New Deal America.* Cambridge, Mass.: Harvard UP, 1994.

Stratemann, Klaus. *Duke Ellington Day by Day and Film by Film.* Copenhagen: Jazz-Media, 1992.

Stuckey, Sterling. *Slave Culture: Nationalist Theory and the Foundations of Black America.* 1987. New York: Oxford UP, 1988.

Sun Ra. "Astro Black." Poem on LP jacket of *Astro Black* by Sun Ra. Impulse!-ABC AS 9255, 1973.

———. CD insert notes. *Sun Song.* By Sun Ra. Includes the poems "Enticement," "New Horizon," and "Sun Song." Delmark DD-411, 1990. Reissue of *Jazz by Sun Ra.* Transition TRLP J-10, 1957.

———. *Extensions Out: The Immeasurable Equation,* vol. 2. Chicago: Ihnfinity/Saturn Research, 1972.

———. *The Immeasurable Equation.* Philadelphia: Sun Ra, 1980.

———. "The Potential." Poem on LP jacket of *Art Forms of Dimensions Tomorrow* by Sun Ra and His Solar Arkestra. Saturn 9956, 1965.

———. "Spiral Outwardly." ca. 1966? Poem in CD insert notes to *Other Planes of There* by Sun Ra and His Solar Arkestra. Evidence ECD 22037-2, 1992.

———. *Sun Ra.* Milbrae, Calif.: Omni Press, 1989.

———. "To the Peoples of Earth." In *Black Fire: An Anthology of Afro-American Writing.* Ed. LeRoi Jones and Larry Neal. New York: William Morrow, 1968. 217.

———. "Your Only Hope Now Is a Lie." *Hambone* 2 fall 1982: 98–114. Partial transcription of a talk, "The Possibility of Altered Destiny," given at Soundscape, New York City, 10 Nov. 1979. A recording of the opening seventy minutes of this talk was included on the limited edition CD *Live from Soundscape* by the Sun Ra Arkestra. DIW 388, 1994.

Szasz, Thomas S. "The Sane Slave: An Historical Note on the Use of Medical Diagnosis as Justificatory Rhetoric." *American Journal of Psychotherapy* 25 (1971): 228–39.

Szwed. John F. CD insert notes. *The Magic City.* By Sun Ra and His Solar Arkestra. Evidence ECD 22069-2, 1993.

———. CD insert notes. *Soundtrack to the Film Space Is the Place.* By Sun Ra and His Intergalactic Solar Arkestra. Evidence ECD 22070-2, 1993.

———. "The Local and the Express: Anthony Braxton's Title-Drawings." In Lock, *Mixtery,* 207–12.

————. *Space Is the Place: The Lives and Times of Sun Ra.* New York: Pantheon, 1997.

————. "Sun Ra, 1914–1993." Obituary. *Village Voice* 15 June 1993: 3, 70.

Taylor, Arthur. *Notes and Tones: Musician-to-Musician Interviews.* 1982. London: Quartet, 1983.

Taylor, Cecil. "Sound Structure of Subculture Becoming Major Breath/Naked Fire Gesture." 1966. CD insert notes. *Unit Structures.* By Cecil Taylor. Blue Note CDP 7 84237 2, 1987.

Theis, Rich. "Sun Ra." *OP* Sept./Oct. 1983: 48–51.

Thiele, Bob. "The Case of Jazz Music." *Jazz* July 1943. In Tucker, *DER*, 175–78.

Thompson, Robert Farris. *Flash of the Spirit: African and Afro-American Art and Philosophy.* 1983. New York: Vintage/Random House, 1984.

————. "The Song That Named the Land: The Visionary Presence of African-American Art." In *Black Art: Ancestral Legacy: The African Impulse in African-American Art.* Ed. Robert V. Rozelle, Alvia Wardlaw, Maureen A. McKenna. Dallas: Dallas Museum of Art; New York: Harry N. Abrams, 1990. 97–141.

Toll, Robert C. *Blacking Up: The Minstrel Show in Nineteenth-Century America.* New York: Oxford UP, 1974.

Towler, Edward. "Reflections on Hearing 'A Drum Is a Woman.'" *Jazz Monthly* Sept. 1957: 30–31.

Townsend, Irving. "Ellington in Private." *Jazz Journal International* Oct. 1976: 4–8.

————. "When Duke Records." *Just Jazz* 4. Ed. Sinclair Traill and Gerald Lascelles. London: Souvenir, 1960. In Tucker, *DER*, 319–24.

Tucker, Mark. "Duke Ellington, 1940–42." CD insert notes. *The Blanton-Webster Band.* By Duke Ellington. Bluebird-BMG 74321 13181 2, 1986.

————. *Ellington: The Early Years.* Urbana: U of Illinois P, 1991.

————. "Ellington's 'Jungle Music.'" In *Duke Ellington and New Orleans: A 90th Birthday Tribute.* Ed. Caroline Richmond. Lugano: Festa New Orleans Music Production, 1989. 13–15.

————. "The Genesis of Black, Brown and Beige." *Black Music Research Journal* 13 (1993): 67–86.

————, ed. *The Duke Ellington Reader* [DER]. New York: Oxford UP, 1993.

Tynan, John. "Take 5." *Down Beat* 23 Nov. 1961: 40.

Ulanov, Barry. *Duke Ellington.* 1946. London: Musicians Press, 1947.

————. "Ellington's Carnegie Hall Concert a Glorified Stage Show." *Metronome* Jan. 1944. In Tucker, *DER*, 210–12.

Ullman, Michael. *Jazz Lives: Portraits in Words and Pictures.* 1980. New York: Perigree, 1982.

Voce, Steve. "Sun Ra." Obituary. *Independent* 1 June 1993: 20.

Wachmeister, Hans. *A Discography and Bibliography of Anthony Braxton.* Stocksund, Sweden: Blue Anchor Jazz Book Shop, 1982.

Walser, Robert. "'Out of Notes': Signification, Interpretation, and the Problem of Miles Davis." In Gabbard, *Jazz*, 165–88.

Washington, Booker T. *Up from Slavery.* 1901. New York: Penguin, 1986.

Watrous, Peter. LP liner notes. *Reflections in Blue.* By the Sun Ra Arkestra. Black Saint BSR0101, 1987.

———. "A Saxophonist Veering Between Poles." Review of solo saxophone concert by Anthony Braxton. Knitting Factory, New York. *New York Times* 24 Nov. 1995: C3.

Watson, Andrew P. "Negro Primitive Religious Services." In Clifton H. Johnson, ed., 1–12.

Wein, George. CD insert notes. 1962. *Money Jungle*. By Duke Ellington. Blue Note CDP 7 46398 2, 1987.

Weinstein, Norman C. *A Night in Tunisia: Imaginings of Africa in Jazz*. New York: Limelight, 1993.

West, Cornel. *Prophetic Reflections: Notes on Race and Power in America*. Monroe, Maine: Common Courage, 1993.

White, Shane, and Graham White. "Slave Clothing and African-American Culture in the Eighteenth and Nineteenth Centuries." *Past and Present* 148 (1995): 149–86.

Whitehead, Kevin. Review of *Composition Notes* by Anthony Braxton. *Cadence* Nov. 1990. Revised version in Lock, *Mixtery*, 155–58.

"Why Duke Ellington Avoided Music Schools." PM 9 Dec. 1945. Uncredited interview. In Tucker, DER, 252–55.

Willard, Patricia. LP booklet. *Jump for Joy*. By Duke Ellington and His Orchestra. Smithsonian Collection of Recordings R037 DMM 1-0722, 1988.

Williams, Martin. *The Jazz Tradition*. Rev. ed. Oxford: Oxford UP, 1983.

Wilmer, Val. *As Serious as Your Life: The Story of the New Jazz*. 1977. London: Pluto, 1987.

———. "Musicians Talking—Anthony Braxton." *Jazz and Blues* May 1971: 27–28.

———. "Sun Ra." *Independent* 1 July 1993: 26.

Wilson, Olly. "The Heterogenous Sound Ideal in African-American Music." In *New Perspectives in Music: Essays in Honor of Eileen Southern*. Ed. Josephine Wright with Samuel A. Floyd Jr. Warren, Mich.: Harmonie Park, 1992. 327–38.

Wilson, Peter Niklas. "Firmly Planted in Mid-Air: Notes on the Syntax and Aesthetics of Anthony Braxton's 'Composition 151' (1991)." In Lock, *Mixtery*, 133–44.

Woodward, C. Vann. *The Strange Career of Jim Crow*. 3rd rev. ed. New York: Oxford UP, 1974.

Work, John. *American Negro Songs and Spirituals*. New York: Bonanza, 1940.

Wright, Richard. *The Outsider*. New York: Harper & Row, 1953.

Zamir, Shamoon. *Dark Voices: W. E. B. DuBois and American Thought, 1888–1903*. Chicago: U of Chicago P, 1995.

Zunser, Florence. "'Opera Must Die,' Says Galli-Curci! Long Live the Blues!" *New York Evening Graphic Magazine* 27 Dec. 1930. In Tucker, DER, 44–45.

Videos and Media Broadcasts

Duke Ellington and His Orchestra (1929–1943). Includes *Black and Tan*, *Symphony in Black*, excerpts from *Check and Double Check*, and other Ellington film appearances. Videocassette. Storyville, 1991.

Duke Ellington: Reminiscin' in Tempo. Prod. and dir. Robert S. Levi. Omnibus, BBC 1, 1994.

Impressions. Interview with Anthony Braxton by Alyn Shipton. Prod. Derek Drescher. BBC Radio 3, 22 Feb. 1997.

Mothership Connection. Prod. Avril Johnson. Dir. John Akomfrah. Black Audio Film Collective production for Channel 4, 1995.

Space Is the Place. Prod. Jim Newman. Dir. John Coney. Perf. Sun Ra and His Intergalactic Solar Arkestra, Ray Johnson, Christopher Brooks, Barbara Delaney. 1974. Videocassette. Rhapsody Films, 1993.

Sun Ra: A Joyful Noise. Prod. and dir. Robert Mugge. Perf. Sun Ra Arkestra. 1980. Videocassette. Rhapsody Films, 1993.

Tempo — Meet the Duke. Narr. Derek Jewell. Granada Television, 6 Mar. 1966.

Index of Compositions and Recordings

This index lists only compositions and recordings by Anthony Braxton, Duke Ellington, and Sun Ra. References to other musicians are listed in the Index.

Index

Braxton, Anthony (*continued*)
175; extended forms of, and cultural authenticity, 157–61; Ghost Trance music of, 272 n.113; jazz journalism, criticisms of, 4, 6, 8, 169, 170–71, 173, 182–83 (see also *Tri-axium Writings*: jazz journalism, critique of); language, criticisms of, 6, 163–64, 167, 219 n.19 (see also *Tri-axium Writings*: language of); marches and parades, love of, 184, 193; and mathematics and numerology, 163–64, 176–77, 275 n.150; and meta-reality, aspects of, 150–51, 161, 165, 167, 168, 171, 173, 184, 195–96, 209 (*see also* Braxton, Anthony: diagram titles of; *Tri-axium Writings*: creativity, philosophy of); multi-orchestra music of, 3, 184 (see also *Composition 82* in Index of Compositions); on music as a place, 165, 186–95; on postmodernism, 220 n.25; prose style, criticisms of, 168–69; pulse track structures of, 156–57; and racial stereotyping, 154–55, 179, 182–83, 266 n.51, 266 n.52 (see also *Tri-axium Writings*: specific concepts discussed in— "the across the tracks syndrome," "the grand trade-off"); ritual and ceremonial musics of, 185–86, 195, 197, 279 n.15; rhythm, new approaches to, 155–57; and science and vibrational science, 162–63, 171–72, 271 n.99 (see also *Tri-axium Writings*: creativity, philosophy of); and seeing sounds, 166, 167–68, 278 n.14; solo saxophone music of, 146–47, 149, 170, 177; "story" compositions of, 164–65, 186, 197, 214, 271 n.103; "swing" (and notation), 153–

57; "swing" (as personal style), 149–53, 277 n.165; and synthesis, ideal of, 208; travel themes and metaphors in music of, 193–94, 280 n.30; tribute and "in the tradition" recordings of, 160, 273 n.132; *Trillium Operas* of, 145–46, 186, 196–209 (for individual titles, see Index of Compositions). See also *Tri-axium Writings*

Broomer, Stuart, 273 n.132
Brown, Lawrence, 98, 121–23
Brown, Sterling A., 131

Calloway, Cab, 88
Campbell, Robert L., 14, 226 n.81, 228 n.111
Cartwright, Samuel A., 56
Change of Mind (film) 101–2
Chase, Allan, 13, 15, 17, 37, 42, 62
Check and Double Check (film), 90
Chicago Defender (newspaper) 22, 33, 37
Clarke, Donald, 257 n.22
Clinton, George, 58–60
Cohen, Alan, 107, 112
Collier, James Lincoln, 56, 82–84, 98–99, 137, 140, 218 n.11
Coltrane, John, 147, 150, 182, 264 n.17, 275 n.150
Cone, James, 232 n.151
Corbett, John, 13, 22, 40, 42–43, 58–60, 62, 63, 237 n.65, 278 n.15
Counce, Curtis, 30
Cripps, Thomas, 90
Crispell, Marilyn, 153, 176
Crouch, Stanley, 159
Cutler, Chris, 226 n.78

Dance, Stanley, 137
Darrell, R. D., 85–86, 120, 122–23
Davis, Francis, 38–39
Davis, Jefferson, 72
Dawbarn, Bob, 275 n.150

Graham Lock is Special Lecturer in American Music
in the School of American & Canadian Studies at
the University of Nottingham. He is the author of
numerous articles, reviews, and books, including
Forces in Motion: Anthony Braxton and the Meta-reality of
Creative Music and *Chasing the Vibration: Meetings*
with Creative Musicians.

Library of Congress Cataloging-in-Publication Data
Lock, Graham
Blutopia : visions of the future and revisions of the past in the
work of Sun Ra, Duke Ellington, and Anthony Braxton /
Graham Lock.
p.   cm.
Includes bibliographical references (p.   ) and index.
ISBN 0-8223-2404-0 (cloth : alk. paper).
ISBN 0-8223-2440-7 (paper : alk. paper)
1. Sun Ra—Criticism and interpretation.
2. Ellington, Duke, 1899–1974—Criticism and interpretation.
3. Braxton, Anthony—Criticism and interpretation.
4. Jazz—History and criticism.
I. Title.
ML390.L79   1999
781.65′092′2—dc21   99-34402   CIP